Dedication

For my wife, Kathy

Acknowledgments

I would like to thank the people of the Waite Group for their help in making this book possible. Special thanks go to Robert Lafore and Joel Fugazzotto for their contributions. Nan Borreson from Borland International also deserves my thanks for keeping me up to date with the latest versions of Turbo C++.

About the Author

Gary Syck lives and works in the Pacific Northwest. He has spent the last 11 years working with various computers and software. He has developed several commercial packages for Windows and OS/2. Lately, he has been designing educational software for children. His other books include The Waite Group's *Turbo Assembler Bible* and The Waite Group's *Turbo Pascal How-To*.

Preface

For most programmers learning to program in Windows is far from easy. In the past you could count on the computer to run your program from beginning to end only deviating to execute the loops and conditions that you programmed. In the event driven model of Windows the computer jumps in and out of your program as events, such as a mouse move or a timer tick, occur. You must change the way you think about a program to handle this sometimes random order of execution.

The power available to Windows programs also makes it difficult for the beginner. There are nearly 600 function calls in the Windows library. If you can find the one you need, you can make Windows do many wonderful things. The problem is that you must spend most of your time poring through the Windows Programming Reference looking for the right function.

The payoff for all of this work is in the quality of the application produced. Pull-down menus, consistent controls, and the Windows help facility make Windows applications easy to use. The Clipboard and Dynamic Data Exchange make different applications work together. The graphical interface lets you create visually appealing applications.

The ObjectWindows Library that comes with Borland C++ with Applications Framework and Turbo C++ for Windows is designed to simplify Windows programming. The key to the success of the ObjectWindows Library is the natural fit between Windows and object-oriented programming.

A window on the screen works much the same as an object in Borland C++. Each window encapsulates all of the routines and data that the window uses, just as an object encapsulates its routines and data. A window can inherit and build on the features of other windows, so can objects. Each window handles messages from the operating system in its own way this is similar to the polymorphism of Borland C++.

The first object in ObjectWindows represents an application. All that you need to do to make your own application is to inherit this object and add in the bits that make your application unique. For example, to create a window in your application you add a window object to the application object. If you want round windows instead of square ones, you can make a new window object that inherits most of its features from the basic window object but has its own way of drawing itself.

Even with ObjectWindows helping you there are still many new things to learn to make Windows programs. This book shows you step-by-step how to create powerful applications using ObjectWindows and Windows. Each example is the answer to a common question about how to do something in Windows. For the beginning Windows programmers, there are solutions to questions such as, "How do I make a menu?" and, "How do I make a dialog box?" More advanced programmers might want to know, "How do I make a DDE server?" or "How do I create custom controls?"

New Windows programmers should read the first chapter to learn the basics of Windows and ObjectWindows. Then, look at the examples in Chapter 2 to learn how to make simple Windows programs. After that, the novice and the experienced programmer can use the rest of the book as a reference to answer your "How do I..." questions.

COMPATIBILITY NOTE

The programs in this book work with Borland C++ 3.1 & Application Frameworks, and are backward compatible with Borland C++ version 3.0. This book is also fully compatible with Turbo C++ for Windows version 3.1, which uses a compatible IDE. You, of course, must have Borland's ObjectWindows Library as well.

Dear Reader:

We have witnessed a revolution in programming. There have been major changes in the way PC programs look, they way they work, and the way they are written.

Computers have given us the power to think in a fundamentally non-linear fashion. For example the ability to cut and paste has allowed us to create at random and to organize our randomness at a later time. As the state of computing matured, users began to see through the simple miracles of cut and paste operations, lightning-speed calculation, and random-access organization. They wanted programs that were visually appealing and intuitive to use. Today we feel the consequences all around us—any program that does not have a GUI (graphical user interface) looks primitive.

C++ and object-oriented programming have been natural advancements. In theory, OOP should make programming more simple because you can create objects, clone them, reuse them, etc. But in practice, this is not necessarily the case because the amount of information needed to undertake that process has grown. A whole new methodology means you must know even more abstract concepts such as inheritance, polymorphism, overloading, etc.

OOP is a natural for Windows. If every Windows program needs certain essentials: menus, scroll bars, dialog boxes etc., why not provide them and let programmers just plug them in? That is exactly what Borland has done with its ObjectWindows library. ObjectWindows gives you the power of object-oriented programming without the need to master the paradigm. Easy, eh? Well, not exactly as easy it sounds, but still a step up from creating everything from scratch. Even if you only know the C language, you'll learn OOP without the pain of the learning curve using ObjectWindows and this book.

We'd like to hear what you think. Fill out and return our Reader Satisfaction Card at the back of this book to obtain a catalog and see what else we are brewing up for you!

Sincerely,

Mitchell Waite

Mitchell Waite
Publisher

WAITE GROUP PRESS™

Introduction

This book is designed for programmers who already have some experience programming in C and would like toknow how to use ObjectWindows to create Windows programs. Chapter 1 shows how to set up and use Borland C++ with the ObjectWindows library. If you do not already have Borland C++ running with ObjectWindows, you should read this chapter to make sure you get off on the right foot. In addition to showing the options settings to use, Chapter 1 shows how to make a simple ObjectWindows program so you can make sure everything is set up right.

As the title of this book indicates, the purpose of this book is to show you "how to" do things using Borland C++ and ObjectWindows. Chapters 2 through 10 contain the solutions to many questions that begin "How do I." Following each question is a description of the problem, then an overview of the solution. Next there is a step-by-step procedure for solving the problem. Finally, there is a discussion of how the solution works and some comments on special uses for the solution.

Chapter 2 covers the basics of creating an application. This chapter is important not only to the beginning Windows programmer looking for some easy examples, but it is the foundation on which the later examples rest. The solutions in Chapter 2 show you how to create windows then, add scroll bars, buttons, and menus. There are also examples of Multiple Document Interface (MDI) applications and using and creating Dynamic Link Libraries (DLL).

Windows gets data from the user in a special window called a dialog box. Dialog boxes use special windows called control windows that let you enter text, choose from a list or set options. The examples in Chapter 3 show you how to use dialog boxes in your programs. There are examples of all of the standard controls used in Windows programs. The controls and format of a dialog box are stored in a file called a resource file that is attached to the end of the executable file. Resource Workshop that comes with Borland C++ makes it easy to change the resources in a program. The examples in Chapter 3 show how to use Resource Workshop to define and maintain dialog boxes.

Chapter 4 shows how to use Windows menus. Windows programs can use very simple pull-down menus, or you can make very elaborate menus. There are examples that show how to make multicolumn menus, floating menus, and graphical menus. These examples show how to make your programs more useful and distinctive.

Chapter 5 explains how to do I/O in Windows. Because Windows is event driven, I/O is handled differently from in conventional programs. Instead of the program calling the operating system to get data, Windows programs let the operating system call them when data is available. Chapter 5 shows you how to handle this "backwards" I/O method with examples for the keyboard, the mouse, and the serial port.

Windows is a graphical user interface. Chapter 6 shows how to use graphics in your own programs. Windows provides functions to draw different shapes, show detailed images, and use different fonts. This chapter shows how each type of function works. The first example shows the basics of getting graphics into a window. From there the chapter shows more complex objects and images. One of the most useful examples shows how to use the various fonts that Windows provides.

Chapter 7 shows you how to customize your own windows. This chapter shows off the power of object-oriented programming by taking the basic Windows object and expanding it into a number of interesting custom windows. The examples demonstrate how to improve existing controls such as the scroll bar and list boxes. Other examples show you how to make round and irregular shaped windows. Of particular interest is an example that shows how to make the gray "3-D" dialog boxes like the ones used in the Borland C++ IDE.

Chapter 8 includes examples of persistent objects. These are objects that save their data so that they can be used every time you run the program. The first example shows how to save the data portion of an object in a file. The rest of the examples expand on this idea to create a database of saved objects. Programs can use this database to swap objects in and out of memory as required.

One of the most useful features of Windows is the fact that applications can easily exchange data. For example, a spreadsheet application that supports the data exchange mechanism can get data from a database application that also supports the data exchange mechanism. Chapter 9 shows the older exchange mechanism called, Dynamic Data Exchange (DDE). The examples show how to make applications that provide data (servers) and applications that use the data (clients). There are examples of each type of transaction possible.

Chapter 10 covers the latest data exchange mechanism called Object Linking and Embedding (OLE). This mechanism not only sends data between applications, but it also lets the server provide routines that manipulate the data to the client. Creating OLE applications is a long and complex process. This chapter eases the difficulty of the task by providing complete, but simple OLE servers and clients. You can use these examples as the basis for your own, more sophisticated OLE applications.

Table of Contents

Contents

Windows and Object-Oriented Programming 1

O ne of the first things you notice as a Windows user is how easy it is to use the consistent, graphical interface. Writing a program for Windows is not so easy. Even a simple program to print "Hello, World" in a window takes several pages of code. To write your first simple program, you must understand Windows, event-driven programming, messages, and other esoteric details. As your program grows, you must correctly choose which of the over 600 functions from the Windows API will make your program do what you want it to do.

One way to reduce the work load of writing Windows programs is to reuse portions of programs that you have written before. This is fine if you keep writing the same program over and over, but what if you only need little bits and pieces of various programs to make a completely new program? In this case you can use an object-oriented language like Borland C++ to create reusable objects. The advantage of object-oriented programming in this situation is that you can modify parts of an object to change specific things while keeping the rest of the object.

There is a natural fit between Windows programming and object-oriented programming. Windows defines everything on the screen as a window. Each window is an object that inherits some of its features from other windows. The data that goes with a window is encapsulated into the window object. Window objects are polymorphic, they can all receive common messages and take action that is appropriate for that window.

Another way to make Windows programming easier is to use a commercial library of routines that handle windows. The ObjectWindows library that comes with Borland C++ is such a library. The routines in the ObjectWindows library are object oriented so you can use them as is, or extend them as much or as little as required. To create a simple program with ObjectWindows, you simply create an application object and a window object. As the program grows, you add menu objects, dialog objects, and others. If these objects don't work exactly the way you want, you can change the part of the object involved and you're in business.

This chapter shows how to use the ObjectWindows library to create Windows programs. The first part shows how to set up Borland C++ to use ObjectWindows. Correctly setting up in the first place can save you hours of frustration. The second part shows how to write a simple application that uses ObjectWindows. This application uses the two basic objects common to all ObjectWindows applications. The next part describes the rest of the objects in the ObjectWindows library. These objects are described in detail in the examples in the rest of the book. The last section gives you some tips on using the tools available for Borland C++ Windows programs. Powerful tools, such as the Resource Workshop, make Windows programming much easier.

The discussion that follows and the examples in this book assume that you have some experience with C++ and Windows programming. Some good references on C++ include: *The Waite Group's Turbo C++ Bible* and *Object-Oriented Programming in Turbo C++*. For information on Windows programming, you should read *Windows Programming Primer Plus* and *Windows API Bible*, both by Jim Conger and published by Waite Group Press.

Setting Up Borland C++ to Use ObjectWindows

If you skip this section, you may have some frustrating experiences getting the examples in this book to run. Borland C++ does not come completely configured for use with ObjectWindows. A few moments spent following the steps in this section can save you hours of guesswork.

The first step is to install the files from the Borland C++ diskettes. The first diskette includes a program called INSTALL.EXE that you must use to copy the required files onto your hard drive. If you have about 50 megabytes of free disk space, the easiest way to get the install right is to install all of the options. If you have less than the required amount of disk space, you must eliminate some of the options. The main installation screen lets you specify the options to install. The options you must have to compile ObjectWindows programs are: Windows support, the ClassLib library, the ObjectWindows library, and the large memory model library.

If you have the disk space, you should install the sample programs. These files, along with this book, are the best ways to find out how ObjectWindows works. There are some problems, such as the one in How-To 3.8 in this book, that cannot be solved without referring to the ObjectWindows sources.

When the install program is done, you must modify your CONFIG.SYS file to set the FILES variable to at least 20. Use a line like this:

```
FILES = 20
```

Also add the directory C:\BORLANDC\BIN to the path in the AUTOEXEC.BAT file with a line like this:

```
PATH = C:\BORLANDC\BIN
```

If you told the install program to put the files in some other directory, you must change the PATH statement to use the directory you used.

If you have installed the files properly, there is a new group in the Program Manager window that includes the programs Borland C++, Resource Workshop, and ImpLib. These are the tools you can use to create Windows programs.

The next step is to set up the Borland C++ compiler and linker to use ObjectWindows. Begin by double-clicking the Borland C++ icon to run the IDE. One of the menu selections in this program is labeled *Options*. Before you can compile an ObjectWindows program, you must set some of these options. The first option to set is the Code generation option under the Compiler submenu. In the dialog that appears check the box labeled *Precompiled headers*. Windows programs use thousands of lines of symbol definitions. Recompiling these lines takes much of the compiling time. By setting the precompiled header option, Borland C++ compiles header files once, and uses the precompiled version for later compiles, saving you time.

The code generation dialog also includes a text entry control for defines. Names entered into this field become defined symbols in each program compiled. Enter the string _CLASSDLL;STRICT;WIN31 in this control. The _CLASSDLL symbol causes ObjectWindows programs to create calls to a Dynamic Link Library (DLL) instead of direct calls to a library. Without this symbol, Borland C++ will link all of the routines from the ObjectWindows library that your program uses. This can add 80K to 100K to your programs. Using the DLL version saves all of this memory. You must also select the large memory model option in this dialog. STRICT tells Borland C++ to use strict type checking across modules. If one module uses STRICT, all modules must use STRICT. Your programs must use STRICT because ObjectWindows uses STRICT. The WIN31 symbol tells Borland C++ to allow Windows version 3.1 extensions.

Select Smart Callbacks in the ~~advanced~~ *ENTRY/EXIT* code generation dialog . This tells the compiler to make sure that it loads the DS register with the correct data segment for all functions that are called from the dynamic link library. Defining the symbol _CLASSDLL helps mark the required functions in your program as callback functions.

The other step you need for using the DLL version of ObjectWindows is to set the linker library options. In the settings dialog, be sure that you have not checked the Case Sensitive Link option. In the dialog that comes up when you select *Libraries* from the *Linker* menu, select Dynamic for each of the three library options.

If you make these settings, you will not have to take any special action in your programs to use the DLL version of the ObjectWindows library. In fact , if you decide to use the standard library, all you need to do is remove the _CLASS-DLL definition, change the Libraries settings, and recompile. One reason to do this is that it simplifies moving your programs to another computer. If you have compiled to use the DLL version, you must copy the DLLs to the other computer along with the programs. Further, you must make sure the other computer includes the directory that contains the DLLs in the PATH statement. If you do not use the DLL version, all you need to do is copy the program itself to the target computer.

The final setup step is to tell Borland C++ about the directories to use. Select the *Directory* option from the menu. You must set the include file and library paths to the following:

```
C:\BORLANDC\OWL\INCLUDE;C:\BORLANDC\CLASSLIB\INCLUDE;C:\BORLANDC\INCLUDE
```

```
C:\BORLANDC\OWL\LIB;C:\BORLANDC\CLASSLIB\LIB;C:\BORLANDC\LIB
```

If you have installed Borland C++ in a different directory, you must change C:\BORLANDC to the name of your directory wherever it appears in these strings.

That's all there is to it. Now Borland C++ is ready to compile the sample programs in this book.

Figure 1-1
The FirstApp
Program Display

Creating a Simple ObjectWindows Application

When you create a Windows program in C, you must handle many details such as checking for previous instances of the program, registering window classes, and defining window procedures. The ObjectWindows library simplifies making a Windows application by reducing the number of steps needed to create two objects that are descendants of the TApplication and TWindow classes.

Using TApplication and TWindow classes makes it easy to create simple Windows applications. The following program shows how to use these objects to create a simple program that displays a window.

```
#include <owl.h>

class TFirstApp : public TApplication
{
    public:
        TFirstApp(LPSTR ApName, HANDLE Inst, HANDLE PrevInst
            , LPSTR CmdLine, int CmdShow) : TApplication(ApName
            , Inst, PrevInst, CmdLine, CmdShow) {};
        virtual void InitMainWindow();
};

void TFirstApp::InitMainWindow()
{
    MainWindow = new TWindow(NULL, "Hello, World");
}

int PASCAL WinMain(HANDLE Inst, HANDLE PrevInst, LPSTR CmdLine
    , int CmdShow)
{
    TFirstApp FirstApp("My First Windows Application", Inst
        , PrevInst, CmdLine, CmdShow);

    FirstApp.Run();
    return FirstApp.Status;
}
```

The first line of this program includes a file that defines the ObjectWindows objects and constants. This include file adds over 8,000 lines of code to your program which means that most of the time it takes to compile this program is spent compiling the include file. This is the reason for setting the precompiled headers option when setting up the compiler. With this option set, the compiler will compile the include file the first time it compiles the program, after that the compiler will use a precompiled version of the include file to save time.

The next part of the program defines a descendant of TApplication called TFirstApp. The definition says that this class has a constructor that calls the constructor for TApplication and a member function that overloads the InitMainWindow member function. The InitMainWindow function shown next in the program creates a TWindow object whose caption bar contains the words "Hello, World."

The last part of the program is the WinMain function that Windows calls when it starts the program. The first thing that WinMain does is create a TFirstApp object. Creating this object calls the constructor which sets up the application. The next thing WinMain does is call the member function Run. This function starts by calling the InitMainWindow member function, which creates the window you see when you run the program. Next, Run processes messages from Windows that let you do such things as move, resize, repaint ,and close the window.

When Windows sends the program a WM_QUIT message, the Run function returns to WinMain which returns the Status variable from the TApplication object to Windows.

To run this program, start the Turbo C++ program by double-clicking its icon. This program puts all of the files required for a program into a collection called a project. To start working on a program, you must create a new project by selecting the *Open project* command from the *Project* menu and entering a project name in the dialog that appears. Next you must add the files to the project by selecting the *Add item* command from the *Project* menu. This program requires two files, one called FIRST.CPP and the other called STANDARD.DEF. Add these names to the project, then select Done to return to the Borland C++ program. The project window now shows the names you entered. Double-click on the FIRST.CPP line in the project window to make the editor open an edit window. Enter the text of the program into this window and select *Save* from the *File* menu. Next, double-click the file in the project menu and enter this text into the edit window that appears:

```
EXETYPE WINDOWS
CODE PRELOAD MOVEABLE DISCARDABLE
DATA PRELOAD MOVEABLE MULTIPLE
HEAPSIZE 4096
STACKSIZE 5120
```

This is a definition file just like those used with other Windows development tools. The first line of this file indicates that this program is a Windows application. The next line puts code into the program that tells Windows that the code segments for this program can be moved around memory or discarded from memory as Windows needs to manage memory usage. The third line says that the data segment can be moved and that each instance gets its own copy of the data area.

These memory selections give Windows the most flexibility possible in using memory. Windows can move either type of segment around to create larger areas of free memory. It can get rid of a code segment that is not executing in order to free up even more memory. Note that Windows automatically reloads code segments when your program calls a routine in a segment that is not in memory. Because Windows cannot automatically load data segments as required, the discardable option cannot be used.

Windows attempts to save memory by loading only one copy of a program no matter how many times the user executes the program. What makes each instance of a program different is that each instance gets a different data segment. The multiple option for the data segment makes this possible. Once you have made these selections in the definition file, Windows handles all of the details. Most programs do not have to know when Windows moves a segment or discards a code segment.

The last two lines in the definition file set the heap size and the stack size for the program. The heap is an area in the data segment in which Windows programs can allocate and free memeory as needed. The heap size represents the amount of memory set aside for this use. Chapter 8, "Storing Objects in Files," gives several examples of how to handle memory allocations in Windows programs. The stack is an area of memory used to store return addresses and local variables. It is not a good idea to save memory by reducing the size of the stack. Although you can determine the exact amount of stack space used by your own program, it is difficult to know what happens when you call a function in the ObjectWindows library or the Windows API.

Now that you have entered the required files, you can compile and run the program. Select the *Run* command from the *Run* menu. The status dialog that appears shows the progress of the compilation and linking. The first time you compile a program you will see the number of lines climb into the thousands as Borland C++ compiles the headers. After compiling the program, Borland C++ links routines from the ObjectWindows library, the ClassLib library, and the standard C library. Finally, Borland C++ runs the resulting program and you see a window such as the one in Figure 1-1.

Admittedly this application is not very useful by itself. The power of this application is its potential. The simple step of replacing the TWindow object in InitMainWindow with an object descended from TWindow opens up many possibilities for the program. For example, if you overload the Paint member function, you can display text or graphics in the window. By adding some of the other objects available in ObjectWindows, you can add menus, control windows, and dialog boxes to the program. Chapter 2, "ObjectWindows Basics," shows how to make some of these basic additions to the program.

The TApplication class represents the application. It includes data members such as the application instance (hInstance), a pointer to the main window object (MainWindow), and a pointer to the accelerator table (HAccTable). The member functions for the TApplication class handle the details of initializing the application and receiving messages from Windows. Your program must call the constructor for TApplication to set up the data members and the Run member function to process Windows messages. Most applications make a descendant class of TApplication so that they can overload certain member functions to handle the specific needs of the application. For example, every program in this book overloads the InitMainWindow member function with one that creates a TWindow object.

ObjectWindows calls the TApplication member functions InitApplication and InitInstance during the call to the Run function to initialize the application. If this is the first instance of the application, ObjectWindows calls InitApplication. If your program performs a lengthy setup, you can put it in the InitApplication function so that each instance does not have to repeat the setup. ObjectWindows calls InitInstance for every instance of the application, including the first one. TApplication::InitInstance calls the member functions to set up the main window; so if you define your own InitInstance, you should make sure it calls TApplication::InitInstance.

Windows programs should never execute a function that goes for very long without checking for messages from Windows. For example, if you write a program to compute and display fractal images and the program attempts to compute the entire fractal as the result of a menu command message, the program will prevent you from entering any commands or letting any other Windows program run. The correct procedure is to break up the fractal calculation into many quick calculations that the program can make in between checking for messages. In ObjectWindows programs, the fast calculation can be made in a TApplication member function called IdleAction. ObjectWindows calls this function when there are no messages for the application.

Just before an application exits, ObjectWindows calls the TApplication member function CanClose to see if it is OK to stop the application. Your program can overload this function with a routine that checks for open files, confirms the exit with the user, or whatever other processing is required before the application terminates. If the application can close safely, CanClose should return TRUE.

The other object class found in most ObjectWindows programs is a descendant of TWindow. This class represents a window on the screen. Typically, a program creates a TWindow object in the InitMainWindow function. The constructor for this class sets up the object variables, such as Attr, that contain the position and size of the window, the window style, the control ID for control windows, and a far pointer that you can use any way you want. Most programs use a descendant of TWindow for the windows in the program so they can overload functions such as the constructor to change the way the window appears.

An important thing to remember about the TWindow constructor is that the actual window does not exist yet. You can set up variables in the TWindow object in the constructor, but you cannot send the window messages or reference the HWindow variable, which will contain the handle to the window when it is created. When the window is created, Windows sends the application a WM_CREATE message that invokes the member function. This is the function you can use to send the window messages, or set up scroll bars, or any other Windows function that requires a handle to a window. ObjectWindows uses this function for some of its own setup so you should call TWindow::SetupWindow from your SetupWindow function.

Many of the member functions for TWindow objects handle messages from Windows. Borland C++ includes an extension to C++ called *message response* functions that make it easy to define a member function that handles a Windows message. A typical definition of an message response function is:

```
virtual void WMPaint(RTMessage Msg) = [WM_FIRST + WM_PAINT];
```

This definition describes a member function called WMPaint that takes a reference to a TMessage structure as an argument. ObjectWindows calls this member function when it receives a WM_PAINT message from Windows. There are several ranges of numbers that ObjectWindows uses for indexed member functions. The constant WM_FIRST puts the index into the range set aside for Windows messages. The TMessage structure that is passed to all message handling member functions contains extra information about the message. The TMessage structure is defined as:

```
struct TMessage {
    HWND Receiver;          // The handle of the window receiving the message
    WORD Message;           // The type of message
    union {
        WORD WParam;        // The word parameter for the message
        struct tagWP {
            BYTE Lo;        // Low byte of the word parameter
            BYTE Hi;        // High byte of the word parameter
        } WP;
    };
    union {
        DWORD LParam;       // The long parameter for the message
```

OBJECT NAME	EXAMPLE	DESCRIPTION
Object	N/A	Base class inherited by all other classes.
TApplication	How To 2-1	Base class for applications.
TButton	How To 5-3	Class for a push button.
TCheckBox	How To 3-5	Class for a check box button.
TComboBox	How To 3-5	Class for combo box controls.
TControl	How To 3-5	Base class for control windows.
TDialog	How To 3-1	Base class for dialog boxes.
TEdit	How To 3-5	Class for an editable text window.
TEditWindow	How To 4-1	Class for a window that lets the user edit text.
TFileDialog	How To 3-2	Class for a dialog box that lets the user select files.
TFileWindow	How To 4-1	Class for a window that lets the user load, save, and edit text files.
TGroupBox	How To 3-5	Class for a group box.
TInputDialog	How To 3-5	Class for a window that gets text from the user.
TListBox	How To 5-2	Class for a list box.
TMDIClient	How To 2-4	Base class for the client area of an MDI application.
TMDIFrame	How To 2-4	Base class for the main window of an MDI application.
TModule	How To 2-5	Base class for Dynamic Link Libraries.
TRadioButton	How To 3-5	Class for a radio button.
TScrollBar	How To 5-1	Class for a scroll bar.
TScroller	How To 5-1	Class for windows that can be scrolled.
TSearchDialog	How To 3-3	Class for a dialog that gets input for a text search.
TStatic	How To 3-5	Class for a static text window.
TStreamable	How To 7-1	Base class for putting objects into a stream.
TWindow	How To 2-1	Base class for control, frame, and edit windows.
TWindowsObject	N/A	Base class inherited by TWindow and TDialog.

Table 1-1 ObjectWindows Object Classes

```
        struct tagWP {
              WORD Lo;    // The low word of the long parameter
              WORD Hi;    // The high word of the long parameter
        } LP;
    };
    long Result;          // Value to return to Windows
};
```

The TWindow class registers the window class and creates a window that uses that class. Many programs can get by with the default class used by ObjectWindows; however, if you want to set the icon for the minimized window, use a nonstandard device context to draw on the screen, change the mouse cursor used in the window, or change the default window background, you must change the way ObjectWindows registers the window. There are two member functions that you need to overload to change the registration of a window.

The first member function is GetClassName, which returns a pointer to a string that is the name of the new window class. ObjectWindows uses this name whenever it has anything to do with the window class. Giving your class a unique name lets you create a unique class. The second function is GetWindowClass, which fills in the WNDCLASS structure with information about the window class. The WNDCLASS structure is the same one used by Windows in the RegisterClass function. Its definition is:

```
typedef struct {
    WORD Style;                         // Style flags for the window
                                        // (Set by ObjectWindows)
    long (FAR PASCAL *lpfnWndProc)();   // Message handling function
                                        // (Set by ObjectWindows)
    int cbClsExtra;                     // Number of extra bytes to be allocated for
                                        // the class. (Set by ObjectWindows)
    int cbWndExtra;                     // Number of extra bytes to be allocated for
                                        // the window. (Set by ObjectWindows)
    HANDLE hINstance;                   // Instance for the application
                                        // (Set by ObjectWindows)
    HICON hIcon;                        // Handle to the icon for the window
    HCURSOR hCursor;                    // Handle for the mouse cursor
    LPSTR lpszMenu;                     // Name of the menu
    LPSTR lpszClassName;                // Name of the window class
                                        // (Set by ObjectWindows)
} WNDCLASS;
```

ObjectWindows requires certain values in some of the WNDCLASS elements. To make sure that the correct values are used, your GetWindowClass function must call TWindow::GetWindowClass. The examples in Chapter 2, "ObjectWindows Basics," show how a program can use the WNDCLASS structure to modify the appearance and behavior of a window.

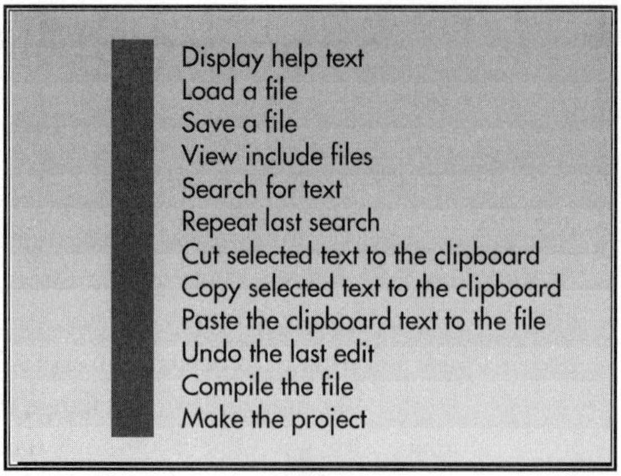

Figure 1-2
The Borland C++
Speed Bar Buttons

Display help text
Load a file
Save a file
View include files
Search for text
Repeat last search
Cut selected text to the clipboard
Copy selected text to the clipboard
Paste the clipboard text to the file
Undo the last edit
Compile the file
Make the project

Using the ObjectWindows Library

The key to creating a good program with ObjectWindows is selecting the right classes. ObjectWindows makes this easy by making the objects match the things you see on the screen. For example, to create a dialog box, you use the TDialog object. For a scroll bar, use TScroller. Table 1-1 shows the object classes defined in ObjectWindows.

You have already seen how the TApplication and TWindow objects work in an ObjectWindows program. The next object classes to look at are the control window objects. A comprehensive example of these objects is presented in How-To 2.3, Chapter 3, "Dialog Boxes," includes detailed examples of each of the control window objects.

Control windows are objects, such as edit windows, that Windows programs use to interact with the user. Control windows are used most frequently as the elements of a dialog box. You can also use control windows as part of the main window. The best examples of this are the scroll bars that appear on the edges of many windows.

ObjectWindows treats control windows as a variation of regular windows and it uses descendants of the TWindow class to handle the controls. This means that you can use the same techniques for moving, resizing, handling messages, and performing other operations that you use for TWindow objects.

Control windows are always associated with another window called the parent window. ObjectWindows maintains this relationship by keeping a list of all of the child windows created for any window. You can use the ForEach member function of the parent window to perform some operation on all of the child windows. How-To 2.5 shows how and why to do this.

Another feature of the list of child windows is that you can issue a single function call to copy information from a list of control windows to a storage area. This is useful in dialog boxes where you want to get all of the user's responses after he presses the OK button. The member function that does this is called TransferData and is demonstrated in Chapter 3, "Dialog Boxes."

The examples for using the data transfer mechanism in Chapter 3 use the TDialog class to make using the transfer operation even easier. The TDialog class is a descendant of the TWindow class that is designed to handle dialog boxes. One feature of this class is that it can handle the OK and Cancel buttons found in most dialogs automatically. When the user presses the OK button, the TDialog class routines invoke the transfer mechanism to copy the data somewhere where it can be used by the program. The Cancel button TDialog ends the dialog and returns a value indicating that the user rejected the dialog.

The TDialog class also includes special message response member functions to handle WM_COMMAND notification messages from controls. This means that all you need to do to handle a message from a control in a dialog is to define an indexed member function with the sum of the constant CF_FIRST and the ID of the control window. You can use notification messages for such things as changing the dialog when certain options are selected, verifying text input, or many other tasks.

Some dialogs are so common that they have their own objects in ObjectWindows. These dialogs handle selecting files (TFileDialog), and getting search information (TSearchDialog). These objects save you programming time on almost every project because they are used so often.

Saving time for programming common operations is the idea behind the TEditWindow and TFileWindow objects. These objects handle editing text in memory and editing disk files. In the past, these operations were not part of many applications due to the time it took to implement them. Many applications required you to leave the application, start an editing program, edit a file, and return to the original program. Now that the work is already done, text editing can become a much more common part of applications. Chapter 4, "Menus," shows how to use these objects.

How-To 2.5 shows how to use the TMDIClient and TMDIFrame classes to create Multiple Document Interface (MDI) applications. The Borland C++ IDE is a good example of an MDI application. It lets you have a number of child windows contained within a main application window. This type of interface is very popular because it makes it easy to work with several files simultaneously. The TMDIClient and TMDIFrame classes handle the details of this interface such as maintaining a list of the child windows and handling the menu com-

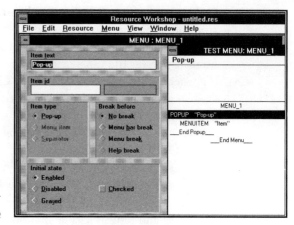

Figure 1-3
The Menu Editor

mands to create new windows, tile or cascade windows, iconize windows, and delete windows.

Using the Borland C++ Windows Programming Tools

The two tools used most often in this book are the Borland C++ IDE program and the Resource Workshop. You already have used Borland C++ IDE to create the simple program presented earlier in this chapter. This program lets you manage projects, edit source files, and compile programs. Learning this program is important because it is where you will spend most of your programming time.

In addition to using the pull-down menus, you can use the Speed Bar in the Borland C++ window to give commands to the program. Figure 1-2 shows the Speed Bar buttons and what they do.

Once you get the Borland C++ options, the first thing you do is create a project. Borland C++ uses projects to group files together that make up a program. You can use the tool bar or the menu to add and delete files from the project window. There are several types of files that you can add to the project window. The three types used in this book are C++ sources (.CPP), resource files (.RES), and definition files (.DEF).

When you select the *Run* command, Borland C++ goes through the files in the project window to see if they are up-to-date. Each type of source file in the project window has a corresponding object file. Borland C++ looks to see if the source file is newer than the object file; if so Borland C++ invokes the required compiler to update the object file. When all of the sources have been compiled, Borland C++ calls the linker to link the program.

The project file also keeps track of the options used during the project. It is very easy to set the options incorrectly and make Borland C++ unable to compile or link your programs. If you followed the directions at the beginning of this chapter, you should not have any problems. Most of the examples in this book can be run using the options given in this chapter. In the cases where different options are needed, the instructions for resetting the options are given with the program.

The editor used in Borland C++ is similar to the editor in the Windows Notepad application. You use the keyboard and the mouse to issue commands to move the cursor, select text, and delete or copy text. The scroll bars let you move the window around to see different parts of the file. There are menu commands that let you move selected text between the Clipboard and the file, and to let you search the file for text. All of these commands are the same as those you have used in other Windows applications, such as Notepad.

Once you have entered a program, you can use the *Run* command to compile, link, and run the program. In some cases, you may not want to do the whole compile-link-run sequence. The *Compile* menu has commands that let you control what part of the sequence you want to run. The *Compile* command compiles the program in the active window regardless of how new the source is. The *Make* command compiles all of the files in the project window if the source is newer than the object file. The *Link* command links all of the object files implied by the source files in the project file. The *Build all* command compiles all of the programs in the project regardless of the newness of the source.

One reason to do only part of the compile-link-run cycle is to check for errors. When Borland C++ detects an error during a compile, it puts the error message into a window called the message window. When you click on one of the messages in this window, Borland C++ shifts the focus to an edit window

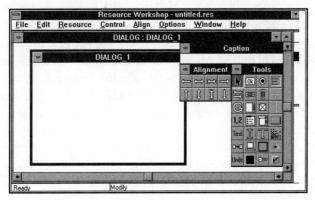

Figure 1-4
The Dialog Editor

containing the source with the error and highlights the line with the error. This makes correcting errors very quick because you can move automatically from the error to the place in the program to be fixed.

The Resource Workshop lets you edit the visible features of programs such as bitmaps, icons, and menus. This is a very versatile program that lets you create resource files to be combined with your own programs. You can change the resources of other programs. For example, if you do not like the way a program's menus are arranged, you can use the resource editor to change the menu around. Use caution when attempting this because not all programs are written in a way that lets the resources be edited arbitrarily.

The programs in this book all use the Resource Workshop to create .RES files that can be linked directly to programs created with the compiler. Other development systems have you create a text file called an .RC file that contains commands that can be compiled to create an .RES file. If you are converting programs from this type of development system, you can edit the .RC file with the Resource Workshop by giving the .RC extension when you load the file. Once you have the file in the Resource Workshop, you can keep the file in the .RC text format or convert the file to a .RES file. If you leave the file in the .RC format, you must use the .RC extension in the Borland C++ project file to make sure it is compiled before it is combined with a program.

To begin editing a new resource file, use the *New* command from the *File* menu. This command brings up a dialog that lets you pick the type of file to create. For the programs in this book, select .RES. The other formats let you create files that are compatible with other development systems. These formats are more limited in the types of resources they can hold. For example, the .RC format cannot directly hold a bitmap. The .BMP format can hold only bitmaps.

Each of the different types of resources you can put into an .RES file uses a different editor. When you select *New* from the *Resource* menu, the Resource Workshop asks you what type of resource you want to create. It uses this information to determine what type of editor to give you. As you create new resources, the names of the resources appear in the window at the right of the main window. You can click on the entry in this window to re-edit it.

When you create a new resource, the Resource Workshop assigns a name to the resource. The name of the resource is important because the program that uses the resource refers to it by name. The name assigned by the Resource Workshop is rarely the name used in the program. Each solution gives the names of the resources expected by the program. To assign these names to the corresponding resource, use the *Rename* command from the *Resource* menu.

Resource editors for menus and dialog boxes show you what the resource looks like as you edit it. Information such as control IDs or styles are available only by bringing up dialogs. This means that there is no single convenient picture of how to enter a control that can be put in this book. To solve this problem, this book gives the text commands for these resources. To enter the text versions of the resource into the resource editor, you must select the *Edit as text* command from the *Resource* menu. Once you have entered the resource as text, you can bring up the regular editor to see what the resource looks like.

Figure 1-3 shows the menu editor from the Resource Workshop. The gray window on the left is where you enter commands to change the name, ID, or style of the menu item selected in the window at the lower right. The menu appears as it will look in your program in the window at the upper right of the editor window.

To add a new menu item, press the *Insert* key. The editor adds the new menu item immediately after the current menu item. You can add new pop-up menus to the menu by pressing the Control-P key. The editor automatically adds a menu item to the new pop-up. You can add pop-up menus to the main menu bar or to one of the pop-ups already created. The editor lets you nest menus as deeply as you like, but remember the purpose of a menu is to make it easy for the user to see the available choices. Creating deeply nested menus defeats this purpose.

To change a menu item, click on the item in the lower right window, and edit the information in the window on the left. Pay close attention to the ID field in the menu item information. If you change this value, you must also change the program that uses the menu to handle the new value. How-To 2.4 shows how to write a program that uses menu IDs.

To delete a menu item, press the delete key. The menu must always have a menu item or pop-up, the editor will not let you delete the last one from the menu. Pop-up menus must always include a menu item or pop-up. Some programs need empty pop-up menus to which they add custom features. In this case, you must create a pop-up with an item, then have the program delete that item before it adds its custom commands. Chapter 4, "Menus," shows how to do this.

Figure 1-4 shows the Resource Workshop dialog editor. This is the most complex editor in the Resource Workshop and also one of the most used editors. The editor shows the dialog box you are editing at the left of the editor window. On the right are windows for editing the dialog caption, aligning controls, and creating new controls. Each of these windows can be moved around however you like or even closed so you do not have to see it.

The two most frequently used windows in the dialog editor are the sample dialog and the tools window. To begin making a dialog box, select the type of control you want in the dialog from the tool box, then click at the location in the dialog box for the control. The editor places the new control at the indicated location and draws a sizing border around the control. You can use the sizing border to change the size of the control as required. You can also click on the control and drag it to a new location. When you double-click on the control, the editor displays a dialog box of options for that control. Chapter 3, "Dialog Boxes," describes the options for each type of control window.

Depending on your skill with the mouse, you may find it difficult to line up the controls just the way you want them. In this case, go to the *Align* menu and select *Show grid*. This command draws lines on the dialog window that you can use to help line up the controls.

Some controls (such as static text, group box, and buttons) include text. You can edit the text by double-clicking the control and entering the text in the dialog box that appears. A quicker way to edit the text is to select the control by clicking on it, and then typing in the text.

The Resource Workshop uses intuitive visual editors for graphical resources such as cursors, icons, and bitmaps. This book shows these resources as figures that you can copy to the editor. The figures have been blown up to make it easier for you to see the pixels. The only piece of information that is lost by this technique is the color of the resource. In most cases, the actual color (or even the shape) does not matter to the program, so you can use your own creativity in entering colors. If you want the exact resources for these programs, you can order the companion disk for this book from The Waite Group.

Perhaps the best feature of the Resource Workshop is that you can use it to experiment with different resources to see what happens. The programs in this book are very tolerant of variations in the resources they use. In most programs, the interface between the program and the resource file is limited to the names of the resources and the ID numbers for menu selections and for control windows.

Summary

The early development environments for Windows did little to help the programmer deal with the daunting task of creating a Windows program. Even a simple Windows program requires over a page of C code. When you are ready to create more interesting programs, you must sift through over 500 API functions to find the one that does the job. Borland C++ with ObjectWindows takes some of the pain out of Windows programming by providing predefined object classes that handle many of the details of Windows programming. You can make a simple program with just a few lines of code. Adding features to the program is often just a matter of adding the appropriate object to the program. Because ObjectWindows is an object-oriented library, you are not forced to decide between limiting your program to things that the library can do, or abandoning the library and writing all your own routines. Instead, you can inherit the features you need from the library and overload the routines that you need to change.

The rest of this book shows you how to go from some simple examples of the basic features of ObjectWindows to very sophisticated programs that take advantage of the most advanced features of Windows.

ObjectWindows Basics 2

2

O ne of the benefits of using object-oriented programming is how easy it is to modify existing programs into new programs. A new program can inherit from objects developed for other programs, then change a few data elements and methods to get the desired results. Because new programs stand on the shoulders of the programs that come before, it is important that you get started on the right foot. This chapter shows you how to write some simple programs that use some of the major features of Windows and the ObjectWindows library.

The solutions in later chapters of this book use object-oriented techniques to modify the programs found in this chapter. Once you have mastered the programs in this chapter and the object-oriented techniques used to modify them, you use them as the basis for your own Windows applications. The programs in this chapter show you how to create windows, add menus and control windows, handle messages, and use Dynamic Link Libraries (DLLs).

These capabilities are enough to get you started writing simple Windows applications of your own.

2.1 Make an ObjectWindows Application

When you learn Zen, you are told that your cup of knowledge cannot be filled until you empty it of everything that you already know. Learning to program in Windows is similar. You must forget what you already know about programming and start over at the beginning. This solution shows you how to begin to create a Windows application. The road to Windows knowledge begins here.

2.2 Change the Class Information and Style of a Window

Windows uses the term *class* to refer to the type of window on the screen. Be careful to notice the difference between a *window class*, which keeps track of a window on the screen, and an *object class*, which describes a C++ object. This solution shows you how to use the ObjectWindows object classes to modify the window class of windows in your programs. Being able to change the window class is important because it tells Windows such things as the menu to use in the window, the mouse cursor, the icon, when to redraw the window, and several other bits of window information.

A program can use a window class for several windows, each of which can have its own variations on the window class called the window style. The style of a window controls things such as the type of border drawn around the window, the controls on the title bar, and whether the window has scroll bars. This solution shows the possible styles for a window and how your program can change the style.

2.3 Add Control Windows to a Window

Control windows are the windows (such as scroll bars, text boxes, and radio buttons) that the user uses to input data to a program. The ObjectWindows library includes object classes for each of these windows that make them easy to add to your program. Control windows are most often found in dialog boxes, but they can be inserted in any window. A good example of this is the scroll bar control used by many programs to let the user move the information in the window. This solution shows how to add scroll bar controls to a window.

2.4 Add Menus to a Program

One of the features that make Windows programs so easy to use is the drop-down menu. Windows programs define the items that appear in the menu in the resource file for the program. Then the program waits for messages from Windows indicating that the user selected a menu command. This solution shows you how to create and use menus.

2.5 Create an MDI Application

This book was written using a word processor that can display several files at once, each in its own window. This capability is called the Multiple Document Interface (MDI) and is built into Windows and the ObjectWindows library. This solution shows you how to use MDI to create applications that display more than one window.

2.6 Make and Use Dynamic Link Libraries

When you write a program for MS-DOS, you must link it with a library that becomes part of the executable program. The more programs you write, the more copies of the library you make. This takes up disk space; and if you make a change to the library, you must relink every program that uses the library.

Windows has a better way: instead of linking a library to the program at linktime, you can create a Dynamic Link Library (DLL) that Windows links to your program at run time. This means that you need only one copy of the library on disk or in memory, no matter how many programs use the library. Also if you change the library, the programs that use the library use the updated library the next time you run them.

2.1 How Do I...
Make an ObjectWindows Application?

Complexity: EASY

PROBLEM

Almost every aspect of Windows programming is different from conventional programming. You cannot use such time-honored conventions as starting the

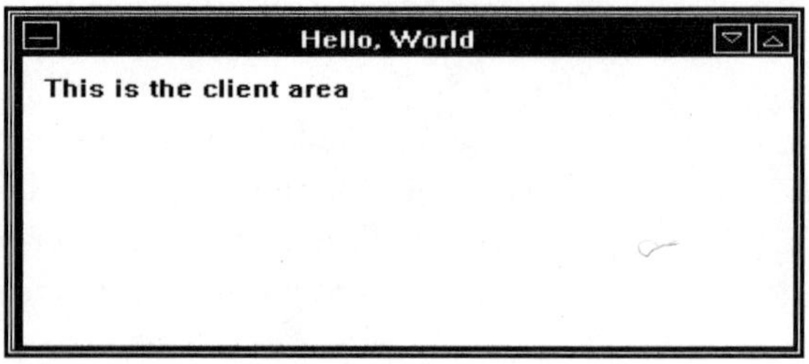

Figure 2-1
The Window
for OWLAPP

program with a function called *main*. Using ObjectWindows also changes the way you have to think about writing programs. This solution shows you the basics of creating a Windows application using the ObjectWindows library. Other solutions in this chapter use object-oriented techniques to add features to this simple program.

TECHNIQUE

The first thing to know about Windows programs is that they begin at a function called WinMain. The purpose of WinMain is to let your program initialize its variables, tell Windows about the windows the program will use, and then repeatedly ask Windows for events until Windows tells it to shut down. With ObjectWindows, you do all of this by creating an instance of a class descended from the TApplication class and calling the Run member function.

Everything else that your program does occurs in response to some event that Windows tells it about. Windows informs your program of events by passing messages to windows that your program has registered. In ObjectWindows, each window is an object descended from the TWindow class. You must create member functions for messages that affect your program.

In this example, the application gets the message from Windows that tells it to repaint the client area. By default, ObjectWindows tells Windows to make the background of the client area blank. This program writes a string of text on the blank background when it gets the paint message. The result is a window that looks like Figure 2-1.

STEPS

1. Create a new project called OWLAPP.PRJ that includes the files OWLAPP.CPP, OWLAPP.RES, and STANDARD.DEF (see Chapter 1, "Windows and Object-Oriented Programming," for how to create projects).

2. Create the source file OWLAPP.CPP with this program:

```
/* A simple OWL program */
#include <owl.h>

/* Definition of the main window object */
class TMyWindow : public TWindow
{
    public:
        /* Constructor for the window object */
        TMyWindow(PTWindowsObject AParent, LPSTR ATitle): TWindow(AParent, ATitle) {};
        /* Handle paint messages from Windows */
        virtual void WMPaint(RTMessage) = [WM_FIRST + WM_PAINT];
};

/* Handle the WM_PAINT message from Windows */
void TMyWindow::WMPaint(RTMessage)
{
    PAINTSTRUCT ps;
    HDC hDC;

    /* Clear the ps structure */
    memset(&ps, 0x00, sizeof(PAINTSTRUCT));
    /* Get a device context handle */
    hDC = BeginPaint(HWindow, &ps);
    /* Print a string in the window */
    TextOut(hDC, 10, 10, "This is the client area", 23);
    /* Release the device context and tell Windows the painting is complete */
    EndPaint(HWindow, &ps);
}


/* definition for the application object */
class TFirstApp : public TApplication
{
    public:
        TFirstApp(LPSTR ApName, HINSTANCE Inst
            , HINSTANCE PrevInst
            , LPSTR CmdLine, int CmdShow) : TApplication(ApName
            , Inst, PrevInst, CmdLine, CmdShow) {};
        virtual void InitMainWindow();
};

/* Initialize the main window */
void TFirstApp::InitMainWindow()
{
    /* Create the main window object and put the pointer into the application object */
    MainWindow = new TMyWindow(NULL, "Hello, World");
}

/* Entry point for the program */
int PASCAL WinMain(HINSTANCE Inst, HINSTANCE PrevInst, LPSTR CmdLine
    , int CmdShow)
{
    /* Create the application object */
    TFirstApp FirstApp("", Inst
        , PrevInst, CmdLine, CmdShow);

    /* Run the application */
    FirstApp.Run();
    return FirstApp.Status;
}
```

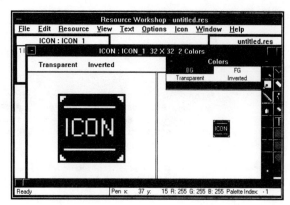

Figure 2-2
The Icon for the
Sample Program

3. Make sure the STANDARD.DEF file from Chapter 1 is in the current directory.
4. Use the Resource Workshop to create the resource file OWLAPP.RES. Add the icon from Figure 2-2.
5. Use the *Run* command to compile and run the program.

HOW IT WORKS

The OWLAPP program uses two objects descended from classes in the ObjectWindows library. The WinMain routine at the end of the listing creates the first object called FirstApp. The class of this object is TFirstApp, which is descended from the ObjectWindows class TApplication. ObjectWindows programs use objects to set up the program and get messages from Windows. This program replaces the InitMainWindow member function to create the main window object for the program. The constructor for TApplication calls InitMainWindow as part of the program setup. After WinMain creates the FirstApp object, it calls the Run member function to get and dispatch messages. When Windows sends a WM_QUIT message to the application, the Run function returns to WinMain, which returns the status to whatever program started this one.

The InitMainWindow member function of the FirstApp object creates the main window for the program. The main window is represented in the program by the object class TMyWindow, which is descended from the ObjectWindows class TWindow. An important part of what TWindow objects do is to act on messages received from Windows. In this program the TMyWindow class is set up to act on the WM_PAINT message from Windows. This message tells the program that it needs to paint the client area of the window. The message is handled by a special type of member function called a *message response member function*. This is a typical message response member function declaration:

```
virtual void WMPaint(RTMessage) = [WM_FIRST + WM_PAINT];
```

The portion of the declaration following the equal sign determines to what message the function responds. The constant WM_FIRST is defined in and indicates that the message is a Windows message. How To 2.2 and 2.3 show how to make message response functions that respond to controls and menu commands. The constant WM_PAINT is defined in an include file called WINDOWS.H and is the number that Windows sends to the program when the window needs to be repainted.

The WMPaint function prints the string "This is the client area" in the client area of the window. The first statement in this function uses the C library function memset to initialize the structure ps to all zeros. This structure gets filled with information about the area to paint in the next statement. The main purpose of the next step is to get a handle to a *device context*. The device context is how Windows keeps track of graphical devices such as screens and printers. This program gets the handle to the device context by calling the Windows function BeginPaint.

The device context handle returned by BeginPaint is set up for efficient repainting of portions of the window. When the user moves windows around the screen, parts of windows are covered and uncovered. Whenever a part of a window gets uncovered, Windows keeps track of the uncovered part and sends a WM_PAINT message to the application that owns the window. If another part gets uncovered before the application can process the WM_PAINT message, Windows adds the two parts together and does not send a second WM_PAINT message. The device context returned by BeginPaint has a clipping region set to the part of the window that needs repainting. Windows does not attempt to paint outside of the clipping region. BeginPaint also fills in the PAINTSTRUCT structure with the coordinates of the clipping region so you can make your program more efficient by not calling functions that draw outside of the clipping region. The format of the PAINTSTRUCT structure is:

```
typedef struct {
        HDC    HDC;              // Handle to the device context for this window
        BOOL   fErase;           // True  if the background has been erased
        struct {
                int left;        // Left edge of the clipping region
                int top;         // Top edge of the clipping region
                int right;       // Right edge of the clipping region
                int bottom;      // Bottom edge of the clipping region
        } rcPaint;
        BOOL   fRestore;         // Reserved field used by Windows
        BOOL   fIncUpdate;       // Reserved field used by Windows
        BYTE   rgbReserved[16];  // Reserved field used by Windows
} PAINTSTRUCT;
```

The OWLAPP program uses the handle to the device context as an argument to TextOut, which prints text in the window. The arguments to TextOut are the x- and y-coordinates of the beginning of the string to print, the text of the string, and the number of characters in the string.

Any function that calls BeginPaint must call EndPaint when it is done drawing on the screen. This tells Windows that the device context is free and can be used by other programs.

The default main window style for ObjectWindows programs includes a system menu on the title bar. The user can use this menu to close the window. When the user closes the main window, Windows sends a WM_CLOSE mes-

MESSAGE CONSTANT	SOLUTION	DESCRIPTION
WM_CHAR	4.2	Sent when the user generates a keyboard character.
WM_CTLCOLOR	5.1	Sent just before drawing a control window.
WM_ENABLE	5.3	Sent when the window is disabled or enabled.
WM_HSCROLL	2.2	Sent when the user clicks on the horizontal scroll bar.
WM_KEYDOWN	4.2	Sent when the user presses a key.
WM_KEYUP	4.2	Sent when the user releases a key.
WM_KILLFOCUS	5.3	Sent when the window loses the keyboard focus.
WM_LBUTTONDBLCLK	4.3	Sent when the user double-clicks the left mouse button.
WM_LBUTTONDOWN	4.3	Sent when the user presses the left mouse button.
WM_LBUTTONUP	4.3	Sent when the user releases the left mouse button.
WM_MBUTTONDBLCLK	4.3	Sent when the user double-clicks the middle mouse button.
WM_MBUTTONDOWN	4.3	Sent when the user presses the middle mouse button.
WM_MBUTTONUP	4.3	Sent when the user releases the middle mouse button.
WM_MOUSEMOVE	4.3	Sent whenever the user moves the mouse.
WM_RBUTTONDBLCLK	4.3	Sent when the user double-clicks the right mouse button.
WM_RBUTTONDOWN	4.3	Sent when the user presses the right mouse button.
WM_RBUTTONUP	4.3	Sent when the user releases the right mouse button.
WM_SETFOCUS	5.3	Sent when Windows gives the window the input focus.
WM_SYSCHAR	4.2	Sent when the user presses a system key (ALT keys).
WM_TIMER	5.6	Sent when a timer has timed out.
WM_VSCROLL	2.2	Sent when the user clicks on the vertical scroll bar.

Table 2-1 Windows Messages

sage to the window. The default action for this message is to destroy the window. Destroying the main window of a program causes Windows to send a WM_QUIT message to the application, which tells the application to stop processing messages and return to the program that launched it. All of this processing is handled by routines in the TApplication class.

Step 4 of the solution tells you to create an icon for the program. Windows uses icons to visually identify a program in the program manager. Icons are useful because most people can find a picture faster than they can find a name in a list. If you do not want to use an icon for this program, you can skip the steps that involve the file OWLAPP.RES.

COMMENT

This simple program is the basis of all ObjectWindows programs. All you need to do to create more complex programs is to add features to the TMyApplication and TMyWindow classes. The most important extension to a Windows program is to add the ability to act on messages from Windows. This capability lets your program use menus, get mouse and keyboard input, keep track of the window size and position, and much more. Table 2-1 lists some of the messages that are used in the examples in this book.

Windows includes information with each message that gives details about the message. ObjectWindows puts this information into a structure called TMessage. The definition of this type is:

```
typedef struct {
     HWND Receiver;              // The window to receive this message
     WORD Message;               // The type of message
     union {
          WORD WParam;           //  The First message parameter
          struct {
               BYTE Lo;          // Low byte of the first parameter
               BYTE Hi;              // High byte of the first parameter
          } WP;
     };
     union {
          DWORD LParam;          // The second message parameter
          struct {
               WORD Lo;          // Low word of the second parameter
               WORD Hi;          // High word of the second parameter
          } LP;
     };
     long result;                     // Value to return to windows
} TMessage;
```

Your program already knows the window handle because it is the HWindow element of the TWindow class. The program also knows the message type because that is how ObjectWindows determines what indexed member function to call.

The next two elements are the ones that have important information for your program. If you have not done much programming with C++, you may have noticed that the unions are missing an identifier. In a C program, every union must have a name that you must include in any reference to one of the elements of the union. For example, if the first union in the structure was named First, then to access the Lo element you would have to use something like Msg.First.WP.Lo. With C++ you can have *anonymous unions* that do not use a union name. The reference to Lo in C++ looks like Msg.WP.Lo.

Each message in Windows uses the parameters differently. For example, in the WM_MOUSEMOVE message, Msg.WParam contains flags that indicate the state of the mouse buttons. In the WM_KEYDOWN message, Msg.WParam is the virtual key code of the key pressed. To see how to use the parameters for the messages in Table 2-1, see the indicated examples.

There are hundreds of messages sent by Windows to applications. You can detect and act on just about anything that happens in the Windows environment by handling the right message. This book includes examples of the most commonly used messages. For a complete description of all of the Windows messages available, see *The Waite Group's Windows API Bible*.

2.2 How Do I ... Change the Class Information and Style of a Window?

Complexity: EASY

PROBLEM

The TWindow class in the ObjectWindows library creates a standard application window suitable for displaying simple text or graphics. For most programs, you need to change this window to add such things as a menu or scroll bars. Clearly, this is the sort of thing for which object-oriented programming is intended. You want to use all of the features of TWindow, but you want the window to include a menu or scroll bars in the window. All you need to do is find the member functions that control how the window looks and modify them. It really is as easy as it sounds.

TECHNIQUE

One of the first things that a Windows program must do is to register the window classes used in the program. In an ObjectWindows program, this step is done for you when you create an object descended from TWindow. ObjectWindows registers a class for windows that are redrawn when the window size changes, use the standard application icon, have the arrow cursor for the mouse, use the standard window background color, and have no menu. To change these features, you must change the methods GetClassName and GetWindowClass, which are used to set up the window class. TWindow objects use the GetClassName method to get the name that Windows uses to identify a class and GetWindowClass to fill a structure with the data for the class.

Registering a window class does not tell Windows everything it needs to know about a window. When a program creates a window, it must specify the style, the position, any special data for the window, and an identifier that Windows can use to find the window. In ObjectWindows programs, you put this information in a structure called Attr before the window is actually created. A good place to set up the Attr structure is in the constructor for the window object.

The program in this solution registers a window class that changes the icon, cursor, menu, and background of the window. Then it changes the Attr structure to make the window smaller than usual. The resulting window looks like the window in Figure 2-3.

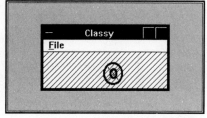

FIGURE 2-3
The Modified
Window

STEPS

1. Create a new project called CLASS.PRJ that includes the files CLASS.CPP, CLASS.RES, and STANDARD.DEF. The STANDARD.DEF file is the same one created in How To 2.1.

2. Use the IDE editor to create the CLASS.CPP file with the following program:

```
/* class.cpp change the class and status information for a window */
#include <owl.h>

/* definition of the main window object class */
class TMyWindow : public TWindow
{
    public:
        TMyWindow(PTWindowsObject AParent, LPSTR ATitle);
        virtual LPSTR GetClassName();
        virtual void GetWindowClass(WNDCLASS& AWndClass);
};
```

```
/* Set up the main window */
TMyWindow::TMyWindow(PTWindowsObject AParent, LPSTR ATitle)
        : TWindow(AParent, ATitle)
{
      Attr.Style |= WS_CAPTION;    // Add a caption to the window
      Attr.W = 200;                // Make it 200 pixels wide
      Attr.H = 100;                // and 100 pixels tall
}


/* Return a unique class name for the window class */
LPSTR TMyWindow::GetClassName()
{
      return "MyClass";
}


/* Set up the WNDCLASS structure for registering the window */
void TMyWindow::GetWindowClass(WNDCLASS& AWndClass)
{
      /* Run the default routine to set up most of the WNDCLASS elements */
      TWindow::GetWindowClass(AWndClass);
      /* Get the cursor from the resource file */
      AWndClass.hCursor = LoadCursor(GetApplicationObject()->hInstance
           , "CLASS_CURSOR");
      /* Get the icon from the resource file */
      AWndClass.hIcon = LoadIcon(GetApplicationObject()->hInstance
           , "CLASS_ICON");
      /* Create a brush to use for the window background */
      AWndClass.hbrBackground
           = CreateHatchBrush(HS_BDIAGONAL, 0xFF);
      /* Assign a menu from the resource file */
      AWndClass.lpszMenuName = "CLASS_MENU";
}


/* Definition of the application object */
class TMyApp : public TApplication
{
      public:
            TMyApp(LPSTR ApName, HINSTANCE Inst, HINSTANCE PrevInst
                 , LPSTR CmdLine, int CmdShow) : TApplication(ApName
                 , Inst, PrevInst, CmdLine, CmdShow) {};
            virtual void InitMainWindow();
};


/* Create the main window object */
void TMyApp::InitMainWindow()
{
      MainWindow = new TMyWindow(NULL, "Classy");
}


/* Entry point for the program */
int PASCAL WinMain(HINSTANCE Inst, HINSTANCE PrevInst, LPSTR CmdLine
     , int CmdShow)
{
      /* Create the application object */
      TMyApp TheApp("", Inst, PrevInst, CmdLine, CmdShow);
```

```
/* Run the application */
TheApp.Run();
return TheApp.Status;
}
```

3. Use the Resource Workshop to create CLASS.RES with an icon named CLASS_ICON, a menu named CLASS_MENU, and a cursor named CLASS_CURSOR. Figure 2-4 shows examples for the icon and the cursor. An easy way to make a menu is to select "Create new File menu" from the "Menu" menu.

4. Use the *Run* command from the *Run* menu to run the program.

HOW IT WORKS

The first thing this program does is define a new object class called TMyWindow that is descended from the ObjectWindows object class TWindow. TMyWindow re-defines the virtual member functions GetClassName and GetWindowClass so that it can change the registration for the window. The GetClassName member function returns a pointer to the string "MyClass" to identify the new class. The GetWindowClass member function fills in elements of the AWndClass structure to specify the features to register.

A Cursor

An Icon

Figure 2-4
Images for the CLASS Resource File

Note the use of the declarations WNDCLASS& in the parameters for GetWindowClass. This is a feature of C++ called *pass by reference* that lets a program pass a pointer to a structure but then refer to the structure as if the whole structure had been passed. This means that GetWindowClass can change AWndClass by using references such as AWndClass.hCursor instead of AWndClass->hCursor as would be required with pointers in a standard C program.

The first thing that GetWindowClass does is call the GetWindowClass method from the TWindow object class. This fills in the parts of the AWndClass structure not handled by this program. This step is vital to the correct operation of the program because one of the fields in AWndClass is the address of the routine Windows calls when it has a message for the window. The message handler for ObjectWindows programs is part of the TWindow object class and must be set up by GetWindowClass.

The constructor for TMyWindow changes the width and height values in the Attr structure. This makes the window much smaller than normal. The rest of the program is identical to the program in How-To 2.1.

STYLE	DESCRIPTION
CS_BYTEALIGNCLIENT	Always position the window so that the left edge of the client area is always on a byte boundary in screen memory. This style can make repainting the client area faster.
CS_BYTEALIGNWINDOW	Always position the window so that the left edge of the whole window is always on a byte boundary in screen memory. This style may make repainting the window frame faster, but it may also slow client area repaints.
CS_CLASSDC	Allocate a device context to be shared by all windows with this window class. A window does not need to release the DC until it is needed by another window in the class.
CS_DBLCLKS	Send double-click mouse messages to the window. Without this style, the window only receives button down and button up messages.
CS_GLOBALCLASS	Make this class usable by all applications. This style is often used in Dynamic Link Libraries that handle windows to be used by several applications.
CS_HREDRAW	Set the repaint area to the whole client area and send a WM_PAINT message whenever the horizontal window size changes.
CS_NOCLOSE	Remove the close option from the window's system menu.
CS_OWNDC	Allocate a device context for each window created with this style. OWNDC windows do not need to release the DC when finished drawing on the screen. Each DC created requires about 800 extra bytes of memory.
CS_PARENTDC	This window uses the DC for its parent window.
CS_SAVEBITS	Save the screen pixels before drawing the

(continued from page 38)

	window. The saved bits are used to repaint the
	screen when the window is destroyed.
CS_VREDRAW	Set the repaint area to the whole client area and
	send a WM_PAINT message whenever the
	vertical window size changes.

Table 2-2 Window Class Styles

COMMENT

Changing the registration parameters for a window is a common practice in Windows programs. For example, any program that uses a menu can place the menu name in the WNDCLASS structure so that it is automatically displayed in the window. The other features you can change are indicated by the elements of the WNDCLASS structure:

```
typedef struct {
    WORD style;                         // The window class style
    Long (FAR PASCAL *lpfnWndPorc)();   // The function to call with messages
    int cbClsExtra;                     // Bytes to add to the window class structure
    int cbWndExtra;                     // Bytes to add to the window
    HANDLE hInstance;                   // Instance of the program that owns the window
    HICON hIcon;                        // The icon to display for the minimized window
    HCURSOR hCursor;                    // The mouse cursor to display in this window
    HBRUSH hbrBackground;               // Pattern for the window background
    LPSTR lpszMenuName;                 // Name of the menu resource
    LPSTR lpszClassName;                // Name of the window class
} WNDCLASS;
```

The style element gives Windows information about how the window works. Table 2-2 lists the possible window class styles. Two or more of the window styles can be combined with the bitwise OR operator (|). The default style is CS_HREDRAW|CS_VREDRAW.

The lpfnWndProc member of the WNDCLASS structure is the address of the routine that Windows calls when it has a message for the window. ObjectWindows sets this address to a routine in the TWindow object class. You should not modify this value.

The next two elements let you add extra bytes to the window class and the window itself. This area is important to standard Windows programs because it is an excellent place to store data that should be encapsulated with the window. In ObjectWindows, this area is redundant because you can simply add fields to the object class for the window.

hInstance holds the instance of the program that owns the window. This value is set up by ObjectWindows and does not need to be changed.

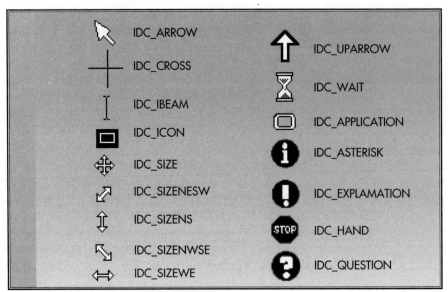

Figure 2-5
Built-in Icons
and Cursors

In the program for How-To 2.1, you put an icon in the resource file so that the icon would appear in program manager. Icons are also displayed when the window is minimized. To associate an icon with a window, you put the handle for the icon in the hIcon element of the WNDCLASS structure. If the icon is in the resource file, it must be loaded into memory with the LoadIcon function before it can be entered into the WNDCLASS structure. If you set this element to 0, no icon will be displayed. Instead, Windows makes the client area of the window the size of an icon and sends a WM_PAINT message to let your program paint the minimized window. There are several icons built into Windows that you can use if you do not want to draw your own. Figure 2-5 shows these icons.

As you move the mouse cursor around the Windows desktop, the cursor changes shape depending on the window under the cursor. The cursor to use for a window is determined by the handle in the hCursor element of the WND-CLASS structure. As with icons, you can put cursors in the resource file. To get a cursor from the resource file into memory use the LoadCursor function. You also can use any of the built-in cursors shown in Figure 2-5.

Windows paints the background of the window differently from the way it paints the text or graphics of a window. You can tell Windows to paint the background by putting a brush handle in the hbrBackground element. A brush is a pattern that Windows uses with some graphics commands. A solid brush sets

Style	Description
WS_BORDER	Draw a border around the window.
WS_CAPTION	Add a title bar to the window.
WS_CHILD	Make a child window.
WS_CHILDWINDOW	Make a child window.
WS_CLIPCHILDREN	Don't draw over child windows.
WS_CLIPSIBLINGS	Don't draw over windows with the same parent.
WS_DISABLED	Disable the window (cannot get input).
WS_DLGFRAME	Draw a double border.
WS_GROUP	Mark this window as the first in a group.
WS_HSCROLL	Add a horizontal scroll bar to the window.
WS_ICONIC	Make the window an icon.
WS_MAXIMIZE	Maximize the window.
WS_MAXIMIZEBOX	Include a control to maximize the window.
WS_MINIMIZE	Minimize the window.
WS_MINIMIZEBOX	Include a control to minimize the window.
WS_OVERLAPPED	Create a window with a sizing border and a title.
WS_POPUP	Create a pop-up window (does not have a parent).
WS_POPUPWINDOW	Create a pop-up window.
WS_SYSMENU	Include a system menu on the title bar.
WS_TABSTOP	Mark this window as one to get the input focus when the user presses the Tab key.
WS_THICKFRAME	Create a sizing border around the window.
WS_VISIBLE	Make the window visible.
WS_VSCROLL	Add a vertical scroll bar to the window.
WS_EX_DLGMODALFRAM	Draw a double border around the window.
WS_EX_NOPARENTNOTIFY	Do not send notify message to the parent window when this window is created or destroyed.
WS_EX_TOPMOST	Makes this window stay on top of others.

Table 2-3 Window Styles

every pixel to the brush color. A clear brush sets every pixel to the current background color. This program uses a hatched brush that sets diagonal lines to the brush color and all other pixels to the background color. For details on how to use brushes see Chapter 6, "Graphics."

The lpszMenuName is the name of the menu to load from the resource file. Whenever the window is drawn, Windows adds the indicated menu to the window. If this element is set to NULL, no menu is added. How-To 2.4 shows you how to use menus in ObjectWindows programs.

The last element is the name of the window class. ObjectWindows sets this field to the name returned by the GetClassName member function. When a program creates a window, it tells Windows the name of the window class to use. ObjectWindows uses the result of GetClassName when creating a window to ensure that the window uses the class you intended.

When a program creates a window, it tells Windows how the window looks and where it should be displayed. ObjectWindows programs store this information in a structure called Attr. The definition of Attr is:

```
typedef struct {
     DWORD Style;          // The style of the window
     DWORD ExStyle;        // The extended style
     int X;                // X-coordinate of the upper left corner of the window
     int Y;                // Y-coordinate of the upper left corner of the window
     int W;                // Width of the window
     int H;                // Height of the window
     LPSTR Menu;           // Name of the menu resource
     int Id;               // Id value used to identify control windows
     LPSTR Param;          // Data to be included in the WM_CREATE message for the window
} Attr;
```

The Style and ExStyle members tell Windows what kind of window to create. Table 2-3 lists the window styles and extended styles available.

The X, Y, W, and H elements tell Windows the position and size of the window. X and Y are the coordinates of the upper left corner of the window. W and H are the width and height of the window. By default, ObjectWindows sets these variables to the Windows constant CW_USEDEFAULT, which tells Windows to assign a value to the parameter.

A window can override the menu selection for its class by calling the AssignMenu member function (see How-To 2.4). The name of the menu in use is indicated by the Menu element of the Attr structure.

The Id element is a number usually assigned to control windows that programs can use to identify the control. The program in How-To 2.3 shows how to use control windows and refer to them by the ID.

The last element is a value that is sent to a window as part of the WM_CREATE message. In ObjectWindows, the WM_CREATE message is handled by the ObjectWindows library. Part of the processing for WM_CREATE is to call the SetupWindow member function, which you can overload if you need to process the WM_CREATE message.

2.3 How Do I...
Add Control Windows to a Window?

Complexity: EASY

PROBLEM

Windows applications get input from the user through special windows called control windows. Examples of control windows include list boxes, edit fields, and radio buttons. The most common place to find control windows is in dialog boxes, but they can be found in the main window also. The best example of this is the scroll bar found in many main windows.

ObjectWindows treats control windows as descendants of the TWindow class. Because control windows inherit features from TWindow objects, many of the things you learned about TWindow objects apply to control window objects. For example, the function that moves windows (MoveWindow) works equally well with regular windows or control windows.

This solution shows you how to add scroll bars and a static text control to the main window of an ObjectWindows program. The program gets messages from the scroll bars that indicate how to move the static text control. Figure 2-6 shows the main window of the program.

TECHNIQUE

ObjectWindows includes object classes for each of the control window types available in Windows. Table 2-4 lists the control types and the object class for the control. These classes are individually described in Chapter 3, "Dialog Boxes." The program in Chapter 3 creates the actual control windows by reading information from the resource file. Then, objects are associated with the controls so the program can handle the control.

In the following program, the scroll bar controls are created by changing the class of the main window and the static text control is created by creating a TStatic object. Scroll bars are such a common addition to windows

Figure 2-6
The Main Window of CONTROL.CPP

43

CONTROL TYPE	OBJECT	DESCRIPTION
Check box	TCheckBox	Small box with text next to it. When the user clicks on the control, the box is checked.
Combo box	TComboBox	Compound control that has an edit field and a list box.
Edit text	TEdit	A text control that can be edited.
Group box	TGroupBox	Rectangle that goes around other controls. The controls inside the box can be treated as a single group.
List box	TListBox	Box that contains a list of strings. The user can select strings from the list with the mouse.
Push button	TButton	Rectangular button that the user can push by clicking on it with the mouse.
Radio button	TRadioButton	Small circle with text next to it. When the user clicks on the control, the circle is filled in. Only one radio button in a group can be selected at a time.
Scroll bar	TScrollBar	Position selection control.
Static text	TStatic	A text control that cannot be edited.

Table 2-4 Controls

that you can tell Windows to add them to the window as easily as you add a caption or system menu. In ObjectWindows programs, this means modifying the Attr.Style member of the TWindow class by ORing it with the constants WS_HSCROLL and WS_VSCROLL.

Every control window object in ObjectWindows has at least two different constructors, one for associating the new object with an existing control and another for creating a new window to go with the object. Programs that create controls from instructions in the resource file use the first type of constructor. Because this program must create any controls it uses, it uses the second type of constructor.

Once the program has created the controls, it must handle messages from the controls and send them commands. Messages from control windows are sent to the parent window of the control (in this case, the main window). Most controls send a WM_COMMAND message to the parent window with the specific message type in the high word of the lParam argument. Scroll bars send their own type of message to the parent window, WM_VSCROLL for vertical scroll bars and WM_HSCROLL for horizontal scroll bars. The wParam argument of these messages indicates what happens to the scroll bar.

To issue commands to a control, you must know either its ID number, the window handle, or the address of the object for the control, depending on what command you want to send. For example, to change the text of a static text control you can use the member function SetText. To access a member functions you need the address of the object as in this example where the address is in the variable TheStatic:

```
TheStatic->SetText("New text");
```

This statement changes the text of the static text object in TheStatic to "New text." Another way to change the text is to use the Windows function SetWindowText. In this case, you need to know the window handle of the control. The window handle of any window is in the HWindow member. Using this information, you can also set the text with this statement:

```
SetWindowText(TheStatic->HWindow, "New text");
```

The third way to send a command to a control is by using the ID number. The Windows function SetDlgItemText sets the text of a control in a given dialog box that has a given control ID. If the control is in a dialog whose handle is hDlg and the ID for the control is 101, this command changes the text for the control:

```
SetDlgItemText(hDlg, 101, "New text", 8);
```

The last argument in this statement is the number of characters in the string. The commands that you can send to controls are not limited to changing the text. The program in this section shows how to use the MoveWindow function to move the control window. Chapter 3, "Dialog Boxes, " shows how to give other commands to controls.

STEPS

1. Create a new project called CONTROL.PRJ that includes the files CONTROL.CPP, CONTROL.RES, and STANDARD.DEF.
2. Use the IDE editor to create a source file called CONTROL.CPP with the following program:

```
/* program to test controls */
#include <owl.h>
#include <scrollba.h>
#include <static.h>

#define IDC_STATIC      101

class TMyWindow : public TWindow
{
    int   HPos;       // Position of the horizontal scroll bar
    int   VPos;       // Position of the vertical scroll bar
```

```
public:
      TMyWindow(PTWindowsObject AParent, LPSTR ATitle);
      virtual void SetupWindow();
      virtual void WMVScroll(RTMessage Msg)
            = [WM_FIRST + WM_VSCROLL];
      virtual void WMHScroll(RTMessage Msg)
            = [WM_FIRST + WM_HSCROLL];
};


/* Constructor for the main window */
TMyWindow::TMyWindow(PTWindowsObject AParent, LPSTR ATitle)
      : TWindow(AParent, ATitle)
{
      long BaseUnits;

      /* Set up the position of the '*' */
      VPos = 0;
      HPos = 0;
      /* Set up attributes and position of the window */
      Attr.Style = WS_OVERLAPPED | WS_SYSMENU | WS_VISIBLE
            | WS_VSCROLL | WS_HSCROLL;
      Attr.X = CW_USEDEFAULT;
      Attr.Y = CW_USEDEFAULT;
      Attr.W = 200;
      Attr.H = 200;
      /* Add a static control to the window */
      new TStatic(this, IDC_STATIC, "Static control"
            , 12, 0, 100, 20, 14);
}


/* Set up the scrollbars */
void
TMyWindow::SetupWindow()
{
      /* Do the default Setup */
      TWindow::SetupWindow();
      /* Use the Windows fucntion to set the range for the scroll bars */
      SetScrollRange(HWindow, SB_VERT, 0, 150, FALSE);
      SetScrollRange(HWindow, SB_HORZ, 0, 138, FALSE);
}


/* Respond to messages from the Vertical scroll bar */
void
TMyWindow::WMVScroll(RTMessage Msg)
{
      switch(Msg.WParam)
      {
            case SB_BOTTOM:                   // Move to the bottom of the window
                  VPos = 150;
                  break;
            case SB_LINEDOWN:                 // Move down one pixel
                  if(VPos < 150)
                        ++VPos;
                  break;
            case SB_LINEUP:                   // Move up one pixel
                  if(VPos)
                        --VPos;
                  break;
            case SB_PAGEDOWN:                 // Move down 10 pixels
```

```
                      if(VPos + 10 < 150)
                            VPos += 10;
                      else
                            VPos = 150;
                      break;
                case SB_PAGEUP:                     // Move up 10 pixels
                      if(VPos - 10 > 0)
                            VPos -= 10;
                      else
                            VPos = 0;
                      break;
                case SB_THUMBPOSITION:              // Move to the indicated position
                      VPos = Msg.LP.Lo;
                      break;
                case SB_TOP:                        // Move to the top of the window
                      VPos = 0;
                      break;
                default:
                      return;
          }
    /* Set the new thumb position in the scroll bar */
    SetScrollPos(HWindow, SB_VERT, VPos, TRUE);
    /* Move the static window control */
    MoveWindow(((PTStatic)ChildWithId(IDC_STATIC))->HWindow
          , HPos+12, VPos, 100, 20, TRUE);
}


/* Respond to messages from the Horizontal scroll bar */
void
TMyWindow::WMHScroll(RTMessage Msg)
{
    switch(Msg.WParam)
    {
          case SB_BOTTOM:                     // Move to the right edge
                HPos = 138;
                break;
          case SB_LINEDOWN:                   // Move right one pixel
                if(HPos < 138)
                      ++HPos;
                break;
          case SB_LINEUP:                     // Move left one pixel
                if(HPos)
                      --HPos;
                break;
          case SB_PAGEDOWN:                   // Move right 10 pixels
                if(HPos + 10 < 138)
                      HPos += 10;
                else
                      HPos = 138;
                break;
          case SB_PAGEUP:                     // Move left 10 pixels
                if(HPos - 10 > 0)
                      HPos -= 10;
                else
                      HPos = 0;
                break;
          case SB_THUMBPOSITION:              // Move to the indicated position
                HPos = Msg.LP.Lo;
                break;
```

```
        case SB_TOP:                                // Move to the left edge
            HPos = 0;
            break;
        default:
            return;
    }
    /* Move the thumb in the scroll bar */
    SetScrollPos(HWindow, SB_HORZ, HPos, TRUE);
    /* Move the static window */
    MoveWindow(((PTStatic)ChildWithId(IDC_STATIC))->HWindow
        , HPos+12, VPos, 100, 20, TRUE);
}


/* Define the application class for this program */
class TMyApp : public TApplication
{
public:
    TMyApp(LPSTR AName, HINSTANCE Inst, HINSTANCE PrevInst
        , LPSTR CmdLine, int Show)
        : TApplication(AName, Inst, PrevInst, CmdLine, Show)
        {};
    virtual void InitMainWindow();
};


void TMyApp::InitMainWindow()
{
    MainWindow = new TMyWindow(NULL, Name);
}


int PASCAL
WinMain(HINSTANCE Inst, HINSTANCE PrevInst, LPSTR CmdLine, int Show)
{
    TMyApp MyApp("Test program", Inst, PrevInst, CmdLine, Show);

    MyApp.Run();
    return MyApp.Status;
}
```

3. Use the Resource Workshop to create a resource file called CONTROL.RES that includes an icon for this program.

4. Select *Run* from the *Run* menu to compile and run the program.

HOW IT WORKS

The definition for the main window is at the beginning of the program. The definition shows that the program overloads the constructor, the SetupWindow function, and functions to handle messages from the scroll bars. There are also two variables, HPos and VPos, that give the location of the static text control. The first thing the constructor does is initialize these variables. Next, the constructor puts values into the Attr member that tell ObjectWindows the style,

Message	Description
SB_BOTTOM	The thumb was moved to the bottom.
SB_LINEDOWN	The user clicked the down arrow.
SB_PAGEDOWN	The user clicked the area below the slider.
SB_PAGEUP	The user clicked the area above the slider.
SB_THUMBPOSITION	The user moved the thumb by dragging it.
SB_TOP	The user moved the slider to the top.

Table 2-5 Scroll Bar Message Types

size, and location of the window. Note that the style includes the Windows constants WS_HSCROLL and WS_VSCROLL. These constants tell Windows to add scroll bar controls to the window. Finally, the constructor creates a TStatic object that creates the static control window.

The member function SetupWindow sets the range of the scroll bars. A scroll bar is a graphical representation of a range of integers. The lowest integer is at the top or left and the greatest is at the bottom or right. The value selected by the user is indicated by the position of the *thumb*, the gray square that moves inside the scroll bar. The Windows function SetScrollRange sets the actual numbers for the lowest and highest values represented by the scroll bar. The Windows function SetScrollPos sets the position of the thumb.

The member functions WMVScroll and WMHScroll handle messages from the scroll bars. A scroll bar can send five different messages depending on what the user does. Table 2-5 shows the messages. Note that the terms all refer to a vertical scroll bar, but horizontal scroll bars send the same messages. Imagine the horizontal scroll bar as a vertical scroll bar that has fallen over so that the top is now at the left.

The program determines what type of message it received and recomputes the position of the static control window. It uses this new position in the call to the Windows MoveWindow function that moves the control window. Windows functions such as MoveWindow require the handle to the window receiving the command. ObjectWindows keeps the handle to the window in the member variable HWindow. To get at this variable, you need to know the address of the window. The program gets the address by calling the function ChildWithId, which is a member function in the parent window. This function searches the child windows looking for one with the given ID.

The rest of the program is the TApplication class that creates the main window and runs the program. This part is similar to previous programs.

COMMENT

Using control windows highlights an important feature of Windows, everything is a window. Scroll bars, menus, and icons all follow the same rules and react to the same commands. ObjectWindows preserves this paradigm by defining objects that are descendants of TWindow for each window type.

You can use this feature to help learn Windows programming. Once you have learned the functions that work with a window, you can use them to operate on other objects. For example, in this solution you learned how to change the text of a static text control. It should not surprise you to learn that you can use the same commands to change the title of dialog boxes or the text in an edit control.

2.4 How Do I...
Add Menus to a Program?

Complexity: EASY

PROBLEM

Drop-down menus are an important part of the Windows application interface. They are how users tell a program what to do next. There are two parts to adding a menu to your program. The first part is to create a menu resource in the resource file. The second part is to add code to the program to load the menu and get messages from it. This solution shows you the basics of adding a menu to a program. For more information on menus, see Chapter 4, "Menus."

TECHNIQUE

The Resource Workshop makes creating a menu resource easy. As you add new commands to the menu, the Resource Workshop shows you what the menu will look like in the program. If you don't like what you see, you can move things around until the menu is just right.

One of the things that you tell the Resource Workshop is the command ID for each command in the menu. ObjectWindows uses the command ID to create a message that your program acts on when the user selects a command. The use of IDs means that you can move a menu command anywhere you want in the menu without affecting the program that uses the menu. The program uses the ID to identify the command instead of the position of the command in the menu.

Loading a menu from a resource file is not the only way to make a menu. There are over 20 Windows functions that affect menus. These functions let you add or delete items from menus, create new menus, change the check mark used in menus, and even add graphics to menus.

This program shows how to use menus from the resource file and then go beyond that with Windows functions to add functionality to your menus. You can add these functions to your own programs to make your menus into something more than just a way to enter commands.

STEPS

1. Create a new project called MENUAPP.PRJ that includes the files MENU-APP.CPP, MENUAPP.RES, and STANDARD.DEF.

2. Use the IDE editor to create the source file MENUAPP.CPP using the following source:

```
/* MENUAPP An OWL program with menus */
#include <owl.h>

#define MID_BEEP          101
#define MID_PRINT         102

/* Definition of the main window */
class TMyWindow : public TWindow
{
    public:
          TMyWindow(PTWindowsObject AParent, LPSTR ATitle);
          /* Handle messages from the menu */
          virtual void DoBeep(RTMessage) = [CM_FIRST + MID_BEEP];
          virtual void DoPrint(RTMessage) = [CM_FIRST + MID_PRINT];
};

/* Initialize the menu */
TMyWindow::TMyWindow(PTWindowsObject AParent, LPSTR ATitle)
      : TWindow(AParent, ATitle)
{
      AssignMenu("MENUAPP");
}

/* Respond to the Beep menu command */
void TMyWindow::DoBeep(RTMessage)
{
      MessageBeep(0);
}

/* Respond to the Print menu command */
void TMyWindow::DoPrint(RTMessage)
{
      HDC hDC;

      hDC = GetDC(HWindow);
      TextOut(hDC, 10, 10, "Some Text", 9);
      ReleaseDC(HWindow, hDC);
}
```

```
/* Define the application object */
class TMenuApp : public TApplication
{
     public:
             TMenuApp(LPSTR ApName, HINSTANCE Inst, HINSTANCE PrevInst
                 , LPSTR CmdLine, int CmdShow) : TApplication(ApName
                 , Inst, PrevInst, CmdLine, CmdShow) {};
             virtual void InitMainWindow();
};

void TMenuApp::InitMainWindow()
{
     MainWindow = new TMyWindow(NULL, "Menu, please");
}

int PASCAL WinMain(HINSTANCE Inst, HINSTANCE PrevInst, LPSTR CmdLine
     , int CmdShow)
{
     TMenuApp TheApp("", Inst
             , PrevInst, CmdLine, CmdShow);

     TheApp.Run();
     return TheApp.Status;
}
```

3. Use the Resource Workshop to create the resource file MENUAPP.RES. This resource file must include a menu named MENUAPP. To create MENUAPP, select "Edit as Text" from the resource menu and enter this text:

```
MENUAPP MENU
BEGIN
     POPUP "&First", CHECKED
     BEGIN
          MENUITEM "&Beep", 101
     END

     POPUP "&Second"
     BEGIN
          MENUITEM "&Print", 102
     END
END
```

You can use the menu editor in the Resource Workshop to see how each of these commands creates parts of a menu. Note the use of the ampersand (&) to mark the accelerator key for the menu selection. By pressing Alt and the letter following the ampersand in a selection, the user can choose a menu command from the keyboard.

4. Select *Run* from the *Run* menu to run the program.

HOW IT WORKS

The statements at the beginning of the program create symbols for the menu command ID numbers. These numbers match the ID numbers in the menu in the resource file. The program uses the ID numbers to create message response member functions that handle the menu commands. This line defines an indexed member function for the IDM_BEEP ID:

```
virtual void DoBeep(RTMessage) = [CM_FIRST + MID_BEEP];
```

The constant CM_FIRST puts the index number into the range set aside for menu commands. When the user selects a menu command, Windows generates a WM_COMMAND message for the parent window that has the ID for the menu command in the wParam parameter. ObjectWindows gets the WM_COMMAND message, gets the ID, and finds the member function for the menu command.

The MENUAPP program includes two member functions for handling menu commands. The first is DoBeep, which calls the Windows function MessageBeep to beep the speaker. The second function, called DoPrint, prints a string on the main window. ObjectWindows handles all of the details of making sure these functions get called at the right time.

The rest of the program handles the TApplication object and is the same as for previous programs.

COMMENT

This example shows just how simple it can be to add menus to a program. Your programs will undoubtedly have more complicated response functions and most programs have more than two menu commands, but the basic concept stays the same. If your program has a more complex structure with submenus in submenus, you still end up with menu commands with IDs that indicate what member function to call in the program.

For most programs, this simple menu scheme works fine. If your program requires something extra, such as the ability to change a menu during run time, or pictures in the menu, you need to add calls to Windows that change the menus. These advanced menu commands are covered in Chapter 4, "Menus."

2.5 How Do I...
Create an MDI Application?

Complexity: MODERATE

PROBLEM

Some applications can work on more than one data file at a time. Windows provides two ways to handle this situation. One way is to let the user start multiple instances of the program and have each instance work on a different file. The

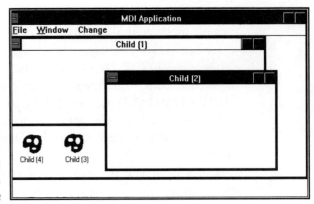

Figure 2-7
An MDI
Application

other is to make the application conform to the Multiple Document Interface (MDI) standard. MDI applications have a single frame and menu bar that can work on any number of child windows, each of which holds a file. Figure 2-7 shows the MDI application described in this example.

ObjectWindows helps you make MDI applications by giving you an object class that handles the details of working MDI applications. You can modify this class to make menu selections that work on selected windows or all of the child windows at once.

TECHNIQUE

The previous programs in this chapter used only one window class. That was enough to handle the single main window used in those programs. MDI applications, on the other hand, have many windows. The child windows that hold the documents in an MDI application are often similar to each other so each one is just an instance of the same object class. The window that has the menu and contains all of the child windows is called the frame window and is quite different from the child windows and needs its own object class.

The frame window in MDI applications has special properties that let it keep track of the child windows. The ObjectWindows library provides this functionality in an object class called TMDIFrame. This class is a descendant of TWindow, so you can use it as the main window of your application. The frame window includes the menu for the application and receives all of the WM_COMMAND messages from the menu. If the frame window does not handle a particular menu selection, the TMDIFrame object class passes the message to the child window that has the focus.

The child windows of an MDI application can be any window descended from TWindow. The standard MDI child window has a title bar with a system menu and minimize and maximize buttons, and a sizing border. This is the same as for a standard TWindow object. When the user minimizes a child window of an MDI application, the application draws an icon for that window in the frame window. You can set the icon for the window using the GetWindowClass member function as demonstrated in How-To 2.2.

MDI Child windows get a WM_COMMAND message from menu selections if the message is not handled by the frame window and if the child window has the input focus. Windows gives the input focus to the last window clicked with the mouse or the window made active by a programmed command. Windows marks the window with the input focus visually by changing the color of the title bar.

STEPS

1. Create a new project file called MDIAPP.PRJ that includes the files MDI-APP.CPP, MDIAPP.RES, and STANDARD.DEF.

2. Use the IDE editor to create a source file called MDIAPP.CPP with the following program:

```
/* MDIAPP.CPP An example of an MDI application */
#include <owl.h>
#include <mdi.h>

#define CM_SHRINK          101
#define CM_GROW            102
#define CM_GROWALL         103
#define CM_SHRINKALL       104

class TMyApp : public TApplication
{
public:
      TMyApp(LPSTR AName, HINSTANCE Inst, HINSTANCE Prev
            , LPSTR lpCmdLine, int nCmdShow)
            : TApplication(AName, Inst, Prev, lpCmdLine, nCmdShow) {};
  virtual void InitMainWindow();
};

class TMyMDIChild : public TWindow
{
public:
  TMyMDIChild(PTWindowsObject AParent, int ChildNum);
  virtual LPSTR GetClassName() { return "MDIChild"; };
  virtual void GetWindowClass(WNDCLASS& AWndClass);
  virtual void Shrink(RTMessage) = [CM_FIRST + CM_SHRINK];
  virtual void Grow(RTMessage) = [CM_FIRST + CM_GROW];
};

typedef TMyMDIChild _FAR *PChild;

/* Constructor for child window objects */
TMyMDIChild::TMyMDIChild(PTWindowsObject AParent, int ChildNum)
  : TWindow(AParent, "")
{
      char TitleStr[12];
```

```
      wsprintf(TitleStr, "Child (%d)", ChildNum);
      SetCaption(TitleStr);
}


/* Make the child window smaller */
void TMyMDIChild::Shrink(RTMessage)
{
      HWND PrntHand;
      RECT r, RectParent;

      /* Don't resize if minimized or maximized */
      if(!IsIconic(HWindow) && !IsZoomed(HWindow))
      {
            PrntHand = GetParent(HWindow);
            GetWindowRect(PrntHand, &RectParent);
            GetWindowRect(HWindow, &r);
            r.left -= RectParent.left;
            r.top -= RectParent.top;
            r.right -= RectParent.left;
            r.bottom -= RectParent.top;
            /* Change the size of the window */
            MoveWindow(HWindow, r.left+10, r.top+10
                  , r.right-r.left-20, r.bottom-r.top-20, TRUE);
      }
}


/* Make the child window larger */
void TMyMDIChild::Grow(RTMessage)
{
      HWND PrntHand;
      RECT r, RectParent;

      if(!IsIconic(HWindow) && !IsZoomed(HWindow))
      {
            PrntHand = GetParent(HWindow);
            GetWindowRect(PrntHand, &RectParent);
            GetWindowRect(HWindow, &r);
            r.left -= RectParent.left;
            r.top -= RectParent.top;
            r.right -= RectParent.left;
            r.bottom -= RectParent.top;
            MoveWindow(HWindow, r.left-10, r.top-10
                  , r.right-r.left+20, r.bottom-r.top+20, TRUE);
      }
}


/* Set up the icon for the child window */
void TMyMDIChild::GetWindowClass(WNDCLASS& AWndClass)
{
      TWindow::GetWindowClass(AWndClass);
      AWndClass.hIcon = LoadIcon(AWndClass.hInstance, "ChildPict");
}

class TMyMDIFrame : public TMDIFrame
{
      int ChildCount;
public:
      TMyMDIFrame(LPSTR ATitle);
      void SetupWindow();
```

```
        virtual PTWindowsObject CreateChild();
        virtual void ShrinkAll(RTMessage) = [CM_FIRST + CM_SHRINKALL];
        virtual void GrowAll(RTMessage) = [CM_FIRST + CM_GROWALL];
};


/* Construct the frame window object */
TMyMDIFrame::TMyMDIFrame(LPSTR ATitle)
        : TMDIFrame(ATitle, "MDIMenu")
{
        /* Indicate which menu gets the window information */
        ChildMenuPos = 1;
}


/* Create the initial child window */
void TMyMDIFrame::SetupWindow()
{
        TMDIFrame::SetupWindow();
        ChildCount = 0;
        CreateChild();
}


/* Make a child window */
PTWindowsObject TMyMDIFrame::CreateChild()
{
        return GetApplication()->MakeWindow(new TMyMDIChild(this
              , ++ChildCount));
}


/* Function that ForEach can use to shrink a child window */
void
ShrinkOne(Pvoid P, Pvoid)
{
        HWND PrntHand;
        RECT r, RectParent;

        if(!IsIconic(((PChild)P)->HWindow)
              && !IsZoomed(((PChild)P)->HWindow))
        {
              PrntHand = GetParent(((PChild)P)->HWindow);
              GetWindowRect(PrntHand, &RectParent);
              GetWindowRect(((PChild)P)->HWindow, &r);
              r.left -= RectParent.left;
              r.top -= RectParent.top;
              r.right -= RectParent.left;
              r.bottom -= RectParent.top;
              MoveWindow(((PChild)P)->HWindow, r.left+10, r.top+10
                    , r.right-r.left-20, r.bottom-r.top-20, TRUE);
        }
}


/* Shrink all of the child windows */
void
TMyMDIFrame::ShrinkAll(RTMessage)
{
        /* Apply the ShrinkOne function to each child window */
        ForEach(ShrinkOne, NULL);
}


/* Function that ForEach can use to grow a window */
```

```
void
GrowOne(Pvoid P, Pvoid)
{
     HWND PrntHand;
     RECT r, RectParent;

     if(!IsIconic(((PChild)P)->HWindow)
          && !IsZoomed(((PChild)P)->HWindow))
     {
          PrntHand = GetParent(((PChild)P)->HWindow);
          GetWindowRect(PrntHand, &RectParent);
          GetWindowRect(((PChild)P)->HWindow, &r);
          r.left -= RectParent.left;
          r.top -= RectParent.top;
          r.right -= RectParent.left;
          r.bottom -= RectParent.top;
          MoveWindow(((PChild)P)->HWindow, r.left-10, r.top-10
               , r.right-r.left+20, r.bottom-r.top+20, TRUE);
     }
}

/* Grow all of the child windows */
void
TMyMDIFrame::GrowAll(RTMessage)
{
     ForEach(GrowOne, NULL);
}

void TMyApp::InitMainWindow()
{
  MainWindow = new TMyMDIFrame(Name);
}

int PASCAL WinMain(HINSTANCE hInstance, HINSTANCE hPrevInstance,
  LPSTR lpCmdLine, int nCmdShow)
{
     TMyApp MyApp("MDI Application", hInstance
     , hPrevInstance, lpCmdLine, nCmdShow);

     MyApp.Run();
     return MyApp.Status;
}
```

3. Use the Resource Workshop to create a resource file called MDIAPP.RES that has a menu resource called MDIMenu and an icon resource called ChildPict. The icon can be any picture you like. The menu resource should have these commands:

```
MDIMENU MENU
BEGIN
     POPUP "&File"
     BEGIN
          MENUITEM "&New", 24339
          MENUITEM "&Exit", 24340
     END

     POPUP "&Window"
```

```
      BEGIN
            MENUITEM "&Cascade", 24337
            MENUITEM "&Tile", 24336
            MENUITEM "&Arrange icons", 24335
            MENUITEM "&Close all", 24338
      END

      POPUP "Change"
      BEGIN
            MENUITEM "&Grow", 102
            MENUITEM "&Shrink", 101
            MENUITEM "G&row all", 103
            MENUITEM "S&hrink all", 104
      END

END
```

4. Use the *Run* command to compile and run the program.

HOW IT WORKS

The object class TMyMDIChild, which represents the MDI child windows, is similar to the windows used in previous examples. It is a descendant of TWindow. It uses the GetClassName and GetWindowClass to set up the icon for the window. It also includes two message response functions to handle menu messages.

The constructor is a little different in that you pass it a window number that it places in the title of the window. This number enables the user to tell one window from another. The program can tell one window from another by the address of the object that goes with the window, but it is also important to let the user know what window is what. In applications such as word processors or spreadsheets, the program can put the file name in the title bar to distinguish one window from another.

The indexed member functions in TMyMDIFrame handle a command from the menu to grow or shrink. These functions use Windows functions to change the size of the window. The first step is to get the handle of the parent window using the Windows function GetParent. Next, the program uses the parent window handle to get the size and location of the parent window on the desktop by calling the GetWindowRect Windows function. The program also uses GetWindowRect to get the size and position of the child window. The last step is to update the size and position of the child window and call MoveWindow to move it.

The rectangle that GetWindowRect returns is always relative to the desktop. The position used in MoveWindow is relative to the parent window. MDIAPP handles this problem by subtracting the parent window coordinates from the child window coordinates before calling MoveWindow.

MDIAPP uses the object class TMyMDIFrame to represent the MDI frame window. This object class is descended from the ObjectWindows class TMDIFrame, which handles many of the details of MDI programs. The first thing TMDIFrame handles is the application menu. MDIAPP passes the name of the menu resource as an argument to the constructor for TMDIFrame. ObjectWindows also handles some of the menu selections for MDI applications. These selections create new windows, arrange windows and icons, and delete windows. All you need to do to access these features is to include items in the menu with the appropriate ID. Table 2-6 lists the functions and the ID to use.

The frame window object in MDIAPP keeps track of the number of child windows created in a data member called ChildCount. This variable is passed to the child window constructor to be used in the window title. Then, ChildCount is incremented for the next window. Note that ChildCount is not necessarily the number of child windows because it is not decremented when windows are closed.

One of the data members in TMDIFrame objects is ChildMenuPos. This variable indicates which menu includes the list of child windows. The constructor for TMyMDIFrame objects sets ChildMenuPos to 1 indicating the first menu item on the menu bar.

MDIAPP uses the SetupWindow member function of TMyMDIFrame to initialize ChildCount and create the first child window. The member function

FUNCTION	ID	DESCRIPTION
CM_CREATECHILD	24339	Make a new child window.
CM_TILECHILDREN	24336	Arrange the child windows so they do not overlap.
CM_CASCADECHILDREN	24337	Arrange the child windows so the cascade is from the upper left corner.
CM_ARRANGEICONS	24335	Arrange the iconized windows in rows at the bottom of the frame window.
CM_CLOSECHILDREN	24338	Close all of the child windows.

Table 2-6 MDI Menu Functions

CreateChild creates a new TMyMDIChild object and passes the object address to MakeWindow to create the window. Then the frame window can put the new window in a list of child windows.

The frame object handles menu commands that grow or shrink all of the child windows. To do these operations, the frame object calls the member function ForEach. The arguments to ForEach are the address of a function to apply to each child window and a pointer to data that the function needs. In this program, the data pointer is set to NULL. The function that ForEach uses gets a pointer to the child window and the pointer given to ForEach. It is called once for each child window.

The rest of the program is similar to the other ObjectWindows programs in this chapter. Note that the main window is a TMyMDIFrame object, the rest is handled by routines in ObjectWindows.

COMMENT

MDI applications have several advantages over standard applications for handling multiple files. The alternative to an MDI application is to let the user invoke multiple instances of the application, each with its own data file. When you do this, each instance must load its own copy of the menu, icons, bitmaps, and other resources. By switching to an MDI application, your program can share these resources, reducing the memory requirements of the application.

Another advantage of MDI applications is that the program can prevent the user from opening more than one copy of a file. With multiple instances, you must write special code that lets one instance check with other instances to see what files are open. With an MDI application, you can use a ForEach command to check what files are loaded and prevent the user from loading another copy and potentially losing changes.

If you program Windows without ObjectWindows, creating an MDI application is a difficult job. Starting with Windows version 3.0, there is some support for MDI applications built into Windows but it is not as easy to use as the ObjectWindows support. For example, there is no command like ForEach to apply a command to all windows. You must create a loop that looks up the child window handles and performs the command for each window found.

Considering the advantages of MDI applications over multiple instances and the ease of using ObjectWindows to make MDI applications, you should consider MDI for all applications that use multiple files.

2.6 How Do I...
Make and Use Dynamic Link Libraries?

Complexity: MODERATE

PROBLEM

When you use a library such as ObjectWindows, the linker finds all of the routines in the library that your program uses and adds them to the executable file. In the case of ObjectWindows, this means that even a simple program can use as much as 50,000 bytes of disk space. Because programming with ObjectWindows is so easy, it won't be long before you have a dozen new programs and are looking for a way to squeeze another megabyte onto your hard drive.

The quick solution to the problem is to use Dynamic Link Libraries (DLL). They are libraries that are linked to a program when the program runs. This means you can keep one copy of the library on the disk and use it in as many programs as you want. All of the libraries for ObjectWindows come in DLL form. You can use them by setting some switches in the *Options* menu of the IDE.

This solution shows you how to create and use your own DLL modules. You can put any functions that you might have put in a conventional library into a DLL and keep a single copy of the routines on your hard drive.

TECHNIQUE

There are only a few changes you need to make to a program to make it use DLL modules. This solution shows you how to convert the program in How-To 2.1 to a program and a DLL. In this case, the DLL includes the TMyWindow object class. This not only makes the TMyWindow object available to other programs, but it lets you change the window routines without recompiling the main program.

The first step in converting OWLAPP.CPP is to move the definition of the TMyWindowClass to an include file. The reason for this is so that it can be included in the DLL and in the program that uses the DLL. Then add the keyword _EXPORT to the class. This tells Borland C++ that the address of the class should be available to programs that use the DLL. Windows only allows routines that have been exported from a DLL to be called. This is similar to using the PUBLIC directive in an assembly language program.

The next step is to create the source for the DLL. Windows has some requirements that you must be aware of. The first is that you provide the entry and exit routines LibMain and WEP. Windows calls LibMain when it loads the DLL and WEP when it unloads the DLL. For ObjectWindows programs, you can use these routines to create a TModule object and destroy it when the library is unloaded. The program in this solution gives examples of these routines that you can copy into your own libraries.

There is only one difference between the code used in How-To 2.1 and the DLL. In the DLL program, the GetClassName and GetWindowClass routines have been added to set the icon for the window. The reason for this is to demonstrate how to use resources in a DLL. Look at the LoadIcon statement in the GetWindowClass function. It gets the instance from the DLL module object to indicate that the icon is in the resources attached to the DLL. To get the DLL from the main program, you can use a statement like:

```
AWndClass.hIcon = LoadIcon(AWndClass.hInstance, "DLLPROG");
```

The .DEF file, used in linking Windows programs, is different for a DLL. The first statement in this file is as LIBRARY statement to indicate that this is a DLL instead of an executable program. You also need to tell the Borland C++ compiler that it should make a DLL. The easiest way to do this is to go to the *Application...* selection in the *Options* menu and press the Windows DLL button in the dialog that comes up. This sets the various options in the compiler that make it create a DLL.

To use the routines in a DLL requires no changes to the main program source. The difference is that you must link in a special library called an import library that lets the linker resolve calls to routines in the DLL. To create an import library, use the program IMPLIBW.EXE that is included with Turbo C++ for Windows, and Borland C++ with Applications Framework.

STEPS

1. Create a new project file called THEDLL.PRJ that includes the files THEDLL.CPP, THEDLL.RES, and THEDLL.DEF.

2. Use the Borland C++ IDE editor to create the file with the following text:

```
/* Definition of DLL window object */

class _EXPORT TMyWindow : public TWindow
{
      public:
            TMyWindow(PTWindowsObject AParent, LPSTR ATitle)
                  : TWindow(AParent, ATitle) {};
            virtual LPSTR GetClassName();
            virtual void GetWindowClass(WNDCLASS& AWndClass);
            virtual void WMPaint(RTMessage)
                  = [WM_FIRST + WM_PAINT];
};
```

3. Use the IDE editor to create the source file THEDLL.CPP with the following program:

```
/* DLL program */
#include <owl.h>
#include "thedll.h"

PTModule TheModule;

int FAR PASCAL LibMain(HANDLE Inst, WORD
    , WORD, LPSTR CmdLine)
{
    int TheStatus;

    TheModule = new TModule("THEDLL", Inst, CmdLine);
    TheStatus = TheModule->Status;
    if(TheStatus)
    {
        delete TheModule;
        TheModule = NULL;
    }
    return (TheStatus==0);
}

int FAR PASCAL WEP(int)
{
    if(TheModule)
        delete TheModule;
    return 1;
}

LPSTR TMyWindow::GetClassName()
{
    return "DLLWindow";
}

void TMyWindow::GetWindowClass(WNDCLASS& AWndClass)
{
    TWindow::GetWindowClass(AWndClass);
    AWndClass.hIcon = LoadIcon(TheModule->hInstance, "DLLICON");
}

void TMyWindow::WMPaint(RTMessage)
{
    PAINTSTRUCT ps;
    HDC hDC;

    memset(&ps, 0x00, sizeof(PAINTSTRUCT));
    hDC = BeginPaint(HWindow, &ps);
    TextOut(hDC, 10, 10, "This is the client area", 23);
    EndPaint(HWindow, &ps);
}
```

4. Use the Resource Workshop to create a resource file called THEDLL.RES with an icon called DLLICON. You can use one of the icons from Figure 2-8.

5. Use the IDE editor to create a source file called THEDLL.DEF that includes this text:

```
LIBRARY THEDLL
DESCRIPTION     'Sample DLL'
EXETYPE    WINDOWS
CODE PRELOAD MOVEABLE DISCARDABLE
DATA PRELOAD MOVEABLE SINGLE
HEAPSIZE 1024
```

Note that this .DEF file is different from the standard .DEF file used in other programs in this chapter. The first line describes the program as a LIBRARY and gives it a name. This is what tells the linker to create a .DLL file instead of an .EXE file.

Figure 2-8
Icons for the DLL Program

6. Go to the *Options* menu of the Turbo C++ IDE and select *Application....* Press the button for Windows DLL in the dialog that appears.

7. Select *Make* from the *Compile* menu to create the DLL.

8. Use the Implibw program to make an import library for this DLL.

9. Create a new project called USEDLL.PRJ that includes the files: US-EDLL.CPP, USEDLL.RES, STANDARD.DEF, and THEDLL.LIB.

10. Use the IDE to create a source file called USEDLL.CPP with the following program:

```
/* Program that uses THEDLL.DLL */
#include <owl.h>
#include "thedll.h"

/* The application object */
class TFirstApp : public TApplication
{
    public:
        TFirstApp(LPSTR ApName, HINSTANCE Inst, HINSTANCE PrevInst
            , LPSTR CmdLine, int CmdShow) : TApplication(ApName
            , Inst, PrevInst, CmdLine, CmdShow) {};
        virtual void InitMainWindow();
};

/* Create the main window */
void TFirstApp::InitMainWindow()
{
    MainWindow = new TMyWindow(NULL, "Hello, World");
}

/* Windows entry point */
int PASCAL WinMain(HINSTANCE Inst, HINSTANCE PrevInst, LPSTR CmdLine
    , int CmdShow)
{
    TFirstApp FirstApp("", Inst
        , PrevInst, CmdLine, CmdShow);

    FirstApp.Run();
    return FirstApp.Status;
}
```

11. Use the Resource Workshop to create a resource file called USEDLL.RES with an icon named DLLPROG.

12. Use the *Run* command to compile and run the program. The result should look just like the program in How-To 2.1.

HOW IT WORKS

The DLL module for this program is called THEDLL.DLL. It contains all of the routines that are used by the TMyWindow object class. The definition of the class is in the include file THEDLL.H. The reason for moving the class definition is so that it can be included in programs that use the DLL. Note that the definition includes the symbol _EXPORT. When used in DLL modules, the symbol _EXPORT tells the compiler to make the symbol available to other programs. In regular programs, _EXPORT does nothing. The dual nature of this symbol makes it ideal for use in include files that must be used with DLL modules and the programs that call them.

The source for the DLL, called THEDLL.CPP, contains the source for the member functions of the TMyWindow object class. These routines are the same as those used in other programs from this chapter. The only special consideration is in the use of instance handles. Windows requires that a window have the same instance handle as the program that includes the message loop. Normally, this is handled automatically by ObjectWindows, but there is a problem when it comes to getting resources. In the other programs in this chapter, routines such as LoadIcon and LoadMenu that get information from the program's resource file, get the instance handle from the window. In this program, the icon resource for the window is in the DLL module not in the main program. THEDLL.CPP uses the module object TheModule to get the correct instance handle.

The program that uses THEDLL.DLL is called USEDLL.EXE. The source for this program is the same as for the program in How-To 2.1 except that the TMyWindow object class code is gone and the program includes the file THEDLL.H. When you link the program you must include the import library THEDLL.LIB to access the routines in the DLL.

COMMENT

DLL modules are one of the great programming features of Windows. Not only do they keep the size of programs down, but they make it easy to add optional features to programs, make updates to programs, and make interchangable modules. Program size is kept low by removing library code from the program and putting it in the DLL module. This reduces the use of disk space for storing programs and, since the DLL is shared by all running programs, it keeps memory usage down as well.

You can use DLL modules to implement optional features in your program. For example, if you want to create an optional macro language for your program, you can put the macro language code in a DLL module. For users who want the macro language, you include the DLL file. For others, do not include the DLL. The users without the DLL cannot use macros.

With traditional library files, when you update the library you must recompile all of the programs that use the library before they will use the update. With DLL modules, as soon as you change the DLL, all programs use the new DLL. There is also an advantage when it comes to distributing updates. If you use modems to update users, just sending the updated DLL can give big savings in time over updating the entire program.

Some programs can use DLL modules to create interchangable modules. For example, a terminal emulation program can have a number of DLL modules each of which implements a different terminal emulation. Each of the DLL modules exports the same routines so that the main program uses them the same way. By loading a different DLL, the program emulates a different terminal. This feature is used to implement foreign language dialog boxes in How-To 3-8.

There are some things to be careful of when using DLL modules. The first thing is that you cannot have multiple instances of a DLL. Although several programs can access a single DLL, the DLL always uses the same data segment. This affects global variables used in the DLL. To see how this affects your programs, imagine a system in which there are two programs, "A" and "B," using a single DLL. If the DLL uses a global variable to keep track of the color of windows in the programs and program A changes the color, program B also changes color because the color variable is in the same instance. This does not happen in regular programs because Windows creates a new data segment for each instance.

The most common source of trouble in DLL modules is the fact that the data segment for the DLL is not the same as the stack segment. In regular programs, the data segment, which holds global variables, is the same as the stack segment, which holds automatic variables. This fact lets the compiler make assumptions that improve performance in the small and medium memory models. For example, when saving the address of a string or array, the compiler can just save the offset of the string or array from the beginning of the data segment. It makes no difference if the string or array is local or global, saving the offset always works.

With DLL modules, there is a difference between the segment for local and global data. In this case, the compiler cannot make any assumptions about the segment of an address. The compiler must always include the segment along with the offset when using pointers. You must keep this in mind if your program uses pointers. In DLL modules, all pointers should be far pointers to avoid problems. One way to make sure you handle pointers correctly is to always use the large memory module when programming DLL modules.

Dialog Boxes **3**

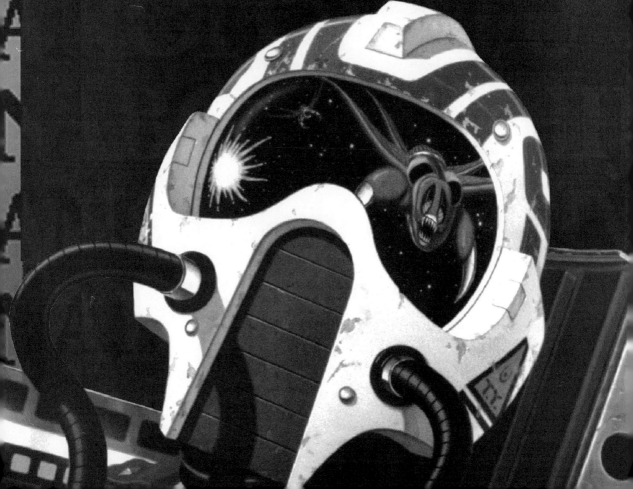

3

Windows applications use dialog boxes to get information from the user. A dialog box contains controls that let the user enter text or choose options. Because these controls are standardized across all applications, the user can use experience gained in one application to help learn a new application. By adding dialog boxes to your programs, you do not have to invent your own interface and explain it to users.

There are two parts to a Windows dialog box. The first part is the description of controls that appear in the dialog box. Most applications keep this information in the resource file so that it can be changed without recompiling the program. The second part of a dialog box is the code that tells Windows what to do with the controls in the dialog. Conventional Windows programs use a message handling function to control the dialog. ObjectWindows programs create an object class descended from the ObjectWindows class TDialog.

The TDialog object class is derived from TWindow, so many of the same techniques you learned in Chapter 2, "ObjectWindows Basics," for handling windows apply to dialog boxes. For example, you use the same control object classes described in How-To 2.3 to handle the controls in a dialog box. This chapter shows how to use the features unique to TDialog objects and gives complete information about each of the control object classes.

3.1 Use the TDialog Object Class

This example shows how to use the features of TDialog objects that are not part of TWindow objects. The program uses a dialog box to get information from the user and copies the information to another dialog box. The first dialog box is *modal*, which means that while the dialog is displayed, the rest of the application does not get event messages. The second dialog is *modeless*, meaning that you can use other windows in the application while the dialog is displayed.

3.2 Make a File Selection Dialog

One of the reasons for using a library like ObjectWindows is to avoid having to write difficult or commonly used routines. One of the commonly used routines handled by ObjectWindows is the file selection dialog. This is a dialog that appears in most Windows applications and it can be difficult to get just right. ObjectWindows includes the object class TFileDialog to handle file dialogs. All that your program needs to do is execute the dialog and use the file name returned. This solution shows you how it works.

3.3 Make a Text Search Dialog

Another commonly used dialog is the text search dialog. ObjectWindows handles this one for you by including the object class TSearchDialog. This dialog gets all of the information you need for a search or replace function. You just add the search routines and you are done.

3.4 Use Text Controls

One of the most versatile Windows controls is the text control. This control can be used for everything from displaying text messages to a complete text editor program. ObjectWindows extends the power of these controls even further by adding member functions to the text edit object class that handles reading and searching the text. This solution shows you several different types of edit controls and what you can do with them.

3.5 Use List Box and Combo Box Controls

There is nothing more intimidating to the new user than to be faced with a blank screen or an empty edit box. Even experienced users must pause to consider the acceptable inputs for this field. You can help users by presenting them with choices whenever possible. The list box control is designed to provide choices for the user. Perhaps the best known example is the list of available files. Picking one from a list box is much easier than remembering the exact spelling of the file and trying to enter it without mistakes. This solution shows the different types of list boxes and how you can use ObjectWindows routines to handle them.

3.6 Use Check Box and Radio Button Controls

Windows programs use check boxes and radio buttons to let the user input options. For example, a program that takes a person's coffee order might use check boxes for items such as cream and sugar and radio buttons to select regular or decaffeinated. Check boxes are independent of each other, while dialogs have groups of radio buttons only one of which can be selected at a time. This solution shows you how to use the ObjectWindows objects that affect check boxes and radio buttons.

3.7 Use String Tables

Windows applications can put everything that the user sees into a resource file. The advantage of this is that when it comes time to change one of the visible features of the program, you can do so without recompiling the whole program. The other solutions in this chapter show you how to include dialog boxes in the resource file. But what if you just need a string to add to a list box or display in a window? The answer is string tables, which are lists of strings saved in the resource file. This solution shows how to get the strings from the resource file into your program.

3.8 Convert Programs to Another Language

There are millions of people in the world who use computers but do not speak English. Some software companies do as much as 70% of their business with non-English speaking countries. Before Windows was available, these companies spent many programming hours converting programs from one language to another. The result was a maintenance nightmare of different versions for each language. This solution shows how you can use resource files and DLLs to create programs that can switch from one language to another with no reprogramming.

3.1 How Do I...
Use the TDialog Object Class?

Complexity: EASY

PROBLEM

Most of the TDialog object class is inherited from the TWindow object class that you learned about in Chapter 2, "ObjectWindows Basics." The features of dialogs that you need to learn include reading control information from the resource file, transferring data from the dialog object to other objects, and executing the dialog box message loop. This program uses two dialog boxes to demonstrate the use of TDialog objects. The first dialog box gets information about fish from the user. The second dialog maintains a list of the fish entered.

TECHNIQUE

Dialog boxes can be divided into two major categories, modal and modeless. Most of the dialogs in Windows applications are modal; when the dialog comes up, no other window in the application can be activated until the dialog goes away. Applications use modal dialogs to get some information needed before continuing. Modeless dialogs let the user activate other windows in the application. They are used when the program can continue without the information in the dialog. In this example, the modeless dialog box is used to display the status of the data in the program.

In ObjectWindows programs, the difference between a modal and a modeless dialog is in the way the dialog is started. The member function ExecDialog in the TModule class starts a modal dialog box. This function does not return until the user closes the dialog box. The return value of the function comes from the dialog box and is often used to return a status (such as the user confirmed the changes or the user wants to discard the changes).

The member function MakeWindow in TModule creates a modeless dialog box. MakeWindow tells Windows to create the dialog, then returns to the calling function so that the program can proceed. You must call the Show member function of the dialog object to get the dialog to appear on the screen. The dialog remains on the screen until closed, but you can give commands to other windows in the application while the dialog is visible.

When a program creates an instance of a TDialog object, it can also create objects for each of the controls in the dialog box. Once the control objects are created, you can use them to handle the controls in the dialog. You are not required to create objects for every control in the dialog. If you choose, you can use the Windows functions for sending messages to the controls to handle them. The examples for each control later in this chapter give detailed information on this topic.

One reason for creating ObjectWindows objects for controls is that it lets you use the TransferData member function to move data from the dialog box to any other data area in the program. Every object derived from TWindowsObject includes a function called TransferData and a data member called TransferBuffer that you can use to move data between objects. TransferData copies data between the memory at TransferBuffer and each of the control objects in the window.

ObjectWindows calls TransferData as part of the SetupWindow member function for all Windows objects to copy data from the transfer buffer to the control windows. Then, ObjectWindows calls TransferData to move the data from the controls to the transfer buffer when the user presses the OK button for dialog objects.

All you have to do to take advantage of the transfer mechanism is to create objects for all of the controls in the dialog and set the TransferBuffer to point to the buffer for the data. This setup should be done in the constructor for the dialog object. Then, as long as the dialog has a button whose ID is the Windows constant IDOK, ObjectWindows does all of the work.

STEPS

1. Create a new project called DLGAPP.PRJ that includes the files DLGAPP.CPP, DLGAPP.RES, and STANDARD.DEF (see Chapter 2, "ObjectWindows Basics," for this file).
2. Use the Borland C++ IDE editor to create the source file DLGAPP.CPP with the following program:

```
/* Dialog example program */
#include <owl.h>
#include <listbox.h>
#include <edit.h>
#include <string.h>

#define IDC_NAME       103
#define IDC_FISHLIST   101

#define IDM_MODELESS   101
#define IDM_MODAL      102

/* Class for the modal dialog box */
class ModalDlg : public TDialog
```

```
{
     public:
          ModalDlg(PTWindowsObject AParent, LPSTR AResource);
};

/* Class for the modeless dialog box */
class ModelessDlg : public TDialog
{
     public:
          PTListBox FishList;    // The list box in the dialog
          ModelessDlg(PTWindowsObject AParent, LPSTR AResource);
};

/* Constructor for the modeless dialog box object */
ModelessDlg::ModelessDlg(PTWindowsObject AParent, LPSTR AResource)
     : TDialog(AParent, AResource)
{
     /* Make an object for the list box */
     FishList = new TListBox(this, IDC_FISHLIST);
}

/* The main window of the program */
class TMyWindow : public TWindow
{
     public:
          ModelessDlg *PDlg;
          /* Varaiables for up to 100 fish */
          struct {
               char Name[20];
          } FishArray[100];
          int FishCnt;
          TMyWindow(PTWindowsObject AParent, LPSTR ATitle);
          /* Menu items to bring up dialogs */
          virtual void DoModeless(RTMessage) = [CM_FIRST + IDM_MODELESS];
          virtual void DoModal(RTMessage) = [CM_FIRST + IDM_MODAL];
          virtual LPSTR GetClassName() { return "MyClass"; };
          virtual void GetWindowClass(WNDCLASS& AWndClass);
};

TMyWindow::TMyWindow(PTWindowsObject AParent, LPSTR ATitle)
     : TWindow(AParent, ATitle)
{
     AssignMenu("DlgMenu");     // Load the menu
     PDlg = NULL;               // Indicate that there is no dialog running
     FishCnt = 0;               // No fish yet
}

/* Set up the icon for the program */
void TMyWindow::GetWindowClass(WNDCLASS& AWndClass)
{
     TWindow::GetWindowClass(AWndClass);
     AWndClass.hIcon = LoadIcon(GetApplicationObject()->hInstance
          , "DlgIcon");
}

/* Toggle modeless dialog on or off */
void TMyWindow::DoModeless(RTMessage)
{
     int i;
     HMENU MnHand;
```

```
        MnHand = GetMenu(HWindow);   // Get the handle of the menu
        if(PDlg)    // If the dialog is running, close eit
        {
                CheckMenuItem(MnHand, IDM_MODELESS, MF_BYCOMMAND|MF_UNCHECKED);
                PDlg->CloseWindow();
                PDlg = NULL;
        }
        else        // Otherwise, start the dialog
        {
                CheckMenuItem(MnHand, IDM_MODELESS, MF_BYCOMMAND|MF_CHECKED);
                PDlg = new ModelessDlg(this, "Modeless");
                GetModule()->MakeWindow(PDlg);
                /* Put the fish names in the list box */
                for(i=0; i<FishCnt; i++)
                        PDlg->FishList->AddString(FishArray[i].Name);
                PDlg->Show(SW_SHOW);
        }
}


/* Do the modal dialog */
void TMyWindow::DoModal(RTMessage)
{
        /* Clear the next fish entry */
        memset(&FishArray[FishCnt], '\0', sizeof(FishArray[FishCnt]));
        /* Run the dialog */
        if(GetModule()->ExecDialog(new ModalDlg(this, "Modal"))==IDOK)
        {
                /* If the modal dialog is running, update its list */
                if(PDlg)
                        PDlg->FishList->AddString(FishArray[FishCnt].Name);
                FishCnt++;
        }
}


/* Create the modal dialog object */
ModalDlg::ModalDlg(PTWindowsObject AParent, LPSTR AResource)
        : TDialog(AParent, AResource)
{
        /* Create an edit control object */
        new TEdit(this, IDC_NAME, 20);
        /* Set up to transfer data with the main window object */
        TransferBuffer = (void far *) &(((TMyWindow *)Parent)->FishArray
                [((TMyWindow *)Parent)->FishCnt]);
}


class TFirstApp : public TApplication
{
        public:
                TFirstApp(LPSTR ApName, HANDLE Inst, HANDLE PrevInst
                        , LPSTR CmdLine, int CmdShow) : TApplication(ApName
                        , Inst, PrevInst, CmdLine, CmdShow) {};
                virtual void InitMainWindow();
};


void TFirstApp::InitMainWindow()
{
        MainWindow = new TMyWindow(NULL, "Dialog examples");
}
```

```
int PASCAL WinMain(HANDLE Inst, HANDLE PrevInst, LPSTR CmdLine
    , int CmdShow)
{
    TFirstApp FirstApp("", Inst
        , PrevInst, CmdLine, CmdShow);

    FirstApp.Run();
    return FirstApp.Status;
}
```

3. Use the Resource Workshop to create the file DLGAPP.RES. This resource file must include a menu named DLGMENU with these items:

```
DLGMENU MENU
BEGIN
    POPUP "Dialogs"
    BEGIN
        MENUITEM "&Modeless", 101
        MENUITEM "Mod&al", 102
    END

END
```

Figure 3-1
The Icon for
DLGAPP.RES

The resource file must also have an icon named DLGCION, such as the one in Figure 3-1.

Finally, the resource file must include two dialog resources named MODAL and MODELESS. Figure 3-2 shows how the dialogs look in the dialog editor. It is important that the controls in the dialogs use the same IDs that the program expects. Also, the order of the controls in the resource file is important because the order determines how the input focus moves from one control to another. So, while you can use the dialog editor to input the dialogs, it is a good idea to enter this text using the *Edit as text* feature of the Resource Workshop:

```
MODAL DIALOG 16, 1, 166, 120
CAPTION "Fish"
STYLE DS_MODALFRAME | WS_POPUP | WS_CAPTION
BEGIN
    CONTROL "Type", -1, "STATIC", SS_LEFT | WS_CHILD | WS_VISIBLE | WS_GROUP, 10, 10, 20, 8
    CONTROL "", 103, "EDIT",
        ES_LEFT|ES_AUTOHSCROLL|WS_CHILD|WS_VISIBLE|WS_BORDER|WS_GROUP
        | WS_TABSTOP, 45, 8, 110, 12
    CONTROL "Quantity", -1, "STATIC", SS_LEFT | WS_CHILD | WS_VISIBLE | WS_GROUP
        , 10, 27, 30, 8
    CONTROL "", 104, "EDIT", ES_LEFT | WS_CHILD | WS_VISIBLE | WS_BORDER | WS_TABSTOP
        , 45, 25, 35, 12
    CONTROL "Agressive", 105, "BUTTON", BS_AUTORADIOBUTTON|WS_CHILD|WS_VISIBLE| WS_GROUP
        | WS_TABSTOP, 15, 68, 45, 12
    CONTROL "Tame", 106, "BUTTON", BS_AUTORADIOBUTTON | WS_CHILD | WS_VISIBLE | WS_TABSTOP
        , 15, 82, 45, 12
    CONTROL "Price", -1, "STATIC", SS_LEFT | WS_CHILD | WS_VISIBLE | WS_GROUP, 10, 44, 16, 8
    CONTROL "", 107, "EDIT", ES_LEFT | WS_CHILD | WS_VISIBLE | WS_BORDER | WS_TABSTOP
        , 45, 42, 35, 12
    CONTROL "Surface", 108, "BUTTON", BS_AUTORADIOBUTTON|WS_CHILD|WS_VISIBLE|WS_GROUP
        | WS_TABSTOP, 105, 50, 50, 12
    CONTROL "Middle", 109, "BUTTON", BS_AUTORADIOBUTTON | WS_CHILD | WS_VISIBLE|WS_TABSTOP
```

```
        , 105, 66, 50, 12
    CONTROL "Bottom", 110, "BUTTON", BS_AUTORADIOBUTTON|WS_CHILD|WS_VISIBLE|WS_TABSTOP
        , 105, 82, 50, 12
    CONTROL "Feeding", 111, "BUTTON", BS_GROUPBOX | WS_CHILD | WS_VISIBLE, 100, 39, 60, 61
    CONTROL "Disposition", 112, "BUTTON", BS_GROUPBOX | WS_CHILD | WS_VISIBLE
        , 10, 56, 55, 44
    CONTROL "OK", 1, "BUTTON", BS_DEFPUSHBUTTON | WS_CHILD | WS_VISIBLE | WS_TABSTOP
        , 20, 104, 40, 13
    CONTROL "Cancel", 2, "BUTTON", BS_PUSHBUTTON | WS_CHILD | WS_VISIBLE | WS_TABSTOP
        , 100, 104, 41, 13
END

MODELESS DIALOG 18, 18, 86, 92
CAPTION "Fish list"
STYLE DS_MODALFRAME | WS_POPUP | WS_CAPTION
BEGIN
    LISTBOX 101, 15, 17, 55, 64
    LTEXT "Fish", -1, 10, 4, 16, 8
END
```

4. Use the *Run* command to compile and run the program.

HOW IT WORKS

The defined constants for the dialog controls and menu selections used in this program are at the beginning. These numbers must match the corresponding controls in the resource file. When the number of controls is small, it is easy to keep the ID numbers correct. For many programs, the number of controls makes it difficult to match the numbers in the resource file to the numbers in the program. One way to solve this problem is to put the defines for ID numbers in an include file. If you tell the Resource Workshop to create .RC files instead of .RES files, you can use the include file and enter the constant name instead of the ID number when creating controls.

The first object class in the program describes the modal dialog box. It defines a single function to be used as the constructor. Note that the actual constructor function appears much later in the program. The reason for this is that the func-

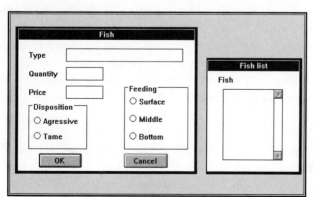

Figure 3-2
The Dialog Boxes
from DLGAPP.RES

tion refers to the TMyWindow object which must be defined before it can be referenced. The constructor creates a TEdit object for the first edit control and points the transfer buffer at an element of an array in the TMyWindow object. Note that the constructor used to create the TEdit object is different from the one used in Chapter 2, "ObjectWindows Basics." Instead of giving the position and size of the edit control, this program gives the ID number in the resource file for the constructor. C++ sees that the arguments are different and calls the appropriate constructor.

The constructor sets up the first dialog control to automatically exchange data with the main window. The function does this by assigning the address of a structure in the parent window to the data member. TransferBuffer. If you create objects for the other controls in the dialog, they can also exchange data with the main window.

The next object in the program handles the modeless dialog box. This object includes a pointer to a list box object and a constructor. The constructor creates a list box object associated with the list box control in the resource file and saves the address in the FishList data member. Other routines can use the FishList variable to send commands to the list box.

The main window object TMyWindow includes data members to hold the list of fish and a pointer to the modeless dialog box object. The member functions include two menu response functions, one to run the modal dialog and another to create and destroy the modeless dialog. The rest of the member functions have been demonstrated in previous programs.

The data member FishArray is a list of the names of the fish entered in the modal dialog box. FishCnt is the number of fish entered. When the program creates a modal dialog, it sets the transfer buffer to the next element in the fish array. If you add more control objects to the modal dialog, you must also add more fields to this structure to hold the data items. The examples of using controls later in this chapter show the type of data item required for each control.

TMyWindow also includes a pointer to the modeless dialog object called PDlg. If the dialog is not created, this pointer is NULL. The member function DoModeless uses this pointer to determine if the modeless dialog should be created or destroyed. The member function DoModal uses this variable to send a fish name to the list box in the modeless dialog.

When DoModeless creates the modeless dialog, it uses the MakeWindow function from the TModule object. The function GetModule gives the address of the TModule object that includes the main window object. After creating the modeless dialog, DoModeless puts the current list of fish into the list box in the dialog. Finally, DoModeless calls the Show member function to make the dialog appear on the screen.

DoModal uses the function ExecDialog to run the modal dialog. The return value from ExecDialog indicates what button the user pressed to exit the dialog.

If the button was the OK button, DoModal adds the new fish to the list box in the modal dialog box and increments the FishCnt. If the user presses the Cancel button, the program ignores the data in the dialog. ObjectWindows sets the return value for ExecDialog to IDOK or IDCANCEL as part of its default processing. You can change the return value by using the TDialog member function ShutDownWindow to close the dialog box and passing the return value to use as an argument to ShutDownWindow.

COMMENT

When you write a program of your own that uses dialog boxes, you will need to add more control objects to get all of the data in and out of the dialog box. You may also want to add some code to verify the data before closing the dialog box. For example, if the fish program puts selections in a database, it should check to see if the name is unique before adding the new entry to the database. You can use the TDialog member function CanClose to handle this processing. ObjectWindows calls CanClose before closing the dialog. If the return value of CanClose is FALSE, ObjectWindows does not close the window. To use this feature, just add a CanClose member function to your dialog object like this:

```
class ModalDlg : public TDialog
{
    public:
        ModalDlg(PTWindowsObject AParent, LPSTR AResource);
        virtual BOOL CanClose();
};

BOOL ModalDlg::CanClose()
{
    /* Check the data in the dialog */
    .
    .
    .
    /* If data no good, return FALSE */
    if(.....)
        return FALSE;
    /* Otherwise return true to allow the dialog to close */
    return TRUE;
}
```

Another way to use dialog objects is as the main window of a program. If your program has controls in the main window, you can make it a TDialog object instead of a TWindow object and take advantage of the dialog processing to handle the controls. The main advantage of this technique is the fact that you can put all of the control descriptions in the resource file and use Resource Workshop to set up the appearance of the window.

If you use a dialog as the main window of your program, you may want to change the class registration of the window as you can with other windows. The GetClassName and GetWindowClass member functions work just as well with modeless dialogs as with other windows—with one caveat. If you change the class name of the dialog, you must put the new class name in the resource file. The dialog editor in Resource Workshop lets you enter the class name in the same dialog used to enter the title of the dialog.

3.2 How Do I...
Make a File Selection Dialog?

Complexity: EASY

PROBLEM

One of the most common dialogs in Windows applications is the file selection dialog. For databases and word processors, this dialog is vital, but other programs often need to load a file as well. This dialog is so common that ObjectWindows includes a special object class that handles a file selection dialog. Figure 3-3 shows the dialogs you can use with this object class. This solution shows you how to add this object to your programs.

TECHNIQUE

The ObjectWindows class TFileDialog is a descendant of TDialog that handles the file selection dialogs. TFileDialog handles two dialog boxes, one to get an existing file and the other to let the user enter a file name for saving. Before you can use the TFileDialog object, you must put the dialog templates in the resource file. The required templates are in the file FILEDIAL.DLG included with ObjectWindows. See the STEPS section for the procedure for loading FILEDIAL.DLG into your resource files.

The TFileDialog declaration and the constants needed are in the file FILEDIAL.H and OWLRC.H. You must include this file at the beginning of your program. To execute the open file dialog, use the ExecDialog member function like this:

```
GetApplication()->ExecDialog(new TFileDialog(this, SD_FILEOPEN, FileName));
```

The variable FileName is a string that contains a file name pattern such as "*.*" before calling the dialog, and the name of the file selected after running the dialog. Use the same line to use the save file dialog, but change the SD_FILEOPEN constant to SD_FILESAVE.

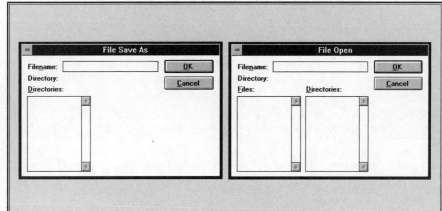

Figure 3-3
The
TFileDialog
Dialogs

STEPS

1. Create a new project file named FILEDLG.PRJ that includes the files FILEDLG.CPP, FILEDLG.RES, and STANDARD.DEF.

2. Use the editor to create the file FILEDLG.CPP with this program:

```
/* Show the file dialog object */
#include <owl.h>
#include <filedial.h>
#include <string.h>

#define IDM_OPEN      102
#define IDM_SAVEAS    104
#define IDM_EXIT      108

/* The main window object */
class TMyWindow : public TWindow
{
    public:
        char FileName[MAXPATH];
        long FileSize;
        TMyWindow(PTWindowsObject AParent, LPSTR ATitle);
        virtual LPSTR GetClassName() { return "MyClass"; };
        virtual void GetWindowClass(WNDCLASS& AWndClass);
        /* Handle menu commands */
        virtual void OpenFile(RTMessage) = [CM_FIRST + IDM_OPEN];
        virtual void SaveFile(RTMessage) = [CM_FIRST + IDM_SAVEAS];
        virtual void Quit(RTMessage) = [CM_FIRST + IDM_EXIT];
        virtual void WMPaint(RTMessage) = [WM_FIRST + WM_PAINT];
};

TMyWindow::TMyWindow(PTWindowsObject AParent, LPSTR ATitle)
    : TWindow(AParent, ATitle)
{
    AssignMenu("FileMenu");             // Load the menu
```

```
      /* Set up the style and size of the window */
      Attr.Style |= WS_CAPTION;
      Attr.W = 400;
      Attr.H = 200;
      /* Initialize data */
      FileName[0] = '\0';
      FileSize = 0L;
}


/* Set up the icon for the program */
void TMyWindow::GetWindowClass(WNDCLASS& AWndClass)
{
      TWindow::GetWindowClass(AWndClass);
      AWndClass.hIcon = LoadIcon(GetApplicationObject()->hInstance, "FileIcon");
}


/* Select a file and open it */
void TMyWindow::OpenFile(RTMessage)
{
      int fd;

      _fstrcpy(FileName, "*.*");
      /* Bring up the file dialog */
      if(GetApplication()->ExecDialog(new TFileDialog(this
            , SD_FILEOPEN, FileName)) == IDOK)
      {
            /* If the user pressed OK, open the file and get the size */
            fd = _lopen(FileName, OF_READ);
            FileSize = _llseek(fd, 0L, 2);
            _lclose(fd);
            /* Make Windows repaint the window */
            InvalidateRect(HWindow, NULL, FALSE);
      }
}


/* Get a file name and display it in a message box */
void TMyWindow::SaveFile(RTMessage)
{
      if(GetApplication()->ExecDialog(new TFileDialog(this
            , SD_FILESAVE, FileName)) == IDOK)
            MessageBox(HWindow, FileName, "Save name", MB_OK);
}


/* Exit the program */
void TMyWindow::Quit(RTMessage)
{
      CloseWindow();
}


/* Show the name and size of the file */
void TMyWindow::WMPaint(RTMessage)
{
      PAINTSTRUCT ps;
      HDC hDC;
      char TmpStr[300];

      memset(&ps, 0x00, sizeof(PAINTSTRUCT));
      hDC = BeginPaint(HWindow, &ps);
      wsprintf(TmpStr, "Name = %s", FileName);
      TextOut(hDC, 5, 5, TmpStr, lstrlen(TmpStr));
```

```
      wsprintf(TmpStr, "Size = %ld", FileSize);
      TextOut(hDC, 5, 25, TmpStr, lstrlen(TmpStr));
      EndPaint(HWindow, &ps);
}


/* The application object */
class TMyApp : public TApplication
{
      public:
            TMyApp(LPSTR ApName, HANDLE Inst, HANDLE PrevInst
                  , LPSTR CmdLine, int CmdShow) : TApplication(ApName
                  , Inst, PrevInst, CmdLine, CmdShow) {};
            virtual void InitMainWindow();
};

void TMyApp::InitMainWindow()
{
      MainWindow = new TMyWindow(NULL, "FileDialog");
}

int PASCAL WinMain(HANDLE Inst, HANDLE PrevInst, LPSTR CmdLine
      , int CmdShow)
{
      TMyApp TheApp("", Inst, PrevInst, CmdLine, CmdShow);

      TheApp.Run();
      return TheApp.Status;
}
```

3. Use the Resource Workshop to create the file FILEDLG.RES. This file must include the file FILEDIAL.DLG, so you have to take special steps when creating the file. First, select *New* from the *File* menu and set the file type to ".RC." This file type lets you load the identifiers used in the FILEDIAL.DLG file. Next, load the identifiers by selecting "Add to project..." from the *File* menu. The identifier file is called OWLRC.H and is in the INCLUDE subdirectory of the ObjectWindows directory. Now you can add in FILEDIAL.DLG with the *Add to project...* command. Finally, *Use the Save as...* command to save the file as FILEDIAL.RES.

The resource file should also include the icon and menu for the program. The menu commands are:

```
FILEMENU MENU
BEGIN
      POPUP "&File"
      BEGIN
            MENUITEM "&Open...", 102
            MENUITEM "Save &as...", 104
            MENUITEM SEPARATOR
            MENUITEM "E&xit", 108
      END

END
```

4. Select *Run* from the *Run* menu in Borland C++ to run the program.

HOW IT WORKS

Most of this program is a standard ObjectWindows program. The parts that make it unique are the indexed member functions in the TMyWindow object class. The OpenFile function uses the TFileDialog object class to display a file selection dialog, then it gets the size of the file, stores the name and size in the TMyWindow object, and uses the Windows function InvalidateRect to make Windows send a WM_PAINT message. The SaveFile function is similar to OpenFile, except it shows a save file dialog and does not get the size of the file.

The Quit and WMPaint member functions close the program and repaint the window. The Quit function calls the ObjectWindows function CloseWindow, which handles all of the details of shutting down the program. WMPaint gets a device context (hDC) from Windows, then uses the Windows function TextOut to print the name and size of the last file entered.

COMMENTS

The TFileDialog object is no more or less complicated than any other dialog object class. You could have created it yourself by modifying examples in this book and using a Windows function called DlgDirList. In a few hours, you would have a dialog box comparable to the one in TFileDialog. By using TFileDialog, you can put those hours into some other part of your program and not worry about file dialogs.

3.3 How Do I...
Make a Text Search Dialog?

Complexity: EASY

PROBLEM

Many programs can use a search command. Word processors can search for text, databases can search for data in fields, and spreadsheets can search for cells that contain certain values. All of these searches need a dialog box that lets the user tell the program what to search for. ObjectWindows provides an object class that presents a dialog box that gets the information a program needs to search for text. This solution shows you how to use that object class.

TECHNIQUE

The ObjectWindows object for search dialogs is called TSearchDialog and is available if you include the file EDITWND.H. One of the differences between

Figure 3-4
The Search
and Replace
Dialogs from
STDWND.DLG

this object and the TFileDialog object is the way information is copied from the dialog to the main program. Instead of using a string as TFileDialog does, TSearchDialog uses a structure called TSearchStruct to copy information. The address of the structure to use is passed to the constructor for TSearchDialog.

The TSearchStruct structure looks like this:

```
struct _CLASSTYPE TSearchStruct {
     char SearchText[81];        // The string to look for
     BOOL CaseSensitive;         // True for case sensitive searches
     char ReplaceText[81];       // The text to substitute into the text
     BOOL ReplaceAll;            // True if all occurrences should be replaced
     BOOL PromptOnReplace;       // True if the program should ask before replacing
};
```

Your program should set the fields of this structure to whatever default values are appropriate before executing the search dialog. If the dialog returns IDOK, then the fields of the TSearchStruct contain the values selected by the user. Otherwise, the structure contains the initial values.

You must put the dialog resource for the search dialog into the resource file for your program. The procedure for this is the same as for the file dialog resource except the file name is STDWND.DLG instead of FILEDIAL.DLG. Figure 3-4 shows the search and replace dialogs found in STDWND.DLG.

STEPS

1. Create a new project file called SEARCH.PRJ that includes the files SEARCH.CPP, SEARCH.RES, and STANDARD.DEF.

2. Create the source file SEARCH.CPP with the following program:

```
/* Show the search dialog object */
#include <owl.h>
#include <editwnd.h>
#include <string.h>
```

```
#define IDM_SEARCH          101
#define IDM_REPLACE         102
#define IDM_EXIT            104


/* The main window for the program */
class TMyWindow : public TWindow
{
    public:
            TSearchStruct SS;
            char TheText[128];
            BOOL HighLight;

            TMyWindow(PTWindowsObject AParent, LPSTR ATitle);
            virtual LPSTR GetClassName() { return "MyClass"; };
            virtual void GetWindowClass(WNDCLASS& AWndClass);
            /* Handle menu commands */
            virtual void SearchText(RTMessage) = [CM_FIRST + IDM_SEARCH];
            virtual void ReplaceText(RTMessage) = [CM_FIRST + IDM_REPLACE];
            virtual void Quit(RTMessage) = [CM_FIRST + IDM_EXIT];
            virtual void WMPaint(RTMessage) = [WM_FIRST + WM_PAINT];
};


TMyWindow::TMyWindow(PTWindowsObject AParent, LPSTR ATitle)
        : TWindow(AParent, ATitle)
{
    AssignMenu("SearchMenu");
    Attr.Style |= WS_CAPTION;
    Attr.W = 500;
    Attr.H = 200;
    /* Set the defaults for searching */
    lstrcpy(TheText, "This is the line of text to search");
    SS.SearchText[0] = '\0';
    SS.CaseSensitive = FALSE;
    SS.ReplaceText[0] = '\0';
    SS.ReplaceAll = FALSE;
    SS.PromptOnReplace = FALSE;
    HighLight = FALSE;
}


/* Set up the program icon */
void TMyWindow::GetWindowClass(WNDCLASS& AWndClass)
{
    TWindow::GetWindowClass(AWndClass);
    AWndClass.hIcon = LoadIcon(GetApplication()->hInstance, "THEICON");
}


/* Do the search dialog */
void TMyWindow::SearchText(RTMessage)
{
    /* Bring up the dialog */
    if(GetApplication()->ExecDialog(new TSearchDialog(this
        , SD_SEARCH, SS)) == IDOK)
        HighLight = TRUE;
    else
        HighLight = FALSE;
    /* Repaint the main window */
    InvalidateRect(HWindow, NULL, FALSE);
}
```

```
/* Do the replace dialog */
void TMyWindow::ReplaceText(RTMessage)
{
      int i, LastPos, SearchLen;   // pointers for searching
      char TmpStr[128];            // Work string for replacing
      char Prompt[80];
      int TmpPos;                  // index into work string
      int Res;                     // Result of message box
      int CmpResult;               // Result of the text compare

      /* Show the dialog */
      if(GetApplication()->ExecDialog(new TSearchDialog(this
          , SD_REPLACE, SS)) == IDOK)
      {
          SearchLen = lstrlen(SS.SearchText);
          LastPos = lstrlen(TheText);
          TmpStr[0] = '\0';
          TmpPos = 0;
          /* Search for the string */
          for(i=0; i<LastPos; i++)
          {
              if(SS.CaseSensitive)
                  CmpResult = _fstrncmp(&TheText[i], SS.SearchText, SearchLen);
              else
                  CmpResult = _fstrnicmp(&TheText[i], SS.SearchText, SearchLen);
              if(CmpResult)    // if not found, go to the next character
                  TmpStr[TmpPos++] = TheText[i];
              else
              {
                  if(SS.PromptOnReplace) // See if replacing requires a prompt
                  {
                      wsprintf(Prompt, "Replace at offset %d?", i);
                      Res = MessageBox(HWindow, Prompt, "Replace check"
                          , MB_YESNO);
                  }
                  else
                      Res = IDYES;
                  if(Res == IDYES) // If OK, replace the text
                  {
                      lstrcpy(&TmpStr[TmpPos], SS.ReplaceText);
                      TmpPos += lstrlen(SS.ReplaceText);
                      if(SS.ReplaceAll)
                          i += SearchLen-1;
                      else
                      {
                          lstrcpy(&TmpStr[TmpPos], &TheText[i+SearchLen]);
                          i = LastPos;
                      }
                  }
                  else
                      TmpStr[TmpPos++] = TheText[i];
              }
          }
      }
      TmpStr[TmpPos] = '\0';
      lstrcpy(TheText, TmpStr);
      HighLight = 0;
```

```
      /* Tell Windows to repaint the main window */
      InvalidateRect(HWindow, NULL, FALSE);
}

/* exit the program */
void TMyWindow::Quit(RTMessage)
{
      CloseWindow();
}

/* Show the string */
void TMyWindow::WMPaint(RTMessage)
{
      PAINTSTRUCT ps;                    // Information about the area to paint
      RECT Rect;                         // The window rectangle
      HDC hDC;                           // Handle to the device context
      int i, FirstPos, LastPos;          // pointers for searching
      int SearchLen;                     // Length of the search string
      int x;                             // column to print text in

      memset(&ps, 0x00, sizeof(PAINTSTRUCT));
      hDC = BeginPaint(HWindow, &ps);
      /* Clear the window */
      GetClientRect(HWindow, &Rect);
      FillRect(hDC, &Rect, GetStockObject(WHITE_BRUSH));
      /* Show the search text in another color */
      if(HighLight)
      {
            SearchLen = lstrlen(SS.SearchText);
            LastPos = lstrlen(TheText) - SearchLen;
            FirstPos = 0;
            x = 5;
            for(i=0; i<=LastPos; i++)
            {
                  if(SS.CaseSensitive)
                  {
                        if(!_fstrncmp(&TheText[i], SS.SearchText, SearchLen))
                        {
                              SetTextColor(hDC, 0); // Set color to black
                              TextOut(hDC, x, 5, &TheText[FirstPos], i - FirstPos);
                              x += GetTextExtent(hDC, &TheText[FirstPos], i - FirstPos);
                              SetTextColor(hDC, 0xFF);    // Set color to blue
                              TextOut(hDC, x, 5, &TheText[i], SearchLen);
                              x += GetTextExtent(hDC, &TheText[i], SearchLen);
                              i += SearchLen;
                              FirstPos = i;
                              --i;
                        }
                  }
                  else
                  {
                        if(!_fstrnicmp(&TheText[i], SS.SearchText, SearchLen))
                        {
                              SetTextColor(hDC, 0); // Set color to black
                              TextOut(hDC, x, 5, &TheText[FirstPos], i - FirstPos);
                              x += GetTextExtent(hDC, &TheText[FirstPos], i - FirstPos);
                              SetTextColor(hDC, 0xFF);    // Set color to blue
                              TextOut(hDC, x, 5, &TheText[i], SearchLen);
```

```
                                x += GetTextExtent(hDC, &TheText[i], SearchLen);
                                i += SearchLen;
                                FirstPos = i;
                                --i;
                        }
                }
        }
        if(FirstPos < lstrlen(TheText))
        {
                SetTextColor(hDC, 0);
                TextOut(hDC, x, 5, &TheText[FirstPos], lstrlen(TheText)-FirstPos);
        }
        SetTextColor(hDC, 0xFF00);
        TextOut(hDC, 5, 25, SS.SearchText, SearchLen);
    }
    else
        TextOut(hDC, 5, 5, TheText, lstrlen(TheText));
    EndPaint(HWindow, &ps);
}

class TMyApp : public TApplication
{
    public:
        TMyApp(LPSTR ApName, HANDLE Inst, HANDLE PrevInst
                , LPSTR CmdLine, int CmdShow) : TApplication(ApName
                , Inst, PrevInst, CmdLine, CmdShow) {};
        virtual void InitMainWindow();
};

void TMyApp::InitMainWindow()
{
    MainWindow = new TMyWindow(NULL, "Search Dialog");
}

int PASCAL WinMain(HANDLE Inst, HANDLE PrevInst, LPSTR CmdLine
    , int CmdShow)
{
    TMyApp TheApp("", Inst, PrevInst, CmdLine, CmdShow);

    TheApp.Run();
    return TheApp.Status;
}
```

3. Use the procedure given in How-To 3.2 to include the resource file STD-WND.DLG in the resource file SEARCH.RES.

4. Add this menu to the resource file:

```
SEARCHMENU MENU
BEGIN
      POPUP "&Search"
      BEGIN
            MENUITEM "&Search", 101
            MENUITEM "&Replace", 102
            MENUITEM SEPARATOR
            MENUITEM "E&xit", 104
      END
```

5. Add an icon named THEICON to the resource file.

6. Use the *Run* command to compile and run the program.

HOW IT WORKS

The differences between this program and FILEDLG.CPP from How-To 3.2 are that this one includes EDITWND.H instead of FILEDIAL.H, the main window includes a TSearchStruct struct to hold data, and the message response functions have been changed to do searches and replaces. The message function SearchText uses the TSearchDialog dialog to get a search string from the user. SearchText sets the member variable HighLight to TRUE or FALSE depending on whether the user pressed the OK or CANCEL button in the dialog. After calling the dialog, SearchText uses the Windows function InvalidateRect to tell Windows to send a WM_PAINT message to the application.

The WMPaint function handles the WM_PAINT message from Windows. The first thing WMPaint does is get a device context from Windows so that it can paint in the window. Next, it paints the window white by calling the Windows function FillRect. Next, WMPaint checks the variable HighLight to see if it should search the text. If so, WMPaint loops through all of the characters in the string being searched to see if there is a match. If the search string is found, WMPaint draws the matching text in red. There are two searches used, one to find an exact match and another that ignores case. The search used depends on the CaseSensitive field in the TSearchStruct structure.

The ReplaceText function executes the replace text dialog in TSearchDialog to get information from the user. If the user presses the OK button in the dialog, ReplaceText loops through the string looking for occurrences of the search string. The CaseSensitive field is used to determine if the search checks case or not. When it finds a match, ReplaceString checks the PromptOnReplace field to see if it should ask the user if it is OK to replace the text. If it is OK or if no prompting is required, ReplaceText substitutes the replace string for the matched text. After replacing, ReplaceText checks the ReplaceAll field to see if it should continue searching or not.

COMMENTS

The TSearchDialog just gets the information required to do the search, you must supply the code to do the actual search. The SEARCH.CPP program uses a simple brute force search to find the search string in a string in memory. You may want to spend the time you save on creating the dialog on implementing a faster search or to search data from a file. If you want the easiest way to implement searching, see the TEditWindow class described in How-To 5.1.

3.4 How Do I...
Use Text Controls?

Complexity : DIFFICULT

PROBLEM

Most dialog boxes include text controls to let the user enter text from the keyboard. In many cases, the text control is a rectangular box that accepts characters typed and allows some simple editing commands. By using the options available for text controls, you can make text controls for passwords, multiline edit boxes, formatted text entry, and more. This solution shows you the possibilities.

TECHNIQUE

The ObjectWindows object TEdit represents text controls. This object includes methods to edit the text, retrieve the text, search the text, and handle the data transfer operation. In a dialog box, you create the actual text control in the dialog editor, then assign a TEdit object to the control.

When you create a text control in a dialog with the resource toolkit, you must set several parameters to describe the control to Windows. To set these parameters in the Resource Workshop, double-click on the text control to bring up the control parameter dialog. The first parameter is the control ID. Be sure to remember the number you use because you will use this number in your program to identify the control when you create a TEdit object and for several Windows functions.

Next, select the attributes for the control. The Tab Stop attribute means that Windows will give this control the focus when the user uses the Tab key to select controls. You should select this attribute for all text entry controls. The Group attribute means that this control marks the beginning of a new group. Groups are used with radio buttons to indicate which radio buttons work together. For Text controls, select this attribute only if the text control is the first control after a group of radio buttons. The next attribute is Disabled, which means that the control is displayed as gray text and the user cannot enter text into the control. Use this attribute if the control should not be used until some other control (such as a check box) has been selected. The last attribute is the border attribute, which draws a rectangle around the control. This attribute is recommended for text controls so that the user can see where he is.

You can also set the justification of the text. Text can be justified to the left or right edges or centered in the space for the control. You can add scroll bars to text controls so that the user can display more text than fits in the space for the control. If you add scroll bars, you may also want to set the automatic scroll feature so that Windows will scroll the text to keep the cursor visible.

Another part of the text control dialog lets you select the case for characters in the field. The possibilities are mixed case, uppercase, or lower case. The next part lets you designate the control as a single or multiple line field. As the name implies, multiple line fields let the user enter more than one line into a single control.

The final choices have to do with conversions of the text the user enters. If you select the Password attribute, anything that the user types will be displayed as asterisks. The Convert OEM attribute converts characters entered from ANSI to the selected keyboard code page and then back to ANSI. This ensures that when you use the AnsiToOem Windows function on the string you get the correct result. This feature is important for data that might be used in MS-DOS that contains foreign language characters. The last attribute is the Keep selection attribute, which tells Windows to leave selected text marked even when the control loses the input focus.

The best way to learn about these attributes is to experiment with different combinations. You can change the attributes of the fields in the program below to see how each of the attributes works.

Once you have used the Resource Workshop to create the dialog with text controls, you must write a program that uses the dialog and handles the controls. The simplest program would create a TDialog object for the dialog box that, in turn, creates TEdit controls for each text control, then uses the ObjectWindows transfer technique to copy data between the main window and the dialog controls. In fact, many dialog boxes can be handled this way, saving you hours of programming time.

For the few times when you need to go beyond the basic text control, ObjectWindows includes many interesting member functions and Windows provides you with control messages that you can use. To use the TEdit member functions from ObjectWindows, you must keep the address of the control when you create it and use that address to call the member function. This is a three-step process. First add a member variable to the dialog box object:

```
class MyDialog : public TDialog
{
    public:
        PTEdit AnEditControl;  // The address of an edit control
        .
        .
        .
};
```

Next, assign the address when you create the TEdit object in the constructor for the dialog box:

```
AnEditControl = new TEdit(this, IDC_THECONTROL, 30);
```

In this statement, IDC_THECONTROL is a defined value that gives the ID number of the control. The number 30 is the maximum number of characters that the user can enter into the control.

The last step is to use the address to call one of the member functions:

```
AnEditControl->SetSelection(3, 5);
```

This statement sets the selected characters in the field to the characters from position 3 to position 5.

Table 3-1 shows some useful member functions for TEdit objects. Once you know what you can do to a text control, you need to know when to do it. Often you want to do something to the control when something else happens. For example, if you want to verify user input as he changes the text, you need to know when the text changes. Windows tells you when something happens to a control by sending a WM_COMMAND message to the parent window for the control. This message includes the ID number of the control and a number that tells you what happened. To handle a control notification message, you must define an indexed member function in the dialog box object. The index for this member function is the ObjectWindows constant ID_FIRST plus the ID number of the control. For example, this program fragment handles all of the possible notification messages for a text control:

```
class MyDialog : public TDialog
{
    public:
        /* A member function to handle notification messages for the text control */
        void HandleNotice(RTMessage Msg) = [ID_FIRST + IDC_TEXTCONTROL];
};

/* Handle notification messages */
void MyDialog::HandleNotice(RTMessage Msg)
{
    switch(Msg.LP.Hi)
    {
        case EN_CHANGE:
            /* The text in the control has changed and been displayed */
            break;
        case EN_ERRSPACE:
            /* The control cannot allocate any more memory */
            break;
        case EN_HSCROLL:
            /* The user has clicked on the horizontal scroll bar for this control */
            break;
        case EN_KILLFOCUS:
            /* The control has lost the input focus */
            break;
        case EN_MAXTEXT:
            /* The control is full and the user is trying to enter more text */
            break;
        case EN_SETFOCUS:
            /* The control just got the input focus */
            break;
```

MEMBER FUNCTION	DESCRIPTION
CanUndo(RTMessage)	Tells if the last edit can be undone.
Clear(RTMessage)	Clear text in the control.
ClearModify(RTMessage)	Reset the modified data variable.
CMEditClear(RTMessage)	Response to CM_EDITCLEAR menu selection. Calls Clear.
CMEditCopy(RTMessage)	Response to CM_EDITCOPY menu selection. Calls Copy.
CMEditCut(RTMessage)	Response to CM_EDITCUT menu selection. Calls Cut.
CMEditDelete(RTMessage)	Response to CM_EDITDELETE menu selection. Calls DeleteSelection.
CMEditPaste(RTMessage)	Response to CM_EDITPASTE menu selection. Calls Paste.
CMEditUndo(RTMessage)	Response to CM_EDITUNDO menu selection. Calls Undo.
Copy()	Copies the selected text to the Windows Clipboard.
Cut()	Copies the selected text to the Windows Clipboard and deletes the selected text from the control.
DeleteLine(int Line)	Deletes the indicated line from a multiline control.
DeleteSelection()	Deletes the selected text.
DeleteSubText(int First, int Last)	Deletes the text from columns First to Last.
ENErrSpace(RTMessage)	Response to the EN_ERRSPACE control message.
GetLine(LPSTR Str, int Size, int Line)	Gets Line from a multiline control. Puts the data in Str.
GetLineFromPos(int Pos)	Returns the line that includes the specified position.
GetLineIndex(int Line)	Returns the position of the first character of Line. If Line is -1, GetLineIndex returns the line with the caret.
GetLineLength(int Line)	Returns the number of characters in Line.
GetNumLines()	Returns the number of lines in the control.
GetSelection(Rint First, Rint Last)	Gets the positions of the first and last selected characters.

(continued from page 96)

GetSubText(LPSTR Str, int Size, int First, int Last)	Copies the text between First and Last to the string Str.
GetText(LPSTR Str, int Size)	Return all of the text in the control.
Insert(LPSTR Str);	Inserts Str at the current caret position.
IsModified( )	Tells if the text has been changed.
Paste( )	Copies data from the Windows Clipboard to the current caret position.
Scroll(int Horz, int Vert)	Scroll the text by Horz columns and Vert rows.
Search(int First, LPSTR Str, BOOL Case)	Search the text starting at First for Str. If Case is TRUE, check case while searching.
SetSelection(int First, int Last)	Select the text between First and Last in the control.
SetText(LPSTR Str)	Change the text in the control to Str.
Undo( )	Undo the last edit.

Table 3-1 TEdit Member Functions

```
            case EN_UPDATE:
                /* The text has changed but it has not been displayed yet */
                break;
            case EN_VSCROLL:
                /* The user has clicked on the vertical scroll bar */
                break;
        }
    }
```

The following program shows several different types of edit controls and uses notification messages and TEdit member functions to manage the controls. Figure 3-5 shows the dialog box.

STEPS

1. Create a new project called TEXT.PRJ that includes the files TEXT.CPP, TEXT.RES, and STANDARD.DEF.
2. Use the IDE editor to enter this program:

```
/* Make a dialog with text controls */
#include <owl.h>
#include <edit.h>
#include <string.h>
#include <ctype.h>

#define IDM_SHOW        101
```

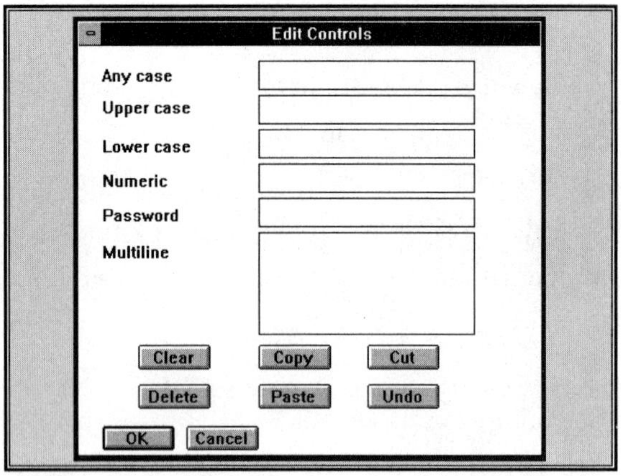

Figure 3-5
The Text Control
Dialog Box

```
#define IDC_MIXED     102
#define IDC_UPPER     103
#define IDC_LOWER     104
#define IDC_NUMBER    105
#define IDC_SECRET    106
#define IDC_MULTI     107
#define IDC_CLEAR     200
#define IDC_COPY      201
#define IDC_CUT       202
#define IDC_DELETE    203
#define IDC_PASTE     204
#define IDC_UNDO      205

/* This object represents the main window */
class TMyWindow : public TWindow
{
    public:
        /* This is where transfer will put the dialog data */
        struct {
            char Mixed[40];  // Sample mixed case text
            char Upper[40];  // Sample uppercase text
            char Lower[40];  // Sample Lowercase text
            char Number[40]; // Sample numeric text
            char Secret[40]; // Sample hidden text
            char Multi[200]; // Sample multiline text
        } Text;
        TMyWindow(PTWindowsObject AParent, LPSTR ATitle);
        virtual LPSTR GetClassName();
        virtual void GetWindowClass(WNDCLASS& AWndClass);
        virtual void ShowDialog(RTMessage) = [CM_FIRST + IDM_SHOW];
};

/* This object represents the dialog box */
class TextDlg : public TDialog
{
    public:
        PTEdit Fields[6];       /* Pointers to the text controls */
        int CurFld;             /* The last control that had the focus */
        char LastNumber[40];
```

```
        TextDlg(PTWindowsObject AParent, LPSTR AResource);
        /* Handle dialog controls */
        void ClearButton(RTMessage) = [ID_FIRST + IDC_CLEAR];
        void CopyButton(RTMessage) = [ID_FIRST + IDC_COPY];
        void CutButton(RTMessage) = [ID_FIRST + IDC_CUT];
        void DeleteButton(RTMessage) = [ID_FIRST + IDC_DELETE];
        void PasteButton(RTMessage) = [ID_FIRST + IDC_PASTE];
        void UndoButton(RTMessage) = [ID_FIRST + IDC_UNDO];
        void CheckFocus1(RTMessage Msg) = [ID_FIRST + IDC_MIXED];
        void CheckFocus2(RTMessage Msg) = [ID_FIRST + IDC_UPPER];
        void CheckFocus3(RTMessage Msg) = [ID_FIRST + IDC_LOWER];
        void VerifyNumb(RTMessage Msg) = [ID_FIRST + IDC_NUMBER];
        void CheckFocus4(RTMessage Msg) = [ID_FIRST + IDC_SECRET];
        void CheckFocus5(RTMessage Msg) = [ID_FIRST + IDC_MULTI];
};

/* Initialize the dialog controls and set up the transfer buffer */
TextDlg::TextDlg(PTWindowsObject AParent, LPSTR AResource)
    : TDialog(AParent, AResource)
{
    /* Create control objects */
    Fields[0] = new TEdit(this, IDC_MIXED, 40);
    Fields[1] = new TEdit(this, IDC_UPPER, 40);
    Fields[2] = new TEdit(this, IDC_LOWER, 40);
    Fields[3] = new TEdit(this, IDC_NUMBER, 40);
    Fields[4] = new TEdit(this, IDC_SECRET, 40);
    Fields[5] = new TEdit(this, IDC_MULTI, 200);
    CurFld = 0;
    /* Set up to transfer data with the main window object */
    TransferBuffer = (void far *) &((TMyWindow *) Parent)->Text;
}

/* Clear the last selected field */
void TextDlg::ClearButton(RTMessage)
{
    Fields[CurFld]->SetText("");
}

/* Copy text from the current field to the clipboard */
void TextDlg::CopyButton(RTMessage)
{
    Fields[CurFld]->Copy();
}

/* Cut text from the current field to the clipboard */
void TextDlg::CutButton(RTMessage)
{
    Fields[CurFld]->Cut();
}

/* Delete selected text in the current field */
void TextDlg::DeleteButton(RTMessage)
{
    Fields[CurFld]->DeleteSelection();
}

/* Paste text into the current case field */
void TextDlg::PasteButton(RTMessage)
```

```
{
      Fields[CurFld]->Paste();
}

/* Undo the last action in the current field */
void TextDlg::UndoButton(RTMessage)
{
      Fields[CurFld]->Undo();
}

/* Set the current field to the first field */
void TextDlg::CheckFocus1(RTMessage Msg)
{
      if(Msg.LP.Hi == EN_SETFOCUS)
            CurFld = 0;
}

/* Set the current field to the second field */
void TextDlg::CheckFocus2(RTMessage Msg)
{
      if(Msg.LP.Hi == EN_SETFOCUS)
            CurFld = 1;
}

/* Set the current field to the third field */
void TextDlg::CheckFocus3(RTMessage Msg)
{
      if(Msg.LP.Hi == EN_SETFOCUS)
            CurFld = 2;
}

/* Check to see if the numeric field contains a number */
void TextDlg::VerifyNumb(RTMessage Msg)
{
      char Text[40], *p;

      /* See if the text is about to change */
      if(Msg.LP.Hi == EN_UPDATE)
      {
            /* Get the text */
            Fields[3]->GetText(Text, 40);
            /* See if the string is all digits */
            for(p = Text; *p && isdigit(*p); p++);
            /* see if a nondigit found */
            if(*p)
            {
                  /* If a nondigit found, beep and put back the last valid number */
                  MessageBeep(0);
                  Fields[3]->SetText(LastNumber);
            }
            else /* If the string is a number, copy it to the last good number */
                  lstrcpy(LastNumber, Text);
      }
      else if(Msg.LP.Hi == EN_SETFOCUS) // See if getting focus
            CurFld = 3;
}

/* Set the current field to the forth field */
```

```
void TextDlg::CheckFocus4(RTMessage Msg)
{
     if(Msg.LP.Hi == EN_SETFOCUS)
          CurFld = 4;
}

/* Set the current field to the fifth field */
void TextDlg::CheckFocus5(RTMessage Msg)
{
     if(Msg.LP.Hi == EN_SETFOCUS)
          CurFld = 5;
}

/* Initialize the main window */
TMyWindow::TMyWindow(PTWindowsObject AParent, LPSTR ATitle)
     : TWindow(AParent, ATitle)
{
     AssignMenu("TextMenu");
     Attr.Style |= WS_CAPTION;
     Attr.W = 300;
     Attr.H = 200;
     memset(&Text, '\0', sizeof(Text));
}

/* return the unique class name */
LPSTR TMyWindow::GetClassName()
{
     return "MyClass";
}

/* Set the main window ICON to the one in the resource file */
void TMyWindow::GetWindowClass(WNDCLASS& AWndClass)
{
     TWindow::GetWindowClass(AWndClass);
     AWndClass.hIcon = LoadIcon(GetApplication()->hInstance, "TEXTICON");
}

/* Display the dialog then paint the results in the main window */
void TMyWindow::ShowDialog(RTMessage)
{
     HDC hDC;

     /* Do the dialog */
     GetModule()->ExecDialog(new TextDlg(this, "TextDialog"));
     /* Print the results */
     hDC = GetDC(HWindow);
     /* Display the sample text */
     TextOut(hDC, 3, 0, Text.Mixed, lstrlen(Text.Mixed));
     TextOut(hDC, 3, 15, Text.Upper, lstrlen(Text.Upper));
     TextOut(hDC, 3, 30, Text.Lower, lstrlen(Text.Lower));
     TextOut(hDC, 3, 45, Text.Number, lstrlen(Text.Number));
     TextOut(hDC, 3, 60, Text.Secret, lstrlen(Text.Secret));
     TextOut(hDC, 3, 75, Text.Multi, lstrlen(Text.Multi));
     ReleaseDC(hDC, HWindow);
}

class TMyApp : public TApplication
{
```

```
    public:
        TMyApp(LPSTR ApName, HANDLE Inst, HANDLE PrevInst
            , LPSTR CmdLine, int CmdShow) : TApplication(ApName
            , Inst, PrevInst, CmdLine, CmdShow) {};
        virtual void InitMainWindow();
};

void TMyApp::InitMainWindow()
{
    MainWindow = new TMyWindow(NULL, "Text controls");
}

int PASCAL WinMain(HANDLE Inst, HANDLE PrevInst, LPSTR CmdLine
    , int CmdShow)
{
    TMyApp TheApp("", Inst, PrevInst, CmdLine, CmdShow);

    TheApp.Run();
    return TheApp.Status;
}
```

3. Use the Resource Workshop to create a resource file named TEXT.RES that includes an icon named TEXTICON. Use the *edit as text* command to make a menu like this:

```
TEXTMENU MENU
BEGIN
    MENUITEM "&Show dialog", 101
END
```

Finally, use the *edit as text* command to create a dialog like this:

```
TEXTDIALOG DIALOG 11, 53, 193, 174
CAPTION "Edit Controls"
STYLE DS_MODALFRAME | WS_POPUP | WS_CAPTION | WS_SYSMENU
BEGIN
    CONTROL "Clear",200,"BUTTON",BS_PUSHBUTTON|WS_CHILD|WS_VISIBLE|WS_TABSTOP,25,122,30,10
    CONTROL "OK",1,"BUTTON",BS_DEFPUSHBUTTON|WS_CHILD|WS_VISIBLE|WS_TABSTOP, 10, 155, 30, 10
    CONTROL "Cancel",2,"BUTTON",BS_PUSHBUTTON|WS_CHILD|WS_VISIBLE | WS_TABSTOP, 45,155,30,10
    CONTROL "Copy",201,"BUTTON",BS_PUSHBUTTON|WS_CHILD|WS_VISIBLE|WS_TABSTOP,75,122,30,10
    CONTROL "Cut",202,"BUTTON",BS_PUSHBUTTON|WS_CHILD|WS_VISIBLE|WS_TABSTOP,120,122,30,10
    CONTROL "Paste",204,"BUTTON",BS_PUSHBUTTON|WS_CHILD|WS_VISIBLE|WS_TABSTOP, 75,138,30,10
    CONTROL "Undo",205,"BUTTON",BS_PUSHBUTTON|WS_CHILD|WS_VISIBLE|WS_TABSTOP,120,138,30, 10
    CONTROL "Delete",203,"BUTTON",BS_PUSHBUTTON|WS_CHILD|WS_VISIBLE|WS_TABSTOP, 25,138,30,10
    CONTROL "", 102, "EDIT", ES_LEFT|WS_CHILD|WS_VISIBLE|WS_BORDER | WS_TABSTOP,75,6, 90, 12
    CONTROL "Any case", -1, "STATIC", SS_LEFT | WS_CHILD | WS_VISIBLE|WS_GROUP, 10, 8,30, 8
    CONTROL "",103,"EDIT",ES_LEFT|ES_UPPERCASE|WS_CHILD|WS_VISIBLE|WS_BORDER,75,20,90,12
    CONTROL "Upper case",-1,"STATIC",SS_LEFT|WS_CHILD|WS_VISIBLE|WS_GROUP, 10, 21, 40, 8
    CONTROL "Lower case",-1, "STATIC", SS_LEFT|WS_CHILD|WS_VISIBLE|WS_GROUP, 10, 37, 40, 8
    CONTROL "",104,"EDIT",ES_LEFT|ES_LOWERCASE|WS_CHILD|WS_VISIBLE|WS_BORDER,75,34,90,12
    CONTROL "Numeric",-1,"STATIC", SS_LEFT | WS_CHILD |WS_VISIBLE|WS_GROUP, 10, 51, 30, 8
    CONTROL "",105,"EDIT",ES_LEFT|WS_CHILD|WS_VISIBLE|WS_BORDER|WS_TABSTOP, 75, 48, 90, 12
    CONTROL "Password",-1,"STATIC",SS_LEFT | WS_CHILD | WS_VISIBLE | WS_GROUP, 10, 65, 35, 8
    CONTROL "",106,"EDIT",ES_LEFT|ES_PASSWORD|WS_CHILD|WS_VISIBLE|WS_BORDER,75,62,90,12
    CONTROL "Multiline", -1, "STATIC", SS_LEFT|WS_CHILD| WS_VISIBLE|WS_GROUP,10,80,35,8
    CONTROL "",107,"EDIT",ES_LEFT|ES_MULTILINE|WS_CHILD|WS_VISIBLE|WS_BORDER,75,76,90,42
END
```

4. Use the *Run* command from the IDE to compile and run the program.

HOW IT WORKS

The first thing that TEXT.CPP does is define constants for all of the IDs used in the program. This helps make the rest of the program easy to understand. The object TMyWindow is the main window of the program. Note the structure Text that is used to hold data transferred from the dialog box. Also note the message response member function ShowDialog that shows the dialog when the user clicks on the menu command.

The TextDlg object represents the dialog box that contains several text controls. The definition includes an array of pointers to TEdit objects called Fields. This array holds the addresses of each of the control objects. Other data items in the object are CurFld, which is an index into Fields, and LastNumber, which is a string that holds the last acceptable entry into the number control. The program makes sure that CurFld always indicates the last text control that had the focus. The fourth text control in the dialog accepts only numeric data. The program enforces this by checking the data whenever it changes. If the data is a number, it is copied to LastNumber so that it can be put back into the control if the user enters a nonnumeric value.

The constructor for the TextDlg object creates TEdit objects for each of the edit controls in the dialog. It saves pointers to each function in the Fields array. Then it sets the transfer buffer to copy data between the main window object and the text controls.

There is a member function in the TestDlg class for each control in the dialog. ObjectWindows calls these member functions when Windows sends a WM_COMMAND message that refers to the control. The button controls call one of the TEdit object member functions for the last control that had the focus. For example, when the user presses the Copy button, ObjectWindows calls the member function CopyButton that calls the Copy member function for the control indicated by CurFld.

The member functions that handle WM_COMMAND messages for text controls check the message type to see if the message is an EN_SETFOCUS message. If it is, the member function sets CurFld to indicate the control. The member function VerifyNumb also handles the EN_UPDATE message by getting the data from the control, checking whether it is a number, and setting or using LastNumber as appropriate.

The TMyWindow object class member function ShowDialog executes the dialog by calling the ExecDialog function. When the user exits the dialog, the transfer mechanism copies the data or doesn't copy the data depending on whether the user selected OK or Cancel to exit the dialog. ShowDialog uses

Windows functions to print the data in the main window. In a complete application, there would also be a function to print the data as the result of a WM_PAINT message from Windows.

COMMENTS

The text control is a very powerful Windows feature. In fact, the Notepad editor supplied with Windows is nothing more than an edit control turned into a whole window. The first How-To in Chapter 4, "Menus," shows how to make an editor application similar to Notepad by combining the ObjectWindows TEdit object class with the TFile class.

If your needs for text entry are less ambitious, the TEdit class can be very easy to use. All that is required is to put an edit control in a dialog in the resource file and set up the transfer mechanism for it. Because of object-oriented techniques, going from a simple text control to a more complex (for example, translating the text to Spanish) does not require starting over. Instead, you just need to handle a few messages.

3.5 How Do I ...
Use List Box and Combo Box Controls?

Complexity : DIFFICULT

PROBLEM

One way to make a user interface easier to use and ensure that you get correct data from the user is to let him pick items from a list. For example, if you want the user to enter the name of his favorite musical group, you can give him a list to choose from instead of hoping that he spells the name correctly in a text field. This solution shows you what you can do with lists in Windows programs.

TECHNIQUE

The first step for using list boxes is to pick the right kind of list box for the job. The parameters dialog for list boxes in the Resource Workshop's dialog editor shows you the possibilities. Some of these parameters, such as scroll bars or the tab stop attribute, should be familiar from working with text controls in the previous solution. The parameters in the group box labeled "List box" are used only with list boxes. Table 3-2 describes each of these parameters.

Your choices do not end with the list box parameters. If you want to allow the user the choice of entering a string or choosing from a list, you can use a combo box control that combines a text control with a list box. Combo boxes have most of the options of both list boxes and text controls.

Once you have decided what kind of list box to use and have created a dialog box in the resource file that includes the list box, you need to add instructions to your program to handle the list box. The ObjectWindows object that handles list boxes is called TListBox, and for combo boxes is TComboBox. Table 3-3 lists some of the member functions provided by these objects.

The first thing to look at with these objects is how to get the list of items into the control and how to get the user's selection out. One way to put strings into the list is to use the member functions AddString and InsertString. AddString adds a string to the end of the list if the control is an unsorted list, or puts the list in alphabetical order for sorted lists. InsertString always adds the string at the indicated position regardless of the sorting parameter for the control. The trick with these functions is to use them at the right time. If you put them in the constructor for the dialog that contains the list box, you will find that none of the strings actually makes it to the list. The reason for this is that these functions work by sending messages to the controls. The actual control does not exist until after the constructor is finished, so there is nothing to recieve the message. Fortunately, ObjectWindows calls the member function SetupWindow after the window and all of its controls are created to handle this situation.

Another way to set up the list for a list box is to use the transfer mechanism. With text controls, you can copy a string into the structures set up for transferring, and ObjectWindows makes sure that the string gets into the text control. You can do a similar thing with data for list boxes. Clearly, you cannot use a simple variable to transfer an unknown number of strings to the list box. ObjectWindows overcomes this problem by making the transfer buffer for list boxes be a pointer to an object called TListBoxData that handles the list of data. The example program in this solution shows how to set this up. The TListBoxData object also handles the problem of getting the selected items back from the control when the user is done selecting.

With text controls you could keep track of what the user was doing to the control by handling WM_COMMAND messages. The same is true with list boxes and combo boxes. In fact, combo boxes provide all of the notification messages that text controls do plus the special messages for list boxes. The two messages unique to list boxes are LBN_DBLCLK, which indicates that the user double-clicked an item in the list, and LBN_SELCHANGE,used when the user selects or de-selects an item in the list.

The last thing you should be aware of with list boxes is that you can create owner-drawn list box items similar to the owner-drawn menu items presented in Chapter 2, "ObjectWindows Basics." If a list box has the owner-drawn style, Windows sends WM_MEASUREITEM and WM_DRAWITEM messages to the owner of the control, so that it can draw the item. One thing to think about with owner-drawn list boxes is what happens to all of the strings you add to the control? If you set the "has strings" parameter for the list box, the strings are saved in memory and you can access them as with any other list box. If you did

Parameter	Description
Notify	Send a WM_COMMAND message to the owner window if the user clicks or double-clicks in the control.
Sort	Sort the strings that are added to the control using the AddString function.
Multiple select	More than one item in the list can be selected at a time.
Don't redraw	Do not redraw the control when changes are made. For long lists you should set this parameter, load all of the strings (they aren't displayed so loading goes faster), then send a WM_SETREDRAW message to the control. Finally, tell Windows to redraw the control.
Tab stops	Lets your program set tab stops in the list box.
Integral height	Makes sure that the height of the list box is a multiple of the height of the items in the list.
Multicolumn	The list box has several columns.
Pass keyboard input	Sends WM_VKEYTOITEM or WM_CHARTOITEM messages to the owner window when the user presses a key. The owner window can interpret the key to see if it indicates that one of the items in the list should be selected.
Extend select	Lets the user select more than one item by holding the Shift key while dragging the mouse.
Has strings	Indicates that the owner draw list box should keep track of strings.
Not owner draw	Standard list box with strings in the list.
Fixed	Each item in the list is drawn by the owner window, all items are the same size.
Variable	Each item in the list is drawn by the owner window, each item is a different size.

Table 3-2 List Box Parameters

not set "has strings," you can pass a long integer when you add or insert a string instead of the address of a string. This long integer will be passed to the owner during the WM_DRAWITEM message. One possibility is to pass handles of bitmaps that will appear in the list. The program below uses owner-drawn list boxes to change the color of items in the list.

The program below includes a dialog box that has three list boxes and a combo box. Figure 3-6 shows you what the dialog looks like. The first list box is a single selection dialog. The program gets notification messages when the user selects or double-clicks an item in this list. The second list box is a multiple selection list box. The third list box has owner-drawn items. The last control is a combo box.

Function	Description
AddString(LPSTR Str)	Adds the string in Str to the list.
ClearList()	Clears all items from the list.
DeleteString(int Index)	Removes the string at Index from the list (first string is 0).
FindExactString(LPSTR Str, int Index)	Searches for a string that matches Str starting at Index.
FindString(LPSTR Str, int Index)	Searches for a string that starts with Str starting at Index.
GetCount()	Returns the number of items in the list box.
GetSelString(LPSTR Str, int Size)	Puts up to Size characters from the selected string into Str.
GetSelStrings(LPSTR *StrLst, int Cnt, int Size)	Puts up to Size characters into Cnt strings into the array at StrLst.
GetSelIndex()	Returns the index of the selected item.
GetSelIndexes(Pint List, int Cnt)	Returns a list of selected indexes.
GetString(LPSTR Str, int Index)	Puts the string at Index into Str.
GetStringLen(int Index)	Returns the length of the string at Index.
InsertString(LPSTR Str, int Index)	Puts Str into the list at Index.
SetSelIndex(int Index);	Selects the item at Index.

Table 3-3 Member Functions for TListBox and TComboBox Objects

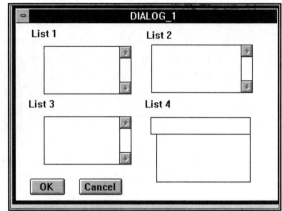

Figure 3-6
The List Box
Dialog

STEPS

1. Create a new project called LIST.PRJ that includes the files LIST.CPP, LIST.RES, and STANDARD.DEF.

2. Create the source file LIST.CPP with the following program:

```
/* Make a dialog with text controls */
#include <owl.h>
#include <listbox.h>
#include <combobox.h>
#include <string.h>
#include <ctype.h>

#define IDM_SHOW        101
#define IDC_LIST1       102
#define IDC_LIST2       103
#define IDC_LIST3       104
#define IDC_LIST4       105

/* This object represents the main window */
class TMyWindow : public TWindow
{
    public:
        /* This is where transfer will put the dialog data */
        PTListBoxData Lists[3];
        PTComboBoxData Combo;
        TMyWindow(PTWindowsObject AParent, LPSTR ATitle);
        virtual LPSTR GetClassName() { return "MyClass"; };
        virtual void GetWindowClass(WNDCLASS& AWndClass);
        /* Handle the menu command */
        virtual void ShowDialog(RTMessage) = [CM_FIRST + IDM_SHOW];
};

/* This object represents the dialog box */
class ListDlg : public TDialog
{
    public:
        PTListBox ListBox[3];
        PTComboBox ComboBox;
```

```
            ListDlg(PTWindowsObject AParent, LPSTR AResource);
            void SetupWindow();
            /* Handle messages */
            virtual void HandleLBox1(RTMessage Msg) = [ID_FIRST + IDC_LIST1];
            virtual void MeasureItem(RTMessage Msg) = [WM_FIRST + WM_MEASUREITEM];
            virtual void WMDrawItem(RTMessage Msg) = [WM_FIRST + WM_DRAWITEM];
};


/* Initialize the dialog controls and set up the transfer buffer */
ListDlg::ListDlg(PTWindowsObject AParent, LPSTR AResource)
    : TDialog(AParent, AResource)
{
    ListBox[0] = new TListBox(this, IDC_LIST1);
    ListBox[1] = new TListBox(this, IDC_LIST2);
    ListBox[2] = new TListBox(this, IDC_LIST3);
    ComboBox = new TComboBox(this, IDC_LIST4, 50);
    TransferBuffer = (void far *) &((TMyWindow *) Parent)->Lists;
}


void ListDlg::SetupWindow()
{
    TDialog::SetupWindow();
    ListBox[0]->AddString("at a time");
}


void ListDlg::HandleLBox1(RTMessage Msg)
{
    char TmpStr[50];

    /* Determine what type of notification */
    switch(Msg.LP.Hi)
    {
        case LBN_DBLCLK:
            ListBox[0]->GetSelString(TmpStr, 50);
            ListBox[1]->AddString(TmpStr);
            break;
        case LBN_SELCHANGE:
            ListBox[0]->GetSelString(TmpStr, 50);
            ComboBox->AddString(TmpStr);
            break;
    }
}


/* Get the size of the items to draw */
void ListDlg::MeasureItem(RTMessage Msg)
{
    MEASUREITEMSTRUCT far *MI;

    MI = (MEASUREITEMSTRUCT far *) Msg.LParam;
    /* See if this message is about the owner-drawn list box */
    if(MI->CtlID == IDC_LIST3)
    {
        /* Return the dimensions of an entry in the list box */
        MI->itemWidth = 100;
        MI->itemHeight = 15;
    }
}


/* Draw an item in the owner-drawn dialog */
```

```
void ListDlg::WMDrawItem(RTMessage Msg)
{
    DRAWITEMSTRUCT far *DI;
    char TmpStr[50];

    DI = (DRAWITEMSTRUCT far *) Msg.LParam;
    /* See if this message is about the owner-drawn list box */
    if(DI->CtlID == IDC_LIST3)
    {
        SetBkMode(DI->hDC, OPAQUE);
        if(DI->itemState&ODS_SELECTED)
        {
            SetBkColor(DI->hDC, 0xFF00);
            SetTextColor(DI->hDC, 0xFF);
        }
        else
        {
            SetBkColor(DI->hDC, 0xFF);
            SetTextColor(DI->hDC, 0xFF00);
        }
        if(DI->itemState&ODS_FOCUS)
            SetTextColor(DI->hDC, 0);
        ListBox[2]->GetString(TmpStr, DI->itemID);
        TextOut(DI->hDC, DI->rcItem.left, DI->rcItem.top
            , TmpStr, lstrlen(TmpStr));
    }
}


/* Initialize the main window */
TMyWindow::TMyWindow(PTWindowsObject AParent, LPSTR ATitle)
    : TWindow(AParent, ATitle)
{
    AssignMenu("ListMenu");
    Attr.Style |= WS_CAPTION;
    Attr.W = 300;
    Attr.H = 200;
}


/* Set the main window ICON to the one in the resource file */
void TMyWindow::GetWindowClass(WNDCLASS& AWndClass)
{
    TWindow::GetWindowClass(AWndClass);
    AWndClass.hIcon = LoadIcon(GetApplication()->hInstance, "LISTICON");
}


/* Display the dialog then paint the results in the main window */
void TMyWindow::ShowDialog(RTMessage)
{
    HDC hDC;
    char TmpStr[50];
    int i, Row;
    RECT Rect;

    /* Set up the data transfer area */
    Lists[0] = new TListBoxData();
    Lists[0]->AddString("Only one");
    Lists[0]->AddString("of these");
    Lists[0]->AddString("can be selected");
    Lists[1] = new TListBoxData();
```

```
        Lists[1]->AddString("You can", TRUE);
        Lists[1]->AddString("select");
        Lists[1]->AddString("several strings");
        Lists[1]->AddString("from this");
        Lists[1]->AddString("list");
        Lists[2] = new TListBoxData();
        Lists[2]->AddString("This");
        Lists[2]->AddString("Listbox");
        Lists[2]->AddString("is in", TRUE);
        Lists[2]->AddString("full color");
        Combo = new TComboBoxData();
        Combo->AddString("Combo boxes", TRUE);
        Combo->AddString("are like a");
        Combo->AddString("list box and");
        Combo->AddString("a text control");
        Combo->AddString("in one");
        /* Do the dialog */
        GetModule()->ExecDialog(new ListDlg(this, "ListDialog"));
        /* Print the results */
        hDC = GetDC(HWindow);
        GetWindowRect(HWindow, &Rect);
        FillRect(hDC, &Rect, GetStockObject(WHITE_BRUSH));
        TextOut(hDC, 0, 0, "First selection:", 14);
        /* Print the selected item in the first list box */
        if(Lists[0]->SelCount)
                Lists[0]->GetSelString(TmpStr, 50);
        else
                lstrcpy(TmpStr, "No string selected");
        TextOut(hDC, 5, 18, TmpStr, lstrlen(TmpStr));
        TextOut(hDC, 0, 36, "Multiple selections:", 20);
        Row = 54;
        for(i=0; i<Lists[1]->SelCount; i++)
        {
                Lists[1]->GetSelString(TmpStr, 50, i);
                TextOut(hDC, 5, Row, TmpStr, lstrlen(TmpStr));
                Row += 18;
        }
        TextOut(hDC, 0, Row, "Combo box selection:", 20);
        Row += 18;
        TextOut(hDC, 5, Row, Combo->Selection, lstrlen(Combo->Selection));
        ReleaseDC(hDC, HWindow);
        delete Lists[0];        // Release the memory used by the list boxes
        delete Lists[1];
        delete Lists[2];
        delete Combo;
}

class TMyApp : public TApplication
{
        public:
                TMyApp(LPSTR ApName, HANDLE Inst, HANDLE PrevInst
                        , LPSTR CmdLine, int CmdShow) : TApplication(ApName
                        , Inst, PrevInst, CmdLine, CmdShow) {};
                virtual void InitMainWindow();
};

void TMyApp::InitMainWindow()
{
        MainWindow = new TMyWindow(NULL, "Listbox controls");
```

```
}

int PASCAL WinMain(HANDLE Inst, HANDLE PrevInst, LPSTR CmdLine
     , int CmdShow)
{
     TMyApp TheApp("", Inst, PrevInst, CmdLine, CmdShow);

     TheApp.Run();
     return TheApp.Status;
}
```

3. Create the resource file named LIST.RES with a menu named LISTMENU, an icon named LISTICON, and a dialog named LISTDIALOG. Here are the text versions of the menu and the dialog:

```
LISTMENU MENU
BEGIN
     MENUITEM "ShowList", 101
END

LISTDIALOG DIALOG 5, 9, 183, 121
CAPTION "DIALOG_1"
STYLE DS_MODALFRAME | WS_POPUP | WS_CAPTION | WS_SYSMENU
BEGIN
     CONTROL "",102,"LISTBOX",LBS_NOTIFY|WS_CHILD|WS_VISIBLE|WS_BORDER|WS_VSCROLL|WS_TABSTOP
          , 20, 16, 60, 33
     CONTROL "List 1", -1, "STATIC", SS_LEFT | WS_CHILD | WS_VISIBLE | WS_GROUP, 11, 3, 30, 8
     CONTROL "OK", 1, "BUTTON", BS_PUSHBUTTON | WS_CHILD | WS_VISIBLE | WS_TABSTOP
          , 10, 106, 24, 11
     CONTROL "List 2", -1, "STATIC", SS_LEFT | WS_CHILD | WS_VISIBLE | WS_GROUP, 91, 4, 25, 8
     CONTROL "",103,"LISTBOX"
          ,LBS_NOTIFY|LBS_MULTIPLESEL|WS_CHILD|WS_VISIBLE|WS_BORDER|WS_VSCROLL
          , 95, 15, 70, 33
     CONTROL "List 3", -1, "STATIC", SS_LEFT | WS_CHILD | WS_VISIBLE | WS_GROUP, 9, 51, 25, 8
     CONTROL "",104,"LISTBOX"
          ,LBS_NOTIFY|LBS_OWNERDRAWFIXED|LBS_HASSTRINGS|WS_CHILD|WS_VISIBLE|WS_BORDER
          |WS_VSCROLL
          , 20, 64, 60, 33
     CONTROL "List 4", -1, "STATIC",SS_LEFT | WS_CHILD | WS_VISIBLE | WS_GROUP, 90, 51, 25, 8
     CONTROL "", 105, "COMBOBOX",CBS_SIMPLE |WS_CHILD | WS_VISIBLE | WS_TABSTOP,94,64,70,52
     CONTROL "Cancel",2,"BUTTON",BS_PUSHBUTTON|WS_CHILD|WS_VISIBLE|WS_TABSTOP,44,106,30,11
END
```

4. Compile and run the program.

HOW IT WORKS

This program has many of the same features as the text control example in the previous solution. The only differences are those required to make this program work with list boxes instead of text controls. The main window in this program includes pointers to TListBoxData and TComboBoxData objects instead of string variables. These objects are used in transferring data between the main window and the list boxes.

The dialog box window object includes pointers for the list box controls and indexed member functions to handle the notification messages and owner-drawn messages. The dialog object defines a SetupWindow member function that demonstrates how to add strings to a list box from within the dialog object. The rest of the list boxes are initialized via the transfer mechanism.

The HandleLBox1 member function handles notification messages from the first list box. When the user double-clicks an item in the first list, this function copies the selected item from the first list box to the second list box. When the user changes the selection, the function copies the selected item to the combo box list.

The MeasureItem and WMDrawItem member functions handle the owner-drawn items in the third list box. When Windows creates the list box, it sends a message that calls the MeasureItem function. The function checks to see if Windows is drawing the list box in question. This step is included only as an example of what you would have to do if there were more than one owner-drawn control in the dialog. The next step is to fill in the MEASUREITEM structure with the height and width of an item in the list.

After getting the size of the list box items, Windows sends a message for each item in the list box that calls the WMDrawItem function. This function picks colors for the text and background based on the selection state of the item. Next, the function gets the string that goes with the item. Finally, it prints the text in the selected colors.

The ShowDialog member function executes the dialog and prints the results in the main window. The first step is to load the data to be transferred to list boxes. ShowDialog allocates a TListBoxData object and adds strings to it for each list box and makes a TComboBoxData object for the combo box. Once all of the data items are loaded, the function executes the dialog. When the user presses the OK button, ShowDialog prints the selected items on the main window. Before exiting, ShowDialog deletes the transfer objects to return the memory they use to the heap.

COMMENTS

List boxes are a bit more difficult to implement than other controls, but they are worth the effort. Not only do they make the user's job easier, but they can actually simplify your programs. If you do not use list boxes, you must go to the extra effort of checking all input data for correctness and providing a way to prompt the user for corrections.

Of course there will always be cases where typing in the data is faster than finding it in the list. In these cases, you should consider a combo box. This gives the user the option of typing in the data or searching for the response in the list. It also allows the user to enter data that is not in the list. For example, in file selection dialogs, the list might contain all of the files with a certain extension but the user can enter a file with whatever extension is required.

3.6 How Do I...
Use Check Box and Radio Button Controls?

Complexity : EASY

PROBLEM

Two of the simplest controls are the check box and its close relative the radio button. These controls are either selected or not selected making them easy for both the user and the programmer. This solution shows you the ObjectWindows objects that handle these buttons.

TECHNIQUE

There are fewer options for check boxes than for controls text controls and list boxes. There are only three possibilities: automatic, tri-state, and normal. Automatic check boxes handle notification messages for you so that you only have to check the state of the control when the user presses the OK button in a dialog. Tri-state check boxes can be checked, unchecked, or grayed. Normal check boxes can be checked or unchecked and you must handle the notification messages.

Radio buttons are slightly more complex. They are usually used in groups in which only one button is selected at a time. If you set the WS_GROUP style for the first radio button in a group and for the control that follows the group, and you use automatic radio buttons, Windows makes sure that only the last button clicked by the user is selected. When the dialog is finished, you need to check each of the radio buttons in the group to find the one that was set.

Both button types have only two notification messages, BN_CLICKED, for when the user clicks the button, and BN_DOUBLECLICKED, for when the user double-clicks the button. If you do not use automatic buttons, you must handle the BN_CLICKED message if you want to have the control change appearance when the user clicks it. You can use these notifications with automatic controls if your program needs to do special processing.

The ObjectWindows objects for these buttons are TCheckBox and TRadioButton. They both provide the member functions in Table 3-4. For most programs, you can use automatic buttons and the transfer mechanism to copy data between the control and other windows. This is the technique used in the program below.

STEPS

1. Create a new project called BUTTON.PRJ that includes the files BUTTON.CPP, BUTTON.RES, and STANDARD.DEF.

2. Create the source file BUTTON.CPP with the following program:

```
/* Make a dialog with text controls */
#include <owl.h>
#include <checkbox.h>
#include <radiobut.h>
#include <string.h>
#include <ctype.h>


#define IDM_SHOW          101
#define IDC_THEGROUP      103
#define IDC_CHOICE        104
#define IDC_OPTION        107


/* This object represents the main window */
class TMyWindow : public TWindow
{
     public:
            /* This is where transfer will put the dialog data */
            struct ButStru {
                  WORD Choices[3];
                  WORD Option1;
                  WORD Option2;
            } Buttons;
            TMyWindow(PTWindowsObject AParent, LPSTR ATitle);
            virtual LPSTR GetClassName();
            virtual void GetWindowClass(WNDCLASS& AWndClass);
            virtual void ShowDialog(RTMessage) = [CM_FIRST + IDM_SHOW];
};


/* This object represents the dialog box */
class ButtonDlg : public TDialog
{
     public:
            PTGroupBox TheGroup;
            PTRadioButton Choices[3];
            PTCheckBox  Options[2];
            ButtonDlg(PTWindowsObject AParent, LPSTR AResource);
            void virtual Clicked(RTMessage) = [ID_FIRST + IDC_OPTION];
};


/* Initialize the dialog controls and set up the transfer buffer */
ButtonDlg::ButtonDlg(PTWindowsObject AParent, LPSTR AResource)
     : TDialog(AParent, AResource)
{
     int i;

     TheGroup = new TGroupBox(this, IDC_THEGROUP);
     for(i=0; i<3; i++)
          Choices[i] = new TRadioButton(this, IDC_CHOICE+i, TheGroup);
     for(i=0; i<2; i++)
          Options[i] = new TCheckBox(this, IDC_OPTION+i, NULL);
     TransferBuffer = (void far *) &((TMyWindow *) Parent)->Buttons;
```

FUNCTION	DESCRIPTION
Check( )	Sets the button to the checked state.
GetCheck( )	Returns the state of the button (TRUE = Checked).
SetCheck(WORD State)	Sets the button to the state in State (BF_CHECKED, BF_UNCHECKED, or BF_GRAYED).
Toggle( )	Toggles the state of the button.

Table 3-4 TCheckBox Member Functions

```
}

void ButtonDlg::Clicked(RTMessage)
{
     /* If the first choice is selected, toggle the second option */
     if(Choices[0]->GetCheck())
          Options[1]->Toggle();
}

/* Initialize the main window */
TMyWindow::TMyWindow(PTWindowsObject AParent, LPSTR ATitle)
     : TWindow(AParent, ATitle)
{
     AssignMenu("ButMenu");
     Attr.Style |= WS_CAPTION;
     Attr.W = 300;
     Attr.H = 200;
     /* Set up the dialog buttons */
     memset(&Buttons, '\0', sizeof(struct ButStru));
     Buttons.Choices[0] = TRUE;
}

/* Return the unique class name */
LPSTR TMyWindow::GetClassName()
{
     return "MyClass";
}

/* Set the main window ICON to the one in the resource file */
void TMyWindow::GetWindowClass(WNDCLASS& AWndClass)
{
     TWindow::GetWindowClass(AWndClass);
     AWndClass.hIcon = LoadIcon(GetApplication()->hInstance, "BUTICON");
}

/* Display the dialog then paint the results in the main window */
void TMyWindow::ShowDialog(RTMessage)
{
     HDC hDC;
     int i;
     char TmpStr[50];
```

```
        /* Do the dialog */
        GetModule()->ExecDialog(new ButtonDlg(this, "ButDialog"));
        /* Print the results */
        hDC = GetDC(HWindow);
        lstrcpy(TmpStr, "Choice #1");
        /* Find the selected choice */
        for(i=0; i<3 && !Buttons.Choices[i]; i++);
        TmpStr[lstrlen(TmpStr)-1] += i;
        TextOut(hDC, 0, 0, TmpStr, lstrlen(TmpStr));
        if(Buttons.Option1)
                lstrcpy(TmpStr, "Option A selected");
        else
                lstrcpy(TmpStr, "Option A not selected");
        TextOut(hDC, 0, 18, TmpStr, lstrlen(TmpStr));
        if(Buttons.Option2)
                lstrcpy(TmpStr, "Option B selected");
        else
                lstrcpy(TmpStr, "Option B not selected");
        TextOut(hDC, 0, 36, TmpStr, lstrlen(TmpStr));
        ReleaseDC(hDC, HWindow);
}

class TMyApp : public TApplication
{
        public:
                TMyApp(LPSTR ApName, HANDLE Inst, HANDLE PrevInst
                        , LPSTR CmdLine, int CmdShow) : TApplication(ApName
                        , Inst, PrevInst, CmdLine, CmdShow) {};
                virtual void InitMainWindow();
};

void TMyApp::InitMainWindow()
{
        MainWindow = new TMyWindow(NULL, "Button controls");
}

int PASCAL WinMain(HANDLE Inst, HANDLE PrevInst, LPSTR CmdLine
        , int CmdShow)
{
        TMyApp TheApp("", Inst, PrevInst, CmdLine, CmdShow);

        TheApp.Run();
        return TheApp.Status;
}
```

3. Create the resource file BUTTON.RES that includes an icon named BUTICON, a menu named BUTMENU, and a dialog named BUTDIALOG. Use this menu and dialog:

```
BUTMENU MENU
BEGIN
        MENUITEM "&Show dialog", 101
END

BUTDIALOG DIALOG 18, 18, 163, 113
CAPTION "Button dialog"
```

```
STYLE DS_MODALFRAME | WS_POPUP | WS_CAPTION | WS_SYSMENU
BEGIN
      CONTROL "OK",1,"BUTTON",BS_DEFPUSHBUTTON|WS_CHILD|WS_VISIBLE|WS_GROUP|WS_TABSTOP
          ,10,95,35,12
      CONTROL "Cancel", 2, "BUTTON", BS_PUSHBUTTON | WS_CHILD | WS_VISIBLE | WS_GROUP |  WS_TAB
          STOP, 55, 95, 35, 12
      CONTROL "", 103, "BUTTON", BS_GROUPBOX | WS_CHILD |WS_VISIBLE, 10, 19, 60, 58
      CONTROL "Radio buttons",-1,"STATIC",SS_LEFT|WS_CHILD|WS_VISIBLE | WS_GROUP, 6, 8, 50, 8
      CONTROL "Choice 1",104,"BUTTON"
          ,BS_AUTORADIOBUTTON|WS_CHILD|WS_VISIBLE|WS_GROUP|WS_TABSTOP
          , 16, 32, 45, 10
      CONTROL "Choice 2",105,"BUTTON",BS_AUTORADIOBUTTON|WS_CHILD|WS_VISIBLE|WS_TABSTOP
          ,15, 46, 45, 10
      CONTROL "Choice 3",106,"BUTTON",BS_AUTORADIOBUTTON|WS_CHILD|WS_VISIBLE|WS_TABSTOP
          , 15, 61, 45, 10
      CONTROL "Option A",107,"BUTTON",BS_AUTOCHECKBOX|WS_CHILD|WS_VISIBLE|WS_GROUP| WS_TABSTOP
          , 85, 18, 55, 12
      CONTROL "Option B",108,"BUTTON",BS_AUTOCHECKBOX|WS_CHILD|WS_VISIBLE|WS_TABSTOP
          ,85,36,55,12
END
```

HOW IT WORKS

In this program, the main window object includes the structure Buttons that has a word entry for each button in the dialog. This structure is the memory area used by transfer to exchange data between the main window and the dialog controls. It is initialized during the main window constructor by clearing the structure to zeros, then the program sets the first radio button.

When the user selects the Show dialog choice from the menu, ObjectWindows calls the ShowDialog function. This function executes the dialog, then it looks in the Buttons structure to get the results. It prints the results in the main window before exiting.

The dialog object constructor creates objects for all of the controls in the dialog, then sets up the transfer buffer. Note that the function creates an object for the group box that surrounds the radio buttons, then passes the address of the object to the radio buttons it creates. The reason for this is that ObjectWindows uses the group box as its way of keeping track of which radio buttons are in what group. All radio buttons associated with the same group box control are in the same group.

Although this program would work fine without looking at the notification messages, the member function Clicked is included to demonstrate handling a notification message and how to use some of the TCheckBox member functions. When the user clicks on the first check box, ObjectWindows calls Clicked. The first thing that Clicked does is to check the state of the first radio button. If it is set, Clicked toggles the state of the second check box.

3.7 How Do I...
Use String Tables?

Complexity : EASY

PROBLEM

String tables are a feature of resource files that let you store strings used in your program in the resource file with all of the other visible features of the program. The more features that you can put into the resource file, the easier it is to customize the program. Users are not dependent on the software provider to change the appearance of a program to meet their needs. Instead, they can edit the resources with a tool like the Resource Workshop to change the program themselves. Using string tables requires an extra step before using the string in a program, but the advantages often outweigh this small inconvenience.

TECHNIQUE

The only function you need in order to use string tables is the Windows function LoadString. The arguments for this function are the instance handle of the module that includes the string, a numeric identifier for the string, and the address and size of a buffer for the string. When your program calls this function, Windows looks in the string table of the specified module for a string with the requested ID. If the string is available, LoadString copies the string to the buffer and returns the number of characters copied. If the string is not available, LoadString returns 0. The following program gets strings from the resource file and prints them in the main window.

STEPS

1. Create a new project called STRINGS.PRJ that includes the files STRINGS.CPP, STRINGS.RES, and STANDARD.DEF.

2. Create the source file STRINGS.CPP with this program:

```
/* Program that gets strings from the resource file */
#include <owl.h>

#define IDC_STRING 101

class TMyWindow : public TWindow
{
```

```
     public:
          TMyWindow(PTWindowsObject AParent, LPSTR ATitle)
               : TWindow(AParent, ATitle) {};
          virtual LPSTR GetClassName();
          virtual void GetWindowClass(WNDCLASS& AWndClass);
          virtual void WMPaint(RTMessage)
               = [WM_FIRST + WM_PAINT];
};

/* return the unique class name */
LPSTR TMyWindow::GetClassName()
{
     return "MyClass";
}

/* Set the main window ICON to the one in the resource file */
void TMyWindow::GetWindowClass(WNDCLASS& AWndClass)
{
     TWindow::GetWindowClass(AWndClass);
     AWndClass.hIcon = LoadIcon(GetApplication()->hInstance, "StringIcon");
}

void TMyWindow::WMPaint(RTMessage)
{
     PAINTSTRUCT ps;
     HDC hDC;
     int Row, i;
     char TmpStr[80];

     memset(&ps, 0x00, sizeof(PAINTSTRUCT));
     hDC = BeginPaint(HWindow, &ps);
     Row = 0;
     /* Load strings and print them */
     for(i=0; i<2; i++)
     {
          LoadString(GetModule()->hInstance, IDC_STRING+i, TmpStr, 80);
          TextOut(hDC, 0, Row, TmpStr, lstrlen(TmpStr));
          Row += 18;
     }
     EndPaint(HWindow, &ps);
}

class TFirstApp : public TApplication
{
     public:
          TFirstApp(LPSTR ApName, HANDLE Inst, HANDLE PrevInst
               , LPSTR CmdLine, int CmdShow) : TApplication(ApName
               , Inst, PrevInst, CmdLine, CmdShow) {};
          virtual void InitMainWindow();
};

void TFirstApp::InitMainWindow()
{
     MainWindow = new TMyWindow(NULL, "Strings");
}

int PASCAL WinMain(HANDLE Inst, HANDLE PrevInst, LPSTR CmdLine
     , int CmdShow)
{
     TFirstApp FirstApp("", Inst
```

```
        , PrevInst, CmdLine, CmdShow);

      FirstApp.Run();
      return FirstApp.Status;
}
```

3. Create the resource file STRINGS.RES that includes an icon named STRINGICON and a string table with these strings:

```
101      This is the first string
102      This is the second string
```

4. Compile and run the program.

HOW IT WORKS

Figure 3-7 shows the window created by this program. The action occurs in the function WMPaint. Whenever Windows sends the program a WM_PAINT message, ObjectWindows calls WMPaint to handle the message. This function reads the strings from the string table into the variable TmpStr, then calls TextOut to print the strings in the window.

3.8 How Do I...
Convert Programs to Another Language?

Complexity: MODERATE

PROBLEM

In the past, converting a program to another language presented many problems. One problem was the need to maintain separate versions of the program for each supported language. Another problem was finding programmers who understood the language well enough to make the required changes. Perhaps the biggest problem was finding a way to fit long foreign words in the space previously occupied by short English words.

All of these problems are solved in Windows applications by using resource files. There is no need for separate programs, just separate resource files. The resource file can be sent to a linguist for translation instead of a programmer. By letting the translator modify whole dialogs instead of just the strings in them, extra space can be found where needed for the translated text.

The only remaining problem is that you now must have several versions of the .EXE file, each with its own language. This approach uses a lot of disk space and requires you to relink the program for each supported language when you make changes. To solve this problem, put all of the resources into a DLL that

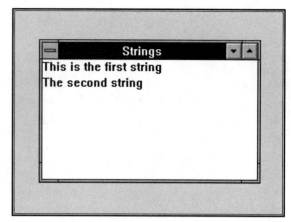

Figure 3-7
The String Table
Program

can be loaded by the application. To get a new language, just load a different DLL. This has the extra advantage that you can load languages at run time based on commands from the user.

TECHNIQUE

In theory, the technique is simple: load a DLL and read its resources for things such as menus and dialog boxes. In practice, there is more to it than that. The ObjectWindow library routines do most of the loading of resources and they all require the resources to be in the main program. Fortunately, this is an object-oriented library so we can overload the functions that load resources with functions of our own that get resources from the DLL.

In the DLL examples in Chapter 2, "ObjectWindows Basics," the DLLs were loaded automatically by linking library modules to the main program that knew what DLLs to load. This program cannot use this technique because you do not know the name of the DLL to load until the user asks for it. Windows provides the function LoadLibrary for loading DLLs at run time. You pass the name of the DLL to the function and it returns an instance handle to the library. You can use the instance handle with any of the Windows functions that load resources to indicate that you want resources from the DLL.

To load resources to be used by the program, you must use the Windows functions for loading resources so that you can specify the instance. For string resources, you can use LoadString because ObjectWindows is not interested in string resources. Loading menus is a bit harder. ObjectWindows wants you to call the ObjectWindows routine AssignMenu to properly initialize its menu routines. Once you have done this, you can call the Windows routine LoadMenu to replace the menu with one from the DLL.

The trickiest resource to load from a DLL is a dialog. You could call the Windows function DialogBox to run the dialog, but you would lose all of the ca-

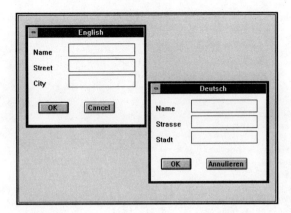

Figure 3-8
International
Dialogs

pabilities of the dialog object. The answer is to overload the ObjectWindows member function that loads the dialog. The member function that does this is TDialog::Execute. With some member functions, you can call the original function somewhere in the replacement function to make sure everything that is supposed to be done gets done. Unfortunately, this is not the case here; the entire function must be duplicated and the line that loads the dialog must be modified.

The TDialog::Execute function needs another function called RegisterFails and a global variable called DlgCreationWindow. The easiest way to get RegisterFails is to copy it into your program. The global variable presents a small problem. The problem is that global variables are not global across DLLs. This means that you cannot use the DLL version of the ClassLib and ObjectWindows libraries when you link your program. Be sure to check the linker library settings in the *Options* menu before compiling this program.

Even though this program does not use any code in the DLL, Windows requires that the DLL have the functions LibMain and WEP. You can use the same LibMain and WEP used in Chapter 2 to satisfy this requirement. The important part is the resources linked to the DLL. You create and link these resources the same as you do for any other program, Windows makes no distinction in this regard between DLLs and regular programs.

The program below includes two DLLs, one in English and the other in German. Depending on which DLL you use, you will get one of the dialogs shown in Figure 3-8.

STEPS

1. Create a project file called LANG.PRJ that includes the files LANG.CPP, LANG.RES, and STANDARD.RES. Be sure that the linker options are set to use static libraries.

2. Create the source file LANG.CPP with this program:

```
/* Make a dialog with text controls */
#include <owl.h>
#include <edit.h>
#include <string.h>
#include <ctype.h>

#define IDM_SHOW 101

/* Variable used by OWL to handle dialogs */
extern PTWindowsObject DlgCreationWindow;

/* This object represents the main window */
class TMyWindow : public TWindow
{
     public:
          HANDLE LangDLL;
          TMyWindow(PTWindowsObject AParent, LPSTR ATitle);
          ~TMyWindow();
          virtual void SetupWindow();
          virtual LPSTR GetClassName();
          virtual void GetWindowClass(WNDCLASS& AWndClass);
          virtual void ShowDialog(RTMessage) = [CM_FIRST + IDM_SHOW];
};

/* This object represents the dialog box */
class TextDlg : public TDialog
{
     public:
          TextDlg(PTWindowsObject AParent, LPSTR AResource);
          virtual int Execute();
};

/* Initialize the dialog controls and set up the transfer buffer */
TextDlg::TextDlg(PTWindowsObject AParent, LPSTR AResource)
     : TDialog(AParent, AResource)
{
}

/* Used when creating dialogs */
static BOOL RegisterFails(void *AWindowsObject, void *)
{
  return !((PTWindowsObject)AWindowsObject)->Register();
}

/* Replacement dialog execute routine to get dialog from the DLL */
int TextDlg::Execute()
{
  HWND HParent;
  int ReturnValue = -1;
  PTWindowsObject OldKBHandler;

  IsModal = TRUE;
  if( Status == 0  && Register() )
  {
      DisableAutoCreate();

      /* Enable the keyboard handler. Although modal dialogs do
         their own keyboard handling, we use the WB_KBHANDLER
         flag for WM_COMMAND processing. */
      EnableKBHandler();
```

```
      if(GetApplication() )
        OldKBHandler = GetApplication()->KBHandlerWnd;

      if(!Parent)
        HParent = 0;
      else
        HParent = Parent->HWindow;
      DlgCreationWindow = this;
      /* Register all the dialog's child objects (for custom control
          support) */
      if(FirstThat(RegisterFails, NULL) == NULL )
      {
        ReturnValue = DialogBoxParam(((TMyWindow far *)Parent)->LangDLL, Attr.Name,
            HParent, GetInstance(), Attr.Param);
        // -1 if the function cannot create the dialog box
        if ( ReturnValue == -1)
            Status = EM_INVALIDWINDOW;
      }
      else
        Status = EM_INVALIDCHILD;
      DlgCreationWindow = NULL;
      if( GetApplication() )
        GetApplication()->SetKBHandler(OldKBHandler);
      HWindow = 0;
  }
  if( Status == 0 )
      delete this;
  else
      if (ReturnValue != -1)
            ReturnValue = BAD_DIALOG_STATUS;  // dialog ran, but status != 0
  return ReturnValue;
}

/* Initialize the main window */
TMyWindow::TMyWindow(PTWindowsObject AParent, LPSTR ATitle)
      : TWindow(AParent, ATitle)
{
      /* Load the resource library */
      LangDLL = LoadLibrary("GERMAN.DLL");
      /* Load a dummy menu */
      AssignMenu("LangMenu");
      Attr.Style |= WS_CAPTION;
      Attr.W = 300;
      Attr.H = 200;
}

/* Release the DLL before exiting */
TMyWindow::~TMyWindow()
{
      FreeLibrary(LangDLL);
}

/* Load the menu after the window is created */
void TMyWindow::SetupWindow()
{
      TWindow::SetupWindow();
      SetMenu(HWindow, LoadMenu(LangDLL, "LANGMENU"));
}

/* Return the unique class name */
```

```
LPSTR TMyWindow::GetClassName()
{
     return "MyClass";
}


/* Set the main window ICON to the one in the resource file */
void TMyWindow::GetWindowClass(WNDCLASS& AWndClass)
{
     TWindow::GetWindowClass(AWndClass);
     AWndClass.hIcon = LoadIcon(GetApplication()->hInstance, "LangIcon");
}


/* Display the dialog then paint the results in the main window */
void TMyWindow::ShowDialog(RTMessage)
{
     HDC hDC;
     char TmpStr[80];

     /* Do the dialog */
     GetModule()->ExecDialog(new TextDlg(this, "LangDialog"));
     /* Print the results */
     hDC = GetDC(HWindow);
     LoadString(LangDLL, 101, TmpStr, 80);
     TextOut(hDC, 0, 0, TmpStr, lstrlen(TmpStr));
     ReleaseDC(hDC, HWindow);
}


class TMyApp : public TApplication
{
     public:
          TMyApp(LPSTR ApName, HANDLE Inst, HANDLE PrevInst
               , LPSTR CmdLine, int CmdShow) : TApplication(ApName
               , Inst, PrevInst, CmdLine, CmdShow) {};
          virtual void InitMainWindow();
};


void TMyApp::InitMainWindow()
{
     MainWindow = new TMyWindow(NULL, "Languages");
}


int PASCAL WinMain(HANDLE Inst, HANDLE PrevInst, LPSTR CmdLine
     , int CmdShow)
{
     TMyApp TheApp("", Inst, PrevInst, CmdLine, CmdShow);

     TheApp.Run();
     return TheApp.Status;
}
```

3. Create the resource file LANG.RES that includes an icon named
   LANGICON and a menu called LANGMENU. The contents of the menu
   are not important because the menu is just here to give AssignMenu something with which to work. The actual menu comes from the DLL.
4. Create a new project called ENGLISH.PRJ that includes the files
   ENGLISH.CPP, ENGLISH.RES, and ENGLISH.DEF. Set the Borland
   C++ options to create a DLL.

5. Create the source file ENGLISH.CPP with this program:

```
/* DLL program */
#include <owl.h>

PTModule TheModule;

int FAR PASCAL LibMain(HANDLE Inst, WORD
    , WORD, LPSTR CmdLine)
{
    int TheStatus;

    TheModule = new TModule("THEDLL", Inst, CmdLine);
    TheStatus = TheModule->Status;
    if(TheStatus)
    {
        delete TheModule;
        TheModule = NULL;
    }
    return (TheStatus==0);
}

int FAR PASCAL WEP(int)
{
    if(TheModule)
        delete TheModule;
    return 1;
}
```

6. Create the resource file ENGLISH.RES with these resources:

```
LANGMENU MENU
BEGIN
    MENUITEM "&Show dialog", 101
END

LANGDIALOG DIALOG 18, 18, 114, 84
CAPTION "English"
STYLE DS_MODALFRAME | WS_POPUP | WS_CAPTION | WS_SYSMENU
BEGIN
    CONTROL "OK", 1, "BUTTON", BS_DEFPUSHBUTTON | WS_CHILD | WS_VISIBLE | WS_TABSTOP
        , 10, 62, 30, 11
    CONTROL "Name", -1, "STATIC", SS_LEFT | WS_CHILD | WS_VISIBLE | WS_GROUP, 5, 10, 30, 8
    CONTROL "Street", -1, "STATIC", SS_LEFT | WS_CHILD | WS_VISIBLE | WS_GROUP, 5, 25, 30, 8
    CONTROL "City", -1, "STATIC", SS_LEFT | WS_CHILD | WS_VISIBLE | WS_GROUP, 5, 40, 30, 8
    CONTROL "", 101, "EDIT", ES_LEFT | WS_CHILD | WS_VISIBLE | WS_BORDER | WS_TABSTOP
        , 40, 6, 65, 12
    CONTROL "", 102, "EDIT", ES_LEFT | WS_CHILD | WS_VISIBLE | WS_BORDER | WS_TABSTOP
        , 40, 21, 65, 12
    CONTROL "", 103, "EDIT", ES_LEFT | WS_CHILD | WS_VISIBLE | WS_BORDER | WS_TABSTOP
        , 40, 36, 65, 12
    CONTROL "Cancel", 104, "BUTTON", BS_PUSHBUTTON | WS_CHILD | WS_VISIBLE | WS_TABSTOP
        , 55, 62, 30, 11
END

STRINGTABLE LOADONCALL MOVEABLE DISCARDABLE
BEGIN
    101, "A test string"
END
```

7. Create the definition file ENGLISH.DEF:

```
LIBRARY ENGLISH
DESCRIPTION    'Sample DLL'
EXETYPEWINDOWS
CODE PRELOAD MOVEABLE DISCARDABLE
DATA PRELOAD MOVEABLE SINGLE
HEAPSIZE 1024
```

8. Create a new project file called GERMAN.PRJ that includes the files GERMAN.CPP, GERMAN.RES, and GERMAN.DEF. Set the Borland C++ options to create a DLL.

9. Copy the source and definition files from the ENGLISH DLL to the corresponding files for the GERMAN DLL. Change the library name to GERMAN in the definition file.

10. Create the resource file GERMAN.RES with these resources:

```
LANGMENU MENU
BEGIN
     MENUITEM "&Ziegan Dialog", 101
END

LANGDIALOG DIALOG 18, 18, 114, 84
CAPTION "Deutsch"
STYLE DS_MODALFRAME | WS_POPUP | WS_CAPTION | WS_SYSMENU
BEGIN
     CONTROL "OK", 1, "BUTTON", BS_DEFPUSHBUTTON | WS_CHILD | WS_VISIBLE | WS_TABSTOP
          , 10, 62, 30, 11
     CONTROL "Name", -1, "STATIC", SS_LEFT | WS_CHILD | WS_VISIBLE | WS_GROUP
          , 5, 10, 30, 8
     CONTROL "Strasse", -1, "STATIC", SS_LEFT | WS_CHILD | WS_VISIBLE | WS_GROUP
          , 5, 25, 30, 8
     CONTROL "Stadt", -1, "STATIC", SS_LEFT | WS_CHILD | WS_VISIBLE | WS_GROUP
          , 5, 40, 30, 8
     CONTROL "", 101, "EDIT", ES_LEFT | WS_CHILD | WS_VISIBLE | WS_BORDER | WS_TABSTOP
          , 40, 6, 65, 12
     CONTROL "", 102, "EDIT", ES_LEFT | WS_CHILD | WS_VISIBLE | WS_BORDER | WS_TABSTOP
          , 40, 21, 65, 12
     CONTROL "", 103, "EDIT", ES_LEFT | WS_CHILD | WS_VISIBLE | WS_BORDER | WS_TABSTOP
          , 40, 36, 65, 12
     CONTROL "Annulieren",104,"BUTTON", BS_PUSHBUTTON | WS_CHILD | WS_VISIBLE | WS_TABSTOP
          , 55, 62, 40, 11
END

STRINGTABLE LOADONCALL MOVEABLE DISCARDABLE
BEGIN
     101, "Ein Prufung"
END
```

11. Compile the program LANG and the DLLs ENGLISH and GERMAN.

HOW IT WORKS

The structure of this program is similar to the others in this chapter. There is a main window with a simple menu that brings up a dialog box. The dialog box has three text entry fields and an OK button. The main difference in this program from the user's point of view is that all of the text is in German. To change the program to English, modify the LoadLibrary function call in the main window constructor to load the English DLL. You could just as easily load the library as the result of a selection in a dialog box, a menu selection, or some other set of circumstances. The only consideration is that you must free the library by calling the Windows function FreeLibrary when you are done with the library, as the main window object destructor in this program does.

After loading the library, the program gets the menu resource from the DLL. The Windows function LoadMenu cannot be run from the constructor because the window does not exist at this point. Instead, the program uses the SetupWindow member function to load the menu.

When the user selects the menu item, ObjectWindows calls the function ShowDialog. This function is just like other ShowDialog functions in this chapter, it uses the ExecDialog function to run the modal dialog, then loads a string from the DLL and prints the string in the main window. The ExecDialog function in ShowDialog creates the dialog object that has been modified to load the dialog from the DLL.

With a traditional library, you would have to modify the library to get it to read the dialog from the DLL or abandon the library and start from scratch. Changing the library would affect the behavior of all programs that use the library. Starting from scratch would waste all of the work that went into creating the library.

Because the ObjectWindows library is object oriented, there is a third possibility: rewrite the routine that loads dialogs and use this new routine in the program that needs it. This is the purpose for the member function Execute in the TextDlg object. It is a copy of the Execute function used by the ObjectWindows TDialog object with the DialogBoxParam function call modified to load the dialog from the DLL. The source for this routine came from the DIALOG.CPP source supplied with the ObjectWindows library.

Using this function means that this program must use the static libraries for ObjectWindows routines instead of the DLL version. The reason for this is that the Execute function uses the global variable DlgCreateWindow from the library. This variable is used by other routines when creating child windows. The problem is that a global variable in a program is not linked to variables in DLLs so the libraries must not be DLLs if they need DlgCreateWindow.

COMMENTS

PC-compatible computers are now available worldwide, creating an international demand for software. This software must be localized for each country in which it is used. Even in the United States, it is a good idea to provide versions of programs in both Spanish and English. For Windows programs, this means putting everything that the user sees into resource files. Using a technique like the one in this solution helps ensure that your program will be ready when the time comes for it to go international.

Menus 4

Users give commands to Windows programs primarily by using menus. The pull-down menu structure in a Windows application is familiar and easy to use. As you saw in Chapter 2, "ObjectWindows Basics," adding a menu to an application is easy. First, design the menu you want in the Resource Workshop, then add some message response member functions to the main window that handles the menu commands.

This simple procedure produces simple menus. It does not allow some options that you may have seen in other Windows applications. You cannot change the menus from the program, mark selected menu items with check marks, or put pictures into menus. To get all of these features in your program, you must use Windows functions that handle menus. This chapter shows many of the menu functions available in Windows and how to use them.

4.1 Load Different Menus from the Resource File

The Resource Workshop program is an example of a program that modifies its own menus. Notice that the menus change depending on what type of resource you are editing. These different menus are all stored in the resource file, each with its own name. The program that uses the resource file asks for the menu by name and adds it to the main window. This How-To shows how you can use multiple menus in your ObjectWindows programs.

4.2 Add and Delete Menu Items

Some Windows applications let the user customize menus by adding, deleting, and moving menu items. In this case, it is impractical to have all of the possibilities stored in the resource file. A menu with as few as 10 commands can be arranged in hundreds of different ways. Other applications let the user add menu items for items, such as command files, that cannot be anticipated by the programmer.

To handle these situations, you need to be able to add and delete items in the menu while the program is running. When adding menu items, you need a way to assign ID numbers to the new items and handle the messages generated by these new items. To delete an item, you need some way of finding the item to delete. This solution shows how to add and delete items, handle messages from the new items, and examine the items in a menu.

4.3 Change the Attributes of a Menu Item

Some menu commands let the user set an option on or off. The menu item has a check mark next to it when the option is active. For example, a text editor may have a menu How-To that puts the editor in insert mode. When insert mode is on, there is a check mark next to the menu item.

Another way to make a menu item that turns something on and off is to change the text of the menu item. For example, a program that can save user commands as they are entered may have a menu item called *Save commands*. When the user selects the item, it changes to *Stop saving commands*.

There are times when a menu command should not be selected. Windows applications indicate this by changing the color of the menu item to gray. A gray menu item does not send messages when it is selected. When you satisfy the prerequisite for the command, the program enables the item and Windows changes the color of the item back to black.

This How-To shows you how to change the attributes of menu items. It uses Windows functions to draw and remove check marks, enable and disable menu selections, and change the text of the menu item. It also shows you the other menu attributes that Windows provides for menus such as multiline and multi-column menus.

4.4 Change the Check Marks Used in Menus

One of the features of Windows is that each application uses the same general interface as other applications. The advantage of common interfaces is that once you learn one application, you can use what you learned to work another. The disadvantage is that it is boring. It is difficult to make a program that stands out from the others if all the programs look the same.

You can make your programs stand out by adding your own graphics to such things as the main window, dialog controls, and menus. This How-To shows an easy way to add graphics to menus by changing the bitmap used as a check mark in the menu.

4.5 Use Bitmaps as Menu Items

Another way to make your menus stand out is to use graphics for the menu commands. You can set the owner-drawn style for a menu item and use the same techniques to draw the menu items that you used to draw list box items in Chapter 3, "Dialog Boxes." Windows includes a much simpler option for adding bitmaps to menu items. You can set a style flag that indicates that the menu item is a bitmap. You must also replace the string for the menu item with a handle to a bitmap. Windows reads the handle and draws the bitmap in the menu. This How-To illustrates the technique.

4.6 Create Pop-Up Menus

Most menus are connected to the main menu bar. This does not have to be the case. Windows lets you display a menu anywhere on the screen that you need a menu. This How-To pops up a menu wherever the user clicks the mouse.

4.1 How Do I...
Load Different Menus from the Resource File?

Complexity: EASY

PROBLEM

There are several reasons to change menus while a program is running. One is to provide commands for optional modules. Another is to provide different menus for users of different skill levels. In these cases, you can have each of the different menus in the resource file and load the one that is required. This solution shows how.

TECHNIQUE

In previous programs with menus, you used the ObjectWindows function AssignMenu to load and display the menu for the program. This function puts the name of the menu in class information about the window so that Windows will load the menu when it creates the window. To change the menu, you must load the menu yourself and replace the old menu with the new one.

The Windows function LoadMenu loads a menu from the resource file and returns a handle to the menu. Menus in the resource file can be identified by a name or a number. If you have a choice, names such as ExpertMenu are easier to remember than numbers. In this case, all you need to do to load the menu is call LoadMenu with the instance of the program and the name of the menu, like this:

```
MenuHandle = LoadMenu(GetApplicationObject()->hInstance, "ExpertMenu");
```

The variable MenuHandle gets the handle for the menu loaded. The ObjectWindows function GetApplicationObject returns the address of the TApplication object for the program, which includes the instance handle for the object in the member hInstance. The second argument to LoadMenu is the name of the menu.

If you use numbers to identify a menu, you must use the Windows macro MAKEINTRESOURCE on the number before passing it to LoadMenu. This statement loads menu number 12:

```
MenuHandle = LoadMenu(GetApplicationObject()->hInstance, MAKEINTRESOURCE(12));
```

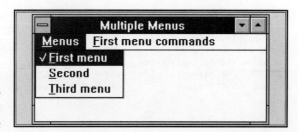

Figure 4-1
The Multiple
Menu Program

Once you have loaded the menu, you can get rid of the current menu and put the new menu in the window. Getting rid of the current menu is a two-step process. The first step is to get the handle of the current menu by calling the Windows function GetMenu. Then use the Windows function DestroyMenu to remove the menu from memory. This statement combines these two functions to get rid of the menu:

```
DestroyMenu(GetMenu(HWindow));
```

In this statement, the GetMenu function gets the menu for HWindow and passes it to DestroyMenu, which gets rid of the menu.

Finally, call the Windows function SetMenu to put the new menu into the main window. The arguments for SetMenu are a handle to a window and a handle to a menu:

```
SetMenu(HWindow, MenuHandle);
```

The following program has three menus in the resource file. Each of the menus includes commands to switch to the other two menus. The user knows which menu is loaded because the corresponding menu command has a check mark next to it. Figure 4-1 shows the program with the first menu loaded.

STEPS

1. Create a new project called MULTIMNU.PRJ that includes the files MULITMNU.CPP, MULTIMNU.RES, and STANDARD.DEF.

2. Create the source file MULTIMNU.CPP with this program:

```
/* MENUAPP An OWL program with menus */
#include <owl.h>

#define MID_MENU1    101
#define MID_MENU2    102
#define MID_MENU3    103

class TMyWindow : public TWindow
```

```
{
    public:
        TMyWindow(PTWindowsObject AParent, LPSTR ATitle);
        /* menu command routines */
        virtual void LoadMenu1(RTMessage) = [CM_FIRST + MID_MENU1];
        virtual void LoadMenu2(RTMessage) = [CM_FIRST + MID_MENU2];
        virtual void LoadMenu3(RTMessage) = [CM_FIRST + MID_MENU3];
};

/* Assign the initial menu when creating the window */
TMyWindow::TMyWindow(PTWindowsObject AParent, LPSTR ATitle)
    : TWindow(AParent, ATitle)
{
    AssignMenu("MENU1");
}

/* Handle the first menu command */
void TMyWindow::LoadMenu1(RTMessage)
{
    HMENU MnHand;

    MnHand = GetMenu(HWindow);   // Get the handle of the menu
    DestroyMenu(MnHand);         // Get rid of the old menu
    /* Load the menu */
    MnHand = LoadMenu(GetApplicationObject()->hInstance, "MENU1");
    SetMenu(HWindow, MnHand);    // Add the menu to the window
}

/* Handle the second menu command */
void TMyWindow::LoadMenu2(RTMessage)
{
    HMENU MnHand;

    MnHand = GetMenu(HWindow);   // Get the handle of the menu
    DestroyMenu(MnHand);         // Get rid of the old menu
    /* Load the menu */
    MnHand = LoadMenu(GetApplicationObject()->hInstance, "MENU2");
    SetMenu(HWindow, MnHand);    // Add the menu to the window
}

/* Handle the third menu command */
void TMyWindow::LoadMenu3(RTMessage)
{
    HMENU MnHand;

    MnHand = GetMenu(HWindow);   // Get the handle of the menu
    DestroyMenu(MnHand);         // Get rid of the old menu
    /* Load the menu */
    MnHand = LoadMenu(GetApplicationObject()->hInstance, "MENU3");
    SetMenu(HWindow, MnHand);    // Add the menu to the window
}

/* Define the application object */
class TMenuApp : public TApplication
{
    public:
        TMenuApp(LPSTR ApName, HINSTANCE Inst, HINSTANCE PrevInst
            , LPSTR CmdLine, int CmdShow) : TApplication(ApName
```

```
                      , Inst, PrevInst, CmdLine, CmdShow) {};
            virtual void InitMainWindow();
};

/* Create the main window object */
void TMenuApp::InitMainWindow()
{
    MainWindow = new TMyWindow(NULL, "Multiple Menus");
}

/* Program entry point */
int PASCAL
WinMain(HINSTANCE Inst, HINSTANCE PrevInst
    , LPSTR CmdLine, int CmdShow)
{
    TMenuApp TheApp("", Inst
        , PrevInst, CmdLine, CmdShow);

    TheApp.Run();
    return TheApp.Status;
}
```

3. Use the Resource Workshop to create a resource file named MULTI-MNU.RES. The file includes three menus like these:

```
MENU1 MENU
BEGIN
    POPUP "&Menus"
    BEGIN
        MENUITEM "&First menu", 101, CHECKED
        MENUITEM "&Second", 102
        MENUITEM "&Third menu", 103
    END

    POPUP "&First menu commands"
    BEGIN
        MENUITEM "Item", 104
    END

END

MENU2 MENU
BEGIN
    POPUP "Menus"
    BEGIN
        MENUITEM "&First menu", 101
        MENUITEM "&Second menu", 102, CHECKED
        MENUITEM "&Third menu", 103
    END

    POPUP "&Second menu commands"
    BEGIN
        MENUITEM "Item", 104
    END

END
```

```
MENU3 MENU
BEGIN
     POPUP "&Menus"
     BEGIN
          MENUITEM "&First menu", 101
          MENUITEM "&Second menu", 102
          MENUITEM "&Third menu", 103, CHECKED
     END

     POPUP "&Third menu commands"
     BEGIN
          MENUITEM "Item", 104
     END

END
```

4. Use the *Run* command to compile and run the program.

HOW IT WORKS

The object definition at the beginning of the program is a standard main window object that handles three menu commands. The constructor for the object loads the first menu with the AssignMenu member function. Each of the menu command handler functions changes the menu by destroying the old menu, loading the new menu, and adding the menu to the main window. Note that these functions do not have to change the settings of the check mark. (See How-To 4.3 for more information on check marks.) Each menu has the appropriate check mark set in the resource file; when the new menu is loaded, the check mark settings get loaded also.

When the user clicks on a menu command, Windows sends a message to the main window. ObjectWindows gets this message and turns it into a call to one of the message response member functions depending on the ID of the menu command. The member function uses the Windows functions described in the "Technique" section to change menus.

COMMENT

When designing a menu for a Windows program, keep one important principle in mind: menus are supposed to make it simpler for the user to give commands to programs. The ability to change menus for different circumstances gives you the ability to make using menus very complex and difficult. If the user cannot find an important command because it is in a menu that is difficult to find, he is likely to have a low opinion of the program.

Programs that have multiple menus should include a menu that allows the user to change to any menu used by the program. This program uses this technique, all three of the available menus are always in the first menu. The user can always go to that menu to load different menus while searching for a command.

4.2 How Do I...
Add and Delete Menu Items?

Complexity: MODERATE

PROBLEM

Some menu changes are not complex enough to justify loading a whole new menu from the resource file. For example, a program that has optional modules that add one or two commands to the menu does not need to load a whole new menu. Other menu changes cannot be anticipated by the programmer, so they cannot be included in the resource file. An example of this situation is an MDI application (see How-To 2.5). The title of each child window in the application is added to the *Window* menu when the window is created. This solution shows how to make these minor changes to a menu.

TECHNIQUE

The first thing that you have to do to add an item is get the handle of the menu. The previous solution shows how to get the handle of the menu bar by calling the Windows function GetMenu. You can use this handle to add items to the menu bar. To add items to a pop-up menu, you need to get the handle of that pop-up with the Windows function GetSubMenu. This statement gets the handle of the third pop-up menu on the menu bar:

```
MenuHandle = GetSubMenu(GetMenu(HWindow), 2);
```

The first argument to GetSubMenu is the handle to the menu bar and the second is the index of the pop-up. The first pop-up is at index 0, so 2 is the third pop-up.

Once you have the menu handle, you can use the Windows function InsertMenu to add an item to the menu. This is a very versatile function that lets you add any of the types of menu items such as strings, bitmaps, separators, or pop-ups to the menu. One of the arguments for InsertMenu is a set of flags that tell Windows what type of item to add and where to add it. The general form of InsertMenu is:

```
BOOL InsertMenu(HMENU MenuHandle, WORD ItemPosition, WORD Flags, WORD ItemID, LPSTR ItemData);
```

MenuHandle is the handle from GetSubMenu. Depending on the value in Flags, ItemPosition is either the position of the new menu item or the ID of the item before which the new item is to be inserted. Flags indicates how to interpret ItemPosition and the type of item to add. ItemID is the ID for the new item.

FLAG	DESCRIPTION
MF_BITMAP	The menu item is a bitmap. ItemData is a handle to a bitmap.
MF_BYCOMMAND	Put the new item before the item with the ID in ItemPosition.
MF_BYPOSITION	Put the new item at the position in ItemPosition.
MF_CHECKED	The new item is checked.
MF_DISABLED	The new item cannot be selected by the user.
MF_ENABLED	The new item can be selected by the user.
MF_GRAYED	The new item cannot be selected and is gray.
MF_MENUBARBREAK	The new item begins a new line or column in the menu. If it starts a new column, there is a bar between the columns.
MF_MENUBREAK	The new item begins a new line or column in the menu.
MF_OWNERDRAW	Windows sends messages to the window to let your program draw the menu selection.
MF_POPUP	The new item is a pop-up menu. ItemData is a handle to a menu.
MF_SEPARATOR	The new item is a separator.
MF_STRING	The new item is a string. ItemData is a pointer to the string to display.
MF_UNCHECKED	The new item is not checked. This is the default case.

Table 4-1 Menu Item Flags

ItemData is a 32-bit value that has different meanings depending on the value of Flags. Table 4-1 shows the possible values for Flags.

The program in this solution adds a string item by position to the menu. The InsertMenu call for this looks like this:

```
InsertMenu(GetSubMenu(GetMenu(HWindow), 1), -1, MF_BYPOSITION | MF_STRING, 1000, "&New item");
```

This statement adds the string "New item" to the end of the second pop-up menu and uses the ID 1000. Note the use of the number -1 as the position to indicate that the new item goes at the end of the menu.

To delete a menu item, pass the menu handle, the position, and either MF_BYPOSITION or MF_BYCOMMAND to the Windows function DeleteMenu. To delete the item added in the previous statement, you can use:

```
DeleteMenu(GetSubMenu(GetMenu(HWindow), 1), 1000, MF_BYCOMMAND)
```

This statement deletes the item in the second pop-up menu whose ID is 1000. You cannot use the position of the item in this case, because you do not know the index of the last item.

The program in this solution uses two other Windows functions to find the item to delete. The first is GetMenuItemCount which returns the number of items in a menu. The second is GetMenuString that returns the string for a menu item. The program gets the number of items in the menu, then checks each one by getting the string and comparing it to the item to delete. When the item is found, the program calls DeleteMenu to get rid of the item.

One problem with adding and deleting menu items is handling the messages generated by the new items. Normally, you would create a message response member function for each item in the menu. Although it is easy to add new items while a program is running, it is impossible to add new message response member functions. If you are making a small number of changes, you can add enough message response member functions to handle all the possible additions. This is not a practical idea if you do not know how many items might be added.

The program in this solution handles this problem by handling the WM_COMMAND message from Windows. Windows sends this message whenever the user selects a menu command. ObjectWindows converts this message into a call to the appropriate message response member function. By handling the WM_COMMAND message, the program can look at the ID before ObjectWindows and handle commands from the added menu items.

STEPS

1. Create a new project file called EDITMNU.PRJ that includes the files EDITMNU.CPP, EDITMNU.RES, and STANDARD.DEF.

2. Create the source file EDITMNU.CPP with this program:

```
/* EDITMNU How add and delete menu items */
#include <owl.h>

#define MID_ADD            101
#define MID_DELETE         102

class TMyWindow : public TWindow
{
    public:
        int NextID;        // The ID for the next menu item
        TMyWindow(PTWindowsObject AParent, LPSTR ATitle);
        virtual void SetupWindow();        // Handle WM_CREATE
        /* menu command routines */
        virtual void AddItem(RTMessage) = [CM_FIRST + MID_ADD];
        virtual void DeleteItem(RTMessage) = [CM_FIRST + MID_DELETE];
```

```
                    virtual void WMCommand(RTMessage Msg) = [WM_FIRST + WM_COMMAND];
};

/* Dialog box for getting menu text */
class AddDlg : public TDialog
{
     public:
           AddDlg(PTWindowsObject AParent, LPSTR AResource)
                : TDialog(AParent, AResource){};
           virtual void Ok(RTMessage) = [ID_FIRST + IDOK];
};

void AddDlg::Ok(RTMessage)
{
     HMENU HnMenu;
     char MenuText[20];

     /* Get the handle of the menu to edit */
     HnMenu = GetSubMenu(GetMenu(Parent->HWindow), 1);
     /* Get the name of the menu item */
     GetDlgItemText(HWindow, 101, MenuText, 20);
     /* Add the new item to the end of the menu */
     InsertMenu(HnMenu, -1, MF_BYPOSITION|MF_STRING
           , ((TMyWindow *)Parent)->NextID++, MenuText);
     /* Get out of the dialog */
     CloseWindow(IDOK);
}


/* Dialog box for getting menu text */
class DeleteDlg : public TDialog
{
     public:
           DeleteDlg(PTWindowsObject AParent, LPSTR AResource)
                : TDialog(AParent, AResource){};
           virtual void Ok(RTMessage) = [ID_FIRST + IDOK];
};

void DeleteDlg::Ok(RTMessage)
{
     HMENU HnMenu;
     char DelText[20], MenuText[20];
     int ItemCnt;
     int i;

     /* Get the handle of the menu to edit */
     HnMenu = GetSubMenu(GetMenu(Parent->HWindow), 1);
     /* Get the name of the menu item */
     GetDlgItemText(HWindow, 101, DelText, 20);
     /* Find out how many items are in the menu */
     ItemCnt = GetMenuItemCount(HnMenu);
     /* Search for a matching string */
     for(i=0; i<ItemCnt; i++)
     {
           GetMenuString(HnMenu, i, MenuText, 20, MF_BYPOSITION);
           if(!lstrcmp(MenuText, DelText))
           {
                DeleteMenu(HnMenu, i, MF_BYPOSITION);
```

```
                    break;
            }
    }
    /* Get out of the dialog */
    CloseWindow(IDOK);
}


/* Assign the initial menu when creating the window */
TMyWindow::TMyWindow(PTWindowsObject AParent, LPSTR ATitle)
    : TWindow(AParent, ATitle)
{
    NextID = 1000;              // Set an initial value for menu IDs
    AssignMenu("MENU1");        // Load an assign the menu
}


/* Set up the main window */
void TMyWindow::SetupWindow()
{
    HMENU HnMenu;

    TWindow::SetupWindow();
    /* Get the handle of the menu to edit */
    HnMenu = GetSubMenu(GetMenu(HWindow), 1);
    /* Delete the item in the menu */
    DeleteMenu(HnMenu, 0, MF_BYPOSITION);
}


/* Handle the add an item command */
void TMyWindow::AddItem(RTMessage)
{
    /* Do the dialog */
    GetModule()->ExecDialog(new AddDlg(this, "ItemDialog"));
}


/* Handle the delete an item command */
void TMyWindow::DeleteItem(RTMessage)
{
    /* Do the dialog */
    GetModule()->ExecDialog(new DeleteDlg(this, "ItemDialog"));
}


/* Handle commands from the edited menu */
void TMyWindow::WMCommand(RTMessage Msg)
{
    HDC hDC;
    char TmpStr[80];
    HMENU HnMenu;

    if(Msg.WParam >= 1000)       // Is this an added menu item?
    {
        hDC = GetDC(HWindow);
        lstrcpy(TmpStr, "You selected: ");
        HnMenu = GetSubMenu(GetMenu(HWindow), 1);
        GetMenuString(HnMenu, Msg.WParam, &TmpStr[14], 20, MF_BYCOMMAND);
        TextOut(hDC, 5, 5, TmpStr, lstrlen(TmpStr));
        ReleaseDC(HWindow, hDC);
    }
    else
```

```
            TWindow::WMCommand(Msg);
}


/* Define the application object */
class TMenuApp : public TApplication
{
     public:
          TMenuApp(LPSTR ApName, HINSTANCE Inst, HINSTANCE PrevInst
               , LPSTR CmdLine, int CmdShow) : TApplication(ApName
               , Inst, PrevInst, CmdLine, CmdShow) {};
          virtual void InitMainWindow();
};


/* Create the main window object */
void TMenuApp::InitMainWindow()
{
     MainWindow = new TMyWindow(NULL, "Multiple Menus");
}


/* Program entry point */
int PASCAL
WinMain(HINSTANCE Inst, HINSTANCE PrevInst
     , LPSTR CmdLine, int CmdShow)
{
     TMenuApp TheApp("", Inst
          , PrevInst, CmdLine, CmdShow);

     TheApp.Run();
     return TheApp.Status;
}
```

3. Use the Resource Workshop to create the file EDITMNU.RES that includes this menu:

```
MENU1 MENU
BEGIN
     POPUP "&Edit"
     BEGIN
          MENUITEM "&Add item", 101
          MENUITEM "&Delete item", 102
     END

     POPUP "New items"
     BEGIN
          MENUITEM "Item", 101
     END

END
```

Also include this dialog in the resource file:

```
ITEMDIALOG DIALOG 18, 18, 142, 56
STYLE DS_MODALFRAME | WS_POPUP | WS_CAPTION | WS_SYSMENU
CAPTION "Edit menu"
BEGIN
     CONTROL "Menu item", -1, "STATIC", SS_LEFT | WS_CHILD | WS_VISIBLE | WS_GROUP
          , 10, 10, 35, 8
     CONTROL "", 101, "EDIT", ES_LEFT | WS_CHILD | WS_VISIBLE | WS_BORDER | WS_TABSTOP
```

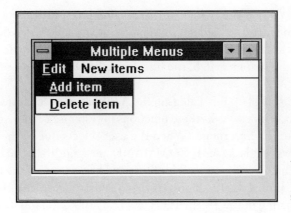

Figure 4-2
The EDITMNU
Program

```
     , 50, 8, 70, 12
  CONTROL "Ok", 1, "BUTTON", BS_DEFPUSHBUTTON | WS_CHILD | WS_VISIBLE | WS_TABSTOP
     , 20, 35, 35, 15
  CONTROL "Cancel", 2, "BUTTON", BS_PUSHBUTTON | WS_CHILD | WS_VISIBLE | WS_TABSTOP
     , 85, 35, 40, 15
END
```

4. Select the *Run* command to compile and run the program.

5. Figure 4-2 shows the main window and the dialog that it uses to get menu item names.

HOW IT WORKS

The object at the beginning of this program handles the main window. The data member NextID is a variable that holds the ID to use when creating a new menu item. It is initialized in the constructor and incremented each time the program adds a new menu item. There are two message response member functions that handle menu commands (AddItem and DeleteItem) and another message response member function to handle the WM_COMMAND message (WMCommand).

The next two objects in the program handle a dialog box that gets the name of the menu item to add or delete. When the user presses the OK button in the dialog, ObjectWindows calls the Ok member function. In the add item dialog, the Ok member function uses the InsertMenu function to add the item to the menu. Note the use of the Windows function GetDlgItemText to get the name of the item from the dialog. This dialog is too simple to justify the overhead of the transfer mechanism used in Chapter 3, "Dialog Boxes." After adding the menu item, the Ok function increments NextID so it will be different for the next item.

The Ok member function of the delete dialog searches the menu for an item that matches the string from the dialog box, and deletes it. First, it uses

GetDlgItemText to get the string from the dialog box. Next, it gets the number of items in the menu by calling GetMenuItemCount. The function uses the number of items as the limit of a for loop that calls GetMenuString for each item in the menu. If the strings match, the function calls DeleteMenu to delete the menu item.

The program brings up the dialogs in the AddItem and DeleteItem member functions. ObjectWindows calls these functions in response to the user selecting a command from the first menu. When the user selects one of the new commands, Windows sends a WM_COMMAND message that ends up in the WMCommand member function. This function checks to see if the menu ID is 1000 or greater. If it is, the function gets the menu string for that item and displays it in the main window. If the ID is less than 1000, the function calls the TWindow::WMCommand function so that ObjectWindows can handle other menu commands.

COMMENT

You can use How-To 4.1 to change the whole menu or this solution to make small changes to a menu. You can combine the two techniques to add new pop-up menus to the menu bar. First, create a resource file that has a main menu and each of the optional pop-ups. Save each pop-up as a separate menu.

In the program, load the main menu as usual with AssignMenu. Then, when you want to add a pop-up, load the pop-up with LoadMenu. Use the handle from LoadMenu in a call to InsertMenu to add the pop-up. This statement shows how:

```
InsertMenu(GetMenu(HWindow), -1, MF_BYPOSITION|MF_POPUP
    , 5, LoadMenu(GetApplicationObject()->hInstance, "PopMenu"));
```

The statement uses GetMenu to get the handle of the menu bar. The flags indicate that the item should be added to the end of the menu bar and is a pop-up. The LoadMenu call gets the menu called PopMenu from the resource file.

4.3 How Do I...
Change the Attributes of a Menu Item?

Complexity: MODERATE

PROBLEM

Menu items do not have to be simple text entries. They can be bitmaps, separators, be checked, and more. Table 4-1 shows the possible attributes for menu

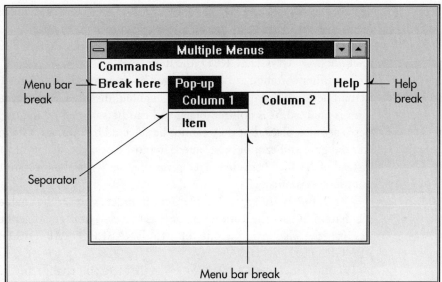

FIGURE 4-3
Menu
Attributes

items. Many of the attributes can be set in the resource file to make the menu look just the way you want. Other attributes, such as check marks, are set by the program to indicate the state of the command. This solution shows you how to handle both situations.

TECHNIQUE

The first place to consider changing menu attributes is in the resource file. You can add separators to group related menu items together, break long menus into multiple columns, and add pop-ups. Figure 4-3 shows some of the attributes you can set in the resource file and what they look like.

The most common menu item attributes changed by programs are check marks and enabled state. Menu items that can be on or off, such as an option to allow duplicate records in a database, can indicate the status of the command by setting or clearing the check mark attribute. The menu in How-To 4.1 used check marks to indicate which menu was loaded. In that case, the check mark attribute was set in the resource file. To set the check mark attribute while the program is running, you can use the Windows function CheckMenuItem. This function can also be used to remove the check mark. Here is an example of how to set the check mark for a menu item:

```
CheckMenuItem(GetMenu(HWindow), 101, MF_BYCOMMAND|MF_CHECKED);
```

This statement uses GetMenu to get the handle of the main menu. Because this statement searches for an item by command, you do not need to get the handle of the specific pop-up, Windows will search all of the pop-ups until it finds an item with a matching ID. The second argument to CheckMenuItem is the ID or position of the item to check. The last argument is the flag that tells how to interpret the position number and whether to check (MF_CHECKED) or uncheck (MF_UNCHECKED) the item.

The other common attribute changed by programs is the enabled state of the item. There are three enabled states: enabled, disabled, and grayed. When an item is enabled, it is colored black and can be selected by the user. Disabled items are also black, but they cannot be selected by the user. Grayed items are colored gray and cannot be selected. In most cases, you will want to use grayed instead of disabled because grayed gives the user a visual indication that he cannot use the command.

The Windows function EnableMenuItem lets you set the enabled state of a menu item. It uses the same arguments as CheckMenuItem, except that the values for the flag can be one of MF_ENABLED, MF_DISABLED, and MF_GRAYED.

Windows includes a general function that lets you change any attribute, the text, and the ID for a menu item called ModifyMenu. The general form of this function is:

```
ModifyMenu(HMENU MenuHandle, WORD Position, WORD ItemFlags, WORD NewID, LPSTR NewData)
```

The arguments for this function are the same as for InsertMenu. The first two arguments are the handle and position of the menu item to change. The flags can be any of the flags from Table 4-1. NewID is the new ID number for the item and NewData is a string, bitmap, or menu handle depending on the value in ItemFlags.

A program that can change menu attributes needs a way to keep track of the current state of menu items. An easy way to do this is to get the menu attributes from Windows by calling the function GetMenuState. This function uses a menu handle, position, and flag arguments to identify an item. It returns a WORD that contains the same flags as in Table 4-1.

The program in this solution includes a menu with three commands. The first command changes the check mark state of the third command. The program uses CheckMenuItem to change the check mark state of the third item and ModifyMenu to change the string in the first item. The second menu item uses EnableMenuItem to flip the third item between the three enabled states. The program gets the current state of the third menu item by calling GetMenuState.

STEPS

1. Create a new project file called ATTRMNU.PRJ that includes the files ATTRMNU.CPP, ATTRMNU.RES, and STANDARD.DEF.

2. Create the source file ATTRMNU.CPP with this program:

```
/* ATTRMNU Demonstrates menu attributes */
#include <owl.h>

#define MID_CHECK      101
#define MID_ENABLE     102
#define MID_SAMPLE     103

class TMyWindow : public TWindow
{
    public:
        TMyWindow(PTWindowsObject AParent, LPSTR ATitle);
        /* menu command routines */
        virtual void CheckIt(RTMessage) = [CM_FIRST + MID_CHECK];
        virtual void EnableIt(RTMessage) = [CM_FIRST + MID_ENABLE];
        virtual void Sample(RTMessage) = [CM_FIRST + MID_SAMPLE];
};

/* Assign the initial menu when creating the window */
TMyWindow::TMyWindow(PTWindowsObject AParent, LPSTR ATitle)
    : TWindow(AParent, ATitle)
{
    AssignMenu("MENU1");
}

/* Toggle the check state of the sample item */
void TMyWindow::CheckIt(RTMessage)
{
    HMENU MnHand;

    MnHand = GetMenu(HWindow);  // Get the handle of the menu
    /* See if the sample is checked */
    if(MF_CHECKED&GetMenuState(MnHand, MID_SAMPLE, MF_BYCOMMAND))
    {
        /* Uncheck the sampled item */
        CheckMenuItem(MnHand, MID_SAMPLE, MF_BYCOMMAND|MF_UNCHECKED);
        /* Change the text of the check command */
        ModifyMenu(MnHand, MID_CHECK, MF_BYCOMMAND|MF_STRING
            , MID_CHECK, "&Check sample");
    }
    else
    {
        CheckMenuItem(MnHand, MID_SAMPLE, MF_BYCOMMAND|MF_CHECKED);
        /* Change the text of the check command */
        ModifyMenu(MnHand, MID_CHECK, MF_BYCOMMAND|MF_STRING
            , MID_CHECK, "&Uncheck sample");
    }
}

/* Toggle the enabled state of the sample */
void TMyWindow::EnableIt(RTMessage)
{
    HMENU MnHand;
    WORD State;

    MnHand = GetMenu(HWindow);  // Get the handle of the menu
    /* Get the state of the sample menu item */
    State = GetMenuState(MnHand, MID_SAMPLE, MF_BYCOMMAND);
    /* See if sample is grayed */
    if(State&MF_GRAYED)
    {
```

```
                /* Disable the sampled item */
                EnableMenuItem(MnHand, MID_SAMPLE, MF_BYCOMMAND|MF_ENABLED);
                /* Change the text of the check command */
                ModifyMenu(MnHand, MID_ENABLE, MF_BYCOMMAND|MF_STRING
                    , MID_ENABLE, "&Disable sample");
        }
        /* See if sample is enabled (Not disabled)*/
        else if(!(State&MF_DISABLED))
        {
                /* Disable the sampled item */
                EnableMenuItem(MnHand, MID_SAMPLE, MF_BYCOMMAND|MF_DISABLED);
                /* Change the text of the check command */
                ModifyMenu(MnHand, MID_ENABLE, MF_BYCOMMAND|MF_STRING
                    , MID_ENABLE, "&Gray sample");
        }
        /* See if sample is disabled */
        else if(State&MF_DISABLED)
        {
                /* Disable the sampled item */
                EnableMenuItem(MnHand, MID_SAMPLE, MF_BYCOMMAND|MF_GRAYED);
                /* Change the text of the check command */
                ModifyMenu(MnHand, MID_ENABLE, MF_BYCOMMAND|MF_STRING
                    , MID_ENABLE, "&Enable sample");
        }
}

/* Handle the sample command */
void TMyWindow::Sample(RTMessage)
{
        MessageBeep(0);
}

/* Define the application object */
class TMenuApp : public TApplication
{
        public:
                TMenuApp(LPSTR ApName, HINSTANCE Inst, HINSTANCE PrevInst
                    , LPSTR CmdLine, int CmdShow) : TApplication(ApName
                    , Inst, PrevInst, CmdLine, CmdShow) {};
                virtual void InitMainWindow();
};

/* Create the main window object */
void TMenuApp::InitMainWindow()
{
        MainWindow = new TMyWindow(NULL, "Multiple Menus");
}

/* Program entry point */
int PASCAL
WinMain(HINSTANCE Inst, HINSTANCE PrevInst
        , LPSTR CmdLine, int CmdShow)
{
        TMenuApp TheApp("", Inst
                , PrevInst, CmdLine, CmdShow);

        TheApp.Run();
        return TheApp.Status;
}
```

3. Most of the menu attributes in this example are in the resource file ATTR-MNU.RES. Here is the menu:

```
MENU1 MENU
BEGIN
     POPUP "Commands"
     BEGIN
          MENUITEM "&Check sample", 101
          MENUITEM "&Disable sample", 102
          MENUITEM "&Sample", 103
     END

     MENUITEM "Break here", 0, MENUBREAK
     POPUP "Pop-up"
     BEGIN
          MENUITEM "Column 1", 200
          MENUITEM SEPARATOR,
          MENUITEM "Item", 2
          MENUITEM "Column 2", 3, MENUBARBREAK
     END

     MENUITEM "Help", 1, HELP
END
```

4. Use the *Run* command to compile and run the program.

HOW IT WORKS

The first object in this program defines the main window for the program. The object includes message response member functions to handle the menu commands. The first function, CheckIt, uses the GetMenuState function to find out if the third menu item is checked or not. In either case, CheckIt calls CheckMenuItem to change the check state and modify the menu to change the string.

The second menu command calls the function EnableIt to change the third item to the next enabled state. This function uses the same basic principles as CheckIt to get the state of the item and change it to the next state. Note that the function does not check for the MF_ENABLED flag to see if the item is enabled. This is because MF_ENABLED is defined as 0; when you logically AND this constant with the state word, you always get zero. MF_DISABLED has the correct bit set so you can AND it with the state and get a meaningful value.

The indexed member function Sample handles the third menu command. It calls the Windows function MessageBeep to make a sound. The purpose of this function is to show you what happens when the menu item is disabled. You will only hear a beep when the menu item is enabled.

4.4 How Do I...
Change the Check Marks Used in Menus?

Complexity: EASY

PROBLEM

One side effect to having consistent user interfaces in Windows programs is that it is hard for a program to distinguish itself. If you want your program to be noticed in this conformist environment, you have to dress it up with some nice graphics. One place to begin is with the check marks used in your menus. Windows lets you replace the check mark with a bitmap of your choosing. This solution shows how to do it.

TECHNIQUE

The Windows function SetMenuItemBitmaps is the key to this solution. It uses the usual menu handle, position number, and flags to identify the item. The last two arguments are handles to bitmaps for the unchecked and checked attributes. Either of these handles can be NULL, indicating that Windows should draw nothing for that attribute. To put back the default check mark, set both handles to NULL.

Before you can use this function, you must have some bitmaps to use for the check mark. The easiest way to get a bitmap is to load it from the resource file. The Resource Workshop includes an easy to use bitmap editor so getting the bitmap into the resource file is no problem. Getting the bitmap into the program is also easy, just call the Windows function LoadBitmap. This function allocates memory and copies the bitmap from the resource file to the memory. Unlike other objects you can load, the memory for bitmaps is not automatically freed when the program exits. This means that you must be sure to use the Windows function DeleteObject to free every bitmap you load.

STEPS

1. Create a new project file called CHECKMNU.PRJ that includes the files CHECKMNU.CPP, CHECKMNU.RES, and STANDARD.DEF.

2. Create the source file CHECKMNU.CPP with this program:

```
/* CHECKMNU Program with custom check marks */
#include <owl.h>

#define MID_CHECK        101
```

```
class TMyWindow : public TWindow
{
        HBITMAP CheckMark;
    public:
        TMyWindow(PTWindowsObject AParent, LPSTR ATitle);
        virtual void SetupWindow();        // Setup the main window
        virtual void CloseWindow();        // Called when exiting the program
        /* menu command routines */
        virtual void CheckIt(RTMessage) = [CM_FIRST + MID_CHECK];
};

/* Assign the initial menu when creating the window */
TMyWindow::TMyWindow(PTWindowsObject AParent, LPSTR ATitle)
    : TWindow(AParent, ATitle)
{
    AssignMenu("MENU1");
}

/* Set up the bitmap for check marks */
void TMyWindow::SetupWindow()
{
    /* Always call the TWindow version of SetupWindow */
    TWindow::SetupWindow();
    /* Load the diamond bitmap from the resource file */
    CheckMark = LoadBitmap(GetApplicationObject()->hInstance, "Diamond");
    /* Set the check mark to the bitmap for the MID_CHECK command */
    SetMenuItemBitmaps(GetMenu(HWindow), MID_CHECK, MF_BYCOMMAND, NULL, CheckMark);
}

/* Free up the memory used by the bitmap */
void TMyWindow::CloseWindow()
{
    DeleteObject(CheckMark);
}

/* Toggle the check state of the menu */
void TMyWindow::CheckIt(RTMessage)
{
    HMENU MnHand;

    MnHand = GetMenu(HWindow);   // Get the handle of the menu
    if(MF_CHECKED&GetMenuState(MnHand, MID_CHECK, MF_BYCOMMAND))
        CheckMenuItem(MnHand, MID_CHECK, MF_BYCOMMAND|MF_UNCHECKED);
    else
        CheckMenuItem(MnHand, MID_CHECK, MF_BYCOMMAND|MF_CHECKED);
}

/* Define the application object */
class TMenuApp : public TApplication
{
    public:
        TMenuApp(LPSTR ApName, HINSTANCE Inst, HINSTANCE PrevInst
            , LPSTR CmdLine, int CmdShow) : TApplication(ApName
            , Inst, PrevInst, CmdLine, CmdShow) {};
        virtual void InitMainWindow();
};

/* Create the main window object */
```

```
void TMenuApp::InitMainWindow()
{
    MainWindow = new TMyWindow(NULL, "Multiple Menus");
}

/* Program entry point */
int PASCAL
WinMain(HINSTANCE Inst, HINSTANCE PrevInst
    , LPSTR CmdLine, int CmdShow)
{
    TMenuApp TheApp("", Inst, PrevInst, CmdLine, CmdShow);

    TheApp.Run();
    return TheApp.Status;
}
```

Figure 4-4
The Diamond
Bitmap

3. Use the Resource Workshop to create a resource file named CHECK-MNU.RES. Add the bitmap shown in Figure 4-4 and name it Diamond. Also include this menu:

```
MENU1 MENU
BEGIN
    POPUP "Menu"
    BEGIN
        MENUITEM "&Check this", 101
    END

END
```

4. Use the *Run* command to compile and run the program.

HOW IT WORKS

The main window object at the beginning of this chapter includes two member functions that are important in programs that use bitmaps. The first member function is SetupWindow. ObjectWindows calls this function when creating the window. This program uses the function to load the check mark bitmap into memory and set it as the check mark for one of the menu items. The other function is CloseWindow, which ObjectWindows calls just before closing the window. This is the place to delete the bitmap object and make its memory available again.

The last member function in the main window object handles the *Check this* command from the menu. When the user selects this command, the program toggles the state of the check mark (see How-To 4.3). This program puts a diamond shape next to the item instead of a check mark. The reason for this is the SetMenuItemBitmaps call in the SetupWindow function. The first three arguments to SetMenuItemBitmaps identify the menu item to change, the last two are the bitmaps to draw for unchecked and check menu items. Note that the argument for the unchecked item is NULL. This tells Windows not to draw anything next to the item.

COMMENT

You can use this feature to make your menus easier to use by providing pictures that show the user how the menu item works. For example, for menu items that turn things on and off, you can show a light switch next to the menu item. You do not have to check and uncheck the menu item to place a bitmap next to it. You can make a bitmap for the unchecked state and it will appear next to the item without any further programming. One use for this feature is to associate menu items with buttons on the tool bar. Programs such as the Borland C++ IDE use tools bars to give the user a shortcut to certain menu commands. The problem is that the user has to decide what command goes with what picture on the tool bar. Putting a picture of the tool bar button next to the menu item teaches the user what tool bar button to press to perform a function.

4.5 How Do I...
Use Bitmaps as Menu Items?

Complexity: EASY

PROBLEM

One problem with menus is that the programmer must choose short commands that tell the user what the command will do. Often the short phrase used in the menu is not enough, you have to go to the manual or a help window to find out what the menu command does. One way to cram 1,000 words into a menu command is to use a picture for the menu command. The program in this solution shows how to use bitmaps for menu commands. The example is a menu that you can use with the language program in How-To 3.8. Instead of showing the name of the language, this program shows the flag of the country.

TECHNIQUE

This program gets the menu and the bitmaps for the menu items from the resource file. You cannot store a menu that uses bitmaps in a resource file, so the program must replace each menu item with the appropriate bitmap after loading the menu. The trick is to match up the right menu item with the bitmap. This program solves the problem by putting the name of the bitmap to use in the menu item text.

The program loops through each menu item replacing the text with a bitmap. The Windows function GetMenuString gets the name of the required bitmap from the menu. Then the program uses LoadBitmap to get the bitmap into memory. Finally, ModifyMenu puts the bitmap into the menu.

STEPS

1. Create a new project file named PICTMNU.PRJ that includes the files PICTMNU.CPP, PICTMNU.RES, and STANDARD.DEF.

2. Create the source file PICTMNU.CPP with this program:

```
/* PICTMNU Program with a graphical menu */
#include <owl.h>

#define MID_USA          101
#define MID_JAPAN        102
#define MID_GERMANY      103


/* The main window object */
class TMyWindow : public TWindow
{
    public:
            /* The menu bitmaps */
            HBITMAP Countries[3];
            TMyWindow(PTWindowsObject AParent, LPSTR ATitle);
            virtual void SetupWindow();       // Load the bitmaps
            virtual void CloseWindow();       // Release the bitmaps
            /* menu command routines */
            virtual void USA(RTMessage) = [CM_FIRST + MID_USA];
            virtual void Japan(RTMessage) = [CM_FIRST + MID_JAPAN];
            virtual void Germany(RTMessage) = [CM_FIRST + MID_GERMANY];
};

/* Assign the initial menu when creating the window */
TMyWindow::TMyWindow(PTWindowsObject AParent, LPSTR ATitle)
      : TWindow(AParent, ATitle)
{
    AssignMenu("MENU1");
}


/* Load the bitmaps when creating the window */
void TMyWindow::SetupWindow()
{
    int i;
    HMENU MnHand;
    char TmpStr[20];

    MnHand = GetMenu(HWindow);
    for(i=0; i<3; ++i)
    {
        /* Get the string from the menu */
        GetMenuString(MnHand, MID_USA + i, TmpStr, 20, MF_BYCOMMAND);
        /* Load the bitmap */
        Countries[i] = LoadBitmap(GetApplicationObject()->hInstance, TmpStr);
        /* Change the menu to a bitmap style */
        ModifyMenu(MnHand, MID_USA+i, MF_BYCOMMAND|MF_BITMAP
            , MID_USA+i, (LPSTR) MAKELONG(Countries[i], 0));
    }
```

```
        /* Always call the TWindow setup */
        TWindow::SetupWindow();
}


/* Delete the bitmaps when exiting the program */
void TMyWindow::CloseWindow()
{
    int i;

    for(i=0; i<3; ++i)
        DeleteObject(Countries[i]);
    /* Always call the TWindow close */
    TWindow::CloseWindow();
}

/* USA Selected */
void TMyWindow::USA(RTMessage)
{
    HDC hDC;

    hDC = GetDC(HWindow);
    TextOut(hDC, 10, 10, "USA              ", 15);
    ReleaseDC(HWindow, hDC);
}


/* Japan Selected */
void TMyWindow::Japan(RTMessage)
{
    HDC hDC;

    hDC = GetDC(HWindow);
    TextOut(hDC, 10, 10, "Japan            ", 15);
    ReleaseDC(HWindow, hDC);
}

/* Germany Selected */
void TMyWindow::Germany(RTMessage)
{
    HDC hDC;

    hDC = GetDC(HWindow);
    TextOut(hDC, 10, 10, "Germany          ", 15);
    ReleaseDC(HWindow, hDC);
}


/* Define the application object */
class TMenuApp : public TApplication
{
    public:
        TMenuApp(LPSTR ApName, HINSTANCE Inst, HINSTANCE PrevInst
            , LPSTR CmdLine, int CmdShow) : TApplication(ApName
            , Inst, PrevInst, CmdLine, CmdShow) {};
        virtual void InitMainWindow();
};

/* Create the main window object */
void TMenuApp::InitMainWindow()
{
    MainWindow = new TMyWindow(NULL, "Multiple Menus");
```

```
}

/* Program entry point */
int PASCAL
WinMain(HINSTANCE Inst, HINSTANCE PrevInst
      , LPSTR CmdLine, int CmdShow)
{
      TMenuApp TheApp("", Inst
            , PrevInst, CmdLine, CmdShow);

      TheApp.Run();
      return TheApp.Status;
}
```

3. Create a resource file called PICTMNU.RES that includes the bitmaps shown in Figure 4.5. Also include this menu:

```
MENU1 MENU
BEGIN
      POPUP "&Countries"
      BEGIN
            MENUITEM "USA", 101
            MENUITEM "JAPAN", 102
            MENUITEM "GERMANY", 103
      END

END
```

Be sure that the menu items and the bitmap names match.

4. Use the *Run* command to compile and run the program.

HOW IT WORKS

The main window object in this program is similar to the one in How-To 4.4. It includes a SetupWindow function to load the bitmaps and put them in the main menu. It also includes a CloseWindow function to delete the bitmaps. The first difference between this object class and the one in How-To 4.4 is that this object includes an array of bitmap handles called Countries to keep track of the bitmaps loaded. The other difference is the three indexed member functions that handle the three menu commands.

The for loop in SetupWindow loads bitmaps from the resource file and associates them with menu items. The first step is to load the text from the menu with the GetMenuString function. This text is the name of the bitmap in the resource file. The program uses this name as an argument to the LoadBitmap function to load a bitmap from the resource file. The handle of the bitmap is saved in the window object so that it can be deleted in the CloseWindow function. Once the bitmap is loaded, the program uses the ModifyMenu function to change the menu item to a bitmap.

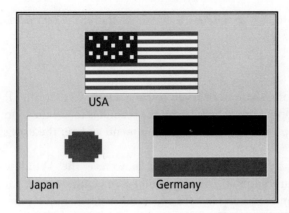

Figure 4-5
Menu Bitmaps

The CloseWindow function deletes the bitmaps by looping through the country array and using DeleteObject to delete the handle in the array. This step is very important because Windows does not automatically remove bitmaps from memory when an application stops. Without this function, every time you ran the program it would use up more memory until eventually there would be no memory left.

The rest of the member functions in the TMyWindow object handle menu command messages from Windows. They work the same way that any other menu function does. When the user selects a command, Windows sends a message to the program that ObjectWindows turns into a call to one of the message response member functions. In this program, the member functions print a string in the main window indicating which menu choice the user selected.

4.6 How Do I...
Create Pop-Up Menus?

Complexity: EASY

PROBLEM

The menus you have seen so far have one basic layout. A menu bar across the top of the window shows the pop-up menus available. Each pop-up appears under the heading on the menu bar for that menu. Windows allows another possibility: unattached pop-up menus. These menus can appear anywhere on the screen. This type of menu can be used to let the user point to an object on the screen and pop up a menu next to that object. This solution shows you how to put a pop-up menu right next to the mouse cursor whenever the user presses the right mouse button.

TECHNIQUE

There are two things you need to do to have unattached pop-up menus. The first is to get a pop-up menu handle and the second is to use the Windows function TrackPopupMenu to create a pop-up menu and get the user's command selection.

One way to make a pop-up menu is to use the Windows function CreateMenu. This function returns a handle to an empty menu. After creating the menu, you can use InsertMenu to add items to the menu. Another way to get a pop-up menu is to load it from the resource file. A menu in the resource file can include any number of pop-up menus. After loading the menu with LoadMenu, you can use GetSubMenu to get the handle to any one of these pop-ups. These statements show how:

```
MenuHandle = LoadMenu(GetApplication()->hInstance, "Menu");
SubMenuHandle = GetSubMenu(MenuHandle, 0);
```

The first statement loads a menu named *Menu* from the resource file and puts the handle in the variable MenuHandle. The second statement uses this handle to get the handle of the first submenu and store it in the variable SubMenuHandle. This is the handle that you give to TrackPopupMenu to make an unattached menu appear on the screen. This statement demonstrates this function:

```
TrackPopupMenu(SubMenuHandle, 0, XPos, YPos, 0, HWindow, NULL);
```

The first argument is the handle of the menu to display. The second argument is a flag that can be 0 or TPM_RIGHTBUTTON if you want the user to use the right button to select items in the menu. The next two arguments are the position of the menu. This position is relative to the upper left corner of the screen. The second to the last argument is a handle to the window that should get messages from Windows when the user selects a command. The other two arguments are reserved and should be 0.

When a program calls TrackPopupMenu, Windows displays the menu and sends all mouse movements and button positions to the pop-up menu. When the user releases the mouse button, Windows sends a message to the window that owns the menu indicating the menu selection. Then Windows destroys the menu. Your program can handle the menu messages with the same indexed member function used by standard menu messages.

The program for this solution waits for the user to press the left mouse button, then calls TrackPopupMenu to place a menu at the position of the mouse cursor. Figure 4-6 shows the pop-up menu.

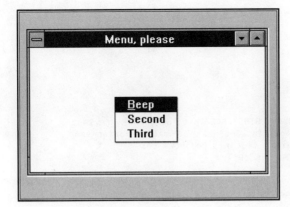

Figure 4-6
An Unattached
Pop-Up Menu

STEPS

1. Create a new project file called POPMNU.PRJ that includes the files POPMNU.CPP, POPMNU.RES, and STANDARD.RES.

2. Create a source file called POPMNU.CPP with this program:

```cpp
/* MENUAPP An OWL program with menus */
#include <owl.h>

#define MID_BEEP        101

/* The main window object */
class TMyWindow : public TWindow
{
     public:
          TMyWindow(PTWindowsObject AParent, LPSTR ATitle)
               : TWindow(AParent, ATitle) {};
          /* Handle left mouse button presses */
          virtual void WMLButtonDown(RTMessage Msg) = [WM_FIRST + WM_LBUTTONDOWN];
          /* Handle a menu command */
          virtual void MenuBeep(RTMessage) = [CM_FIRST + MID_BEEP];
};

/* Pop up the menu at the button position */
void TMyWindow::WMLButtonDown(RTMessage Msg)

     HMENU Pop;
     RECT Rect;

     /* Get the position of the main window */
     GetWindowRect(HWindow, &Rect);
     /* Get a menu from the resource file */
     Pop = LoadMenu(GetApplication()->hInstance, "PopMenu");
     /* Display the pop-up menu */
     TrackPopupMenu(GetSubMenu(Pop, 0), 0, Msg.LP.Lo + Rect.left
          , Msg.LP.Hi + Rect.top + 10, 0, HWindow, NULL);
     /* Get rid of the menu */
     DestroyMenu(Pop);
}

/* Beep when the user selects the first menu item */
```

```
void TMyWindow::MenuBeep(RTMessage)
{
     MessageBeep(0);
}


/* The application object */
class TMenuApp : public TApplication
{
     public:
             TMenuApp(LPSTR ApName, HINSTANCE Inst, HINSTANCE PrevInst
                 , LPSTR CmdLine, int CmdShow) : TApplication(ApName
                 , Inst, PrevInst, CmdLine, CmdShow) {};
             virtual void InitMainWindow();
};

/* Create the main window object */
void TMenuApp::InitMainWindow()
{
     MainWindow = new TMyWindow(NULL, "Menu, please");
}


/* Main entry point for the program */
int PASCAL WinMain(HINSTANCE Inst, HINSTANCE PrevInst, LPSTR CmdLine
     , int CmdShow)
{
     TMenuApp TheApp("", Inst
         , PrevInst, CmdLine, CmdShow);

     TheApp.Run();
     return TheApp.Status;
}
```

3. Create a resource file called POPMNU.PRJ that includes this menu:

```
POPMENU MENU
BEGIN
     POPUP "Pop-up"
     BEGIN
             MENUITEM "&Beep", 101
             MENUITEM "Second", 102
             MENUITEM "Third", 103
     END

END
```

4. Use the *Run* command to compile and run the program.

HOW IT WORKS

The main action of this program is in the WMLButtonDown member function of the main window object. ObjectWindows calls this function when it receives a message from Windows indicating that the user pressed the left mouse button. The first thing this function does is get the position of the main window. The reason for this is that the position of the mouse in the WM_RBUTTON-

DOWN message is relative to the upper left corner of the window, while the TrackPopupMenu requires the position to be relative to the upper left corner of the screen. The button position can be converted to the menu position by adding the upper left corner of the window to the button position.

The WMLButtonDown function loads a menu from the resource file that includes the pop-up needed. The handle of this menu is stored in the variable Pop. The function passes this handle to GetSubMenu to get the handle to the pop-up. Then it passes the pop-up handle, the computed position, and the main window handle to the TrackPopupMenu routine. This routine returns after the user makes a selection and Windows has erased the menu from the screen. The last statement in the WMLButtonDown function deletes the menu to remove it from memory.

COMMENT

One question that a program designer must ask is, "What does it mean when the user clicks on an item?" For example, if you have a list of files, does clicking on a file mean you want to delete the file, view its contents, or copy it to another directory? By using pop-up menus, you can give this choice to the user—making the program more flexible. You can even get carried away with this idea and display different menus depending on which mouse button the user has pressed.

Input/Ouput 5

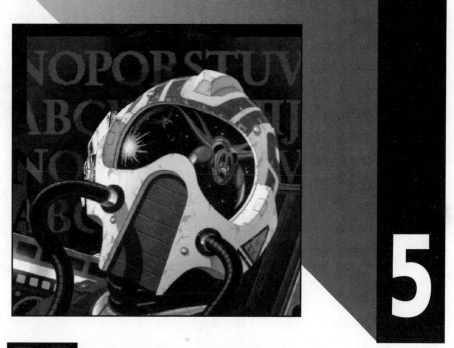

5

MS-DOS programs must handle most of the I/O themselves. The I/O handlers included in MS-DOS all lack certain vital capabilities. The printer driver cannot format text, the video driver cannot do sophisticated graphics, and the serial port driver does not work well at high speeds. Windows makes up for this lack by providing high-level device-independent I/O for such things as printers, graphics displays, and keyboards. Windows version 3.1 even includes drivers for CD players and sound devices.

The Windows I/O drivers let application programs make the most of the devices attached to the computer. You can format printer data with fonts and graphics, you can display screen graphics, and the serial port can receive data at speeds up to 19,200 baud. You do not have to be an expert on these devices to take advantage of these features. Windows includes easy to use functions that handle all of the details.

Another benefit of the Windows drivers is device independence. If you write a program that works with an HP LaserJet, it will work just as well on a PostScript printer, or any other printer for which you have a Windows device driver. The same goes for video screens, sound boards, CD players, and any other device that has a Windows device driver. Device independence means that your program can be used on a wide variety of systems. This gives you and your users more flexibility in designing a computer system.

5.1 Create a Text Editor

Text editors use many of the available I/O devices, keyboard, mouse, screen, and printer. In a book on conventional programming, this solution would be at the end of the chapter as an example of how to tie all of the I/O devices together. With ObjectWindows, creating a text editor is one of the easiest ways to look at I/O. The ObjectWindows library includes an object that handles text editing. This solution shows you how to use this object.

5.2 Get Input from the Keyboard

To read the keyboard in an MS-DOS program, you call one of the keyboard reading routines and then process the key returned. Windows turns this around so that when the user presses a key, Windows calls your program. Windows sends messages about several keyboard events such as key pressed, key released, character generated, etc. This solution shows how to handle the messages that Windows uses to tell your program about the keys pressed.

5.3 Get Input from the Mouse

The mouse is an important part of the Windows interface. Some of the mouse actions with a program, such as resizing and making menu selections, are handled by Windows itself. Once the mouse is inside the client area of the program, it is up to the program to handle mouse actions. This solution shows how to get the mouse position, take action when the user presses a mouse button, and change the mouse cursor.

5.4 Use the Serial Port

To use your computer as an information tool, you must be able to get information from other computers. Data services are available for trading stocks, making travel plans, or sending electronic mail to someone. To use these services, you need to send and receive data through the serial port. One way is to use the terminal program that comes with Windows. Another way is to write your own program that uses the serial port. With your own program, you can set up the computer to automatically collect all of the data you need.

5.5 Use the Sound Interface

The IBM PC does not have a sophisticated sound system built in. This has prevented programmers from adding sound to their programs. In the past, if your program needed sound, you had to write separate sound modules for each sound add-in board. Windows includes sound drivers as part of the multimedia extensions. Now you can write a single sound routine for your program and it will work on any supported hardware. This solution shows you how to record and play sounds.

5.6 Handle the Printer

If you have ever installed an MS-DOS word processing program, take a look at the diskettes that come with the program. For many packages, most of the disks hold nothing but printer drivers for the various printers supported. When you install a new word processor, a drafting program, or any other program that uses the printer, you have to install all new printer drivers. Windows programs do not have this problem because Windows includes its own printer drivers that can be used by applications.

Making a single interface that handles all types of printers is not a simple task. As a result, the printer interface is not simple. You must load the driver, set up parameters, describe pages, and send the data in a way that the printer can handle. This solution shows you everything you need to know about printing text or graphics.

5.1 How Do I...
Create a Text Editor?

Complexity: EASY

PROBLEM

Some programs can benefit from built-in text editing. For example, a database can have long text fields used for descriptions, or the program might use macros that the user can edit. ObjectWindows makes it easy to add text editing to programs by using the TEditWindow and TFileWindow objects. This solution shows how to use these objects in your programs.

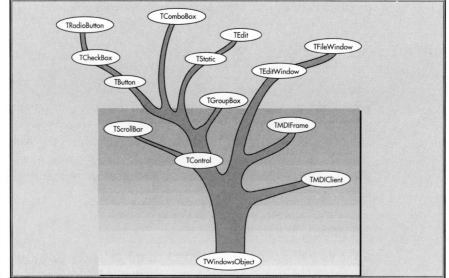

Figure 5-1
Family Tree
of the
TFileWindow
and
TEditWindow
Classes

TECHNIQUE

ObjectWindows includes two object classes for editing text called TEditWindow and TFileWindow. The difference between these classes is that TFileWindow includes routines to load and save the text in files. These classes inherit many things from other objects in ObjectWindows. Figure 5-1 shows how these objects fit together. The easiest way to use these classes is to replace the TWindow object class in the basic ObjectWindows application (see How-To 2.1) with one of the edit window classes.

The edit window classes create a window that has a multiline edit control filling the client area. Windows handles cursor positioning, adding text, and deleting text, just as with any other text control. The edit window classes handle a number of menu commands commonly used in text editing programs. Table 5-1 lists the menu commands handled.

Several of the menu commands require more information from the user. ObjectWindows uses the dialog objects presented in Chapter 3, "Dialog Boxes," to get the information from the user. To use these dialogs, the proper dialog resources must be in the resource file. The dialogs for file handling are in the ObjectWindows file FILEDIAL.DLG and the search dialogs are in STD-WND.DLG.

These dialog resources use constants defined in the file OWLRC.H to identify the fields. To get the resources into your own resource file, you must convert them to the .RES format. First, start the Resource Workshop and select

COMMAND	ID	DESCRIPTION
CM_EDITCUT	24320	Cut the selected text to the Clipboard.
CM_EDITCOPY	24321	Copy the selected text to the Clipboard.
CM_EDITPASTE	24322	Paste text from the Clipboard to the cursor position.
CM_EDITDELETE	24323	Delete the selected text.
CM_EDITCLEAR	24324	Delete all text.
CM_EDITUNDO	24325	Undo the last change.
CM_EDITFIND	24326	Search for text.
CM_EDITREPLACE	24327	Find text and replace it.
CM_EDITFINDNEXT	24328	Repeat the last search.
CM_EXIT	24340	Close the window and exit the program.
CM_FILENEW	24329	Create a new file.
CM_FILEOPEN	24330	Open a file for editing.
CM_FILESAVE	24333	Save the file.
CM_FILESAVEAS	24334	Get a new file name and save the file.

Table 5-1 Menu Commands for the Edit Window Classes

New from the *File* menu. Select the file type .RC in the dialog that appears. Now use *Add to project* to include the files OWLRC.H, FILEDIAL.DLG, and STDWND.DLG. You can find these files in the OWL directories. To convert the resource file to a .RES file, select the *Save as* command and select the .RES file type.

Once you have put the ObjectWindows dialog objects in your resource file, you can add a menu that includes items for the commands handled by the edit window objects. If you add the menu before you convert the resource file to a .RES file, you can use the command names from the first column of Table 5-1 as the menu ID. Otherwise, use the ID numbers from the second column.

STEPS

1. Create a new project file called EDITFILE.PRJ that includes the files EDITFILE.CPP, EDITFILE.RES, and STANDARD.DEF.
2. Create the source file EDITFILE.CPP with this program:

```
/* TEXTEDIT an ObjectWindows editor */
#include <owl.h>
#include <filewnd.h>

/* Definition of the editor object */
class TMyEditor : public TFileWindow
{
    public:
          TMyEditor(LPSTR Title, LPSTR File);
};

/* Get the menu from the resource file */
TMyEditor::TMyEditor(LPSTR Title, LPSTR File)
      : TFileWindow(NULL, Title, File)
{
    AssignMenu("TextMenu");
}

/* definition for the application object */
class TFirstApp : public TApplication
{
    public:
          TFirstApp(LPSTR ApName, HINSTANCE Inst
                , HINSTANCE PrevInst
                , LPSTR CmdLine, int CmdShow) : TApplication(ApName
                , Inst, PrevInst, CmdLine, CmdShow) {};
          virtual void InitMainWindow();
};

/* Initialize the main window */
void TFirstApp::InitMainWindow()
{
    /* Allocate memory for the main window object and put the pointer into the application
    object */
    MainWindow = new TMyEditor("Text editor", "");
}

/* Entry point for the program */
int PASCAL WinMain(HINSTANCE Inst, HINSTANCE PrevInst, LPSTR CmdLine
    , int CmdShow)
{
    /* Create the application object */
    TFirstApp FirstApp("", Inst
          , PrevInst, CmdLine, CmdShow);

    /* Run the application */
    FirstApp.Run();
    return FirstApp.Status;
}
```

3. Use the procedure outlined in the TECHNIQUES section to create the resource file EDITFILE.RES. Include the ObjectWindows files OWLRC.H, FILEDIAL.RC, and STDWND.RC. Also include this menu:

```
TEXTMENU MENU
BEGIN
      POPUP "&File"
```

```
BEGIN
      MENUITEM "&New file", 24329
      MENUITEM "&Open file...", 24330
      MENUITEM SEPARATOR,
      MENUITEM "&Save file", 24333
      MENUITEM "Save &as...", 24334
      MENUITEM SEPARATOR,
      MENUITEM "&Exit", 24340
END

POPUP "&Edit"
BEGIN
      MENUITEM "&Undo", 24325
      MENUITEM SEPARATOR,
      MENUITEM "Cu&t", 24320
      MENUITEM "&Copy", 24321
      MENUITEM "&Paste", 24322
      MENUITEM SEPARATOR,
      MENUITEM "&Delete", 24323
      MENUITEM "C&lear", 24324
      MENUITEM SEPARATOR,
      MENUITEM "&Find", 24326
      MENUITEM "&Replace", 24327
      MENUITEM "Find &next", 24328
END

END
```

4. Use the *Run* command to compile and run the program.

HOW IT WORKS

This program is very similar to the simple menu example in Chapter 2 (How-To 2.4). Instead of the TWindow class, this program uses the TFileWindow class. Note that at the beginning of the program is a line to include the file FILEWND.H This include file contains the definition of the TFileWindow class. The TMyEditor class defined in this program inherits from TFileWindow, which handles all of the editing functions.

Most of the member functions in TFileWindow handle the menu commands in the resource file. This keeps the editor program very simple. The only member function in TMyEditor is the constructor whose only job is to load the menu for the program.

COMMENT

It is easy to customize the editor by using oject-oriented techniques. For example, by adding a method to handle the timer message, you can automatically save the text at timed intervals. You can also modify the *Undo* command to undo multiple changes. The program in How-To 5.6 shows how to add printing to the editor.

5.2 How Do I...
Get Input from the Keyboard?

Complexity: MODERATE

PROBLEM

Windows manages to run several applications at once because when a Windows application has nothing to do, Windows stops running the program and runs other programs. The application begins running again when some event occurs that the program must handle. One of the possible events is that a user pressed a key. This solution shows how to handle keyboard events.

TECHNIQUE

When the user presses or releases a key, Windows checks to see which application has the keyboard *focus*, and then sends a message to that application about the key. The focus is one of the attributes Windows keeps for each window. Typically, there is some visual clue, such as a different caption color for the window that has the focus. The message gives the virtual key code for the key and the scan code for the key. For keys that represent ASCII characters, Windows creates an additional message that gives the ASCII code for the key.

Windows also checks whether the key is an accelerator. Each key is checked against a list of accelerator keys from the resource file. If the key is in the list, Windows creates a WM_COMMAND message with the ID given in the accelerator list for that key. Applications often use accelerators as shortcuts to certain menu commands.

Windows uses virtual key codes to identify keys. Reference books, such as the *Windows Programming Reference* from Microsoft, list some of the virtual key codes. The program in this solution gives you a more direct way to find the virtual key code for the key. It displays information about every keyboard message received. If you have any question about the messages generated by a key, just run the program and press the key to see what happens.

The first message that Windows sends is WM_KEYDOWN, indicating that the user pressed a key. Then, if the key represents an ASCII character, Windows sends WM_CHAR. Finally, when the user releases the key, Windows sends WM_KEYUP. While the messages for any given key are always in this order, it is possible to have several WM_KEYDOWN messages mixed with WM_KEYUP messages. For example, pressing the shift key generates a WM_KEYDOWN, pressing the Tab key generates another WM_KEY-

DOWN. When you release the keys, you get a WM_KEYUP message for each key.

Keeping track of the state of keys can add complexity to your program. An easier way is to wait for the WM_KEYDOWN message of a nonmodifier key and check the state of the modifiers with the Windows function GetKeyState. You pass this function the virtual key code of the key you are interested in, and it returns the state. If the return value is less than 0, the key is pressed, otherwise it is released. If bit 0 of the return value is set, the key has been pressed an odd number of times since the system started. This bit can be used to determine the state of such keys as Caps Lock and Num Lock.

A program that does something with keys needs to know if the key is going to generate a WM_CHAR message. The reason for this is that the WM_KEY-DOWN message does not tell you what character the key generates, so you should ignore it and wait for the WM_CHAR message. To tell if the key will generate a WM_CHAR message, use the Windows function MapVirtualKey. You pass this function the virtual key code and it returns the ASCII value of the unshifted key. For keys that do not generate a WM_CHAR, this function returns 0. Note that because the result of MapVirtualKey is unshifted, you still have to wait for the WM_CHAR message to get the actual ASCII code intended by the user.

Windows considers any key pressed while the Alt key is pressed to be a system key. These keys generate their own messages: WM_SYSKEYDOWN, WM_SYSCHAR, and WM_SYSKEYUP. If you want to use system keys, you must get these messages. Windows uses system keys to provide keyboard commands for the system menu and to display application menus. If you get system key messages, you may prevent Windows from using these keys.

One way to use keys such as function keys or cursor keys is to put them in an accelerator table and handle the WM_COMMAND messages generated. One advantage of this technique is that you can change the meaning of keys by editing the resource file. The Resource Workshop makes it easy to add keys to an accelerator table. Select *New* from the *Resources* menu to bring up the accelerator editor. Each entry in the accelerator table has an ID and a key value. The ID is the number that Windows sends in the WM_COMMAND message when the user presses an accelerator key. You can enter the key value either by entering the virtual key code for the key, or by selecting the *Key value* command in the menu and pressing the accelerator key.

When the user presses an accelerator key, the TranslateAccelerator Windows function in the ObjectWindows Run member function converts the key messages to the specified WM_COMMAND message. The result is that the accelerator key has the same effect as a menu command.

STEPS

1. Create a new project file called KEYS.PRJ that includes the files KEYS.CPP, KEYS.RES, and STANDARD.RES.

2. Create a source file called KEYS.CPP with this program:

```
/* Keys an ObjectWindows editor */
#include <owl.h>
#include <edit.h>
#include <editwnd.h>

#define MID_ACCEL      101

/* The replacement edit control */
class TMyEdit : public TEdit
{
    public:
        TMyEdit(PTWindowsObject Aparent, int AnID, LPSTR AText
            , int X, int Y, int W, int H, WORD TextLen
            , BOOL Multi, PTModule Module = NULL)
            : TEdit(Aparent, AnID, AText, X, Y, W, H, TextLen
            , Multi, Module) {};
        virtual void Accel(RTMessage) = [CM_FIRST + MID_ACCEL];
        virtual void WMChar(RTMessage Msg) = [WM_FIRST + WM_CHAR];
        virtual void WMKeyDown(RTMessage Msg) = [WM_FIRST + WM_KEYDOWN];
        virtual void WMKeyUp(RTMessage Msg) = [WM_FIRST + WM_KEYUP];
        virtual void WMSChar(RTMessage Msg) = [WM_FIRST + WM_SYSCHAR];
        virtual void WMSKeyDown(RTMessage Msg) = [WM_FIRST + WM_SYSKEYDOWN];
        virtual void WMSKeyUp(RTMessage Msg) = [WM_FIRST + WM_SYSKEYUP];
};

/* Handle the accelerator key */
void TMyEdit::Accel(RTMessage)
{
    Insert("F1 accelerator\r\n");
}

/* Handle WM_CHAR message */
void TMyEdit::WMChar(RTMessage Msg)
{
    char TmpStr[80];

    /* Make a string about this message */
    wsprintf(TmpStr, "WM_CHAR          Key: 0x%0x    Scan: 0x%0x", Msg.WParam
        , Msg.LP.Hi&0xFF);
    /* Check extended keys */
    if(Msg.LP.Hi&0x100)
        lstrcat(TmpStr, " Extended");
    /* Check alt keys */
    if(Msg.LP.Hi&0x2000)
        lstrcat(TmpStr, " Alt");
    /* Add EOL */
    lstrcat(TmpStr, "\r\n");
    /* Add it to the window */
    Insert(TmpStr);
}
```

```
/* Handle WM_KEYDOWN message */
void TMyEdit::WMKeyDown(RTMessage Msg)
{
      char TmpStr[80];

      /* Make a string about this message */
      wsprintf(TmpStr, "WM_KEYDOWN        Key: 0x%0x    Scan: 0x%0x  ASCII: 0x%x"
            , Msg.WParam, Msg.LP.Hi&0xFF
            , MapVirtualKey(Msg.WParam,2));   // Get the ASCII value for the key
      /* Check extended keys */
      if(Msg.LP.Hi&0x100)
            lstrcat(TmpStr, " Extended");
      /* Check alt keys */
      if(Msg.LP.Hi&0x2000)
            lstrcat(TmpStr, " Alt");
      /* Add EOL */
      lstrcat(TmpStr, "\r\n");
      /* Add it to the window */
      Insert(TmpStr);
}


/* Handle WM_KEYUP message */
void TMyEdit::WMKeyUp(RTMessage Msg)
{
      char TmpStr[80];

      /* Make a string about this message */
      wsprintf(TmpStr, "WM_KEYUP            Key: 0x%0x    Scan: 0x%0x", Msg.WParam
            , Msg.LP.Hi&0xFF);
      /* Check extended keys */
      if(Msg.LP.Hi&0x100)
            lstrcat(TmpStr, " Extended");
      /* Check alt keys */
      if(Msg.LP.Hi&0x2000)
            lstrcat(TmpStr, " Alt");
      /* Add EOL */
      lstrcat(TmpStr, "\r\n");
      /* Add it to the window */
      Insert(TmpStr);
}


/* Handle WM_SYSCHAR message */
void TMyEdit::WMSChar(RTMessage Msg)
{
      char TmpStr[80];

      /* Make a string about this message */
      wsprintf(TmpStr, "WM_SYSCHAR          Key: 0x%0x    Scan: 0x%x", Msg.WParam
            , Msg.LP.Hi&0xFF);
      /* Check extended keys */
      if(Msg.LP.Hi&0x100)
            lstrcat(TmpStr, " Extended");
      /* Check alt keys */
      if(Msg.LP.Hi&0x2000)
            lstrcat(TmpStr, " Alt");
      /* Add EOL */
      lstrcat(TmpStr, "\r\n");
      /* Add it to the window */
```

```
        Insert(TmpStr);
}


/* Handle WM_SYSKEYDOWN message */
void TMyEdit::WMSKeyDown(RTMessage Msg)
{
        char TmpStr[80];

        /* Make a string about this message */
        wsprintf(TmpStr, "WM_SYSKEYDOWN  Key: 0x%0x    Scan: 0x%x", Msg.WParam
                , Msg.LP.Hi&0xFF);
        /* Check extended keys */
        if(Msg.LP.Hi&0x100)
                lstrcat(TmpStr, " Extended");
        /* Check alt keys */
        if(Msg.LP.Hi&0x2000)
                lstrcat(TmpStr, " Alt");
        /* Add EOL */
        lstrcat(TmpStr, "\r\n");
        /* Add it to the window */
        Insert(TmpStr);
}


/* Handle WM_SYSKEYUP message */
void TMyEdit::WMSKeyUp(RTMessage Msg)
{
        char TmpStr[80];

        /* Make a string about this message */
        wsprintf(TmpStr, "WM_SYSKEYUP        Key: 0x%0x    Scan: 0x%x", Msg.WParam
                , Msg.LP.Hi&0xFF);
        /* Check extended keys */
        if(Msg.LP.Hi&0x100)
                lstrcat(TmpStr, " Extended");
        /* Check alt keys */
        if(Msg.LP.Hi&0x2000)
                lstrcat(TmpStr, " Alt");
        /* Add EOL */
        lstrcat(TmpStr, "\r\n");
        /* Add it to the window */
        Insert(TmpStr);
}


/* Definition of the editor object */
class TMyEditor : public TEditWindow
{
        public:
                TMyEditor(LPSTR Title);
};

/* Get the menu from the resource file */
TMyEditor::TMyEditor(LPSTR Title)
        : TEditWindow(NULL, Title)
{
        AssignMenu("TextMenu");
        delete Editor;
        Editor = new TMyEdit(this, ID_EDITOR, NULL, 0, 0, 0, 0, 0
                , TRUE, GetModule());
```

```
        Editor->Attr.Style |= ES_NOHIDESEL;
}


/* definition for the application object */
class TFirstApp : public TApplication
{
        public:
                TFirstApp(LPSTR ApName, HINSTANCE Inst
                        , HINSTANCE PrevInst
                        , LPSTR CmdLine, int CmdShow) : TApplication(ApName
                        , Inst, PrevInst, CmdLine, CmdShow) {};
                virtual void InitMainWindow();
                virtual void InitInstance();
};


/* Initialize the main window */
void TFirstApp::InitMainWindow()
{
        /* Create the main window object and put its pointer into the application object */
        MainWindow = new TMyEditor("Keyboard tester");
}


void TFirstApp::InitInstance()
{
        TApplication::InitInstance();
        HAccTable = LoadAccelerators(hInstance, "AccelKeys");
}


/* Entry point for the program */
int PASCAL WinMain(HINSTANCE Inst, HINSTANCE PrevInst, LPSTR CmdLine
        , int CmdShow)
{
        /* Create the application object */
        TFirstApp FirstApp("", Inst
                , PrevInst, CmdLine, CmdShow);

        /* Run the application */
        FirstApp.Run();
        return FirstApp.Status;
}
```

3. Create a resource file named KEYS.RES that includes an accelerator table named AccelKeys. This program only recognizes a single accelerator key with an ID of 101. While in the accelerator editor, select the *Key value* selection from the menu, then press the (F1) key. Finally, press (ALT)-(ESC) to get out of key value mode.

4. Use the *Run* command to compile and run the program. Figure 5-2 shows the output of the program after pressing a few keys.

HOW IT WORKS

This program uses a TEditWindow object as the main window so that it can handle the text generated as the user presses keys. As mentioned in How-To 5.1

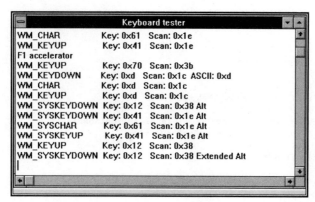

Figure 5-2
The KEYS
Program

the TEditWindow object includes a TEdit object that actually does the editing. The TEdit object is the one that gets keys so this program has to replace it with one that intercepts the keyboard messages. The first object class in the program is the object that will replace the TEdit object normally used by TEditWindow.

You can see how the TEditWindow class normally works by examining the OWL sources. The constructor allocates a TEdit object and stores a pointer to this object in the member Editor. The constructor for the main window in the program above re-creates this code with a minor modification. Instead of allocating a TEdit object, it allocates a TMyEdit object.

The TMyEdit class has member functions for the accelerator and the six keyboard messages. Each of these member functions creates a string that describes the keyboard message and adds it to the main window by calling the Insert member function. The WParam member of the message gives the virtual key code, and LParam gives miscellaneous information about the key. Figure 5-3 shows the format of LParam.

The WMKeyDown function demonstrates the use of MapVirtualKey to see if a key generates a WM_CHAR message. The function passes the virtual key code to the function and adds the result to the string displayed. The second argument to MapVirtualKey tells it what type of mapping to do. A 2 indicates that the function should convert a virtual key to an ASCII value.

The program loads the accelerator table in the InitInstance member function of the application object. All you need to do is call the Windows function LoadAccelerators and put the handle returned into the data member hAccTable.

COMMENT

Windows allows you to use keyboards from different countries. These keyboards often have keys in different locations and they can include special keys to enter accented characters and symbols. The extra character codes are returned in the

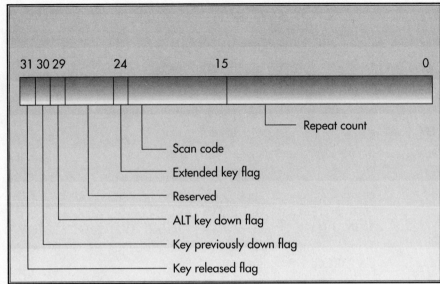

Figure 5-3
The LParam
Member
ofKeyboard
Messages

WM_CHAR message and follow the ISO 8859 code standard. You can ensure that your program will work with these keyboards by using virtual key codes instead of scan codes to identify keys, and always check whether the key generates a WM_CHAR message.

5.3 How Do I...
Get Input from the Mouse?

Complexity: MODERATE

PROBLEM

Part of any graphical user interface is a pointing device such as a mouse. All of the programs in this book use the mouse to select menu items, resize windows, and move objects around the screen. In each of these cases, Windows handles the mouse input and sends the results to the program. This solution shows you how to handle mouse input directly.

TECHNIQUE

When the user moves the mouse or clicks a mouse button, Windows generates messages to tell the application under the mouse cursor what happened. The

FLAG	DESCRIPTION
MK_CONTROL	The control key is pressed.
MK_LBUTTON	The left mouse button is pressed.
MK_MBUTTON	The middle mouse button is pressed.
MK_RBUTTON	The right mouse button is pressed.
MK_SHIFT	The shift key is pressed.

Table 5-2 Flags for the WParam Parameter in Mouse Messages

events that generate messages are button presses (WM_LBUTTONDOWN), button releases (WM_LBUTTONUP), button double-clicks (WM_LBUT-TONDBLCLK), and mouse movements (WM_MOUSEMOVE). Note that Windows only sends double-click messages to windows that have the CS_DBLCLKS style set.

The parameters for mouse messages give information about the mouse when the message is generated. The WParam word contains a combination of the values in Table 5-2. LParam gives the position of the mouse cursor in window co-ordinates (LP.Lo is the x position and LP.Hi is the y position).

Normally, Windows only sends mouse messages to an application if the mouse cursor is over the application window. An application can make Windows send all mouse messages to itself by calling the Windows function SetCapture. If your program does something when the mouse button is pressed, it should call SetCapture to make sure that it gets the button up message. When the application no longer needs the mouse input, it calls ReleaseCapture.

In Chapter 2, "ObjectWindows Bascis," you learned how to change the mouse cursor when it is over the application window (How-To 2.2). The Windows function SetCursor lets you change the mouse cursor at any time. You must pass this function the handle to a cursor that you loaded from the resource file with the LoadCursor function.

The program in this solution handles the mouse messages and shows how to change the mouse cursor. It captures the mouse messages when the mouse button is pressed by calling SetCapture. While the mouse button is pressed, the program uses mouse movements to create lines on the screen. The result is a drawing made from the mouse movements. Figure 5-4 shows the program with a drawing.

STEPS

1. Create a new project file called SCRIBBLE.PRJ with the files SCRIBBLE.CPP, SCRIBBLE.RES, and STANDARD.DEF.

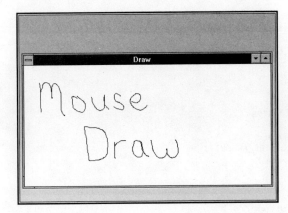

Figure 5-4
Drawing with
the Mouse

2. Create a source file called SCRIBBLE.CPP with this program:

```
/* SCRIBBLE a program to demonstrate use of the mouse */
#include <owl.h>

class TMyWindow : public TWindow
{
     HDC hDC;
     HPEN Pen;
     HCURSOR Cursor;
     public:
          TMyWindow(PTWindowsObject AParent, LPSTR ATitle)
               : TWindow(AParent, ATitle) {};
          /* Routines to handle button messages */
          virtual void WMLButtonDown(RTMessage Msg) = [WM_FIRST + WM_LBUTTONDOWN];
          virtual void WMMouseMove(RTMessage Msg) = [WM_FIRST + WM_MOUSEMOVE];
          virtual void WMLButtonUp(RTMessage) = [WM_FIRST + WM_LBUTTONUP];
          virtual void WMRButtonDown(RTMessage Msg) = [WM_FIRST + WM_RBUTTONDOWN];
          virtual void WMRButtonUp(RTMessage) = [WM_FIRST + WM_RBUTTONUP];
};

/* Start left button drawing */
void TMyWindow::WMLButtonDown(RTMessage Msg)
{
     /* Change the cursor */
     Cursor = LoadCursor(GetApplication()->hInstance, "BlackCursor");
     SetCursor(Cursor);
     /* Capture mouse messages */
     SetCapture(HWindow);
     /* Get a device context */
     hDC = GetDC(HWindow);
     /* Set up the drawing color */
     Pen = CreatePen(PS_SOLID, 1, 0x0);
     SelectObject(hDC, Pen);
     /* Position the pen */
     MoveTo(hDC, Msg.LP.Lo, Msg.LP.Hi);
}

/* Draw a line */
void TMyWindow::WMMouseMove(RTMessage Msg)
```

```
{
      /* See if there is a DC to use */
      if(hDC)
            LineTo(hDC, Msg.LP.Lo, Msg.LP.Hi);
}


/* Stop left button drawing */
void TMyWindow::WMLButtonUp(RTMessage)
{
      /* Replace the normal cursor */
      SetCursor(LoadCursor(NULL, IDC_ARROW));
      /* Delete the special cursor */
      DeleteObject(Cursor);
      /* Delete the pen object */
      DeleteObject(Pen);
      /* Give the DC back to Windows */
      ReleaseDC(HWindow, hDC);
      hDC = NULL;
      /* Stop capturing mouse input */
      ReleaseCapture();
}


/* Start right button drawing */
void TMyWindow::WMRButtonDown(RTMessage Msg)
{
      /* Change the cursor */
      Cursor = LoadCursor(GetApplication()->hInstance, "BlueCursor");
      SetCursor(Cursor);
      /* Capture mouse messages */
      SetCapture(HWindow);
      /* Get a device context */
      hDC = GetDC(HWindow);
      /* Set up the drawing color */
      Pen = CreatePen(PS_SOLID, 1, 0xFF0000);
      SelectObject(hDC, Pen);
      /* Position the pen */
      MoveTo(hDC, Msg.LP.Lo, Msg.LP.Hi);
}


/* Stop right button drawing */
void TMyWindow::WMRButtonUp(RTMessage)
{
      /* Replace the normal cursor */
      SetCursor(LoadCursor(NULL, IDC_ARROW));
      /* Delete the special cursor */
      DeleteObject(Cursor);
      /* Delete the pen object */
      DeleteObject(Pen);
      /* Give the DC back to Windows */
      ReleaseDC(HWindow, hDC);
      hDC = NULL;
      /* Stop capturing mouse input */
      ReleaseCapture();
}


/* Define the application object */
class TMenuApp : public TApplication
{
```

```
    public:
        TMenuApp(LPSTR ApName, HINSTANCE Inst, HINSTANCE PrevInst
            , LPSTR CmdLine, int CmdShow) : TApplication(ApName
            , Inst, PrevInst, CmdLine, CmdShow) {};
        virtual void InitMainWindow();
};

/* Create the main window object */
void TMenuApp::InitMainWindow()
{
    MainWindow = new TMyWindow(NULL, "Draw");
}

int PASCAL WinMain(HINSTANCE Inst, HINSTANCE PrevInst, LPSTR CmdLine
    , int CmdShow)
{
    TMenuApp TheApp("", Inst
        , PrevInst, CmdLine, CmdShow);

    TheApp.Run();
    return TheApp.Status;
}
```

3. Create a resource file named SCRIBBLE.RES that includes two cursors named BlackCursor and BlueCursor. Figure 5-5 shows the cursors.

4. Use the *Run* command to compile and run the program.

Black Cursor   Blue Cursor

Figure 5-5
Cursors for the Mouse Program

HOW IT WORKS

The main window object in this program has member functions that handle the mouse messages. The first function, WMLButtonDown, handles the message for pressing the left mouse button. The first thing this function does is to load a new cursor from the resource file. The function stores the cursor in the member variable Cursor. Next, the function calls SetCursor to change the cursor to the new shape.

WMLButtonDown calls SetCapture to make sure that all mouse messages are sent to this program. This step makes sure that the program gets the WM_LBUTTONUP message so that it can undo the things done in this function.

After capturing the mouse, this function gets a device context so that it can draw on the window. Normally, programs would release the device context before the end of the function, but in this case the program hangs on to the device context until the user releases the mouse button. The reason for this is that the WMLButtonDown sets the color for the device context by creating a colored pen. This pen goes away when the program releases the mouse button. By keeping the device context, the program keeps the pen available.

The last step in the WMLButtonDown function is to place the graphics cursor at the position of the mouse. When the user moves the mouse, Window generates a message that ObjectWindows turns into a call to the WMMouseMove member function. This function uses the device context opened in WMLButtonDown to draw a line by calling the Windows function LineTo.

The WMLButtonUp handles the message for releasing the left mouse button. First, this function restores the normal cursor and deletes the cursor loaded when the user pressed the button. Next, the function gets rid of the pen and releases the device context. Finally, the function releases the mouse so that other windows can get mouse messages.

This program also handles the right mouse button. The routines for this button are similar to the ones for the left button. The only difference is that the WMRButtonDown sets the pen color to blue instead of black. If you have a three-button mouse you can add routines for handling the middle button also.

5.4 How Do I...
Use the Serial Port?

Complexity: DIFFICULT

PROBLEM

The serial port is one of the most versatile devices on the computer. It can connect to printers, plotters, modems, other computers, and many other devices. Windows includes drivers for the serial port that let you send and receive data at speeds up to 19,200 baud. This solution shows you how to set up and use the serial port.

TECHNIQUE

Windows includes several functions for using the serial ports. Table 5-3 summarizes these functions.

The first thing you must do to use a serial port is open the serial device driver with the OpenComm function. This function takes three arguments: the port name, the size of the input buffer, and the size of the output buffer. The port name tells what port to use. Typical names are COM1, COM2, COM3, and COM4.

The serial port itself works on one byte at a time at a much slower rate than the CPU. A program that works directly with the serial port would spend most

Function Name	Description
BuildCommDCB	Creates a device control block.
ClearCommBreak	Stops the port from sending a break signal.
CloseComm	Closes a serial port.
EscapeCommFunction	Does special tasks.
FlushComm	Clears the communications buffers.
GetCommError	Gets the last error from the comm device.
GetCommEventMask	Gets and clears a comm event.
GetCommState	Gets the setting for a comm device.
OpenComm	Opens a comm device for I/O.
ReadComm	Gets data from the comm device.
SetCommBreak	Starts the port sending a break signal.
SetCommEventMask	Sets a comm event flag.
SetCommState	Sets comm device parameters.
TransmitCommChar	Sends a character out the serial port.
UngetCommChar	Adjusts the buffer pointers for the comm device.
WriteComm	Sends characters to the comm device.

Table 5-3 Serial Port Functions

of its time waiting for the port. Windows overcomes this problem by letting programs store data in buffers, and only transferring data to or from the buffer when the port is ready. This frees the CPU to continue running your program.

The buffer sizes you pass in the OpenComm function tell Windows how many bytes to allocate for the input and output buffers. The input buffer holds characters received from the serial port until the program is ready to read the port. If your program has message handling routines that take a long time, you should increase the size of the buffer to make sure you get all the characters received. The output buffer holds data to send out the serial port. If your program sends large amounts of data in a single burst, increase the buffer size to hold all of the characters.

Once you have opened the port, you must set the serial parameters to match those of the device to which the serial port is connected. Windows programs can set the serial parameters by putting the required settings in a structure called the *Device Control Block* (DCB). Table 5-4 lists the members of the DCB structure.

Type Member	Description
BYTE Id	Port ID.
WORD BaudRate	Baud rate.
BYTE ByteSize	Number of bits in each byte sent or received.
BYTE Parity	Type of parity to use. Set to one of these constants:
	EVENPARITY
	MARKPARITY
	NOPARITY
	ODDPARITY
	SPACEPARITY
BYTE StopBits	Number of stop bits following each byte. Set to one of these constants:
	ONESTOPBIT
	ONE5STOPBITS
	TWOSTOPBITS
WORD RlsTimeout	Time to wait for CD signal before generating an error.
WORD CtsTimeout	Time to wait for the CTS signal before generating an error.
WORD DsrTimeout	Time to wait for the DSR signal before generating an error.
BYTE fBinary : 1	TRUE if using EofChar to mark the end of data.
BYTE fRtsDisable : 1	TRUE if RTS should be off.
BYTE fParity : 1	TRUE if checking parity on input.
BYTE fOutxCtsFlow : 1	TRUE if using CTS to control output.
BYTE fOutxDsrFlow : 1	TRUE if using DSR to control output.
BYTE fDummy : 1	Reserved.
BYTE fDtrDisable : 1	TRUE if DTR should not be set.
BYTE fOutX : 1	TRUE if using XON/XOFF flow control on output.
BYTE fInX : 1	TRUE if using XON/OFF flow control on input.
BYTE fPeChar : 1	TRUE if bytes received with parity errors should be replaced with PeChar.

(continued from page 190)

Type Member	Description
BYTE fNull : 1	TRUE if NULL characters should be discarded.
BYTE fDtrFlow : 1	TRUE if using DTR flow control.
BYTE fRtsFlow : 1	TRUE if using RTS flow control.
BYTE fDummy2 : 1	Reserved.
char XonChar	Character to use for XON.
char XoffChar	Character to use for XOFF.
WORD XonLim	Number of characters left when Windows should send XON.
WORD XoffLim	Number of characters to receive before sending XOFF.
char PeChar	Character to substitute on a parity error.
char EofChar	Character that signifies the end of data.
char EvtChar	Character that signifies an event.
WORD TxDelay	Not used.

Table 5-4 The DCB Structure

Instead of trying to find the right settings for all of these parameters, you can use the default settings by reading the current parameters with GetCommState, changing only the baud rate, word size, parity, and stop bit count, and then setting the new parameters with SetCommState. These four parameters are all you need to worry about for most devices.

When the parameters are set, you can read and write data by using the ReadComm and WriteComm routines. Deciding when to use WriteComm is easy; whenever you have data to send, send it with WriteComm.

It is more difficult to decide when to use ReadComm. You never know when data will arrive from the serial port. This means that you must constantly check for incoming data. If you just make a function that repeatedly calls ReadComm, waiting for data, your program will never give control back to Windows. This is not only considered bad Windows programming style; it means that your program can never receive messages, so you cannot stop it.

The answer is to use the IdleAction member function of the TApplication object. ObjectWindows calls this function during the message processing loop in the Run member function when there are no messages for the program. A program can run a brief routine in this function to check for data at the serial port.

ERROR	DESCRIPTION
CE_BREAK	The serial port received a break signal.
CE_CTSTO	CTS was low longer than the timeout period given in the DCB.
CE_DSRTO	DSR was low longer than the timeout period given in the DCB.
CE_FRAME	The serial port did not receive a stop bit at the right time.
CE_MODE	The information in the DCB is bad.
CE_OVERRUN	The driver could not read data from the serial port fast enough.
CE_RLSDTO	CD was low longer than the timeout period given in the DCB.
CE_RXOVER	The driver ran out of room in the receive buffer.
CE_RXPARITY	The parity for a received character is not correct.
CE_TXFULL	The driver ran out of room in the transmit buffer.

Table 5-5 Communications Errors

When you use the ReadComm or WriteComm functions, it is possible to get an error from the serial driver. When this happens, you must check the error by calling the Windows function GetCommError. Windows does not allow any further serial I/O until you check for the error. GetCommError returns an integer whose bits tell what errors have occurred since the last call to GetCommError. Table 5-5 lists the possible errors for serial ports.

The last thing to think about when writing a serial port program is the selection of a program name. Windows will not run a program that has the same name as a Windows device driver. So you cannot name your program SERIAL.

The program in this solution sends a dial command to a Hayes-compatible modem and displays the characters received. It sets the baud rate, word size, and parity in the DCB. Then it uses WriteComm and ReadComm to send and receive data. The ReadComm routine is called from the IdleAction member function. If there is any data, the IdleAction function posts a message to the main window with the data received.

STEPS

1. Create a new project file called MODEM.PRJ with the files MODEM.CPP, MODEM.RES, and STANDARD.DEF.

2. Create the source file MODEM.CPP with this program:

```
/* MODEM Send and receive data at the serial port */
#include <owl.h>
#include <edit.h>
```

```
#define MID_DIAL        101
#define MID_HANGUP      102

#define UM_ERROR WM_USER + 1
#define UM_DATA  WM_USER + 2

class TMyWindow : public TWindow
{
     public:
          char PhoneNumber[20];
          int CPort;        /* Id for the comm port */
          TMyWindow(PTWindowsObject AParent, LPSTR ATitle);
          virtual void SetupWindow();
          virtual void CloseWindow();
          /* menu command routines */
          virtual void DialPhone(RTMessage) = [CM_FIRST + MID_DIAL];
          virtual void HangUp(RTMessage) = [CM_FIRST + MID_HANGUP];
          /* Serial port user messages */
          virtual void SerError(RTMessage Msg) = [WM_FIRST + UM_ERROR];
          virtual void SerData(RTMessage Msg) = [WM_FIRST + UM_DATA];
};

/* Dialog box for getting menu text */
class PhoneDlg : public TDialog
{
     public:
          PhoneDlg(PTWindowsObject AParent, LPSTR AResource);
};

/* Set up the transfer buffer for the dialog */
PhoneDlg::PhoneDlg(PTWindowsObject AParent, LPSTR AResource)
     : TDialog(AParent, AResource)
{
     /* Create an object for the text field */
     new TEdit(this, 101, 20);
     /* Point the transfer buffer at the main window */
     TransferBuffer = (void far *) &((TMyWindow *) Parent)->PhoneNumber;
}

/* Assign the initial menu when creating the window */
TMyWindow::TMyWindow(PTWindowsObject AParent, LPSTR ATitle)
     : TWindow(AParent, ATitle)
{
     PhoneNumber[0] = '\0';      // Blank the phone number
     CPort = -1;                 // Indicate comport is closed
     AssignMenu("ModemMenu");    // Load an assign the menu
}

/* Open and set up the comm port */
void TMyWindow::SetupWindow()
{
     DCB CommData;

     /* Open the comm port */
     CPort = OpenComm("COM1", 1024, 1024);
     /* Get the current port settings */
     GetCommState(CPort, &CommData);
     /* Set 2400 baud */
```

```
        CommData.BaudRate = 2400;
        /* use 8 bit bytes */
        CommData.ByteSize = 8;
        /* Turn off parity */
        CommData.Parity = NOPARITY;
        /* Use one stop bit */
        CommData.StopBits = ONESTOPBIT;
        /* Send the new parameters to the device driver */
        SetCommState(&CommData);
        TWindow::SetupWindow();
}


/* Close the comm port */
void TMyWindow::CloseWindow()
{
        CloseComm(CPort);
        TWindow::CloseWindow();
}


/* Handle the dial command */
void TMyWindow::DialPhone(RTMessage)
{
        HDC hDC;

        /* Do the dialog */
        GetModule()->ExecDialog(new PhoneDlg(this, "PhoneNumber"));
        hDC = GetDC(HWindow);
        TextOut(hDC, 10, 10, "Dialing", 7);
        TextOut(hDC, 60, 10, PhoneNumber, lstrlen(PhoneNumber));
        ReleaseDC(HWindow, hDC);
        /* Send modem dial command */
        WriteComm(CPort, "ATDT ", 5);
        /* Send the phone number */
        WriteComm(CPort, PhoneNumber, lstrlen(PhoneNumber));
        /* End the line */
        WriteComm(CPort, "\r", 1);
        /* Get out of the dialog */
}


/* Handle the hang up command */
void TMyWindow::HangUp(RTMessage)
{
        /* Get the modem's attention */
        WriteComm(CPort, "+++", 3);
        /* Wait */
        MessageBeep(0);
        /* Send the hang up command */
        WriteComm(CPort, "AT HO\r", 6);
}


/* Handle serial port errors */
void TMyWindow::SerError(RTMessage Msg)
{
        HDC hDC;
        char TmpStr[80];

        /* Display the error code in the window */
        hDC = GetDC(HWindow);
```

```
            wsprintf(TmpStr, "Serial error: %x", Msg.WParam);
            TextOut(hDC, 10, 50, TmpStr, lstrlen(TmpStr));
            ReleaseDC(HWindow, hDC);
}


/* Handle serial data */
void TMyWindow::SerData(RTMessage Msg)
{
        HDC hDC;

        /* Display the data received in the window */
        hDC = GetDC(HWindow);
        TextOut(hDC, 10, 30, "Serial data: ", 13);
        TextOut(hDC, 100, 30, (LPSTR) Msg.LParam, Msg.WParam);
        ReleaseDC(HWindow, hDC);
}


/* Define the application object */
class TModemApp : public TApplication
{
        public:
                TModemApp(LPSTR ApName, HINSTANCE Inst, HINSTANCE PrevInst
                    , LPSTR CmdLine, int CmdShow) : TApplication(ApName
                    , Inst, PrevInst, CmdLine, CmdShow) {};
                virtual void InitMainWindow();
                virtual void IdleAction();
};


/* Create the main window object */
void TModemApp::InitMainWindow()
{
        MainWindow = new TMyWindow(NULL, "Modem");
}


/* See if there is any data available */
void TModemApp::IdleAction()
{
        int Ret;
        char Buffer[80];
        int Port;
        COMSTAT ComStat;

        Port = ((TMyWindow *) MainWindow)->CPort;
        if(Port >= 0)
        {
            /* Read any available data */
            Ret = ReadComm(Port, Buffer, 80);
            /* Check for errors */
            if(Ret < 0)
            {
                /* Get the comport error */
                Ret = GetCommError(Port, &ComStat);
                /* Send it to the main window */
                PostMessage(MainWindow->HWindow, UM_ERROR, Ret, NULL);
                /* Get the number of characters */
                Ret = -Ret;
            }
            /* If there is data, send it to the main window */
```

```
                if(Ret)
                        PostMessage(MainWindow->HWindow, UM_DATA, Ret, (long) Buffer);
        }
}

/* Program entry point */
int PASCAL
WinMain(HINSTANCE Inst, HINSTANCE PrevInst
        , LPSTR CmdLine, int CmdShow)
{
        TModemApp TheApp("", Inst, PrevInst, CmdLine, CmdShow);

        TheApp.Run();
        return TheApp.Status;
}
```

3. Use the Resource Workshop to create the resource file MODEM.RES, include this menu:

```
MODEMMENU MENU
BEGIN
        POPUP "Modem"
        BEGIN
                MENUITEM "&Dial...", 101
                MENUITEM "&Hangup", 102
        END

END
```

Also include this dialog:

```
PHONENUMBER DIALOG 18, 18, 142, 67
STYLE DS_MODALFRAME | WS_POPUP | WS_CAPTION | WS_SYSMENU
CAPTION "Phone number"
BEGIN
        CONTROL "Enter number", -1, "STATIC", SS_LEFT | WS_CHILD | WS_VISIBLE | WS_GROUP
                , 7, 11, 50, 8
        CONTROL "", 101, "EDIT", ES_LEFT | WS_CHILD | WS_VISIBLE | WS_BORDER | WS_TABSTOP
                , 16, 22, 115, 12
        CONTROL "Ok", 1, "BUTTON", BS_DEFPUSHBUTTON | WS_CHILD | WS_VISIBLE | WS_TABSTOP
                , 20, 46, 40, 13
        CONTROL "Cancel", 2, "BUTTON", BS_PUSHBUTTON | WS_CHILD | WS_VISIBLE | WS_TABSTOP
                , 85, 46, 40, 13
END
```

4. Connect a Hayes-compatible modem to the serial port of the computer (or use an internal modem). If the modem is not on COM1, change the OpenComm statement in the SetupWindow function to open the correct communications port. If your modem cannot handle data at 2,400 baud, you must change the baud rate in the SetupWindow function.

5. Use the *Run* command to compile and run the program.

HOW IT WORKS

The main window object of this program includes the member functions SetupWindow and CloseWindow. It uses these functions to open and close the serial port. When the program opens the port, it stores the ID of that port in the member variable CPort. After opening the communications port, SetupWindow gets the default parameters into a DCB, and then changes the baud rate, word size, parity, and stop bits in the DCB. SetupWindow sends this modified DCB to the port with the SetCommState function.

The program uses the PhoneDlg object to display a dialog box that gets a phone number from the user. This dialog object uses the transfer mechanism (see How-To 3.4) to copy the phone number from the dialog box to the main window member PhoneNumber. The main window routine DialPhone, which brings up the dialog box, also sends the dial command and the phone number to the serial port.

The main window function HangUp also sends data to the serial port. This data tells the modem to hang up the phone line.

The TApplication object's member function IdleAction checks for data from the serial port. The first step is to call ReadComm to see if any data is ready and if so read it. The return value of ReadComm tells what happened. If the return value is 0, there is no data ready. If the return value is less than zero, there is data but there was an error. In this case, IdleAction calls GetCommError to get the error and clear the device driver's error flag. Then it posts a message for the main window, telling it that an error occurred.

If the return value from ReadComm is greater than zero, then it is the number of characters received. In this case IdleAction posts a message for the main window telling it about the data received. This message goes to the main window function SerData. IdleAction passes the address of the data in the LParam member of the message. SerData prints this data in the main window. Note that each time the program gets data, it overwrites the data that is already displayed.

COMMENT

This program just gives the general idea of a serial program. You can use it as the basis for programs such as file transfer programs, terminal emulators, or programs to exchange data and commands with other computers. To make these programs, you can add code to the SerData function that handles the data as it comes in. Your program will send data as the result of menu commands, keyboard actions, and the data received.

5.5 How Do I...
Use the Sound Interface?

Complexity: DIFFICULT

PROBLEM

Windows 3.0 with Multimedia Extensions and all versions of Windows 3.1 include sophisticated routines for generating sounds using optional sound interfaces. Becasue these interfaces are not typical PC devices, you would have to get detailed information from the interface manufacturer to program the device without Windows. Once you got the program working, it would not work with boards from other manufacturers. Using the Windows sound routines gives you a way to add sound to your programs that works with any sound board that includes a Windows sound driver. This solution shows you how to use the sound driver.

TECHNIQUE

Windows includes a group of functions that let you send commands to the *Media Control Interface* (MCI). This interface handles multimedia devices such as CD players, sound boards, and MIDI interfaces. This solution shows the commands that you can send to control wave forms on the sound board. The wave form commands let you record, play, edit, and store wave forms.

MCI can accept commands as strings or command numbers. This solution uses the command string interface. The MCI function mciSendString sends a command to the interface. The first step is to send a command that tells the interface to open a sound device. The MCI command for this is open. You must tell the open command what device to open, the type of device, and the size of the wave form buffer. Here is a typical open command:

```
mciSendString("open new type waveaudio alias sounder buffer 4");
```

This command tells MCI to open a new device whose type is waveaudio (a sound device). The rest of the program refers to the device by the alias sounder and the buffer holds four seconds of sound. Each second of sound for the buffer uses about 11K of memory with the default settings.

When the device is open, you can send commands to it. Table 5-6 lists the commands that are available.

A wave form is a block of data that contains values that give the position of the speaker cone at various times. By moving the speaker back and forth, the sound

COMMAND	DESCRIPTION
capability	Return information about what the device can do.
close	Finished using the device.
cue	Get ready to play or record. This command can improve performance.
delete	Remove part of the sound in the buffer.
info	Get information about the device.
open	Prepare the device for use.
pause	Waits for a resume before continuing to play or record.
play	Begin playing.
record	Begin recording.
resume	Resume playing or recording after a pause.
save	Copy the sound to a file.
seek	Go to a specified position in the sound.
set	Set parameters for the device.
status	Get parameters from the device.
stop	Stop playing or recording.

Table 5-6 MCI Sound Device Commands

board makes sounds. When recording a wave form, the sound board gets a value for the wave form at a specified interval, this is called a sample. You can set the rate at which the board samples and the number of bits used to store the sampled value.

The sample rate should always be twice the highest frequency in the sound wave. Lower sampling rates can distort the wave form due to a problem known as *aliasing*. Figure 5-6 shows how aliasing can distort a wave form.

For normal recording and playback, the default settings are fine. The record command starts recording and continues until the buffer allocated in the open command is full or the program issues a stop or pause command. All MCI commands work in the background. For example, after sending a record command, your program resumes immediately, but the recording continues without interruption.

If you need to know when an MCI command is finished, you can add the command notify to the MCI command string and specify a handle to the window that should be notified. In this case, the driver sends an MM_MCINOTI-FY message to the window when the command is finished. The WParam

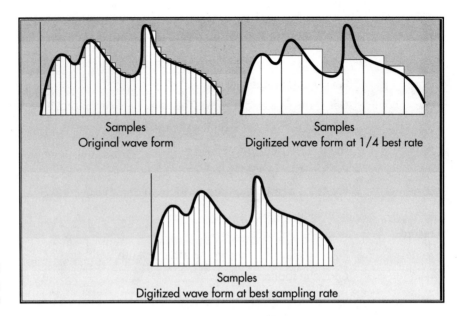

Figure 5-6
Aliasing

Samples
Original wave form

Samples
Digitized wave form at 1/4 best rate

Samples
Digitized wave form at best sampling rate

member of the message object tells how the command terminated. Table 5-7 lists the possible values.

After recording a wave form, you can play it back with the play command. This command accepts arguments specifying the portion of the wave form to play. This command plays the wave form from 128 milliseconds into the buffer to 321 milliseconds into the buffer:

```
mciSendString("play sounder from 128 to 321");
```

If you do not specify the beginning and end points, the play command plays from the current position to the end of the wave form.

WPARAM	DESCRIPTION
MCI_NOTIFY_SUCCESSFUL	The command completed successfully.
MCI_NOTIFY_SUPERSEDED	Another command was issued before the current command finished.
MCI_NOTIFY_ABORTED	The parameters have been changed and the command cannot continue.
MCI_NOTIFY_FAILURE	The device driver detected a hardware error.

Table 5-7 MCI Notification Messages

FLAG	DESCRIPTION
SND_SYNC	Do not return until finished playing the sound.
SND_ASYNC	Return immediately and play the sound in the background.
SND_NODEFAULT	Do not beep if the sound does not exist.
SND_MEMORY	Play a wave form in memory. In this case the file name argument is a pointer to the wave form.
SND_LOOP	Play the sound over and over. This option can only be used with SND_ASYNC so that you can stop the loop by calling sndPlaySound with the name set to NULL.
SND_NOSTOP	Return without playing the sound if there is already a sound playing.

Table 5-8 sndPlaySound Flags

When you get a wave form in memory that you like, you can save it to disk with the save command. This command saves the wave form to the file ASOUND.WAV:

```
mciSendString("save sounder asound.wav");
```

Playing a sound that is saved in a disk file is easy, just use the sndPlaySound function. The arguments to this function are the name of the wave form file and a flag word. Table 5-8 lists the possible flags.

The program in this solution shows you how to use sndPlaySound to play a wave form file. It also shows how to use the MCI string commands to record and play a wave form.

STEPS

1. Create a new project file called SOUNDER.PRJ that includes the files SOUNDER.CPP, SOUNDER.RES, and STANDARD.DEF.

2. Create the source file SOUNDER.CPP with this program:

```
/* SOUNDER a program to record and play sounds */
#include <owl.h>
#include "mmsystem.h"

#define MID_WAVE        101
#define MID_RECORD      102
#define MID_PLAY        103

/* Definition of the main window object */
class TMyWindow : public TWindow
{
    public:
        TMyWindow(PTWindowsObject AParent, LPSTR ATitle);
```

```
                virtual void SetupWindow();
                virtual void CloseWindow();
                /* Menu command handlers */
                virtual void PlayWave(RTMessage) = [CM_FIRST + MID_WAVE];
                virtual void Recorder(RTMessage) = [CM_FIRST + MID_RECORD];
                virtual void MemoryWave(RTMessage) = [CM_FIRST + MID_PLAY];
};

/* Main window constructor */
TMyWindow::TMyWindow(PTWindowsObject AParent, LPSTR ATitle)
        : TWindow(AParent, ATitle)
{
        AssignMenu("SoundMenu");
}

/* Open the wave form device */
void TMyWindow::SetupWindow()
{
        char TmpStr[80];

        /* Open the wave form device */
        if(mciSendString("open new type waveaudio alias sounder buffer 4"
                , TmpStr, 80, NULL))
                MessageBeep(0);
        else if(mciSendString( // Set the time format
                "set sounder time format milliseconds"
                , TmpStr, 80, NULL))
                MessageBeep(0);

}

/* Close the wave form device */
void TMyWindow::CloseWindow()
{
        mciSendString("close sounder", NULL, 0, NULL);
}

/* Play a wave form */
void
TMyWindow::PlayWave(RTMessage)
{
        sndPlaySound("d:\\windows\\CHIME.WAV", SND_SYNC);
}

/* Record a wave */
void
TMyWindow::Recorder(RTMessage)
{
        char TmpStr[80];
        HDC hDC;
        DWORD Ret;

        /* Start recording */
        if((Ret = mciSendString("record sounder", TmpStr, 80, NULL)) != 0)
        {
                /* If an error, display the error code */
                hDC = GetDC(HWindow);
```

```
            wsprintf(TmpStr, "Error: %d", (Ret&0xFFFF));
            TextOut(hDC, 10, 10, TmpStr, lstrlen(TmpStr));
            ReleaseDC(HWindow, hDC);
            MessageBeep(0);
    }
}

/* Play the wave form in memory */
void
TMyWindow::MemoryWave(RTMessage)
{
    mciSendString("play sounder from 1", NULL, 0, NULL);
}

/* definition for the application object */
class TFirstApp : public TApplication
{
    public:
        TFirstApp(LPSTR ApName, HINSTANCE Inst
                , HINSTANCE PrevInst
                , LPSTR CmdLine, int CmdShow) : TApplication(ApName
                , Inst, PrevInst, CmdLine, CmdShow) {};
        virtual void InitMainWindow();
};

/* Initialize the main window */
void TFirstApp::InitMainWindow()
{
    MainWindow = new TMyWindow(NULL, "Sounder");
}


/* Entry point for the program */
int PASCAL WinMain(HINSTANCE Inst, HINSTANCE PrevInst, LPSTR CmdLine
    , int CmdShow)
{
    /* Create the application object */
    TFirstApp FirstApp("", Inst
        , PrevInst, CmdLine, CmdShow);

    /* Run the application */
    FirstApp.Run();
    return FirstApp.Status;
}
```

3. Create a resource file called SOUNDER.RES that includes this menu:

```
SOUNDMENU MENU
BEGIN
    POPUP "Sounds"
    BEGIN
        MENUITEM "&Play wave file", 101
        MENUITEM "&Record wave", 102
        MENUITEM "Play &wave", 103
    END
END
```

4. Use the *Run* command to compile and run the program.

HOW IT WORKS

The second include file in this program, MMSYSTEM.H, contains the function prototypes and constant definitions for the Windows multimedia extensions.

The main window object class TMyWindow defines SetupWindow and CloseWindow member functions. The program uses these functions to open and close the wave form device. Both of these functions use the mciSendString function to send commands to the device driver. The SetupWindow member function sends an open command that opens the device and allocates a four second buffer. The second MCI command sets the time format for the device to milliseconds. After this command, any commands that specify a location in the wave form must give the position in milliseconds from the beginning of the wave form.

The main window class also includes indexed member functions for the three menu commands. The member function PlayWave uses the function sndPlaySound to play the wave form file CHIME.WAV. If you do not have this file, change the file name to the name of a file that you do have.

The member function Recorder uses the MCI record command to begin recording the wave form. Recording continues for four seconds. If there is a problem with the record command, the program prints the error code in the main window.

The last member function is MemoryWave, which plays the recorded wave form. This function sends a command that plays from the first millisecond of the wave form through to the end.

COMMENT

The multimedia extensions to Windows include many more commands than can be fully described here. One source of information about these functions is the help files that come with Borland C++ and Turbo C++ 3.1. To view these files, click the help command from the program manager. Then, select the open command from the file menu in the help window. Next, navigate to the BIN directory in the Borland C++ directories. The files with multimedia information are: WIN31MWH.HLP and MCISTRWH.HLP.

These files describe all of the functions and commands in the multimedia extensions. This information should get you started. For more complete information, you will have to get the *Multimedia Programmer's Reference* and the *Multimedia Programmer's Guide* from Microsoft.

5.6 How Do I...
Handle the Printer?

Complexity: DIFFICULT

PROBLEM

In Windows applications, just about anything you can display in a window on the screen you can draw on paper. Windows handles many of the messy details such as how to select fonts for the printer, issuing graphics commands, and moving the paper. Printing in Windows is not easy; but once you do it, it works for any printer that has a Windows device driver. This solution makes printing easier by showing you step by step how to print.

TECHNIQUE

Before you can print from a Windows application, you have to open a device context for the printer. In many of the previous examples, the programs use device contexts to draw on the screen. The printer device context works in much the same way. You use the same functions for drawing on the printed page that you use for drawing on the screen. For example, to print text you use TextOut just as you have in some of the previous examples in this book.

The Windows function that gets a printer device context is CreateDC. You pass this function the name of the device driver to use, the name of the device in that driver, the port that the printer is connected to, and an optional structure containing setup information. Before you can call CreateDC, you have to look up the correct names for the printer.

The names that CreateDC requires are stored in the Windows WIN.INI file. This file contains configuration information used by Windows. The file is divided into sections for each application that uses the file. The name of the application is at the beginning of the section and enclosed in square brackets. The printer information is in the windows section whose first line looks like this:

```
[windows]
```

The section contains several strings that have a key name followed by an equal sign (=), and a value for the key. The key name for the printer information is device. A typical printer entry looks like this:

```
device=HP DeskJet 500,HPDSKJET,LPT1:
```

The device statement has three parts that are the device name, driver name, and port name. That is all of the information you need to use the CreateDC function to get a device context for printing. All you have to do is locate and open the WIN.INI file, read line by line until you find the line with [windows], continue reading until you find device=, and then read and parse the rest of the line.

Windows includes the function GetProfileString to simplify the task of getting information from the WIN.INI file. This statement shows how to use this function to get the printer information:

```
GetProfileString("windows", "device", ",,,", PrinterInfo, 80);
```

The first argument to GetProfileString is the application name. The next argument is the key name. Next is a default string to use if the key is not in the section. The last two arguments are the string to put the information in and the number of characters that fit in that string. All that is left for you to do is get the three pieces out of the string.

Most programs let the user set some printer parameters by using a printer setup dialog box. This dialog is part of the printer device driver so all your program has to do is call the function that brings up the dialog. The procedure for this is the same as for Dynamic Link Libraries (DLL). To load the printer driver, you must add .DRV to the driver name from the WIN.INI file and pass the result to the Windows LoadLibrary function (see How-To 3.8). Then, use the Windows function GetProcAddress to get the address of a function called DEVICEMODE. Finally, call this function with the handle to the main window, the instance of the library (from LoadLibrary), the device name, and the port name. The program in this solution illustrates this technique.

Printers have to do things that the screen does not have to do. For example, you must eject the paper when finished printing. Windows includes the Escape function to let you send special commands to a device, such as "go to the next page." Each driver supports different escape commands depending on the capabilities of the device, but all printer devices must support the escape commands in Table 5-9.

Before a program can print anything, it must send a STARTDOC escape to the printer device. This tells the driver to set up for printing a document. Now the program can use Windows functions to draw on the device. When the program fills a page, it sends a NEWFRAME escape to eject the page and start the next page. After printing all of the pages, the program sends an ENDDOC escape to tell the driver there is no more data coming for this document. The print spooler uses the ENDDOC escape to indicate that it is OK to begin printing a document from another application.

COMMAND	DESCRIPTION
ABORTDOC	Stops printer no matter what escapes have been given.
ENDDOC	Marks the end of the current document.
NEWFRAME	Go to the next page.
NEXTBAND	Go to the next band.
QUERYESCAPESUPPORT	See if an escape is supported.
SETABORTPROC	Indicate the function to call in case of an error.
STARTDOC	Begin a document.

Table 5-9 Printer Escape Commands

Some printers cannot move the paper backwards so you have to print from the top of the page down to the bottom. If your application prints forms or graphics, you must sort the commands so that they print from top to bottom. Windows programs do not have to worry about this due to a feature called banding. Instead of sending each print command directly to the printer, the driver saves the print command in a metafile (see How-To 6.4). When the program sends a NEXTFRAME escape, the driver executes all of the commands in the metafile, but it clips the output to a band at the top of the printed page. Then, the driver replays the metafile clipping to the next band of the page. The driver repeats this procedure until the entire page is printed.

Although this procedure works for all printers that have a properly written device driver, it is not the most efficient way to print. If you could tell the driver that you have sent it all of the commands that affect the current band, the driver would not have to replay those commands over and over as it prints the page. The NEXTBAND escape tells the driver to print all of the graphics commands received so far and move to the next band. This can have a dramatic effect on performance.

Windows uses a spooler called Print Manager to hold the data that gets sent to the printer so that your program does not have to wait for the printer to finish before it can continue. The only thing your program has to wait for is the driver to process the printer commands. This works well until the driver runs out of memory to hold the metafile or the spool file fills the disk. When this happens, the NEXTFRAME command returns an error. Of course, the spool file will eventually empty by sending the data to the printer, and you can continue printing.

If your program goes into a loop waiting for the spool file to empty, the program cannot receive any messages from Windows so it appears to be hung.

Printer drivers give you an alternative by letting you specify a function to call before returning an error. You can make this function process messages so that Windows can function normally while the spool file is being emptied.

The program in this solution uses the techniques described above to add printing capabilities to the editor described in How-To 5.1. Although this is only a simple example of printing text, the same principles can be used to draw graphics on the page by replacing the TextOut function calls with the required graphics functions.

STEPS

1. Create a new project called PRNEDIT.PRJ with the files PRNEDIT.CPP, PRNEDIT.RES, and STANDARD.RES.

2. Create the source file PRNEDIT.CPP with this program:

```
/* PRNEDIT an editor with printing */
#include <owl.h>
#include <filewnd.h>

#define MID_PRINT     101
#define MID_SETUP     102

/* Definition of the editor object */
class TMyEditor : public TFileWindow
{
     public:
          char Device[40];      // Printer device name
          char Driver[40];      // Printer driver name
          char Port[15];        // Printer port name
          TMyEditor(LPSTR Title, LPSTR File);
          virtual void SetupWindow();
          /* Handle print menu commands */
          virtual void PrintIt(RTMessage) = [CM_FIRST+MID_PRINT];
          virtual void PrnSetup(RTMessage) = [CM_FIRST+MID_SETUP];
};

/* Get the menu from the resource file */
TMyEditor::TMyEditor(LPSTR Title, LPSTR File)
     : TFileWindow(NULL, Title, File)
{
     AssignMenu("TextMenu");
}

/* Get the printer information from the INI file */
void TMyEditor::SetupWindow()
{
     char TmpStr[80];
     char *Src, *Dst;

     /* Get the printer string from the WIN.INI file */
     GetProfileString("windows", "device", ",,,", TmpStr, 80);
     /* Copy the information to the main window object */
     Src = TmpStr;
```

```
      /* Get the device name */
      Dst = Device;
      while(*Src && *Src != ',')
            *Dst++ = *Src++;
      *Dst = '\0';
      if(*Src)
            ++Src;          // Skip the comma
      /* Get the driver name */
      Dst = Driver;
      while(*Src && *Src != ',' && *Src != ' ')
            *Dst++ = *Src++;
      *Dst = '\0';
      if(*Src)
            ++Src;
      /* Get the port name */
      Dst = Port;
      while(*Src)
            *Dst++ = *Src++;
      *Dst = '\0';
      TFileWindow::SetupWindow();
}


/* Abort proc for printing */
BOOL FAR PASCAL AbortProc(HDC, short)
{
      MSG msg;

      /* Handle any messages pending */
      while(PeekMessage(&msg, NULL, 0, 0, PM_REMOVE))
            DispatchMessage(&msg);
      return TRUE;
}

/* Print the text being edited */
void TMyEditor::PrintIt(RTMessage)
{
      HDC PrnDC;
      int Height, Width;
      int LineCount, i;
      char TextLine[200];
      int LineLen;
      int PrintedHeight;
      union {
            struct {
                  WORD LineWidth;
                  WORD LineHeight;
            } Ex;
            long Extent;
      };
      FARPROC AbortInst;


      /* Make a printer device context */
      PrnDC = CreateDC(Driver, Device, Port, NULL);
      /* Get the size of a page */
      Height = GetDeviceCaps(PrnDC, VERTRES);
      Width = GetDeviceCaps(PrnDC, HORZRES);
      /* Don't allow i/o in the window */
```

```
      EnableWindow(HWindow, FALSE);
      /* Set up the abort proc */
      AbortInst = MakeProcInstance((FARPROC) AbortProc
          , GetApplication()->hInstance);
      Escape(PrnDC, SETABORTPROC, 0, (LPSTR) AbortInst, NULL);
      /* Mark the beginning of a document */
      Escape(PrnDC, STARTDOC, 12, "Print editor", NULL);
      /* See how many lines to print */
      LineCount = Editor->GetNumLines();
      /* Keep track of the amount of the page used */
      PrintedHeight = 0;
      for(i=0; i<LineCount; ++i)
      {
          /* Get a line of text */
          if(Editor->GetLine(TextLine, 200, i))
          {
              LineLen = lstrlen(TextLine);
              /* Get the size of the line */
              Extent = GetTextExtent(PrnDC, TextLine, LineLen);
          }
          else  /* blank line */
          {
              LineLen = 0;
              Extent = GetTextExtent(PrnDC, "W", 1);
          }
          /* While the line is too long */
          while(Ex.LineWidth > Width)
          {
              /* Remove a character from the end of the line */
              TextLine[--LineLen] = '\0';
              Extent = GetTextExtent(PrnDC, TextLine, LineLen);
          }
          /* See if at the end of the page */
          if(PrintedHeight + Ex.LineHeight > Height)
          {
              Escape(PrnDC, NEWFRAME, 0, NULL, NULL);
              PrintedHeight = 0;
          }
          /* Print the line */
          if(LineLen)
              TextOut(PrnDC, 0, PrintedHeight, TextLine, LineLen);
          PrintedHeight += Ex.LineHeight;
      }
      /* Finish printing */
      Escape(PrnDC, NEWFRAME, 0, NULL, NULL);
      Escape(PrnDC, ENDDOC, 0, NULL, NULL);
      /* Release the abort proc */
      FreeProcInstance(AbortInst);
      /* Allow i/o in the window */
      EnableWindow(HWindow, TRUE);
      /* Get rid of the printer device context */
      DeleteDC(PrnDC);
}

/* Set up the printer */
void TMyEditor::PrnSetup(RTMessage)
{
```

```
    HINSTANCE DevDriver;
    char TmpStr[20];
   'void (far pascal *DevMode)(HWND, HANDLE, LPSTR, LPSTR);

    /* Make the driver name */
    lstrcpy(TmpStr, Driver);
    lstrcat(TmpStr, ".DRV");
    /* Load the driver */
    DevDriver = LoadLibrary(TmpStr);
    /* See if the load worked */
    if((int) DevDriver >= 32)
    {
        /* Get the address of the device mode function */
        (FARPROC) DevMode = GetProcAddress(DevDriver, "DEVICEMODE");
        /* Call the device mode function */
        (*DevMode)(HWindow, DevDriver, Device, Port);
        /* Release the library */
        FreeLibrary(DevDriver);
    }
}


/* definition for the application object */
class TFirstApp : public TApplication
{
    public:
        TFirstApp(LPSTR ApName, HINSTANCE Inst
            , HINSTANCE PrevInst
            , LPSTR CmdLine, int CmdShow) : TApplication(ApName
            , Inst, PrevInst, CmdLine, CmdShow) {};
        virtual void InitMainWindow();
};

/* Initialize the main window */
void TFirstApp::InitMainWindow()
{
    /* Allocate memory for the main window object and put the pointer into the
    application object */
    MainWindow = new TMyEditor("Text editor", "");
}

/* Entry point for the program */
int PASCAL WinMain(HINSTANCE Inst, HINSTANCE PrevInst, LPSTR CmdLine
    , int CmdShow)
{
    /* Create the application object */
    TFirstApp FirstApp("", Inst
        , PrevInst, CmdLine, CmdShow);

    /* Run the application */
    FirstApp.Run();
    return FirstApp.Status;
}
```

3. Copy the resource file EDITFILE.RES from How-To 5.1 to the file PRNEDIT.RES. Then change the menu to this:

```
TEXTMENU MENU
```

```
BEGIN
    POPUP "&File"
    BEGIN
        MENUITEM "&New file", 24329
        MENUITEM "&Open file...", 24330
        MENUITEM SEPARATOR,
        MENUITEM "&Save file", 24333
        MENUITEM "Save &as...", 24334
        MENUITEM SEPARATOR,
        MENUITEM "&Print", 101
        MENUITEM "Printer se&tup", 102
        MENUITEM SEPARATOR,
        MENUITEM "&Exit", 24340
    END

    POPUP "&Edit"
    BEGIN
        MENUITEM "&Undo", 24325
        MENUITEM SEPARATOR,
        MENUITEM "Cu&t", 24320
        MENUITEM "&Copy", 24321
        MENUITEM "&Paste", 24322
        MENUITEM SEPARATOR,
        MENUITEM "&Delete", 24323
        MENUITEM "C&lear", 24324
        MENUITEM SEPARATOR,
        MENUITEM "&Find", 24326
        MENUITEM "&Replace", 24327
        MENUITEM "Find &next", 24328
    END

END
```

4. Use the *Run* command to compile and run the program.

HOW IT WORKS

This program is the same as the editor program in How-To 5.1 with two message response member functions added to handle the two printer menu commands. This program also has some new code in the SetupWindow member function to get the printer information from the WIN.INI file. The program uses the GetProfileString function to get the printer information, then it copies the parts of the string to the data members Device, Driver, and Port. The program moves the pointer variable Src through the information string, copying each character to the position indicated by the pointer variable Dst. When Src points to a comma, Dst is changed to point to the next data member.

The member function PrnSetup brings up the setup dialog from the printer device driver. The first thing it does is add the .DRV extension to the driver name and put the result in TmpStr. The function uses this name as an argument to the Windows function LoadLibrary, which returns the instance handle of the library. If the handle is less than 32, it is actually an error and this program ignores it. Otherwise, PrnSetup calls the Windows function GetProcAddress to get the address of the function DEVICEMODE in the driver. Then PrnSetup calls DEVICEMODE, which displays the dialog. When DEVICEMODE returns, PrnSetup frees the device driver.

The member function PrintIt prints the text from the main window. The first step is to create a device context for the printer using the CreateDC function. The arguments for this function come from the member variables that were set up in the SetupWindow function. Next PrintIt gets the dimensions of the printable area by calling the Windows function GetDeviceCaps.

The PrintIt function sets up a function to handle errors during printing. The first step is to disable the main window so that the user cannot enter another print command. Next, the function gets an instance of the function AbortProc, which will handle errors. Then, PrintIt passes the instance to the printer device driver by sending it a SETABORTPROC escape. The AbortProc function calls the Windows function PeekMessage to see if there are any messages to process. If so, the function calls DispatchMessage to handle the message. Then, it returns TRUE to the device driver indicating that the driver should try again.

Before printing, PrintIt sends a STARTDOC escape to the device driver. Then it gets the number of lines of text in the window by calling the member function GetNumLines. This number is the end limit of a for loop that prints each line from the window. The for loop begins by getting a line from the window. Then, it passes the line to the Windows function GetTextExtent which returns the height and width of the line in pixels. If the line is too long to fit on a page, the program removes characters from the line, one at a time, until the line is short enough to fit.

The next step is to see if the page is full. The variable PrintedHeight accumulates the total height of the printed lines. When this value is larger than a piece of paper, the program sends a NEWFRAME escape to go to the next page. Finally, the program prints the line of text by calling TextOut.

When PrintIt has printed all of the lines in the window, it sends a final NEWFRAME escape to eject the last page. Then it sends an ENDDOC escape to mark the end of the document. The clean-up steps free the instance for the AbortProc function, re-enable the main window, and get rid of the printer device context.

Graphics 6

6

Graphics is the key to the Windows interface, as the name *Graphical User Interface* (GUI) implies. Windows dedicates many functions to giving powerful graphical functions to applications. Windows refers to this group of functions as the *Graphical Device Interface* (GDI). As with many Windows systems, the power of the GDI comes at the cost of ease of use. You need a native guide to show you the way through the hundreds of functions that are available. This chapter cuts through the jungle and shows you how to do some of the common tasks required in applications.

6.1 Draw in a Window

Windows uses a number of metaphors to describe how to draw on the screen. For example, Windows draws lines using an object called a pen. Like real pens, Windows pens come in different colors and widths. Windows also uses brushes to fill areas. Like real brushes, Windows brushes can paint different colors. Both pens and brushes in Windows can do more than real pens and brushes. Pens can draw segmented lines and brushes can draw simple patterns. This solution shows what you can do with pens and brushes to draw in a window.

6.2 Draw Different Shapes

Many graphics libraries help you draw by providing several basic shapes that you can draw with a single function call. The Windows GDI includes several functions for drawing shapes such as rectangles and ellipses. There are also variations on these basic shapes that let you draw arcs and pie slices. This solution shows you how to draw each of the basic shapes available with Windows.

6.3 Use Bitmaps

Some images cannot be easily drawn with lines and curves because they are too detailed. For example, a picture of an airplane requires more lines and curves than are practical to draw with a program. In this case, you can use bitmaps, which are arrays of pixels, to draw the airplane. The Resource Workshop makes it easy to add bitmaps to programs by providing a sophisticated bitmap editor. These bitmaps are stored with other resources for the program. Some of the previous programs have used bitmaps for things such as menu items. This solution shows how to get information about a bitmap and display the bitmap on the screen.

6.4 Use Fonts

Windows programs are not limited to one kind of text. They can display bold or italics, proportional or monospaced, and fancy or plain characters. Starting with version 3.1, TrueType fonts let you display characters at any size. All of this capability comes from the font functions of Windows. This solution shows you how to find out what fonts are available and select the font to use.

6.5 Use Metafiles

When you draw in a window, you should save all the drawing commands so that you can re-create the drawing when you get a WM_PAINT message. Windows sends this message to an application when something happens that affects the window display. Your program must be ready to respond to this message by repainting the window.

One way to handle this problem is to let Windows keep track of the graphics commands used. Windows saves the information in a memory structure called a metafile. When you need to re-create the graphics, just play the metafile and Windows does the rest. This solution shows you how.

6.6 Use the Color Palette

Many video interfaces can display many different colors, but only a few at a time. These interfaces put the currently selected colors in a palette from which programs select the colors that appear on the screen. If you change the palette, the colors on the screen change automatically. This is fine if the program that is changing the palette is the only one displaying things on the screen. In the Windows environment, letting any one program change the palette interferes with all the other programs being displayed.

Windows handles this problem by keeping total control of the palette. If a program needs to change the palette, it must ask Windows, which checks the available palette entries. If there is an available entry, Windows lets the program change it. If not, Windows tells the program to use the closest color in the current palette. Windows requires the cooperation of all applications to implement this system. This solution shows you how the system works.

6.1 How Do I...
Draw in a Window?

Complexity: EASY

PROBLEM

Before you can make full use of the GDI, you need to learn a few basics. For example, when a Windows program draws a line, it uses an object called a pen. When the program fills an area, it uses a brush. Both of these objects have drawing styles and a color. This solution shows what pens and brushes are and how to use them.

TECHNIQUE

The first thing you have to do before drawing in a window is to get a device context for the Window. Many of the previous solutions used the GetDC function to get a device context so they could write text. The same procedure works for

PARAMETER	SETTING
Background color	White
Background mode	OPAQUE
Brush	WHITE_BRUSH
Brush origin	(0,0)
Character spacing	0
Clipping region	Client area
Color palette	DEFAULT_PALETTE
Font	SYSTEM_FONT
Mapping mode	MM_TEXT
Pen	BLACK_PEN
Pen position	(0,0)
Polygon fill mode	ALTERNATE
Text color	Black
Viewport extent	(1,1)
Viewport origin	(0,0)
Window extents	(1,1)
Window origin	(0,0)

Table 6-1 Device Context Defaults

graphics. The device context includes information about how to draw in the window. Table 6-1 shows the default settings for a new device context.

The default settings are fine for simple text or graphics, but if you want to add features like color to your graphics you must modify the applicable defaults. This solution shows how to use the brush, pen, and background defaults. To show the effects of these items, the program draws rectangles in the main window. When Windows draws a rectangle, it draws the border using the current pen settings and the interior with the current brush. Certain pens and brushes do not draw every pixel in the rectangle. Instead, they fill in gaps with the current background.

The first step in changing the current pen is to create a pen object. Note that this is a Windows object, not a C++ object. Windows refers to pens, bitmaps, and brushes. The term "object" in this case has nothing to do with object-oriented programming. The Windows function CreatePen creates a pen object and returns the handle to the pen. The next step is to select the pen for the device context with the Windows function SelectObject. Now any functions that use pens will use the new pen. When you are finished drawing, you must get rid of the pen with the Windows function DeleteObject to return the memory used by the pen object.

Pens have a style, width, and color. The style determines whether the pen draws a solid or dashed line. Figure 6-1 shows the possible pen styles. The width is the width of the line in logical units. The default logical unit is one pixel. You can change the size of logical units by calling the Windows function SetMappingMode. For example, you can set the mapping mode to MM_LO-ENGLISH to tell Windows that a logical unit is 0.01 inches. Using units other than pixels (mapping mode MM_TEXT) can affect performance because Windows must multiply each coordinate by a scaling factor.

Programs specify colors in Windows with a COLORREF variable. The COLORREF type is really an unsigned long that can have one of three formats depending on the value of the high byte. Figure 6-2 shows the three possible formats of a COLORREF value. If the high byte is 0, then the low three bytes are the red, green, and blue components of the color. Windows checks the video device driver to see if a matching color is available; if not, Windows creates a dithered color by putting pixels of different colors next to each other so that they appear to be the selected color.

If the high byte of a COLORREF value is one, then the low two bytes of the value are an index to the application's palette. Palettes are the list of colors that the application can use. How-To 6.6 shows how you can use palettes to change the available colors.

The last type of COLORREF value has a two in the high byte and red, green, and blue values in the low three bytes. The difference between this type and the first type is that this type looks for a matching color in the logical palette for the application while the first type gets its match from the default Windows palette. See How-To 6.6 for more information on palettes.

PS_SOLID	────────────
PS_DASH	─ ─ ─ ─ ─ ─ ─
PS_DOT	············
PS_DASHDOT	─ · ─ · ─ · ─
PS_DASHDOTDOT	─ ·· ─ ·· ─ ··
PS_NULL	
PS_INSIDEFRAME	────────────

Figure 6-1
Pen Styles

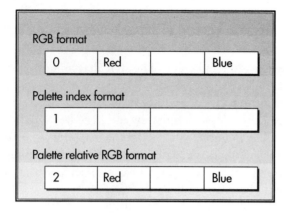

Figure 6-2
The Format of
a COLORREF
Value

Windows uses brushes to fill areas. For example, the program in How-To 2.2 changed the brush used to fill the background of the window. Brushes have a style and color. Depending on the style, brushes have a data field that tells what type of pattern to use. In addition to the predefined styles used in How-To 2.2, brushes can use bitmaps to define the pattern. The bitmap is copied over and over until the area is filled. Figure 6-3 shows how a simple pattern can be repeated to make a nice design.

Some of the styles for pens and brushes have gaps between the parts of the line or area drawn. What goes in the gaps depends on the background settings. The first setting is the background mode which can be OPAQUE or TRANSPARENT. If the mode is OPAQUE, then Windows fills the gaps with the current background color; otherwise, Windows does not draw in the gaps at all.

The program in this solution includes three dialogs that let you select attributes for pens, brushes, and the background. To show you the results of your selections, the program draws random rectangles in the main window.

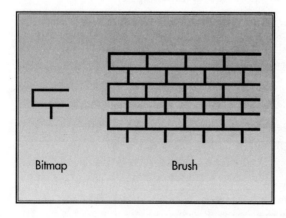

Figure 6-3
Bitmaps and
Brushes

STEPS

1. Create a new project file called DRAW.PRJ that includes the files DRAW.CPP, DRAW.RES, and STANDARD.DEF.

2. Create the source file DRAW.CPP with this program:

```
/* DRAW a program to use pens and brushes */
#include <owl.h>
#include <stdlib.h>
#include <time.h>
#include <radiobut.h>
#include <groupbox.h>
#include <edit.h>

#define MID_PEN         101
#define MID_BRUSH       102
#define MID_BACK        103


#define IDC_STYLES      102
#define IDC_THEGROUP    101
#define IDC_WIDTH       109
#define IDC_COLOR       110
#define IDC_THEGROUP2   111
#define IDC_HSTYLES     112


/* Definition of the main window */
class TMyWindow : public TWindow
{
     public:
          /* Information from the pen dialog */
          struct {
               WORD Style[7];
               char Width[10];
               char Color[10];
          } PenDlgData;
          /* Information from the brush dialog */
          struct {
               WORD Style[4];
               char Color[10];
               WORD HatchStyle[6];
          } BrushDlgData;
          /* Information from the background dialog */
          struct {
               WORD Mode[2];
               char Color[10];
          } BackDlgData;
          HBITMAP TheBitmap;      // Bitmap for brushes
          TMyWindow(PTWindowsObject AParent, LPSTR ATitle);
          virtual void SetupWindow();
          virtual void CloseWindow();
          /* Handle timer messages */
          virtual void WMTimer(RTMessage) = [WM_FIRST + WM_TIMER];
          /* Handle messages from the menu */
          virtual void ChangePen(RTMessage) = [CM_FIRST + MID_PEN];
          virtual void ChangeBrush(RTMessage) = [CM_FIRST + MID_BRUSH];
          virtual void ChangeBack(RTMessage) = [CM_FIRST + MID_BACK];
```

```
};

/* Pen information dialog */
class PenDlg : public TDialog
{
    public:
            PenDlg(PTWindowsObject AParent, LPSTR AResource);
};

/* Initialize the dialog controls and set up the transfer buffer */
PenDlg::PenDlg(PTWindowsObject AParent, LPSTR AResource)
    : TDialog(AParent, AResource)
{
    int i;
    PTGroupBox TheGroup;

    /* Initialize the controls */
    TheGroup = new TGroupBox(this, IDC_THEGROUP);
    for(i=0; i<7; i++)
        new TRadioButton(this, IDC_STYLES+i, TheGroup);
    new TEdit(this, IDC_WIDTH, 10);
    new TEdit(this, IDC_COLOR, 10);
    TransferBuffer = (void far *) &((TMyWindow *) Parent)->PenDlgData;
}

/* Brush information dialog */
class BrushDlg : public TDialog
{
    public:
            BrushDlg(PTWindowsObject AParent, LPSTR AResource);
};

/* Initialize the dialog controls and set up the transfer buffer */
BrushDlg::BrushDlg(PTWindowsObject AParent, LPSTR AResource)
    : TDialog(AParent, AResource)
{
    int i;
    PTGroupBox TheGroup;

    /* Initialize the controls */
    TheGroup = new TGroupBox(this, IDC_THEGROUP);
    for(i=0; i<4; ++i)
        new TRadioButton(this, IDC_STYLES+i, TheGroup);
    new TEdit(this, IDC_COLOR, 10);
    TheGroup = new TGroupBox(this, IDC_THEGROUP2);
    for(i=0; i<6; ++i)
        new TRadioButton(this, IDC_HSTYLES+i, TheGroup);
    TransferBuffer = (void far *) &((TMyWindow *) Parent)->BrushDlgData;
}

/* Background information dialog */
class BackDlg : public TDialog
{
    public:
            BackDlg(PTWindowsObject AParent, LPSTR AResource);
};
```

```
/* Initialize the dialog controls and set up the transfer buffer */
BackDlg::BackDlg(PTWindowsObject AParent, LPSTR AResource)
      : TDialog(AParent, AResource)
{

      int i;
      PTGroupBox TheGroup;

      /* Initialize the controls */
      TheGroup = new TGroupBox(this, IDC_THEGROUP);
      new TRadioButton(this, IDC_STYLES, TheGroup);
      new TRadioButton(this, IDC_STYLES+1, TheGroup);
      new TEdit(this, IDC_COLOR, 10);
      TransferBuffer = (void far *) &((TMyWindow *) Parent)->BackDlgData;
}


/* Initialize the menu and window data */
TMyWindow::TMyWindow(PTWindowsObject AParent, LPSTR ATitle)
      : TWindow(AParent, ATitle)
{

      int i;

      AssignMenu("DRAWMENU");
      /* Set the pen defaults */
      PenDlgData.Style[0] = 1;
      for(i=1; i<7; ++i)
            PenDlgData.Style[i] = 0;
      lstrcpy(PenDlgData.Width, "1");
      lstrcpy(PenDlgData.Color, "0");
      /* Set the brush defaults */
      BrushDlgData.Style[0] = 1;
      for(i=1; i<4; ++i)
            BrushDlgData.Style[i] = 0;
      lstrcpy(BrushDlgData.Color, "255");
      BrushDlgData.HatchStyle[0] = 1;
      for(i=1; i<6; ++i)
            BrushDlgData.HatchStyle[i] = 0;
      /* Set the background defaults */
      BackDlgData.Mode[0] = 1;
      BackDlgData.Mode[1] = 0;
      lstrcpy(BackDlgData.Color, "65280");
}

/* Set up program data */
void TMyWindow::SetupWindow()
{
      TWindow::SetupWindow();
      /* Give the random number generator a random seed */
      randomize();
      /* Load the bitmap for brushes */
      TheBitmap = LoadBitmap(GetModule()->hInstance, "BrushPict");
      /* Start a timer */
      SetTimer(HWindow, 1, 2000, NULL);
}


/* Clean up */
void TMyWindow::CloseWindow()
{
```

```
      /* Stop the timer */
      KillTimer(HWindow, 1);
      /* Get rid of the bitmap */
      DeleteObject(TheBitmap);
      TWindow::CloseWindow();
}

/* Draw a new rectangle */
void TMyWindow::WMTime(RTMessage)
{
      HDC hDC;                         // Device context handle
      RECT Rect;                       // Rectangle coordinates
      HPEN ThePen;                     // Handle to a pen
      int i;                           // Loop index
      int Width;                       // Pen width
      COLORREF Colr;                   // Pen color
      LOGBRUSH BrushInfo;              // Brush parameters
      HBRUSH TheBrush;                 // Handle to a brush

      /* Get the device context */
      hDC = GetDC(HWindow);
      /* Get the pen parameters */
      for(i=0; i<7 && !PenDlgData.Style[i]; ++i);
      Width = atoi(PenDlgData.Width);
      Colr = (COLORREF) atol(PenDlgData.Color);
      ThePen = CreatePen(i, Width, Colr);
      SelectObject(hDC, ThePen);
      /* Get the brush parameters */
      if(BrushDlgData.Style[0])
            BrushInfo.lbStyle = BS_HATCHED;
      else if(BrushDlgData.Style[1])
            BrushInfo.lbStyle = BS_HOLLOW;
      else if(BrushDlgData.Style[2])
            BrushInfo.lbStyle = BS_PATTERN;
      else if(BrushDlgData.Style[3])
            BrushInfo.lbStyle = BS_SOLID;
      BrushInfo.lbColor = (COLORREF) atol(BrushDlgData.Color);
      if(BrushInfo.lbStyle == BS_PATTERN)          // See if pattern
            BrushInfo.lbHatch = (int) TheBitmap;
      else if(BrushInfo.lbStyle == BS_HATCHED)     // See if hatched pattern
      {
            if(BrushDlgData.HatchStyle[0])
                  BrushInfo.lbHatch = HS_BDIAGONAL;
            else if(BrushDlgData.HatchStyle[1])
                  BrushInfo.lbHatch = HS_CROSS;
            else if(BrushDlgData.HatchStyle[2])
                  BrushInfo.lbHatch = HS_DIAGCROSS;
            else if(BrushDlgData.HatchStyle[3])
                  BrushInfo.lbHatch = HS_FDIAGONAL;
            else if(BrushDlgData.HatchStyle[4])
                  BrushInfo.lbHatch = HS_HORIZONTAL;
            else if(BrushDlgData.HatchStyle[5])
                  BrushInfo.lbHatch = HS_VERTICAL;
      }
      TheBrush = CreateBrushIndirect(&BrushInfo);
      SelectObject(hDC, TheBrush);
      /* Get the background parameters */
```

```
        if(BackDlgData.Mode[0])
              SetBkMode(hDC, TRANSPARENT);
        else
              SetBkMode(hDC, OPAQUE);
        SetBkColor(hDC, (COLORREF) atol(BackDlgData.Color));
        /* Get the coordinates of the window */
        GetClientRect(HWindow, &Rect);
        /* Create a rectangle that fits in the window */
        Rect.left = random(Rect.right);
        Rect.top = random(Rect.bottom);
        Rect.right = Rect.left + random((Rect.right - Rect.left));
        Rect.bottom = Rect.top + random((Rect.bottom - Rect.top));
        /* Draw the rectangle */
        Rectangle(hDC, Rect.left, Rect.top, Rect.right, Rect.bottom);
        /* Clean up */
        ReleaseDC(HWindow, hDC);
        DeleteObject(ThePen);
        DeleteObject(TheBrush);
}


/* Get pen parameters */
void TMyWindow::ChangePen(RTMessage)
{
        /* Do the pen dialog */
        GetModule()->ExecDialog(new PenDlg(this, "PenDialog"));
}


/* Get brush parameters */
void TMyWindow::ChangeBrush(RTMessage)
{
        /* Do the brush dialog */
        GetModule()->ExecDialog(new BrushDlg(this, "BrushDialog"));
}


void TMyWindow::ChangeBack(RTMessage)
{
        /* Do the background dialog */
        GetModule()->ExecDialog(new BackDlg(this, "BackDialog"));
}


/* Define the application object */
class TMenuApp : public TApplication
{
        public:
              TMenuApp(LPSTR ApName, HINSTANCE Inst, HINSTANCE PrevInst
                    , LPSTR CmdLine, int CmdShow) : TApplication(ApName
                    , Inst, PrevInst, CmdLine, CmdShow) {};
              virtual void InitMainWindow();
};


/* Create the main window */
void TMenuApp::InitMainWindow()
{
      MainWindow = new TMyWindow(NULL, "Pens and Brushes");
}


int PASCAL WinMain(HINSTANCE Inst, HINSTANCE PrevInst, LPSTR CmdLine
```

```
        , int CmdShow)
{
        TMenuApp TheApp("", Inst, PrevInst, CmdLine, CmdShow);

        TheApp.Run();
        return TheApp.Status;
}
```

3. Create a resource file called DRAW.RES with these resources:

```
DRAWMENU MENU
BEGIN
        POPUP "Options"
        BEGIN
                MENUITEM "&Pen", 101
                MENUITEM "&Brush", 102
                MENUITEM "B&ackground", 103
        END

END


BACKDIALOG DIALOG 18, 18, 128, 70
STYLE DS_MODALFRAME | WS_POPUP | WS_CAPTION | WS_SYSMENU
CAPTION "Background"
BEGIN
        CONTROL "Mode", 101, "BUTTON", BS_GROUPBOX | WS_CHILD | WS_VISIBLE, 5, 5, 60, 38
        CONTROL "Transparent", 102, "BUTTON", BS_AUTORADIOBUTTON|WS_CHILD|WS_VISIBLE|WS_GROUP
            | WS_TABSTOP, 10, 15, 50, 12
        CONTROL "Opaque", 103, "BUTTON", BS_AUTORADIOBUTTON | WS_CHILD | WS_VISIBLE| WS_TABSTOP
            , 10, 26, 35, 12
        CONTROL "Color", -1, "STATIC", SS_LEFT | WS_CHILD | WS_VISIBLE | WS_GROUP, 74, 9, 20, 8
        CONTROL "", 110, "EDIT", ES_LEFT | WS_CHILD | WS_VISIBLE|WS_BORDER|WS_GROUP|WS_TABSTOP
            , 79, 19, 45, 12
        CONTROL "OK", 1, "BUTTON", BS_DEFPUSHBUTTON | WS_CHILD|WS_VISIBLE|WS_GROUP|WS_TABSTOP
            , 7, 56, 30, 11
        CONTROL "Cancel", 2, "BUTTON", BS_PUSHBUTTON | WS_CHILD | WS_VISIBLE | WS_TABSTOP
            , 53, 56, 35, 11
END


BRUSHDIALOG DIALOG 10, 14, 203, 112
STYLE DS_MODALFRAME | WS_POPUP | WS_CAPTION | WS_SYSMENU
CAPTION "Brush information"
BEGIN
        CONTROL "OK", 1, "BUTTON", BS_DEFPUSHBUTTON|WS_CHILD|WS_VISIBLE|WS_GROUP | WS_TABSTOP
            , 15, 97, 30, 12
        CONTROL "Cancel", 2, "BUTTON", BS_PUSHBUTTON | WS_CHILD | WS_VISIBLE | WS_TABSTOP
            , 65, 97, 30, 12
        CONTROL "Style", 101, "BUTTON", BS_GROUPBOX | WS_CHILD | WS_VISIBLE, 9, 9, 60, 66
        CONTROL "Hatched", 102, "BUTTON", BS_AUTORADIOBUTTON|WS_CHILD|WS_VISIBLE|WS_GROUP
            | WS_TABSTOP, 15, 23, 40, 12
        CONTROL "Hollow", 103, "BUTTON", BS_AUTORADIOBUTTON|WS_CHILD|WS_VISIBLE|WS_TABSTOP
            , 15, 35, 35, 12
        CONTROL "Pattern", 104, "BUTTON", BS_AUTORADIOBUTTON|WS_CHILD|WS_VISIBLE|WS_TABSTOP
            , 15, 47, 35, 12
```

```
        CONTROL "Solid", 105, "BUTTON", BS_AUTORADIOBUTTON | WS_CHILD | WS_VISIBLE | WS_TABSTOP
            , 15, 59, 31, 12
        CONTROL "Color", -1, "STATIC", SS_LEFT | WS_CHILD | WS_VISIBLE | WS_GROUP, 75, 9, 20, 8
        CONTROL "", 110, "EDIT", ES_LEFT|WS_CHILD|WS_VISIBLE| WS_BORDER | WS_GROUP | WS_TABSTOP
            , 78, 19, 55, 12
        CONTROL "Hatch style", 111, "BUTTON", BS_GROUPBOX|WS_CHILD|WS_VISIBLE, 77, 36, 120, 53
        CONTROL "Backward", 112, "BUTTON", BS_AUTORADIOBUTTON|WS_CHILD|WS_VISIBLE|WS_GROUP
            | WS_TABSTOP, 80, 45, 40, 12
        CONTROL "Cross", 113, "BUTTON", BS_AUTORADIOBUTTON | WS_CHILD | WS_VISIBLE | WS_TABSTOP
            , 80, 57, 30, 12
        CONTROL "Diagonal cross", 114, "BUTTON",BS_AUTORADIOBUTTON|WS_CHILD|WS_VISIBLE
            | WS_TABSTOP, 80, 69, 60, 12
        CONTROL "Foreward", 115, "BUTTON",BS_AUTORADIOBUTTON|WS_CHILD|WS_VISIBLE | WS_TABSTOP
            , 145, 45, 40, 12
        CONTROL "Horizontal",116,"BUTTON",BS_AUTORADIOBUTTON|WS_CHILD|WS_VISIBLE | WS_TABSTOP
            , 145, 57, 45, 12
        CONTROL "Vertical",117,"BUTTON",BS_AUTORADIOBUTTON |WS_CHILD | WS_VISIBLE | WS_TABSTOP
            , 145, 69, 40, 12
END

PENDIALOG DIALOG 18, 18, 198, 115
STYLE DS_MODALFRAME | WS_POPUP | WS_CAPTION | WS_SYSMENU
CAPTION "Set pen"
BEGIN
        CONTROL "Style", 101, "BUTTON", BS_GROUPBOX | WS_CHILD | WS_VISIBLE, 5, 6, 120, 71
        CONTROL "Solid",102,"BUTTON",BS_AUTORADIOBUTTON|WS_CHILD|WS_VISIBLE|WS_GROUP
            | WS_TABSTOP, 15, 20, 28, 12
        CONTROL "Dash", 103, "BUTTON", BS_AUTORADIOBUTTON | WS_CHILD | WS_VISIBLE | WS_TABSTOP
            , 15, 34, 28, 12
        CONTROL "Dot", 104, "BUTTON", BS_AUTORADIOBUTTON | WS_CHILD | WS_VISIBLE | WS_TABSTOP
            , 15, 48, 28, 12
        CONTROL "Dash-dot",105,"BUTTON",BS_AUTORADIOBUTTON | WS_CHILD | WS_VISIBLE | WS_TABSTOP
            , 15, 60, 40, 12
        CONTROL "Dash-dot-dot",106,"BUTTON",BS_AUTORADIOBUTTON|WS_CHILD|WS_VISIBLE|WS_TABSTOP
            , 65, 21, 50, 12
        CONTROL "Null", 107, "BUTTON", BS_AUTORADIOBUTTON | WS_CHILD | WS_VISIBLE | WS_TABSTOP
            , 65, 33, 28, 12
        CONTROL "Inside frame",108, "BUTTON", BS_AUTORADIOBUTTON | WS_CHILD | WS_VISIBLE
            | WS_TABSTOP, 65, 46, 50, 12
        CONTROL "OK", 1, "BUTTON", BS_DEFPUSHBUTTON | WS_CHILD | WS_VISIBLE | WS_TABSTOP
            , 14, 99, 30, 12
        CONTROL "Cancel", 2, "BUTTON", BS_PUSHBUTTON | WS_CHILD | WS_VISIBLE | WS_TABSTOP
            , 62, 99, 30, 12
        CONTROL "Width", -1, "STATIC", SS_LEFT | WS_CHILD | WS_VISIBLE | WS_GROUP, 133, 9, 20, 8
        CONTROL "", 109, "EDIT", ES_LEFT | WS_CHILD |WS_VISIBLE|WS_BORDER|WS_GROUP|WS_TABSTOP
            , 137, 19, 30, 12
        CONTROL "Color", -1, "STATIC", SS_LEFT | WS_CHILD | WS_VISIBLE | WS_GROUP,
        133,37,20,8
        CONTROL "", 110, "EDIT", ES_LEFT|WS_CHILD|WS_VISIBLE|WS_BORDER|WS_TABSTOP
            , 137, 46, 45, 12
END
```

Also include the bitmap from Figure 6.4 and name it BRUSHPICT.

4. Use the *Run* command to compile and run the program.

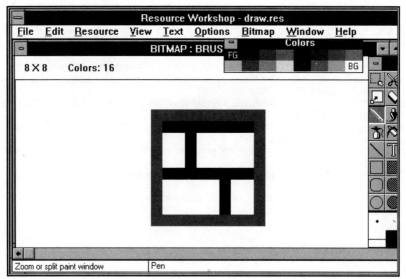

Figure 6-4
The BRUSH-
PICT Bitmap

HOW IT WORKS

The main window object at the beginning of the program includes data members to hold information from the dialog boxes. The first structure holds the pen information, the second holds the brush information, and the third has the background information. The members in these structures match those required by the transfer mechanism for the dialogs (see Chapter 3, "Dialog Boxes"). The data must be converted before it can be passed to Windows. The last data member is a handle to the bitmap that will be used as a pattern for the brush.

The main window class member functions include the ObjectWindows functions SetupWindow and CloseWindow. The SetupWindow function in this program sets up the Borland C++ random number generator, loads the bitmap, and sets a timer. Windows programs use timers to generate messages at timed intervals. The Windows function SetTimer starts a timer. The timer is a Windows resource that sends a message to a window at specified timed intervals. The first argument is a handle to the window that gets the timer message (WM_TIMER). The next argument is an ID number that programs can use to tell one timer from another. The third argument is the number of milliseconds between timer messages. The last argument is the address of a function to call instead of sending a message.

The CloseWindow member function cleans up after the program by killing the timer and deleting the bitmap. Windows can handle only a small number of timers 30 in Windows 3.1, so it is important to kill timers when they are no longer needed by the program so they can be used by other programs.

The main window class includes an indexed member function called WMTimer that handles the timer messages from Windows. The first thing that WMTimer does is get a device context. Then, it selects a pen and a brush, and then sets the background. The data in the main window structures must be converted before it can be passed to Windows. The program uses a for loop to find out which radio button was selected. This gives the pen style. The width and the color can be converted from the strings with the C++ functions atoi and atol. The program passes this information to the CreatePen function to make a pen, then it selects the resulting object in the device context.

The brush styles are not in sequential order, so the program must test each radio button and assign a style constant for the selected radio button. The pattern to use depends on the style. If the style is BS_PATTERN, then the program uses the bitmap for the brush pattern. If the style is BS_HATCHED, then the hatch style from the dialog box gives the pattern to use. The program sends this information plus the color to the CreateBrushIndirect function by putting it in a LOGBRUSH structure and passing the address. Then the program selects the brush with SelectObject.

The program sets the background mode based on the radio button from the background dialog. The background color comes from the color string from the dialog. Note that if the background mode is TRANSPARENT, Windows ignores the background color.

After the program sets up the device context, it creates a random rectangle. The first step is to get the size of the main window by calling GetClientRect. Then the program selects the upper left corner of the rectangle by getting random numbers that fit within the window. Next, the program selects the lower right corner of the rectangle by selecting random numbers between the upper left corner and the bottom right of the window. The program passes these coordinates to the Windows function Rectangle to draw the rectangle. Before exiting, WMTimer releases the device context and deletes the pen and brush.

The information about the pen, brush, and background comes from the dialogs PenDlg, BrushDlg, and BackDialog. These dialogs use their constructors to create objects for the controls and set up the transfer mechanism for the dialog. Each dialog uses the transfer mechanism to exchange data between the dialog and the main window object. The program starts the dialogs in the main window class member functions ChangePen, ChangeBrush, and ChangeBack. This procedure should look familiar if you have looked at the solutions in Chapter 3, "Dialog Boxes."

6.2 How Do I...
Draw Different Shapes?

Complexity: EASY

PROBLEM

The graphics that appear in a window are made up of groups of pixels. You can draw just about anything by specifying the pixels that make up the drawing. Of course if you can specify a picture by drawing a few simple shapes, you can simplify your program. In the previous solution, you learned how to draw a rectangle. This solution shows how to draw other shapes such as polygons and ellipses.

TECHNIQUE

Drawing a line in Windows programs is easy: you move the pen to one end point with MoveTo and use the LineTo function to draw the line to the other end point. Rectangles are also easy, just give the coordinates of the left, top, right, and bottom edges. Things get trickier when you need to draw curves. Not only do you have end points, but you have to specify the amount and shape of the curve.

All curves in Windows are based on an ellipse that isn't rotated. To specify the ellipse, you pass Windows the coordinates of the bounding rectangle (see Figure 6.5). Note that a circle is the same as an ellipse bounded by a square.

You can draw a complete ellipse by passing the bounding rectangle to the Windows function Ellipse. Windows fills the interior of the ellipse using the current brush. There are also three functions for drawing a portion of an ellipse. To specify what portion of the ellipse to draw, you must give the starting and ending points of the portion. If the point you specify is not exactly on the ellipse, Windows finds the point on the ellipse closest to the specified point. The program for this solution picks a point on the bounding rectangle to simplify the calculations.

The Windows function Arc draws the portion of the ellipse from the starting point, moving counterclockwise to the ending point. Arcs do not have an interior, so they are not filled. The Windows function Chord draws an arc and connects the end points with a line. This makes an enclosed area that Windows fills with the current brush. The last function is Pie, which draws lines from the center of the ellipse to the end points. Windows fills the resulting area with the current brush.

This solution also shows two other shape functions: Polyline and Polygon. Programs pass both of these functions a list of points. Windows draws a line

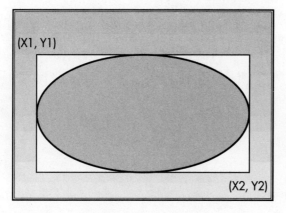

Figure 6-5
Bounding
Rectangles for
Ellipses

from each point to the next. In the case of Polygon, Windows draws a line from the last point back to the first point and fills the resulting polygon with the current brush.

The program in this solution includes a menu of shapes. When you select a shape, the program creates a random item of the specified shape and draws it in the window.

STEPS

1. Create a new project file called SHAPES.PRJ that includes the files SHAPES.CPP, SHAPES.RES, and STANDARD.DEF.

2. Create a source file called SHAPES.CPP with this program:

```
/* SHAPES.CPP program to draw shapes in a window */
#include <owl.h>
#include <time.h>
#include <stdlib.h>

#define MID_ARC        101
#define MID_LINE       102
#define MID_POLYLINE   103
#define MID_CHORD      104
#define MID_ELLIPSE    105
#define MID_PIE        106
#define MID_POLYGON    107

/* Definition of the main window */
class TMyWindow : public TWindow
{
    public:
        TMyWindow(PTWindowsObject AParent, LPSTR ATitle);
        /* Handle messages from the menu */
        virtual void MakeArc(RTMessage) = [CM_FIRST + MID_ARC];
        virtual void MakeLine(RTMessage) = [CM_FIRST + MID_LINE];
        virtual void MakePolyLine(RTMessage) = [CM_FIRST + MID_POLYLINE];
        virtual void MakeChord(RTMessage) = [CM_FIRST + MID_CHORD];
```

```
               virtual void MakeEllipse(RTMessage) = [CM_FIRST + MID_ELLIPSE];
               virtual void MakePie(RTMessage) = [CM_FIRST + MID_PIE];
               virtual void MakePolygon(RTMessage) = [CM_FIRST + MID_POLYGON];
};

/* Initialize the menu and window data */
TMyWindow::TMyWindow(PTWindowsObject AParent, LPSTR ATitle)
      : TWindow(AParent, ATitle)
{
      int i;

      AssignMenu("SHAPEMENU");
      randomize();
}


void TMyWindow::MakeArc(RTMessage)
{
      HDC hDC;
      RECT ClientRect;
      int X1, Y1, X2, Y2, X3, Y3, X4, Y4;

      /* Get the corners of the window */
      GetClientRect(HWindow, &ClientRect);
      /* Compute the upper left corner of the bounding rectangle */
      X1 = random(ClientRect.right);
      Y1 = random(ClientRect.bottom);
      /* Compute the lower right corner of the bounding rectangle */
      X2 = X1 + random(ClientRect.right - X1);
      Y2 = Y1 + random(ClientRect.bottom - Y1);
      /* Computer the start point of the arc */
      X3 = X1 + random(X2-X1);
      Y3 = Y1 + random(Y2-Y1);
      /* Compute the end point of the arc */
      X4 = X1 + random(X2-X1);
      Y4 = Y1 + random(Y2-Y1);
      hDC = GetDC(HWindow);
      Arc(hDC, X1, Y1, X2, Y2, X3, Y3, X4, Y4);
      ReleaseDC(HWindow, hDC);
}


void TMyWindow::MakeLine(RTMessage)
{
      HDC hDC;
      RECT ClientRect;

      GetClientRect(HWindow, &ClientRect);
      hDC = GetDC(HWindow);
      MoveTo(hDC, random(ClientRect.right), random(ClientRect.bottom));
      LineTo(hDC, random(ClientRect.right), random(ClientRect.bottom));
      ReleaseDC(HWindow, hDC);
}


void TMyWindow::MakePolyLine(RTMessage)
{
      POINT PointList[50];
      int Count;
      int i;
      RECT ClientRect;
```

```
        HDC hDC;

        GetClientRect(HWindow, &ClientRect);
        Count = random(50);
        for(i=0; i<Count; ++i)
        {
                PointList[i].x = random(ClientRect.right);
                PointList[i].y = random(ClientRect.bottom);
        }
        hDC = GetDC(HWindow);
        Polyline(hDC, PointList, Count);
        ReleaseDC(HWindow, hDC);
}


void TMyWindow::MakeChord(RTMessage)
{
        HDC hDC;
        RECT ClientRect;
        int X1, Y1, X2, Y2, X3, Y3, X4, Y4;

        /* Get the corners of the window */
        GetClientRect(HWindow, &ClientRect);
        /* Compute the upper left corner of the bounding rectangle */
        X1 = random(ClientRect.right);
        Y1 = random(ClientRect.bottom);
        /* Compute the lower right corner of the bounding rectangle */
        X2 = X1 + random(ClientRect.right - X1);
        Y2 = Y1 + random(ClientRect.bottom - Y1);
        /* Computer the start point of the arc */
        X3 = X1 + random(X2-X1);
        Y3 = Y1 + random(Y2-Y1);
        /* Compute the end point of the arc */
        X4 = X1 + random(X2-X1);
        Y4 = Y1 + random(Y2-Y1);
        hDC = GetDC(HWindow);
        Chord(hDC, X1, Y1, X2, Y2, X3, Y3, X4, Y4);
        ReleaseDC(HWindow, hDC);
}


void TMyWindow::MakeEllipse(RTMessage)
{
        HDC hDC;
        RECT ClientRect;
        int X1, Y1, X2, Y2;

        /* Get the corners of the window */
        GetClientRect(HWindow, &ClientRect);
        /* Compute the upper left corner of the bounding rectangle */
        X1 = random(ClientRect.right);
        Y1 = random(ClientRect.bottom);
        /* Compute the lower right corner of the bounding rectangle */
        X2 = X1 + random(ClientRect.right - X1);
        Y2 = Y1 + random(ClientRect.bottom - Y1);
        hDC = GetDC(HWindow);
        Ellipse(hDC, X1, Y1, X2, Y2);
        ReleaseDC(HWindow, hDC);
}
```

```
void TMyWindow::MakePie(RTMessage)
{
      HDC hDC;
      RECT ClientRect;
      int X1, Y1, X2, Y2, X3, Y3, X4, Y4;

      /* Get the corners of the window */
      GetClientRect(HWindow, &ClientRect);
      /* Compute the upper left corner of the bounding rectangle */
      X1 = random(ClientRect.right);
      Y1 = random(ClientRect.bottom);
      /* Compute the lower right corner of the bounding rectangle */
      X2 = X1 + random(ClientRect.right - X1);
      Y2 = Y1 + random(ClientRect.bottom - Y1);
      /* Computer the start point of the arc */
      X3 = X1 + random(X2-X1);
      Y3 = Y1 + random(Y2-Y1);
      /* Compute the end point of the arc */
      X4 = X1 + random(X2-X1);
      Y4 = Y1 + random(Y2-Y1);
      hDC = GetDC(HWindow);
      Pie(hDC, X1, Y1, X2, Y2, X3, Y3, X4, Y4);
      ReleaseDC(HWindow, hDC);
}

void TMyWindow::MakePolygon(RTMessage)
{
      POINT PointList[10];
      int Count;
      int i;
      RECT ClientRect;
      HDC hDC;

      GetClientRect(HWindow, &ClientRect);
      Count = random(10);
      for(i=0; i<Count; ++i)
      {
            PointList[i].x = random(ClientRect.right);
            PointList[i].y = random(ClientRect.bottom);
      }
      hDC = GetDC(HWindow);
      Polygon(hDC, PointList, Count);
      ReleaseDC(HWindow, hDC);
}

/* Define the application object */
class TMyApp : public TApplication
{
      public:
            TMyApp(LPSTR ApName, HINSTANCE Inst, HINSTANCE PrevInst
                  , LPSTR CmdLine, int CmdShow) : TApplication(ApName
                  , Inst, PrevInst, CmdLine, CmdShow) {};
            virtual void InitMainWindow();
};

/* Create the main window */
void TMyApp::InitMainWindow()
{
```

```
        MainWindow = new TMyWindow(NULL, "Shapes");
}

int PASCAL WinMain(HINSTANCE Inst, HINSTANCE PrevInst, LPSTR CmdLine
    , int CmdShow)
{
    TMyApp TheApp("", Inst, PrevInst, CmdLine, CmdShow);

    TheApp.Run();
    return TheApp.Status;
}
```

3. Create a resource file called SHAPES.RES that includes this menu:

```
SHAPEMENU MENU
BEGIN
    POPUP "&Shapes"
    BEGIN
        MENUITEM "&Arc", 101
        MENUITEM "&Line", 102
        MENUITEM "&Polyline", 103
        MENUITEM "&Chord", 104
        MENUITEM "&Ellipse", 105
        MENUITEM "P&ie", 106
        MENUITEM "P&olygon", 107
    END
END
```

4. Use the *Run* command to compile and run the program

HOW IT WORKS

The main window for this program is very simple, it only includes member functions to handle the menu commands. Each member function draws a different shape. The MakeEllipse function creates random coordinates for a rectangle that fits in the main window client area. Then it calls the Windows function Ellipse to draw the ellipse.

The function MakeArc uses random numbers to make a rectangle that encloses an ellipse. The program selects the corners of the rectangle so that it fits inside the main window client area. Next, the function picks a starting and ending point for the arc. To simplify the calculations, these points lie on the bounding rectangle instead of the actual ellipse. Windows picks the closest point on the arc as the actual point. The Windows function Arc draws the portion of the ellipse that is between the starting and ending point, moving counterclockwise.

The MakeChord and MakePie functions are variations on the MakeArc function. The difference is which Windows function they call. The Windows function Chord, called by MakeChord, draws an arc and connects the end points with a line. The Windows function Pie in MakePie draws the arc and lines from the end points to the center of the ellipse.

The function MakeLine uses random numbers to select the starting and ending points of a line. The function creates points that fit inside the client area. Then the program draws the line by calling the Windows functions MoveTo and LineTo.

The MakePolyline function is similar to the MakeLine function except for the number of points selected. This number is itself a random number less than 50. The program selects random points and stores them in an array of POINT structures. The POINT structure is a Windows structure that holds the x- and y- coordinates of a pixel. The Windows function Polyline draws lines from one point to the next in the array.

The last function, MakePolygon, is similar to MakePolyline except it computes fewer points and uses the Windows function Polygon to draw the object. Windows does its best to fill the resulting polygon, but this is not always possible because the random points can result in edges that cross and confuse the issue of what is inside and what is outside the polygon.

COMMENT

The functions in this chapter can help you draw many different things, but they do not cover everything. There are times when a straight line or elliptical arc just will not do. In this case, you can create your own functions that draw pixel by pixel. The Windows function to use is SetPixel and has this format:

```
SetPixel(hDC, X, Y, Color)
```

The arguments are the device context handle, the x- and y- coordinates of the point, and the color of the pixel (in COLORREF format). This technique has the drawback that any call to a Windows function takes time, and drawing this way can result in many calls to SetPixel. In many cases, this technique will visibly slow your program.

6.3 How Do I...
Use Bitmaps?

Complexity: EASY

PROBLEM

Windows programs are not limited to simple geometric shapes based on lines and elliptical arcs. You can store a complex image in the resource file as a bitmap and display this bitmap in the Window. This solution not only shows you how to draw bitmaps, but also how to find out how the bitmap is stored in memory.

TECHNIQUE

The first step to using bitmaps is to create the data for the bitmap. The most common way to do this is to put the bitmap in the resources for the program. The Resource Workshop makes this easy, just select the *Bitmap* option in the *New resource* command and you are in the bitmap editor. The editor lets you draw and edit the image until it is just what you want. Then you can save the bitmap in the resource file, so it can be included in the program.

The next step is to get the bitmap from the resource file into memory. The Windows function LoadBitmap handles this task. You pass this function the handle to the instance for the module that includes the bitmap resource and the name of the bitmap. In ObjectWindows programs, the instance handle is in the TApplication object. The ObjectWindows function GetApplication returns a pointer to the application object, so a call to LoadBitmap looks like this:

```
BitmapHandle = LoadBitmap(GetApplication()->hInstance, "BitmapName");
```

If you search through the *Windows Programmer's Reference* to find a function that takes a bitmap handle as returned by LoadBitmap and draws the bitmap on the screen, you will be disappointed. The function to copy a bitmap from one place to another is called BitBlt, but it requires a handle to a device context, not to a bitmap. So you need to have a device context that knows about the bitmap. Here is the secret:

```
MemDC = CreateCompatibleDC(hDC);
SelectObject(MemDC, BitmapHandle);
```

The first statement creates a memory device context that is compatible with the screen device context. This device context looks just like a screen to your program, except the output goes to memory instead of the screen. The second statement associates the bitmap with the memory device context. In fact, the bitmap is the memory that the device context uses for storing what would go to the screen for a screen device context.

Once the bitmap is selected in a device context, you can use the Windows function BitBlt to copy all or part of a bitmap to the screen device context. The format of the function is:

```
BitBlt(DestDC, X, Y, Width, Height, SourceDC, SourceX, SourceY, ROP);
```

The first argument is the device context on which to draw the bitmap. To draw on the program window, you can use GetDC to supply this argument. The next four arguments give the location and size of the place to draw the bitmap. After that is the source device context. Usually, this is the memory device context created above. The next two arguments are the place in the source bitmap to start copying. The size must be the same as for the destination, so you do not have to give it. The last argument is the Raster OPeration (ROP) and tells

Windows how to combine the source and destination bitmaps. Table 6-2 lists some of the possible ROP values.

Windows combines each pixel in the source bitmap with the destination bitmap according to the formula in Table 6-2. For example, if the ROP is SRCERASE, Windows takes a pixel from the destination and inverts it, then combines this pixel with one from the source using a logical AND. Windows repeats this process for each pixel in the transfer.

The program in this solution loads a bitmap from the resources and uses BitBlt to copy it to the main window with the SRCCOPY ROP.

STEPS

1. Make a new project file called BITMAP.PRJ that includes the files BITMAP.CPP, BITMAP.RES, and STANDARD.DEF.

2. Create a source file called BITMAP.CPP with this program:

```
/* BITMAP a program to show how to use bitmaps  */
#include <owl.h>
#include <alloc.h>
```

ROP Value	Formula
BLACKNESS	0
DSTINVERT	!Destination
MERGECOPY	Pattern&Source
MERGEPAINT	(!Source)&Destination
NOTSRCCOPY	!Source
NOTSRCERASE	!(Source|Destination)
PATCOPY	Pattern
PATINVERT	Pattern^Destination
PATPAINT	((!Source)|Pattern)|Destination
SRCAND	Source&Destination
SRCCOPY	Source
SRCERASE	(!Destination)&Source
SRCINVERT	Source^Destination
SRCPAINT	Source|Destination
WHITENESS	1

Table 6-2 ROP Values for BitBlt

```
/* Definition of the main window object */
class TMyWindow : public TWindow
{
    public:
        TMyWindow(PTWindowsObject AParent, LPSTR ATitle)
            : TWindow(AParent, ATitle) {};
        virtual void WMPaint(RTMessage)
            = [WM_FIRST + WM_PAINT];
};

/* Handle the WM_PAINT message from Windows */
void TMyWindow::WMPaint(RTMessage)
{
    PAINTSTRUCT ps;
    HDC hDC;
    HDC MemDC;
    HBITMAP TheBitmap;
    BITMAP BitInfo;
    char TmpStr[80];

    /* Clear the ps structure */
    memset(&ps, 0x00, sizeof(PAINTSTRUCT));
    /* Get a device context handle */
    hDC = BeginPaint(HWindow, &ps);
    /* Load the bitmap */
    TheBitmap = LoadBitmap(GetApplication()->hInstance, "Airplane");
    /* Draw the bitmap */
    MemDC = CreateCompatibleDC(hDC);
    SelectObject(MemDC, TheBitmap);
    BitBlt(hDC, 0, 0, 130, 50, MemDC, 0, 0, SRCCOPY);
    /* Show the bitmap information */
    GetObject(TheBitmap, sizeof(BITMAP), &BitInfo);
    wsprintf(TmpStr, "Dimensions X: %d Y: %d"
        , BitInfo.bmWidth
        , BitInfo.bmHeight);
    TextOut(hDC, 5, 60, TmpStr, lstrlen(TmpStr));
    wsprintf(TmpStr, "Bit count: %d Planes: %d"
        , BitInfo.bmBitsPixel, BitInfo.bmPlanes);
    TextOut(hDC, 5, 75, TmpStr, lstrlen(TmpStr));
    /* Release the device context and tell Windows the painting is complete */
    EndPaint(HWindow, &ps);
    DeleteDC(hDC);
    DeleteObject(TheBitmap);
}

/* definition for the application object */
class TFirstApp : public TApplication
{
    public:
        TFirstApp(LPSTR ApName, HINSTANCE Inst
            , HINSTANCE PrevInst
            , LPSTR CmdLine, int CmdShow) : TApplication(ApName
            , Inst, PrevInst, CmdLine, CmdShow) {};
        virtual void InitMainWindow();
};

/* Initialize the main window */
void TFirstApp::InitMainWindow()
```

```
{
    /* Create the main window object */
    MainWindow = new TMyWindow(NULL, "Bitmaps");
}

/* Entry point for the program */
int PASCAL WinMain(HINSTANCE Inst, HINSTANCE PrevInst, LPSTR CmdLine
    , int CmdShow)
{
    /* Create the application object */
    TFirstApp FirstApp("", Inst
        , PrevInst, CmdLine, CmdShow);

    /* Run the application */
    FirstApp.Run();
    return FirstApp.Status;
}
```

3. Create the resource file BITMAP.RES with the bitmap from Figure 6-6.

4. Use the *Run* command to compile and run the program.

HOW IT WORKS

The important action in this program is in the WMPaint member function. ObjectWindows calls this function when Windows sends a WM_PAINT message to the program. The first thing the function does is to get a device context handle by calling the Windows function BeginPaint. Next, WMPaint loads the bitmap from the resources and memory device context to hold the bitmap. Once the bitmap is selected into the memory device context, the function puts it on the screen with the BitBlt function.

After WMPaint draws the bitmap, it prints some information about it in the main window. The first step in this procedure is to call the Windows function GetObject to put information from the bitmap into the structure BitInfo. Next, the program gets the dimensions and number of colors used from the structure and prints the information in the main window.

Before it is done, WMPaint cleans up by getting rid of the memory device context and the bitmap.

COMMENT

There is another function that you can use to copy bitmaps from one device context to another, called StretchBlt. This function lets you specify the height and width of both the destination and source bitmaps. StretchBlt stretches the source bitmap so that it fits in the specified destination area. To make a bitmap larger, the function adds rows or columns of pixels to the bitmap. The new pixels match adjacent pixels from the original bitmap. To make a bitmap smaller, StretchBlt removes rows or columns from the source bitmap. How the function removes lines depends on the last call to SetStretchBltMode. This function selects one

Figure 6-6
A Sample
Bitmap

of three modes, BLACKONWHITE in which adjacent rows or columns are logically ANDed, COLORONCOLOR in which rows or columns are removed, and WHITEONBLACK in which adjacent rows are logically ORed.

To see how this function works, replace the BitBlt line in the previous program with these statements:

```
{
    RECT Rect;

    GetClientRect(HWindow, &Rect);
    StretchBlt(hDC, 0, 0, Rect.right, Rect.bottom, MemDC, 0, 0, 130, 50, SRCCOPY);
}
```

This change makes the program fill the main window with the bitmap. As you resize the window, the program stretches the bitmap to keep the window filled. One thing you may notice as you run this program is that StretchBlt is very slow. You should avoid this function if performance is an issue.

6.4 How Do I...
Use Fonts?

Complexity: MODERATE

PROBLEM

One way to make your programs more visually interesting is to use different fonts for different types of text. For example, the text in this book uses Janson, Frutiger, and OCRB fonts in different sizes and weights depending on what the text is for. Windows fonts come in a variety of styles and sizes making the task of picking the right font complex. The task is also complicated by the fact that Windows does not always use standard typographical terminology to describe fonts. This solution shows you how Windows handles fonts and what your program must do to take advantage of fonts.

TECHNIQUE

When a program asks Windows for a font, it does not say, "Give me this font." Instead, the program says, "Give me a font as close to this as possible." Windows compares the requested font features, such as family name and size, with the fonts available and returns a handle to the closest match. Windows uses 10 characteristics to specify a font. For each characteristic that does not match, Windows adds a penalty to the font. After looking at each possible font, Windows selects the one with the lowest penalty. Windows can synthesize some characteristics such as bold, underline, and italic. Synthesized fonts are assessed additional penalties for each synthesized characteristic.

Your program uses a LOGFONT structure to specify the desired characteristics. The format of the LOGFONT structure is:

```
typedef struct tagLOGFONT {
        short int   lfHeight;        // Penalty = 2, Some heights can be synthesized
        short int   lfWidth;         // Penalty = 2, Some widths can be synthesized
        short int   lfEscapement;    // Not compared
        short int   lfOrientation;   // Not compared
        short int   lfWeight;        // Penalty = 1, Bold can be synthesized
                                     //     400 = Normal
                                     //     700 = Bold
        BYTE        lfItalic;        // Penalty = 1, Can be synthesized
        BYTE        lfUnderline;     // Penalty = 1, Can be synthesized
        BYTE        lfStrikeOut;     // Penalty = 1, Can be synthesized
        BYTE        lfCharSet;       // Penalty = 4, Cannot be synthesized
                                     //     ANSI_CHARSET
                                     //     OEM_CHARSET
                                     //     SYMBOL_CHARSET
        BYTE        lfOutPrecision;  // Always set to OUT_DEFAULT_PRECIS
        BYTE        lfClipPrecision; // Always set to OUT_CLIP_PRECIS
        BYTE        lfQuality;       // Font quality
                                     //     DEFAULT_QUALITY = Don't care
                                     //     DRAFT_QUALITY = Synthesized font sizes are OK
                                     //     PROOF_QUALITY = Do not synthesize font sizes
        BYTE        lfPitchAndFamily;// Pitch penalty = 3, Family penalty = 3
                                     //     DEFAULT_PITCH = Use any pitch
                                     //     FIXED_PITCH = Only use fixed pitch fonts
                                     //     VARIABLE_PITCH = Only use proportional width fonts
                                     //
                                     //     FF_DECORATIVE = Decorative family
                                     //     FF_DONTCHARE = Any family is OK
                                     //     FF_MODERN = Modern family
                                     //     FF_ROMAN = Roman family
                                     //     FF_SCRIPT = Script family
                                     //     FF_SWISS = Swiss family
        BYTE        lfFaceName[LF_FACESIZE];    // Penalty = 3
} LOGFONT;
```

Setting up a LOGFONT structure may seem like a lot of work just to pick a font, but there is method to this madness. The reason is that you do not know what fonts are installed on all the possible systems that might run your program. By using the LOGFONT structure, a program will always get the font closest to the requested font, no matter what fonts are installed.

Once you have filled in a LOGFONT structure, you can use the Windows function CreateFontIndirect to get a handle to the font. Then, select the font into a device context. Any TextOut calls using the device context will use the selected font.

One problem with using different fonts is that you cannot set aside a fixed area of the screen for a given string of text. Different fonts will draw the string at different sizes. You can find out how big a string is in the current font by calling the Windows function GetTextExtent. The return value of this function is a long integer with the height of the string in the high word and the width of the string in the low word. This statement gets the dimensions of a string:

```
Extent = GetTextExtent(hDC, "Test string", 11);
```

The first argument is the handle to the device context, the second is that string to measure, and the last argument is the number of characters in the string. You can use the HIWORD and LOWORD macros to get the dimensions like this:

```
Height = HIWORD(Extent);
Width = LOWORD(Extent);
```

The Windows function EnumFonts lets you find out what fonts are installed on the system. You pass it the font face name and it tells you all of the fonts for that face name that are installed. If you do not give a face name, Windows gives you all of the available face names. EnumFonts calls a function in your program for each matching font. The program for this solution shows how this function works.

The program in this solution displays a dialog box with controls for each of the parts of the LOGFONT structure. When the user presses the OK button in the dialog, the program prints the alphabet in the selected font in the main window.

STEPS

1. Create a new project called PICKFONT.PRJ with the files PICKFONT.CPP, PICKFONT.RES, and STANDARD.DEF.
2. Create the source file PICKFONT.CPP with this program:

```
/* PICKFONT select and display fonts */
#include <owl.h>
#include <listbox.h>
#include <edit.h>
#include <groupbox.h>
#include <radiobut.h>
#include <checkbox.h>
#include <stdlib.h>

#define MID_SELECTFONT 101

/* Font dialog box defines */
#define IDC_FACENAME    101
#define IDC_HEIGHT      102
#define IDC_WIDTH       103
#define IDC_WEIGHT      104
#define IDC_ESCAPE      109
#define IDC_ORIENT      110
#define IDC_PITCH       115
#define IDC_DEFAULTP    116
#define IDC_FIXEDP      117
#define IDC_VARIABLEP   118
#define IDC_CHARSET     111
#define IDC_OEM         112
#define IDC_ANSI        113
#define IDC_SYMBOL      114
#define IDC_STYLE       105
#define IDC_ITALIC      106
#define IDC_UNDERLINE   107
#define IDC_STRIKEOUT   108


/* This object represents the main window */
class TMyWindow : public TWindow
{
    public:
        struct {
            PTListBoxData FaceName;
            char Height[10];
            char Width[10];
            char Weight[10];
            char Escape[10];
            char Orientation[10];
            WORD Default;
            WORD Fixed;
            WORD Variable;
            WORD Oem;
            WORD Ansi;
            WORD Symbol;
            WORD Italic;
            WORD Underline;
            WORD StrikeOut;
        } FontDlgData;
        TMyWindow(PTWindowsObject AParent, LPSTR ATitle);
        virtual void SetupWindow();
        virtual void CloseWindow();
        virtual void ShowDialog(RTMessage) = [CM_FIRST + MID_SELECTFONT];
```

```
};

/* This object represents the dialog box */
class FontDlg : public TDialog
{
    public:
        FontDlg(PTWindowsObject AParent, LPSTR AResource);
};

/* Initialize the dialog controls and set up the transfer buffer */
FontDlg::FontDlg(PTWindowsObject AParent, LPSTR AResource)
    : TDialog(AParent, AResource)
{
    PTGroupBox TheGroup;

    /* Font face name */
    new TListBox(this, IDC_FACENAME);
    /* Numeric settings */
    new TEdit(this, IDC_HEIGHT, 10);
    new TEdit(this, IDC_WIDTH, 10);
    new TEdit(this, IDC_WEIGHT, 10);
    new TEdit(this, IDC_ESCAPE, 10);
    new TEdit(this, IDC_ORIENT, 10);
    /* Font pitch group */
    TheGroup = new TGroupBox(this, IDC_PITCH);
    new TRadioButton(this, IDC_DEFAULTP, TheGroup);
    new TRadioButton(this, IDC_FIXEDP, TheGroup);
    new TRadioButton(this, IDC_VARIABLEP, TheGroup);
    /* Character set group */
    TheGroup = new TGroupBox(this, IDC_CHARSET);
    new TRadioButton(this, IDC_OEM, TheGroup);
    new TRadioButton(this, IDC_ANSI, TheGroup);
    new TRadioButton(this, IDC_SYMBOL, TheGroup);
    /* Font style group */
    TheGroup = new TGroupBox(this, IDC_STYLE);
    new TCheckBox(this, IDC_ITALIC, TheGroup);
    new TCheckBox(this, IDC_UNDERLINE, TheGroup);
    new TCheckBox(this, IDC_STRIKEOUT, TheGroup);
    TransferBuffer = (void far *) &((TMyWindow *) Parent)->FontDlgData;
}

/* Initialize the main window */
TMyWindow::TMyWindow(PTWindowsObject AParent, LPSTR ATitle)
    : TWindow(AParent, ATitle)
{
    AssignMenu("FontMenu");
}

/* Add a face name to the list box */
int FAR PASCAL GetFont(const LOGFONT *LogFont, const TEXTMETRIC *
    , int, long FaceList);

/* Initialize the font data */
void TMyWindow::SetupWindow()
{
    HDC hDC;

    TWindow::SetupWindow();
```

```
    /* Set up the font data transfer area */
    FontDlgData.FaceName = new TListBoxData();
    /* Enumerate face names */
    hDC = GetDC(HWindow);
    EnumFonts(hDC, NULL, GetFont, (long) FontDlgData.FaceName);
    ReleaseDC(HWindow, hDC);
    /* Set other font parameters */
    lstrcpy(FontDlgData.Height, "8");
    lstrcpy(FontDlgData.Width, "0");
    lstrcpy(FontDlgData.Weight, "400");
    lstrcpy(FontDlgData.Escape, "0");
    lstrcpy(FontDlgData.Orientation, "0");
    FontDlgData.Default = 1;
    FontDlgData.Fixed = FontDlgData.Variable = 0;
    FontDlgData.Oem = 1;
    FontDlgData.Ansi = FontDlgData.Symbol = 0;
    FontDlgData.Italic = FontDlgData.Underline = FontDlgData.StrikeOut = 0;
}

int FAR PASCAL GetFont(const LOGFONT *LogFont, const TEXTMETRIC *
    , int, long FaceList)
{
    ((PTListBoxData)FaceList)->AddString((LPSTR) LogFont->lfFaceName);
    return TRUE;
}

/* Clean up the memory usage */
void TMyWindow::CloseWindow()
{
    delete FontDlgData.FaceName;// Release the memory used by the list box
    TWindow::CloseWindow();
}

/* Display the dialog then paint the results in the main window */
void TMyWindow::ShowDialog(RTMessage)
{
    HDC hDC;
    char TmpStr[50];
    int i, Row;
    RECT Rect;
    LOGFONT FontInfo;
    HFONT TheFont;
    HBRUSH TheBrush;
    long TextSize;

    /* Do the dialog */
    GetModule()->ExecDialog(new FontDlg(this, "FontDialog"));
    /* Print the results */
    hDC = GetDC(HWindow);
    GetWindowRect(HWindow, &Rect);
    TheBrush = CreateSolidBrush(0xFFFFFF);
    FillRect(hDC, &Rect, TheBrush);
    DeleteObject(TheBrush);
    /* Get the face name */
    if(FontDlgData.FaceName->SelCount)
        FontDlgData.FaceName->GetSelString(FontInfo.lfFaceName
            , LF_FACESIZE);
    else
```

```
                lstrcpy(FontInfo.lfFaceName, "");
        FontInfo.lfHeight = atoi(FontDlgData.Height);
        FontInfo.lfWidth = atoi(FontDlgData.Width);
        FontInfo.lfWeight = atoi(FontDlgData.Weight);
        FontInfo.lfEscapement = atoi(FontDlgData.Escape);
        FontInfo.lfOrientation = atoi(FontDlgData.Orientation);
        if(FontDlgData.Default)
                FontInfo.lfPitchAndFamily = DEFAULT_PITCH;
        else if(FontDlgData.Fixed)
                FontInfo.lfPitchAndFamily = FIXED_PITCH;
        else
                FontInfo.lfPitchAndFamily = VARIABLE_PITCH;
        if(FontDlgData.Oem)
                FontInfo.lfCharSet = OEM_CHARSET;
        else if(FontDlgData.Ansi)
                FontInfo.lfCharSet = ANSI_CHARSET;
        else
                FontInfo.lfCharSet = SYMBOL_CHARSET;
        FontInfo.lfItalic = FontDlgData.Italic;
        FontInfo.lfUnderline = FontDlgData.Underline;
        FontInfo.lfStrikeOut = FontDlgData.StrikeOut;
        /* Set up the selected font */
        TheFont = CreateFontIndirect(&FontInfo);
        SelectObject(hDC, TheFont);
        /* Draw the alphabet */
        TextSize = GetTextExtent(hDC, "ABCDEFGHIJKLMNOPQRSTUZ|VWXYZ", 26);
        TextOut(hDC, 5, 5, "ABCDEFGHIJKLMNOPQRSTUVWXYZ", 26);
        TextOut(hDC, 5, 6 + HIWORD(TextSize), "abcdefghijklmnopqrstuvwxyz", 26);
        ReleaseDC(HWindow, hDC);
        DeleteObject(TheFont);
}


class TMyApp : public TApplication
{
        public:
                TMyApp(LPSTR ApName, HINSTANCE Inst, HINSTANCE PrevInst
                        , LPSTR CmdLine, int CmdShow) : TApplication(ApName
                        , Inst, PrevInst, CmdLine, CmdShow) {};
                virtual void InitMainWindow();
};


void TMyApp::InitMainWindow()
{
        MainWindow = new TMyWindow(NULL, "Font selector");
}


int PASCAL WinMain(HINSTANCE Inst, HINSTANCE PrevInst, LPSTR CmdLine
        , int CmdShow)
{
        TMyApp TheApp("", Inst, PrevInst, CmdLine, CmdShow);

        TheApp.Run();
        return TheApp.Status;
}
```

3. Create the resource file PICKFONT.RES with these resources:

```
FONTMENU MENU
```

```
BEGIN
     MENUITEM "&Select font", 101
END


FONTDIALOG DIALOG 18, 18, 215, 176
STYLE DS_MODALFRAME | WS_POPUP | WS_CAPTION | WS_SYSMENU
CAPTION "Font Selection"
BEGIN
     CONTROL "Face name", -1, "STATIC", SS_LEFT | WS_CHILD | WS_VISIBLE | WS_GROUP, 7, 7, 40, 8
     CONTROL "", 101, "LISTBOX", LBS_STANDARD | WS_CHILD | WS_VISIBLE | WS_GROUP, 10, 17, 100, 61
     CONTROL "Height", -1, "STATIC", SS_LEFT | WS_CHILD | WS_VISIBLE | WS_GROUP, 145, 12, 25, 8
     CONTROL "", 102, "EDIT", ES_LEFT | WS_CHILD | WS_VISIBLE | WS_BORDER | WS_GROUP | STOP, 175, 9, 25, 12
     CONTROL "Width", -1, "STATIC", SS_LEFT | WS_CHILD | WS_VISIBLE | WS_GROUP, 150, 28, 20, 8
     CONTROL "", 103, "EDIT", ES_LEFT | WS_CHILD | WS_VISIBLE | WS_BORDER | WS_TABSTOP, 175, 24, 25, 12
     CONTROL "Weight", -1, "STATIC", SS_LEFT | WS_CHILD | WS_VISIBLE | WS_GROUP, 145, 42, 25, 8
     CONTROL "", 104, "EDIT", ES_LEFT | WS_CHILD | WS_VISIBLE | WS_BORDER | WS_TABSTOP 39, 25, 12
     CONTROL "Escapement", -1, "STATIC", SS_LEFT | WS_CHILD | WS_VISIBLE | WS_GROUP, 130, 57, 40, 8
     CONTROL "", 109, "EDIT", ES_LEFT | WS_CHILD | WS_VISIBLE | WS_BORDER | WS_TABSTOP, 175, 54, 25, 12
     CONTROL "Orientation", -1, "STATIC", SS_LEFT | WS_CHILD | WS_VISIBLE | WS_GROUP, 135, 8
     CONTROL "", 110, "EDIT", ES_LEFT | WS_CHILD | WS_VISIBLE | WS_BORDER | WS_TABSTOP, 175, 69, 25, 12
     CONTROL "Style", 105, "BUTTON", BS_GROUPBOX | WS_CHILD | WS_VISIBLE, 140, 87, 50, 53
     CONTROL "Italic", 106, "BUTTON", BS_AUTOCHECKBOX | WS_CHILD | WS_VISIBLE |
WS_GROUP | STOP, 145, 101, 28, 12
     CONTROL "Underline", 107, "BUTTON", BS_AUTOCHECKBOX | WS_CHILD | WS_VISIBLE |
WS_TAB STOP, 145, 113, 40, 12
     CONTROL "Strike out", 108, "BUTTON", BS_AUTOCHECKBOX | WS_CHILD | WS_VISIBLE |
WS_TABSTOP, 145, 125, 42, 12
     CONTROL "Characters", 111, "BUTTON", BS_GROUPBOX | WS_CHILD | WS_VISIBLE, 75, 87, 45, 52
     CONTROL "OEM", 112, "BUTTON", BS_AUTORADIOBUTTON | WS_CHILD | WS_VISIBLE | WS_GROUP |
WS_TABSTOP, 80, 99, 28, 12
     CONTROL "ANSI", 113, "BUTTON", BS_AUTORADIOBUTTON | WS_CHILD | WS_VISIBLE |
WS_TAB STOP, 80, 111, 28, 12
     CONTROL "Symbol", 114, "BUTTON", BS_AUTORADIOBUTTON | WS_CHILD | WS_VISIBLE |
WS_TAB STOP, 80, 123, 35, 12
     CONTROL "Pitch", 115, "BUTTON", BS_GROUPBOX | WS_CHILD | WS_VISIBLE, 9, 87, 50, 52
     CONTROL "Default", 116, "BUTTON", BS_AUTORADIOBUTTON | WS_CHILD | WS_VISIBLE |
WS_GROUP | WS_TABSTOP, 14, 96, 35, 12
     CONTROL "Fixed", 117, "BUTTON", BS_AUTORADIOBUTTON | WS_CHILD | WS_VISIBLE |
WS_TAB STOP, 14, 110, 28, 12
     CONTROL "Variable", 118, "BUTTON", BS_AUTORADIOBUTTON | WS_CHILD | WS_VISIBLE |
WS_TABSTOP, 15, 123, 40, 12
     CONTROL "OK", 1, "BUTTON", BS_DEFPUSHBUTTON | WS_CHILD | WS_VISIBLE | WS_GROUP |
WS_TABSTOP, 40, 151, 40, 14
     CONTROL "Cancel", 2, "BUTTON", BS_PUSHBUTTON | WS_CHILD | WS_VISIBLE | WS_GROUP |
WS_TABSTOP, 140, 151, 35, 14
END
```

Figure 6-7 shows how the dialog should look in the dialog editor.

4. Use the *Run* command to compile and run the program.

HOW IT WORKS

By now you should recognize the format of a TDialog object as used in this program. The font dialog in this program is the most complex dialog presented so far, but it follows the basic principles described in Chapter 3, "Dialog Boxes."

The SetupWindow function initializes the dialog data fields. For most of the controls, this is a simple matter of copying strings to the transfer area. The list of face names is more complicated because it requires a call to the EnumFonts Windows function. EnumFonts needs a function that it can call with font information. The function in this program is called GetFont. One of the arguments to GetFont is a LOGFONT structure with information about the font. Another is a long integer that comes from the last argument to the EnumFonts function. This program passes the address of the list box data object. GetFont adds the face name from the LOGFONT structure to the list box data object so that it will appear in the font dialog.

The program executes the dialog in the member function ShowDialog. After executing the dialog, ShowDialog copies the data from the transfer area to a LOGFONT structure. Then it passes the LOGFONT structure to CreateFontIndirect to get the font. After selecting the font, the program draws uppercase and lowercase alphabets in the selected font. Before exiting, the ShowDialog function removes the font from memory by calling DeleteObject.

COMMENT

If you don't like any of the fonts available, you can create your own font with the Resource Workshop or buy third party fonts. You have two choices for how to

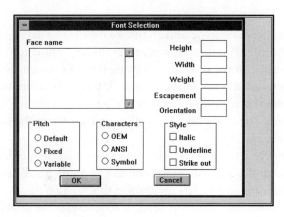

Figure 6-7
The Font Selection
Dialog

use the new font. The first choice is to select .FNT as the file type when you create the font in the Resource Workshop, then you must use the Windows Control panel program to load the font into Windows. After that, the font is available to all programs.

The second choice is to put the font into the resources for your application. Then use the Windows function AddFontResource to load the font into the list of available fonts. Next load the font with CreateFontIndirect. When you no longer need the font, you can remove it by calling RemoveFontResource.

Borland C++ uses the latter technique to provide two special fonts used by the editor. If you run the program in this solution from Borland C++, you see two extra face names in the font selection dialog. These fonts are not available from Program Manager or File Manager.

6.5 How Do I...
Use Metafiles?

Complexity: EASY

PROBLEM

Windows uses metafiles to save GDI commands so they can be played back later. One use for this feature is to save a commonly used sequence of instructions so that the entire sequence can be repeated with a single function call. Another use is to save the commands used to draw in a window so that the window can be repainted in response to the WM_PAINT message. This solution shows how to save GDI commands in a metafile and play them back.

TECHNIQUE

The Windows function CreateMetaFile returns a handle to a device context that represents the metafile. Windows stores any graphics command you use with this device context in memory instead of drawing it on the screen. Note that the command itself is saved, not the image created. If you save a command to draw a line from the current pen position to a new pen position, replaying the metafile gives you a different line every time you call it, depending on the pen position when you replay the metafile.

Before you can replay the metafile, you must close it by calling the Windows function CloseMetaFile. This function returns a metafile handle that you can pass to other metafile functions. The program in this solution passes the metafile handle to the Windows function PlayMetaFile to re-create the drawing.

The program below draws the well-known Mandlebrot set (see Figure 6-8). The computations for creating this image can take several hours. Clearly this is unacceptable for a Windows program that must give up time to the operating system so that other programs can run. The program computes the image in the IdleAction member function one pixel a time. When the program computes a pixel, it sends the command to draw it to a metafile. Then, when the program gets a WM_PAINT message, it only needs to play the metafile, not recompute all of the pixels.

STEPS

1. Create a new project file called META.PRJ that includes the files META.CPP, META.RES, and STANDARD.DEF.

2. Create the source file META.CPP with this program:

```
/* META to show how metafiles work */
#include <owl.h>

#define MID_DRAW        101

/* Definition of the main window */
class TMyWindow : public TWindow
{
    public:
            double Left;            // Left-most coordinate of Mandlebrot set
            double Top;             // Top-most coordinate of Mandlebrot set
            double Right;           // Right-most coordinate of Mandlebrot set
            double Bottom;          // Bottom-most coordinate of Mandlebrot set
            double XInterval, YInterval;    // Size of a pixel in Mandlebrot set units
            HMETAFILE MetaHandle;   // The metafile
            BOOL Drawing;           // True when computing points
            RECT Rect;              // Coordinates of the window
            POINT At;               // The next pixel to compute
            HDC MetaDC;             // Metafile device context
            TMyWindow(PTWindowsObject AParent, LPSTR ATitle);
            /* Handle messages from the menu */
            virtual void DrawIt(RTMessage) = [CM_FIRST + MID_DRAW];
            /* Handle the WM_PAINT message */
            virtual void WMPaint(RTMessage) = [WM_FIRST + WM_PAINT];
};


/* Initialize the menu */
TMyWindow::TMyWindow(PTWindowsObject AParent, LPSTR ATitle)
    : TWindow(AParent, ATitle)
{
    AssignMenu("METAMENU");
    /* Set the range of the fractal area */
    Left = -2.0;
    Top = 1.25;
    Right = 0.5;
    Bottom = -1.25;
    Drawing = FALSE;
}
```

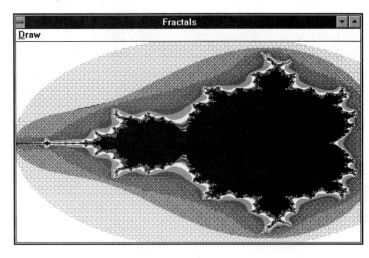

Figure 6-8
The Mandelbrot
Set

```
/* Draw the Mandelbrot set */
void TMyWindow::DrawIt(RTMessage)
{
      GetClientRect(HWindow, &Rect);
      /* Set up initial state */
      At.x = At.y = 0;
      XInterval = (Right - Left)/(double) Rect.right;
      YInterval = (Top - Bottom) / (double) Rect.bottom;
      /* Create a metafile in memory */
      MetaDC = CreateMetaFile(NULL);
      /* Start Computations in IdleAction */
      Drawing = TRUE;
}


void TMyWindow::WMPaint(RTMessage)
{
      PAINTSTRUCT ps;
      HDC hDC;

      /* Clear the ps structure */
      memset(&ps, 0x00, sizeof(PAINTSTRUCT));
      /* Get a device context handle */
      hDC = BeginPaint(HWindow, &ps);
      /* Play the metafile */
      if(!Drawing)
            PlayMetaFile(hDC, MetaHandle);
      /* Release the device context and tell Windows the painting is complete */
      EndPaint(HWindow, &ps);
}

/* Define the application object */
class TMyApp : public TApplication
{
      public:
            TMyApp(LPSTR ApName, HINSTANCE Inst, HINSTANCE PrevInst
```

```
            , LPSTR CmdLine, int CmdShow) : TApplication(ApName
            , Inst, PrevInst, CmdLine, CmdShow) {};
        virtual void InitMainWindow();
        virtual void IdleAction();
};

/* Create the main window */
void TMyApp::InitMainWindow()
{
    MainWindow = new TMyWindow(NULL, "Fractals");
}


void TMyApp::IdleAction()
{
    HDC hDC;
    double Size;
    int Count;
    double ComputeX, ComputeY;
    double XPos, YPos;
    double Tmp;

    /* Calculate the color for a pixel */
    if(((TMyWindow *)MainWindow)->Drawing)
    {
        /* Get the point to compute */
        ComputeY = YPos = ((TMyWindow *)MainWindow)->Top
            - ((TMyWindow *)MainWindow)->At.y
            * ((TMyWindow *)MainWindow)->YInterval;
        ComputeX = XPos = ((TMyWindow *)MainWindow)->Left
            + ((TMyWindow *)MainWindow)->At.x
            * ((TMyWindow *)MainWindow)->XInterval;
        hDC = GetDC(((TMyWindow *)MainWindow)->HWindow);
        /* Iterate the expression Z = Z*Z + C */
        Size = 0.0;
        Count = 0;
        ComputeX = XPos;
        ComputeY = YPos;
        /* Count the iterations */
        while(Size < 4.0 && Count < 512)
        {
            Tmp = 2 * ComputeX * ComputeY;
            ComputeX = ComputeX * ComputeX
                - ComputeY * ComputeY + XPos;
            ComputeY = Tmp + YPos;
            Size = ComputeX * ComputeX + ComputeY * ComputeY;
            ++Count;
        }
        /* Draw the pixel in the window */
        SetPixel(hDC, ((TMyWindow *)MainWindow)->At.x
            , ((TMyWindow *)MainWindow)->At.y, PALETTEINDEX(Count));
        /* Draw the pixel in the metafile */
        SetPixel(((TMyWindow *)MainWindow)->MetaDC
            , ((TMyWindow *)MainWindow)->At.x
            , ((TMyWindow *)MainWindow)->At.y, PALETTEINDEX(Count));
        ReleaseDC(((TMyWindow *)MainWindow)->HWindow, hDC);
        /* Find the next point */
        if(++((TMyWindow *)MainWindow)->At.x
            > ((TMyWindow *)MainWindow)->Rect.right)
```

```
                {
                        if(++((TMyWindow *)MainWindow)->At.y
                                > ((TMyWindow *)MainWindow)->Rect.bottom)
                        {
                                /* When all pixels computed, stop drawing mode
                                    and close the metafile */
                                ((TMyWindow *)MainWindow)->Drawing = FALSE;
                                ((TMyWindow *)MainWindow)->MetaHandle
                                    = CloseMetaFile(
                                    ((TMyWindow *)MainWindow)->MetaDC);
                        }
                        ((TMyWindow *)MainWindow)->At.x = 0;
                }
        }
}


int PASCAL WinMain(HINSTANCE Inst, HINSTANCE PrevInst, LPSTR CmdLine
    , int CmdShow)
{
        TMyApp TheApp("", Inst
                , PrevInst, CmdLine, CmdShow);

        TheApp.Run();
        return TheApp.Status;
}
```

3. Create the resource file META.RES with this menu:

```
METAMENU MENU
BEGIN
        MENUITEM "&Draw", 101
END
```

4. Use the *Run* command to compile and run the program.

HOW IT WORKS

Non-Windows programs can compute the points in the Mandlebrot set by looping through each of the points in the set, and computing the pixel color for each point. This procedure does not work in Windows because the program needs to check for messages periodically to let other programs run. The Windows program must break up the Mandlebrot calculation into small steps that can be computed between messages. This program computes one pixel each time ObjectWindows calls the IdleAction function. The TMyWindow object data member At indicates the next point to compute.

This program uses two different coordinate systems. One represents the pixels of the client area and is bounded by the elements of the member variable Rect. The other coordinate system is the mathematical space that contains the Mandlebrot set. This system is bounded by the data members Left, Top, Right, and Bottom. Note that these coordinates are doubles so that they can represent real numbers. The data members XInterval and YInterval give the size of a window pixel in Mandlebrot set coordinates.

When the user selects the Draw menu command, the program runs the DrawIt menu function. This function sets the current pixel to the upper left corner of the window, computes the values for XInterval and YInterval, creates the metafile device context, and sets the Drawing member variable to TRUE.

The IdleAction function checks the Drawing variable to see if it should be calculating pixels. The first step is to convert the point in At to Mandlebrot set coordinates. The variables XPos and YPos are the coordinates of the point. The while loop in IdleAction does the Mandlebrot computation until the variable Size is less than 4 or the loop has run 512 times. The number of times that the loop runs is used as an index into the palette to get the color for the pixel. IdleAction calls SetPixel twice, once to draw the pixel in the window and once to draw the pixel in the metafile.

After drawing the pixel, IdleAction sets At to point to the next point in the window. Once all of the points are computed, IdleAction closes the metafile, creating a handle that will be used in the WMPaint routine to replay the metafile.

6.6 How Do I...
Use the Color Palette?

Complexity: MODERATE

PROBLEM

Many PC-compatible computers can display as many as 16,777,216 different colors, but only 256 of these colors can be on the screen at one time. The Windows device driver for the screen keeps track of which colors can be displayed in a *system palette*. Each application also has a palette of colors it would like to display. Windows deals out colors from the system palette to different applications in an attempt to prevent one application from changing the colors of another application. This solution shows you how to set up and use a palette in your application.

TECHNIQUE

Windows maintains two types of palettes. One type is the application palette, which is the list of colors from which an application can choose. The second is the system palette, which is the list of all displayed colors. When an application selects a color, it refers to a color in the application palette. Windows gets an index to the system palette from the application palette and gets the actual color to use from the system palette.

A program specifies the colors in the palette by giving the red, green, and blue intensity levels that the video card should combine to create the color. You may be familiar with what happens if you mix red and green paint. You get dark brown or black paint depending on the shades of red and green. The rules are different for mixing light on a CRT screen. In this case, mixing red and green gives yellow. The program in this solution can help you learn how mixing light works by letting you try different combinations.

If an application needs a new color that is not in the system palette, it updates the application palette and tells Windows to realize the palette. Windows looks for matching colors in the system palette and maps the application palette entries to system palette entries. If the color does not exist in the system palette, Windows looks for a system palette entry that is not being used and puts the new color in the system palette. If there are no available system palette entries, Windows attempts to approximate the color by placing different colored pixels next to each other. Because the pixels are small, your eye blends the colors together giving the appearance of a new color.

The Windows function CreatePalette lets you set up a palette in your application. You pass this function a LOGPALETTE structure that contains an array of PALETTEENTRY structures that describe each palette entry. The definitions of these structures are:

```
typedef struct {
      BYTE peRed;          // The amount of red in the color
      BYTE peGreen;        // The amount of green in the color
      BYTE peBlue;         // The amount of blue in the color
      BYTE peFlags;        // PC_EXPLICIT if peRed is an index into the system palette.
                           // PC_NOCOLLAPSE if this color should not be mapped to an existing
                           // entry in the system palette.
                           // PC_RESERVED if this entry will be changed by the application.
} PALETTEENTRY;

typedef struct {
      WORD palVersion;            // Set to 0x300
      WORD palNumEntries;         // How many entries in the palette array
      PALETTEENTRY palPalEntry[]; // Array of entries
} LOGPALETTE;
```

Note that the PALETTEENTRY array in the LOGPALETTE structure does not indicate how many elements are in the array. You must be sure that you allocate space for this array following the structure. Windows will treat any memory following the structure as an array of palNumEntries elements.

The Windows function CreatePalette returns a handle to the palette that can be selected into a device context with the Windows function SelectPalette. You cannot use SelectObject with palettes as you can with other objects such as bitmaps and fonts. After selecting the palette, you have to call the Windows function RealizePalette to get Windows to actually map the colors to the system palette.

In previous examples that used colors, the color was given in a long integer that had red, green, and blue intensities in different bytes. With palettes you also use a long integer to specify the color, but instead of red, green, and blue values, you give an index into the palette. The Windows macro PALETTEINDEX converts an index into the proper COLORREF value.

You can look at the entries in the current application palette by calling the Windows function GetPaletteEntries. This function fills in an array of PALETTEENTRY structures with the palette data for specified entries. To change specified entries, use the Windows function SetPaletteEntries. Note that the changes do not take effect until you call RealizePalette to map in the new colors.

Some video cards can have as many as 256 colors on the screen at a time. For these cards, the system palette is 256 entries, 20 of which are reserved by Windows for system colors. If your application changes colors often, you can quickly use up the remaining 236 colors. To help keep the number of entries used low, Windows lets applications designate an entry as one that it will change from time to time. No other application will use this entry. The Windows function AnimatePalette lets you change this palette entry. You do not have to realize the new palette with AnimatePalette because Windows updates the system palette automatically.

The program below creates a palette of 21 colors. The program draws 20 squares, one for each of the first 20 colors. The 21st color is the window background. The program animates the background color by cycling through all of the possible colors. You can use the mouse to select a square, then bring up a dialog box to edit the red, green, and blue components of the color.

STEPS

1. Create a new project file called COLORS.PRJ that includes the files COLORS.CPP, COLORS.RES, and STANDARD.DEF.

2. Create the source file COLORS.CPP with this source file:

```
/* COLORS.EXE program to demonstrate Windows palettes */
#include <owl.h>
#include <edit.h>
```

```
#define MID_COLOR      101
#define IDC_RED        101
#define IDC_GREEN      102
#define IDC_BLUE       103

/* Definition of the main window */
class TMyWindow : public TWindow
{
     public:
          HPALETTE ThePalette;
          PALETTEENTRY PalColor;
          int SelectedColor;
          struct {
               char Red[5];
               char Green[5];
               char Blue[5];
          } Colors;
          TMyWindow(PTWindowsObject AParent, LPSTR ATitle);
          virtual void SetupWindow();
          virtual void CloseWindow();
          virtual void WMPaint(RTMessage) = [WM_FIRST + WM_PAINT];
          virtual void WMTimer(RTMessage) = [WM_FIRST + WM_TIMER];
          virtual void WMLButtonDown(RTMessage) = [WM_FIRST + WM_LBUTTONDOWN];
          /* Handle messages from the menu */
          virtual void EditColors(RTMessage) = [CM_FIRST + MID_COLOR];
};

/* Color dialog */
class ColorDlg : public TDialog
{
     public:
          ColorDlg(PTWindowsObject AParent, LPSTR AResource);
};

/* Initialize the dialog controls and set up the transfer buffer */
ColorDlg::ColorDlg(PTWindowsObject AParent, LPSTR AResource)
     : TDialog(AParent, AResource)
{
     int i;

     /* Initialize the controls */
     new TEdit(this, IDC_RED, 5);
     new TEdit(this, IDC_GREEN, 5);
     new TEdit(this, IDC_BLUE, 5);
     TransferBuffer = (void far *) &((TMyWindow *) Parent)->Colors;
}

/* Initialize the menu and window data */
TMyWindow::TMyWindow(PTWindowsObject AParent, LPSTR ATitle)
     : TWindow(AParent, ATitle)
{
     int i;

     Attr.W = 350;
     Attr.H = 340;
     AssignMenu("COLORMENU");
}

void TMyWindow::SetupWindow()
```

```
{
     HANDLE Mem;
     LPLOGPALETTE PalData;
     int i;

     Mem = LocalAlloc(LMEM_MOVEABLE, sizeof(LOGPALETTE)
           + sizeof(PALETTEENTRY) * 21);
     PalData = (LPLOGPALETTE) LocalLock(Mem);
     PalData->palVersion = 0x300;
     PalData->palNumEntries = 21;
     /* Set up the colors for the squares */
     for(i=0; i<20; ++i)
     {
          PalData->palPalEntry[i].peRed = 0xFF;
          PalData->palPalEntry[i].peGreen = 0;
          PalData->palPalEntry[i].peBlue = 0;
          PalData->palPalEntry[i].peFlags = 0;
     }
     /* Set up the background colors */
     PalData->palPalEntry[20].peRed = PalColor.peRed = 0;
     PalData->palPalEntry[20].peGreen = PalColor.peGreen = 0;
     PalData->palPalEntry[20].peBlue = PalColor.peBlue = 0;
     PalData->palPalEntry[20].peFlags = PalColor.peFlags = PC_RESERVED;
     ThePalette = CreatePalette(PalData);
     LocalUnlock(Mem);
     LocalFree(Mem);
     SetTimer(HWindow, 1, 500, NULL);
     SelectedColor = 0;
     TWindow::SetupWindow();
}

/* Stop the timer before exiting the program */
void TMyWindow::CloseWindow()
{
     KillTimer(HWindow, 1);
     TWindow::CloseWindow();
}

/* Handle paint messages */
void TMyWindow::WMPaint(RTMessage)
{
     HDC hDC;
     PAINTSTRUCT ps;
     RECT Rect;
     HBRUSH TheBrush;
     int i;

     memset(&ps, 0, sizeof(PAINTSTRUCT));
     hDC = BeginPaint(HWindow, &ps);
     SelectPalette(hDC, ThePalette, 0);
     RealizePalette(hDC);
     GetClientRect(HWindow, &Rect);
     TheBrush = CreateSolidBrush(PALETTEINDEX(20));
     FillRect(hDC, &Rect, TheBrush);
     DeleteObject(TheBrush);
     for(i=0; i<20; ++i)
     {
          TheBrush = CreateSolidBrush(PALETTEINDEX(i));
          Rect.left = 50 + 50 * (i/4);
          Rect.top = 50 + 50 * (i%4);
```

```
                    Rect.right = Rect.left + 40;
                    Rect.bottom = Rect.top + 40;
                    FillRect(hDC, &Rect, TheBrush);
                    DeleteObject(TheBrush);
          }
          EndPaint(HWindow, &ps);
}


/* Change the palette on a timer tick */
void TMyWindow::WMTimer(RTMessage)
{
          PalColor.peRed += 16;
          if(PalColor.peRed == 0)
          {
                    PalColor.peGreen += 16;
                    if(PalColor.peGreen == 0)
                            PalColor.peBlue += 16;
          }
          AnimatePalette(ThePalette, 20, 1, &PalColor);
}


/* Get a button press */
void TMyWindow::WMLButtonDown(RTMessage Msg)
{
          int x, y;

          x = Msg.LP.Lo;
          y = Msg.LP.Hi;
          /* See if the mouse is over one of the squares */
          if(x > 50 && x < 300 && y > 50 && y < 250)
          {
                    /* compute which square */
                    x -= 50;
                    y -= 50;
                    x /= 50;
                    y /= 50;
                    /* Save the square number for editing */
                    SelectedColor = x * 4 + y;
                    SetPaletteEntries(ThePalette, SelectedColor, 1, &PalColor);
                    InvalidateRect(HWindow, NULL, FALSE);
          }
}


void TMyWindow::EditColors(RTMessage)
{
          PALETTEENTRY EditColor;

          /* Get the colors to edit */
          GetPaletteEntries(ThePalette, SelectedColor, 1, &EditColor);
          wsprintf(Colors.Red, "%d", EditColor.peRed);
          wsprintf(Colors.Green, "%d", EditColor.peGreen);
          wsprintf(Colors.Blue, "%d", EditColor.peBlue);
          GetModule()->ExecDialog(new ColorDlg(this, "ColorDialog"));
          EditColor.peRed = atoi(Colors.Red);
          EditColor.peGreen = atoi(Colors.Green);
          EditColor.peBlue = atoi(Colors.Blue);
          SetPaletteEntries(ThePalette, SelectedColor, 1, &EditColor);
```

```
        InvalidateRect(HWindow, NULL, FALSE);
}

/* Define the application object */
class TMyApp : public TApplication
{
    public:
        TMyApp(LPSTR ApName, HINSTANCE Inst, HINSTANCE PrevInst
            , LPSTR CmdLine, int CmdShow) : TApplication(ApName
            , Inst, PrevInst, CmdLine, CmdShow) {};
        virtual void InitMainWindow();
};

/* Create the main window */
void TMyApp::InitMainWindow()
{
    MainWindow = new TMyWindow(NULL, "Colors");
}

int PASCAL WinMain(HINSTANCE Inst, HINSTANCE PrevInst, LPSTR CmdLine
    , int CmdShow)
{
    TMyApp TheApp("", Inst, PrevInst, CmdLine, CmdShow);

    TheApp.Run();
    return TheApp.Status;
}
```

3. Create the resource file COLORS.RES with these resources:

```
COLORMENU MENU
BEGIN
    MENUITEM "&Color", 101
END


COLORDIALOG DIALOG 18, 18, 86, 82
STYLE DS_MODALFRAME | WS_POPUP | WS_CAPTION | WS_SYSMENU
CAPTION "Color edit"
BEGIN
    CONTROL "Red", -1, "STATIC", SS_LEFT | WS_CHILD | WS_VISIBLE | WS_GROUP, 5, 18, 20, 8
    CONTROL "Green", -1, "STATIC", SS_LEFT | WS_CHILD | WS_VISIBLE | WS_GROUP, 5, 33, 20, 8
    CONTROL "Blue", -1, "STATIC", SS_LEFT | WS_CHILD | WS_VISIBLE | WS_GROUP, 5, 48, 20, 8
    CONTROL "", 101, "EDIT", ES_LEFT | WS_CHILD | WS_VISIBLE | WS_BORDER | WS_TABSTOP,
35, 15, 40, 12
    CONTROL "", 102, "EDIT", ES_LEFT | WS_CHILD | WS_VISIBLE | WS_BORDER | WS_TABSTOP,
35, 30, 40, 12
    CONTROL "", 103, "EDIT", ES_LEFT | WS_CHILD | WS_VISIBLE | WS_BORDER | WS_TABSTOP,
35, 45, 40, 12
    CONTROL "Ok", 1, "BUTTON", BS_DEFPUSHBUTTON | WS_CHILD | WS_VISIBLE | WS_TABSTOP, 10,
65, 30, 12
    CONTROL "Cancel", 2, "BUTTON", BS_PUSHBUTTON | WS_CHILD | WS_VISIBLE | WS_TABSTOP,
50, 65, 30, 12
END
```

4. Use the *Run* command to compile and run the program.

HOW IT WORKS

The main window object in this program includes data members for the palette and a structure to transfer data with the dialog. The program initializes the palette data in the SetupWindow member function. The first step in SetupWindow is to allocate space for the LOGPALETTE structure. The LocalAlloc statement allocates room for 21 palette entries. Next, SetupWindow puts the color red in the first 20 palette entries. The function sets the 21st palette entry to black and sets the palette flag to PC_RESERVED so that it can be changed later in the program.

The CreatePalette statement in SetupWindow returns a handle to the application palette. After creating the palette, the program frees the memory block and starts a timer. The timer creates a message every 500 milliseconds until the user stops the program and ObjectWindows calls the CloseWindow member function.

When Windows sends a WM_PAINT message to the program, the WMPaint member function paints the window shown in Figure 6-9. Before drawing the window, WMPaint calls SelectPalette and RealizePalette to use the application palette created in SetupWindow.

The member function WMTimer handles timer messages. This function increments the color for the 21st palette entry. It uses the Windows function AnimatePalette to change the palette color. The result is that the background changes every half second.

The user can save the background color in one of the rectangles by clicking the mouse button over the rectangle to change. The WMLButtonDown function handles this. The if statement determines if the mouse is within the area of the rectangles. If so, the function computes which rectangle the user selected and changes its palette entry.

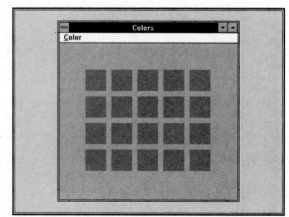

Figure 6-9
The Palette
Program

The dialog box object lets the user edit the red, green, and blue levels for the last rectangle selected. The user starts the dialog by selecting the menu command, which calls the EditColors member function. This function uses the Windows function GetPaletteEntries to get the levels for the selected color. Then it copies these colors to the transfer area and runs the dialog. After running the dialog, the program copies the data from the transfer area back to the application palette.

Customizing Windows 7

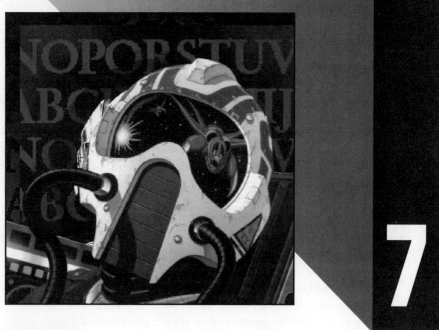

When you first install it, your Windows looks just like everyone else's Windows. Each application that you install looks pretty much like the last one. Before long you will look for ways to decorate Windows with different desktop pictures or change the system colors. This is about as far as a Windows user can go towards customizing Windows. You, as a programmer, can do much more to make your Windows environment unique. This chapter shows you how to add 3-D dialogs to your programs, create custom controls, write your own screen saver and create nonrectangular windows. These techniques are all ways to help you stand out from the crowd by being a little different.

7.1 Make 3-D Dialog Windows

This section shows how to use the 3-D effect used by the dialogs in the Borland C++ IDE in your own programs. Because Borland has already written the routines for these dialogs, this is an easy way to make your programs more interesting.

7.2 Create Custom Controls

One reason to use custom controls is simply to make your program different from others. For example, you can make a custom button that has an animated icon on it. Functionally, such a button adds little to a program; but visually, it makes the program more interesting.

Another reason to use custom controls is to allow a different type of I/O. For example, a sound program could use a custom control that *looks* like a volume control to control the volume. This control not only makes the program more visually interesting, it makes it easier to use by giving the user a control with an obvious function.

The program in this solution shows you how to create a custom scroll bar with a variable-sized thumb. This control not only shows the user the scroll position, but also the proportion of the data that is displayed.

7.3 Make a Screen Saver

Starting with Windows version 3.1, you can install a program to act as a screen saver. You use the control panel program to tell Windows what program to run and how long to wait before running it. When there is no mouse or keyboard command for the specified time interval, Windows runs the program.

The Windows 3.1 SDK includes routines that help you write a screen saver program, but those routines are incompatible with ObjectWindows. This solution shows you how to write an ObjectWindows screen saver.

7.4 Make Nonrectangular Windows

One reason for using rectangular windows is that they are easy to draw. The computer can make a rectangle with just four lines. Clipping graphics so that they fit in the rectangle is easy because it only takes four tests to see if a point is inside the rectangle. When the designers of Windows had to decide what shape to use for Windows, the rectangle was an obvious choice.

With a little extra work, you can use other geometric shapes for your windows. You can use different shapes for different types of windows to identify the window to the user. A nonrectangular window is a surefire attention getter.

This solution uses Windows clipping regions to make different shapes. The possible shapes include ellipses, polygons, and any combination of these shapes. The program in this solution shows the basics by making an elliptical window.

7.5 Use Complex Shapes as Windows

Some shapes are too complex to be represented by a collection of polygons and ellipses. In these cases you cannot use clipping regions to define the window shape. This solution shows how to use a bitmap to define the shape of the window. Using bitmaps makes it possible to create windows of any shape.

7.1 How Do I...
Make 3-D Dialog Windows?

Complexity: EASY

PROBLEM

The Borland C++ IDE uses a nice-looking 3-D effect for its dialog windows. To create this effect, a program must handle paint messages to change the way it draws dialog windows, and create custom controls that fit the 3-D design. Borland programmers have not only done all of this work, but they have made it available to you for use in your own programs. This solution shows how.

TECHNIQUE

The program that uses 3-D dialogs is almost identical to one that uses standard dialogs. The only difference is that the program must load the library BWCC.DLL.

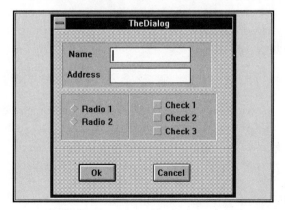

Figure 7-1
A 3-D Dialog

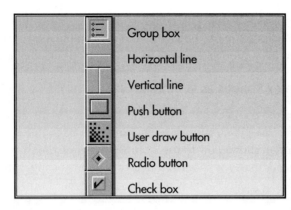

Figure 7-2
The Resource
Workshop
Custom Control

This library registers special window classes for custom dialogs and controls. Once the new window classes are registered, Windows sends any messages for windows created with those classes to the routines in BWCC.DLL. You can create windows that use these classes by returning the class name in the GetClassName member function of a window object. You can also specify the class when you create the dialog or control in the Resource Workshop.

The 3-D effect comes from making the dialog box gray and shading the edges of parts of the dialog box with lighter and darker shades of gray. Figure 7-1 shows a dialog box with several 3-D controls in it. Note how the shading makes some areas appear to stand out and others appear indented.

Putting the normal dialog box controls in the 3-D dialog window would destroy the effect by putting flat controls in the window. To maintain the 3-D illusion, you must use custom controls. Figure 7-2 shows the controls that are available from the Resource Workshop tool window.

The BWCC.DLL library defines the custom controls for 3-D dialog boxes. As far as your program is concerned, these controls are identical to the standard controls. The program below is a standard ObjectWindows program with a dialog window. Pay close attention to the resource file information to see the changes required for 3-D dialogs.

STEPS

1. Create a new project file called DIALOG.PRJ that includes the files DIALOG.CPP, DIALOG.RES, and STANDARD.DEF.

2. Create the program source DIALOG.CPP with this program:

```
/* Dialog example program */
#include <owl.h>

#define IDM_DIALOG          101
```

```
/* The main window class */
class TMyWindow : public TWindow
{
      public:
      HANDLE BWCCMod;
            TMyWindow(PTWindowsObject AParent, LPSTR ATitle);
            ~TMyWindow();
            virtual void DoDialog(RTMessage) = [CM_FIRST + IDM_DIALOG];
            virtual LPSTR GetClassName() {return "MyClass";};
            virtual void GetWindowClass(WNDCLASS& AWndClass);
};

/* Load the menu and the Borland library */
TMyWindow::TMyWindow(PTWindowsObject AParent, LPSTR ATitle)
      : TWindow(AParent, ATitle)
{
      AssignMenu("TheMenu");
      BWCCMod = LoadLibrary("BWCC.DLL");
}

/* Free the Borland library */
TMyWindow::~TMyWindow()
{
      FreeLibrary((HINSTANCE) BWCCMod);
}

/* Set up the icon for the main window */
void TMyWindow::GetWindowClass(WNDCLASS& AWndClass)
{
      TWindow::GetWindowClass(AWndClass);
      AWndClass.hIcon = LoadIcon(GetApplicationObject()->hInstance
            , "ICON_1");
}

/* Execute the dialog */
void TMyWindow::DoDialog(RTMessage)
{
      GetModule()->ExecDialog(new TDialog(this, "TheDialog"));
}

/* The application class */
class TMyApp : public TApplication
{
      public:
            TMyApp(LPSTR ApName, HINSTANCE Inst, HINSTANCE PrevInst
                  , LPSTR CmdLine, int CmdShow) : TApplication(ApName
                  , Inst, PrevInst, CmdLine, CmdShow) {};
            virtual void InitMainWindow();
};

/* Create the main window */
void TMyApp::InitMainWindow()
{
      MainWindow = new TMyWindow(NULL, "3D Dialog");
}

/* Windows entry point */
int PASCAL WinMain(HINSTANCE Inst, HINSTANCE PrevInst, LPSTR CmdLine
      , int CmdShow)
```

```
{
     TMyApp MyApp("", Inst, PrevInst, CmdLine, CmdShow);

     MyApp.Run();
     return MyApp.Status;
}
```

3. Create the resource file DIALOG.RES with these resources:

```
THEMENU MENU
BEGIN
     MENUITEM "&Show dialog", 101
END


THEDIALOG DIALOG 18, 18, 144, 129
STYLE DS_MODALFRAME | WS_POPUP | WS_CAPTION | WS_SYSMENU
CLASS "BorDlg"
CAPTION "TheDialog"
BEGIN
     CONTROL "", 101, "BorShade", 1 | WS_CHILD | WS_VISIBLE, 7, 10, 120, 36
     CONTROL "Name", -1, "STATIC", SS_LEFT | WS_CHILD | WS_VISIBLE | WS_GROUP, 12, 15, 20, 8
     CONTROL "", 102, "EDIT", ES_LEFT|WS_CHILD|WS_VISIBLE|WS_BORDER|WS_TABSTOP,45, 14, 65, 12
     CONTROL "Address", -1, "STATIC", SS_LEFT|WS_CHILD | WS_VISIBLE | WS_GROUP, 11, 31, 30, 8
     CONTROL "", 103, "EDIT", ES_LEFT|WS_CHILD|WS_VISIBLE|WS_BORDER|WS_TABSTOP,45, 30, 65, 12
     CONTROL "", 104, "BorShade", 1 | WS_CHILD | WS_VISIBLE, 6, 50, 125, 37
     CONTROL "Radio 1", 105, "BorRadio", 9 | WS_CHILD | WS_VISIBLE, 13, 57, 35, 10
     CONTROL "Radio 2", 105, "BorRadio", 9|WS_CHILD | WS_VISIBLE, 13, 67, 40, 10
     CONTROL "Check 1", 106, "BorCheck", 3|WS_CHILD | WS_VISIBLE | WS_TABSTOP, 80, 54, 40, 10
     CONTROL "Check 2", 106,"BorCheck", 3| WS_CHILD | WS_VISIBLE | WS_TABSTOP, 80, 64, 40, 10
     CONTROL "Check 3", 106,"BorCheck", 3 | WS_CHILD | WS_VISIBLE | WS_TABSTOP, 80, 75, 40, 9
     CONTROL "", 107, "BorShade", 3 | WS_CHILD | WS_VISIBLE, 60, 50, 2, 36
     CONTROL "Ok", 1, "BUTTON",BS_DEFPUSHBUTTON|WS_CHILD|WS_VISIBLE|WS_TABSTOP, 20,105,30,14
     CONTROL "Cancel", 2, "BUTTON",BS_PUSHBUTTON|WS_CHILD|WS_VISIBLE|WS_TABSTOP,80,105,30,14
     CONTROL "", 110, "BorShade", 2 | WS_CHILD | WS_VISIBLE, 0, 93, 145, 2
END
```

Also include the icon from Figure 7-3. Name it ICON_1.

Figure 7-3
The Dialog
Program Icon

HOW IT WORKS

The program is a very simple program with a dialog window. The main window class, called TMyWindow, includes a member function, called DoDialog, that runs the dialog whenever the user selects the menu command. The constructor for TMyWindow loads the menu and also loads the library BWCC.DLL. Loading the library causes it to register the Windows classes for 3-D dialogs.

The interesting part of this program is the dialog resource. The third line of the dialog definition is the class statement that identifies this dialog as a BorDlg window. This statement tells Windows to send messages for this dialog to the routine registered by BWCC.DLL. Each CONTROL statement also refers to classes registered by

BWCC.DLL. The third field in each statement is the name of the window class to use.

7.2 How Do I...
Create Custom Controls?

Complexity: DIFFICULT

PROBLEM

Some of the controls in How-To 7.1 are custom controls from the BWCC.DLL module. Custom controls let you extend the capabilities of Windows by adding your own devices for displaying information or getting user input. This solution shows you how to create you own control.

TECHNIQUE

A Windows control is a special kind of window, so your new control can come from the TWindow class in ObjectWindows. What makes a control unique is how it draws itself and how it handles messages. Table 7-1 lists some of the Windows messages that a custom control might handle.

In addition to the standard Windows messages, a control may have to handle special messages that only have meaning for that control. For example, a button control handles messages that set and clear the state of the button. With ObjectWindows you can choose to send this type of information to the control with Windows messages or by calling member functions. Using member functions gives much better performance, but may make the control unusable by non-ObjectWindows programs.

Many controls send information to the parent window by sending WM_COMMAND messages. For example, the edit control sends a WM_COMMAND message whenever the user changes the text in the control. The WParam field in a WM_COMMAND message tells the parent window what type of message it is. ObjectWindows controls also exchange information with the parent window through the transfer mechanism. To take advantage of this, the control must define a Transfer member function.

The program in this solution creates an improved scroll bar control. The standard scroll bar control lets you specify a single value by placing the thumb at various positions. When used to control scrolling in a window, the thumb can represent the top, middle, or bottom of the area displayed. The improved con-

MESSAGE	DESCRIPTION
WM_ACTIVATE	Sent when the control becomes active or inactive.
WM_CHAR	Sent when the user presses a character key.
WM_CLOSE	Sent when the control is about to be closed.
WM_CREATE	Sent when the control is created.
WM_DESTROY	Sent when the control is about to be destroyed.
WM_ENABLE	Sent when the control is enabled or disabled.
WM_ERASEBKGND	Sent when Windows wants to redraw the background of the control.
WM_GETDLGCODE	Sent to find out what keys the control uses. This tells Windows if the control or Windows should handle keys such as the arrow keys, Tab, or Enter.
WM_GETTEXT	Sent to find out the text in the control.
WM_GETTEXTLENGTH	Sent to find out how much text is in the control.
WM_KEYDOWN	Sent when the user presses a key.
WM_KEYUP	Sent when the user releases a key.
WM_KILLFOCUS	Sent when the control loses the focus. Many controls change appearance depending on whether they have the focus or not.
WM_LBUTTONDBLCLK	Sent when the user double-clicks the left mouse button.
WM_LBUTTONDOWN	Sent when the user presses the left mouse button.
WM_LBUTTONUP	Sent when the user releases the left mouse button.
WM_MOUSEMOVE	Sent when the mouse moves inside the control.
WM_PAINT	Sent when Windows wants to draw the control.
WM_SETFOCUS	Sent when the control gets the focus. (See WM_KILLFOCUS.)
WM_SETFONT	Sent to set the font that the control should use.
WM_SETTEXT	Sent to set the text in the control.

Table 7-1 Messages Sent to Controls

trol in this solution uses a variable-sized thumb to show the proportion of the displayed area to the total area represented. For example, in a text editor application, if half the text fits in the window, the thumb fills half the control area.

STEPS

1. Create a new project file called THUMB.PRJ that includes the files THUMB.CPP, THUMB.RES, and STANDARD.DEF.

2. Create the source file THUMB.CPP with this program:

```
/* Thumb a program to demonstrate a custom control */
/* define OEMRESOURCE to get constants for built-in bitmaps */
#define OEMRESOURCE
#include <owl.h>
#include <control.h>


#define MID_BIGGER           101
#define MID_SMALLER          102


/* Class for the new scroll bar */
class TMyScroll : public TControl
{
     public:
          int LineMagnitude;
          int ThumbSize;
          int LoRange, HiRange;
          int CntlPos, ThumbPos;
          TMyScroll(PTWindowsObject AParent, int AnID
               , int X, int Y, int W, int H, PTModule AModule = NULL);
          virtual LPSTR GetClassName() {return "NEWSCROLL";};
          virtual void SetupWindow();
          virtual void SetRange(int LoVal, int HiVal);
          virtual void GetRange(int& LoVal, int& HiVal);
          virtual int GetPosition();
          virtual void SetPosition(int ThumbPos);
          virtual void SetThumbSize(int NewSize);
          virtual int GetThumbSize();
          virtual WORD Transfer(Pvoid DataPtr, WORD TransferFlag);
          /* Handle menu commands */
          virtual void WMLButtonDown(RTMessage Msg) = [WM_FIRST + WM_LBUTTONDOWN];
          virtual void WMPaint(RTMessage Msg) = [WM_FIRST + WM_PAINT];
};


/* Initialize the control */
TMyScroll::TMyScroll(PTWindowsObject AParent, int AnID
     , int X, int Y, int W, int H, PTModule AModule)
     : TControl(AParent, AnID, NULL, X, Y, W, H, AModule)
{
     LineMagnitude = 1;        // Amount to add when user presses an arrow
     ThumbPos = 0;             // Start the thumb at the top
     CntlPos = 0;              // Position in range units
     if(Attr.W == 0)           // Use default control size?
          Attr.W = GetSystemMetrics(SM_CXVSCROLL);
     ThumbSize = 20;           // Initial thumb range
}


/* Sets range to 0..100. */
void TMyScroll::SetupWindow()
{
  SetRange(0, 100);
  TControl::SetupWindow();
}


/* Retrieves the range of values that the associated scroll bar can return. */
void TMyScroll::GetRange(int& LoVal, int& HiVal)
{
     LoVal = LoRange;
```

```
        HiVal = HiRange;
}

/* Returns the position of the thumb of the associated scroll bar. */
int TMyScroll::GetPosition()
{
        return CntlPos;
}

/* Sets the range of values that the associated scroll bar can return. */
void TMyScroll::SetRange(int LoVal, int HiVal)
{
        LoRange = LoVal;
        HiRange = HiVal;
}

/* Sets the position of the thumb of the associated scroll bar. */
void TMyScroll::SetPosition(int NewPos)
{
        int LoVal , HiVal;

        /* Get the current control range */
        GetRange(LoVal, HiVal);
        /* See if the new value is in range */
        if(NewPos > HiVal)
                NewPos = HiVal;
        else if (NewPos < LoVal)
                NewPos = LoVal;
        if(CntlPos != NewPos)  // If the position changed
        {
                CntlPos = NewPos;
                ThumbPos = (CntlPos - LoRange)
                        * (Attr.H - ThumbSize - 2 * GetSystemMetrics(SM_CYVSCROLL))
                        / (HiRange - LoRange);
                /* Redraw the control */
                InvalidateRect(HWindow, NULL, FALSE);
        }
}

/* Handle button messages */
void TMyScroll::WMLButtonDown(RTMessage Msg)
{
        /* Check for up arrow */
        if(Msg.LP.Hi < GetSystemMetrics(SM_CYVSCROLL))
                SetPosition(CntlPos - 1);
        /* Check for down arrow */
        else if(Msg.LP.Hi > Attr.H - GetSystemMetrics(SM_CYVSCROLL))
                SetPosition(CntlPos + 1);
}

/* Change the thumb size */
void TMyScroll::SetThumbSize(int NewSize)
{
        int Size;

        /* Scale the size to display units */
        Size = Attr.H - 2 * GetSystemMetrics(SM_CYVSCROLL);
        ThumbSize = NewSize * Size / (HiRange - LoRange);
```

```
        if(ThumbPos + ThumbSize > Size)
            ThumbPos = HiRange - ThumbSize;
        InvalidateRect(HWindow, NULL, FALSE);
}


/* Get the size of the thumb */
int TMyScroll::GetThumbSize()
{
        /* Scale to control units */
        return ThumbSize * (HiRange-LoRange)
            / (Attr.H - 2 * GetSystemMetrics(SM_CYVSCROLL));
}


/* Transfer the thumb position */
WORD TMyScroll::Transfer(Pvoid DataPtr, WORD TransferFlag)
{
        int *NewPtr = (int *)DataPtr;

        if(TransferFlag == TF_GETDATA)
            *NewPtr = CntlPos;
        else
            SetPosition(*NewPtr);
        return sizeof(int);
}


/* Paint the control with a different thumb */
void TMyScroll::WMPaint(RTMessage)
{
        HDC hDC, MemDC;
        HBITMAP OldBitmap;
        HBRUSH OldBrush;
        RECT Rect;
        PAINTSTRUCT ps;
        int BMHeight;

        hDC = BeginPaint(HWindow, &ps);
        /* Create a light gray brush */
        OldBrush = (HBRUSH) SelectObject(hDC, CreateSolidBrush(0xB0B0B0));
        /* Get the height of the arrow bitmaps */
        BMHeight = GetSystemMetrics(SM_CYVSCROLL);
        /* Draw a rectangle filled with light gray */
        GetWindowRect(HWindow, &Rect);
        Rect.bottom -= Rect.top + BMHeight;
        Rect.right -= Rect.left;
        Rect.left = 0;
        Rect.top = BMHeight;
        Rectangle(hDC, Rect.left, Rect.top, Rect.right, Rect.bottom);
        /* Draw the up arrow */
        MemDC = CreateCompatibleDC(hDC);
        OldBitmap = (HBITMAP) SelectObject(MemDC
            , LoadBitmap(NULL, (LPSTR) OBM_UPARROW));
        StretchBlt(hDC, 0, 0, Rect.right, BMHeight
            , MemDC, 0, 0, 15, 15, SRCCOPY);
        /* Draw the down arrow */
        DeleteObject(SelectObject(MemDC, LoadBitmap(NULL, (LPSTR) OBM_DNARROW)));
        StretchBlt(hDC, 0, Rect.bottom, Rect.right, BMHeight-1
            , MemDC, 0, 0, 15, 15, SRCCOPY);
        DeleteObject(SelectObject(MemDC, OldBitmap));
```

```
            DeleteDC(MemDC);
            /* Draw the thumb */
            Rect.top = BMHeight + ThumbPos;
            Rect.bottom = Rect.top + ThumbSize;
            Rect.left += 1;
            Rect.right -= 1;
            DeleteObject(SelectObject(hDC, CreateSolidBrush(0x7F7F7F)));
            Rectangle(hDC, Rect.left, Rect.top, Rect.right, Rect.bottom);
            DeleteObject(SelectObject(hDC, OldBrush));
            EndPaint(HWindow, &ps);
}


/* Definition of the main window */
class TMyWindow : public TWindow
{
     public:
            TMyScroll *TheScroller;
            TMyWindow(PTWindowsObject AParent, LPSTR ATitle);
            /* Handle messages from the menu */
            virtual void Bigger(RTMessage) = [CM_FIRST + MID_BIGGER];
            virtual void Smaller(RTMessage) = [CM_FIRST + MID_SMALLER];
};


/* Initialize the menu and create the control */
TMyWindow::TMyWindow(PTWindowsObject AParent, LPSTR ATitle)
     : TWindow(AParent, ATitle)
{
     AssignMenu("THUMBMENU");
     TheScroller = new TMyScroll(this, 200, 10, 10, 15, 200, FALSE);
}


/* Make the thumb bigger */
void TMyWindow::Bigger(RTMessage)
{
     TheScroller->SetThumbSize(TheScroller->GetThumbSize() + 10);
}


/* Make the thumb smaller */
void TMyWindow::Smaller(RTMessage)
{
     TheScroller->SetThumbSize(TheScroller->GetThumbSize() - 10);
}


/* Define the application object */
class TMyApp : public TApplication
{
     public:
            TMyApp(LPSTR ApName, HINSTANCE Inst, HINSTANCE PrevInst
                 , LPSTR CmdLine, int CmdShow) : TApplication(ApName
                 , Inst, PrevInst, CmdLine, CmdShow) {};
            virtual void InitMainWindow();
};


/* Create the main window */
void TMyApp::InitMainWindow()
{
     MainWindow = new TMyWindow(NULL, "Custom control");
```

```
}

int PASCAL WinMain(HINSTANCE Inst, HINSTANCE PrevInst, LPSTR CmdLine
    , int CmdShow)
{
    TMyApp TheApp("", Inst
            , PrevInst, CmdLine, CmdShow);

    TheApp.Run();
    return TheApp.Status;
}
```

3. Create the resource file THUMB.RES with this menu resource:

```
THUMBMENU MENU
BEGIN
    MENUITEM "&Bigger thumb", 101
    MENUITEM "&Smaller thumb", 102
END
```

4. Use the *Run* command to compile and run the program.

HOW IT WORKS

The TMyScroll object class contains the routines that handle the custom scroll bar control. This class is a descendant of the TControl class so it has all of the features of a standard ObjectWindows control. The constructor for TMyScroll sets up the member data items for the control. The member data items ThumbPos and CntlPos both refer to the position of the thumb. ThumbPos gives the position of the thumb in pixels from the top of the control. CntlPos gives the position relative to the current range. The ThumbSize is the height of the thumb in pixels.

Most of the member functions for TMyScroll set and return values for the data member items. For example, SetRange sets the low and high values that the scroll bar represents. GetRange returns those same values to the calling routine. The member function SetThumbSize not only sets the value of the ThumbSize data item, it invalidates the rectangle so that Windows sends a WM_PAINT message to repaint the control.

The WMPaint member function draws the control. The first step is to draw a light gray rectangle that fills most of the control window. Next, WMPaint gets the system bitmaps for the up and down arrows and draws them at the top and bottom of the control. The constant OEMRESOURCE must be defined at the beginning of the program to use the constants OBM_UPARROW and OBM_DNARROW, which identify the bitmaps. The last step is to draw the thumb. WMPaint uses a dark gray rectangle for the thumb. The member variables ThumbPos and ThumbSize give the position and size of the rectangle.

COMMENT

The custom control shown here shows the basics of creating a control. For most controls, you will want to support more of the messages given in Table 7-1. For example, you should handle the WM_SETFOCUS and WM_KILLFOCUS messages by changing the appearance of the control when it has the input focus.

The quality of the input controls you use determines whether your program is easy or hard to use. Creating a new control involves many iterations of testing and refining until you get it just right. The time you spend here is time well spent if the final result makes your application easier to use.

7.3 How Do I...
Make a Screen Saver?

Complexity: EASY

PROBLEM

The term *screen saver* refers to a program that blanks the screen or draws a moving image when there are no user inputs. The purpose of this type of program is to prevent the phosphor on the video screen from getting an image burned in permanently. Modern screens do not suffer from this problem as much as they used to, but screen saver programs continue to be used. This solution shows how to create a program that Windows 3.1 can install as a screen saver.

TECHNIQUE

The basic structure of a screen saver is the same as for any other Windows program. The differences are that the screen saver draws on the entire screen, exits on any user input message, and includes information in the executable file that identifies the program as a screen saver.

You use the Windows Control Panel program to designate a program as the screen saver program. The Control Panel program looks in the Windows directory for files that have an .SCR extension and include the word SCRNSAVE in the header. To add this information to your program, you must put it in the .DEF file used when linking the program. Here is a sample .DEF file for a screen saver:

```
NAME SAVER
DESCRIPTION 'SCRNSAVE :Circles'
EXETYPE WINDOWS
CODE PRELOAD MOVEABLE DISCARDABLE
DATA PRELOAD MOVEABLE MULTIPLE
HEAPSIZE 4096
STACKSIZE 5120
```

In this .DEF file, the description includes the word SCRNSAVE followed by the name to show in the Control Panel program.

The Control Panel program includes a button to set up the screen saver. If your program includes any options, you can let the user set up the options when he presses this button. The Control Panel tells your program to run the setup dialog by passing the command line option /c or -c. Any options that you set must be stored on the disk so the next time Windows runs the screen saver, the program can read the options. A good place to save setup information is in a profile file such as WIN.INI. Windows includes several functions that read and write profile files so it is easy to put data there.

When Windows has not handled any I/O messages for the time period specified in the Control Panel program, it runs the selected screen saver program. The screen saver should create a window that fills the entire video screen. It can use any Windows functions to draw on the window, make sounds, and handle messages. When Windows sends an I/O message such as a key press or a mouse move, the program should close the window and exit.

The program in this solution draws ellipses or rectangles on the screen. Figure 7-4 shows the results of running this program for a few seconds. There is a setup dialog that lets the user select which object to draw. The program stores its data in a private profile file called SAVER.INI.

STEPS

1. Create a new project called SAVER.PRJ that includes the files SAVER.CPP, SAVER.RES, and SAVER.DEF.

2. Create the source file SAVER.CPP with this program:

```
#include <owl.h>
#include <checkbox.h>

#define IDC_ELLIPSE    101
#define IDC_RECTANGLE  102
```

Figure 7-4
The Screen Saver
Program

```
/* The main window for the screen saver program */
class TMyWindow : public TWindow
{
    public:
        struct {
                WORD DoEllipse;
                WORD DoRectangle;
        } SetupInfo;
        POINT MousePos;
        RECT Screen;
        TMyWindow(PTWindowsObject Parent, LPSTR Title);
        ~TMyWindow();
        virtual LPSTR GetClassName() {return "SaverClass";}
        virtual void GetWindowClass(WNDCLASS& AWndClass);
        virtual void SetupWindow();
        virtual void DefWndProc(RTMessage);
        virtual void WMSysCommand(RTMessage) = [WM_FIRST + WM_SYSCOMMAND];
        virtual void DoDrawing();
};

TMyWindow::TMyWindow(PTWindowsObject Parent, LPSTR Title)
    : TWindow(Parent, Title)
{
    char TmpStr[20];

    /* Get profile information */
    GetPrivateProfileString("Shapes", "Ellipse", "TRUE"
        , TmpStr, 20, "SAVER.INI");
    if(lstrcmp(TmpStr, "TRUE"))
        SetupInfo.DoEllipse = 0;
    else
        SetupInfo.DoEllipse = 1;
    GetPrivateProfileString("Shapes", "Rectangle", "FALSE"
        , TmpStr, 20, "SAVER.INI");
    if(lstrcmp(TmpStr, "TRUE"))
        SetupInfo.DoRectangle = 0;
    else
        SetupInfo.DoRectangle = 1;
    /* Turn off the mouse cursor */
    ShowCursor(FALSE);
    Attr.Style = WS_POPUP;
}

/* Restore the mouse cursor */
TMyWindow::~TMyWindow()
{
    ShowCursor(TRUE);
}

void TMyWindow::GetWindowClass(WNDCLASS& AWndClass)
{
    TWindow::GetWindowClass(AWndClass);
    AWndClass.hIcon = NULL;
    /* Have windows save the screen */
    AWndClass.style |= CS_SAVEBITS;
    AWndClass.hbrBackground = (HBRUSH) GetStockObject(BLACK_BRUSH);
}
```

```c
/* Set up the main window */
void TMyWindow::SetupWindow()
{
    TWindow::SetupWindow();
    /* Save the mouse position */
    GetCursorPos(&MousePos);
    /* Get the dimensions of the screen */
    GetWindowRect(GetDesktopWindow(), &Screen);
    /* Make the window cover the screen */
    MoveWindow(HWindow, Screen.left, Screen.top
        , Screen.right, Screen.bottom, TRUE);
}


/* Look for messages that end the program */
void TMyWindow::DefWndProc(RTMessage Msg)
{
    switch(Msg.Message)
    {
        case WM_MOUSEMOVE:
            /* See if the mouse moved */
            if(LOWORD(Msg.LParam) == MousePos.x
                && HIWORD(Msg.LParam) == MousePos.y)
                break;
        case WM_ACTIVATE:
        case WM_ACTIVATEAPP:
            /* See if the window is activated */
            if(Msg.WParam != 0)
                break;
            /* Check for keypress */
        case WM_KEYDOWN:
        case WM_SYSKEYDOWN:
        /* Check for mouse buttons */
        case WM_LBUTTONDOWN:
        case WM_MBUTTONDOWN:
        case WM_RBUTTONDOWN:
            PostMessage(HWindow, WM_CLOSE, 0, 0L);
    }
    TWindow::DefWndProc(Msg);
}


/* Return true for screen saver system message */
void TMyWindow::WMSysCommand(RTMessage Msg)
{
    if((Msg.WParam&0xFFF0) == SC_SCREENSAVE)
        Msg.Result = TRUE;
    else
        DefWndProc(Msg);
}


/* Draw */
void TMyWindow::DoDrawing()
{
    HDC hDC;
    HBRUSH OldBrush;
    int Left, Top, Right, Bottom;

    hDC = GetDC(HWindow);
    /* Select a solid brush */
```

```
        OldBrush = (HBRUSH) SelectObject(hDC
                , CreateSolidBrush(PALETTEINDEX(random(16))));
        if(SetupInfo.DoEllipse)
        {
                /* Compute the bounding rectangle */
                /* Compute the upper left corner of the bounding rectangle */
                Left = random(Screen.right);
                Top = random(Screen.bottom);
                /* Compute the lower right corner of the bounding rectangle */
                Right = Left + random(Screen.right - Left);
                Bottom = Top + random(Screen.bottom - Top);
                /* Draw the ellipse */
                Ellipse(hDC, Left, Top, Right, Bottom);
        }
        if(SetupInfo.DoRectangle)
        {
                /* Compute the rectangle */
                /* Compute the upper left corner of the bounding rectangle */
                Left = random(Screen.right);
                Top = random(Screen.bottom);
                /* Compute the lower right corner of the bounding rectangle */
                Right = Left + random(Screen.right - Left);
                Bottom = Top + random(Screen.bottom - Top);
                /* Draw the ellipse */
                Rectangle(hDC, Left, Top, Right, Bottom);
        }
        /* Delete the brush */
        DeleteObject(SelectObject(hDC, OldBrush));
        ReleaseDC(HWindow, hDC);
}


/* The setup dialog object */
class TSetupDlg : public TDialog
{
        public:
                struct {
                        WORD DoEllipse;
                                        WORD DoRectangle;
                } SetupInfo;
                PTCheckBox Check1;
                        PTCheckBox Check2;
                TSetupDlg(PTWindowsObject AParent, LPSTR AName);
                virtual void Ok(RTMessage) = [ID_FIRST + IDOK];
};


/* Initialize the dialog data */
TSetupDlg::TSetupDlg(PTWindowsObject AParent, LPSTR AName)
        : TDialog(AParent, AName)
{
        char TmpStr[20];

        /* Get profile information */
        GetPrivateProfileString("Shapes", "Ellipse", "TRUE", TmpStr, 20, "SAVER.INI");
        if(lstrcmp(TmpStr, "TRUE"))
                SetupInfo.DoEllipse = 0;
        else
                SetupInfo.DoEllipse = 1;
        GetPrivateProfileString("Shapes", "Rectangle", "FALSE", TmpStr, 20, "SAVER.INI");
```

```
            if(lstrcmp(TmpStr, "TRUE"))
                  SetupInfo.DoRectangle = 0;
            else
                  SetupInfo.DoRectangle = 1;
            Check1 = new TCheckBox(this, IDC_ELLIPSE, NULL);
            Check2 = new TCheckBox(this, IDC_RECTANGLE, NULL);
            TransferBuffer = (void far *) &SetupInfo;
}


void TSetupDlg::Ok(RTMessage Msg)
{
            char TmpStr[20];

            if(Check1->GetCheck() == BF_CHECKED)
                  lstrcpy(TmpStr, "TRUE");
            else
                  lstrcpy(TmpStr, "FALSE");
            WritePrivateProfileString("Shapes", "Ellipse", TmpStr, "SAVER.INI");
            if(Check2->GetCheck() == BF_CHECKED)
                  lstrcpy(TmpStr, "TRUE");
            else
                  lstrcpy(TmpStr, "FALSE");
            WritePrivateProfileString("Shapes", "Rectangle", TmpStr, "SAVER.INI");
            TDialog::Ok(Msg);
}


/* The application object class */
class TMyApp : public TApplication
{
            public:
                  BOOL Running;
                  TMyApp(LPSTR Name, HINSTANCE hInst, HINSTANCE hPrev
                        , LPSTR Cmnd, int Show)
                        : TApplication(Name, hInst, hPrev, Cmnd, Show) {};
                  virtual void InitMainWindow();
                  virtual void IdleAction();
};


/* Create the main window */
void TMyApp::InitMainWindow()
{
            /* See if running as a dialog or as a screen saver */
            if(*((WORD FAR *) lpCmdLine) == '/c' || *((WORD FAR *) lpCmdLine) == '-c')
            {
                  MainWindow = new TSetupDlg(NULL, "SaveDlg");
                  Running = FALSE;
            }
            else
            {
                  MainWindow = new TMyWindow(NULL, "Screen saver");
                  Running = TRUE;
            }
}


/* Draw Objects*/
void TMyApp::IdleAction()
{
            if(Running)
```

```
      ((TMyWindow *)MainWindow)->DoDrawing();
}

int PASCAL WinMain(HINSTANCE hInst, HINSTANCE hPrev, LPSTR Cmnd, int Show)
{
      TMyApp App("Circle.Saver", hInst, hPrev, Cmnd, Show);

      App.Run();
      return App.Status;
}
```

3. Create the resource file SAVER.RES with this dialog box:

```
SAVEDLG DIALOG 18, 18, 100, 66
STYLE DS_MODALFRAME | WS_POPUP | WS_CAPTION | WS_SYSMENU
CAPTION "Saver Setup"
BEGIN
      CONTROL "Draw ellipses",101,"BUTTON",BS_AUTOCHECKBOX|WS_CHILD | WS_VISIBLE | WS_TABSTOP
          , 16, 15, 55, 12
      CONTROL "Draw rectangles", 102, "BUTTON", BS_AUTOCHECKBOX | WS_CHILD | WS_VISIBLE
          | WS_TABSTOP, 16, 27, 65, 12
      CONTROL "OK", 1, "BUTTON", BS_DEFPUSHBUTTON | WS_CHILD | WS_VISIBLE | WS_TABSTOP
          , 5, 49, 35, 12
      CONTROL "Cancel", 2, "BUTTON", BS_PUSHBUTTON | WS_CHILD | WS_VISIBLE | WS_TABSTOP
          , 60, 49, 35, 12
END
```

4. Create the definition file SAVER.DEF with this information:

```
NAME SAVER
DESCRIPTION 'SCRNSAVE :Circles'
EXETYPE WINDOWS
CODE PRELOAD MOVEABLE DISCARDABLE
DATA PRELOAD MOVEABLE MULTIPLE
HEAPSIZE 4096
STACKSIZE 5120
```

5. Use the *Make* command to compile the program

6. Copy SAVER.EXE to SAVER.SCR in your windows directory.

7. Use the Control Panel program to install the screen saver program.

HOW IT WORKS

There are a number of differences between this program and a standard ObjectWindows program. The first is that the InitMainWindow member function does not just create the main window object. Instead, InitMainWindow checks for a -c or /c command line argument to decide if the main window should be the setup dialog using the TSetupDlg object or the full screen window using TMyWindow. InitMainWindow also sets the member variable Running to determine if the IdleAction member function should draw on the screen.

When the Control Panel program runs this program in setup mode, the main window is the TSetupDlg object. This object uses the dialog in the resource file to ask the user if the program should draw ellipses, rectangles, or both. The constructor for this object reads the private profile file SAVER.INI to get the current settings before showing the dialog. When the user presses the OK button in the dialog, the program calls the Ok member function which puts the data back into SAVER.INI.

When Windows runs this program as a screen saver, the main window is the TMyWindow object. The constructor for this object reads SAVER.INI to find out what to draw. ObjectWindows calls the IdleAction member function whenever there are no messages for this program. IdleAction checks the member variable Running to see if it needs to draw on the screen. If so, it calls the TMyWindow member function DoDrawing to add an object to the screen. DoDrawing uses the techniques from Chapter 6, "Graphics," to draw ellipses and rectangles.

In other examples of ObjectWindows programs in this book, Windows messages are handled by creating an indexed member function for that message. This program does the same thing for several different messages. The normal message handling technique would require a separate function for each message. This program reduces all this to a single function by overloading the DefWndProc member function. This is the function that gets messages directly from Windows. With this function, the program can test for all of the I/O messages to see if it needs to stop the program. When Windows sends one of these messages, the program posts a WM_CLOSE message, which shuts down the program.

The last member function to look at is WMSysCommand. Windows sends a WM_SYSCOMMAND message to exchange system information with applications. ObjectWindows turns this message into a call to WMSysCommand. If the message indicates that Windows is looking for a screen saver program, the program returns TRUE.

COMMENT

Windows comes with several screen savers that anyone can use. You can also get screen saver programs from electronic bulletin boards. But, if you want to be truly unique, you must write your own screen saver. Even though screen savers are not required as much any more, they are still very popular. You will know when you have made a good one because everyone will want to know where they can get a copy.

7.4 How Do I...
Make Nonrectangular Windows?

Complexity: MODERATE

PROBLEM

The big problem with nonrectangular windows is keeping objects within the borders of the window. One approach is to compute the results of everything you are about to draw and draw only the parts that appear inside the window. This solution uses Windows clipping functions to provide a much simpler answer.

TECHNIQUE

The solution to the problem of keeping drawings within the borders of your window is to use Windows clipping regions. A clipping region is an area where drawing is allowed. Any drawing done outside the clipping region is clipped off and not displayed. Windows includes functions that let you create elliptical, rectangular, polygonal, and rounded rectangular regions (see Table 7-2). You can combine regions to make many different shapes (see Figure 7-5).

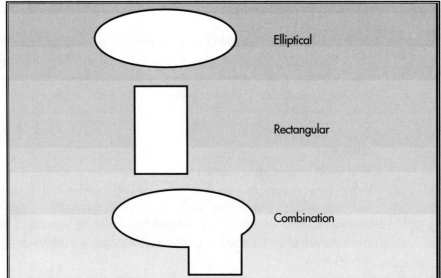

Figure 7-5
Some Possible Clipping Regions

FUNCTION	DESCRIPTION
CombineRgn(&DestRgn, Rgn1, Rgn2, Mode)	Combines Rgn1 and Rgn2.
Rgn = CreateEllipticRgn(X1, Y1, X2, Y2)	Creates an elliptical region.
Rgn = CreateEllipticRgnIndirect(&Rect)	Creates an elliptical region.
Rgn = CreatePolygonRgn(PointArray, Count, FillMode)	Creates a polygonal region.
Rgn = CreatePolyPolygonRgn(PointArray, Polys, Count, Fill)	Creates a region from several polygons.
Rgn = CreateRectRgn(X1, Y1, X2, Y2)	Creates a rectangular region.
Rgn = CreateRectRgnIndirect(&Rect)	Creates a rectangular region.
Rgn = CreateRoundRectRgn(X1, Y1, X2, Y2, X3, Y3)	Creates a rectangular region with rounded corners.
BOOL = EqualRgn(Rgn1, Rgn2)	Returns TRUE if the regions are the same.
FillRgn(hDC, Rgn, Brush)	Fills a region using the brush.
FrameRgn(hDC, Rgn, Brush, Width, Height)	Draws a frame around the region.
GetRgnBox(Rgn, &Rect)	Makes Rect cover the entire region.
InvalidateRgn(HWindow, Rgn, Erase)	Marks a region so it will be repainted.
InvertRgn(hDC, Rgn)	Inverts the colors in the region.
OffsetRgn(Rgn, X, Y)	Moves the region.
PaintRgn(hDC, Rgn)	Fills the region with the selected brush.
BOOL = PtInRegion(Rgn, X, Y)	Checks if the point is in the region.
RectInRegion(Rgn, &Rect)	Checks if part of the rectangle is in the region.
SetRectRgn(Rgn, X1, Y1, X2, Y2)	Changes an existing region to the specified rectangle.

Table 7-2 Region Functions

Once you have created a region, use the Windows function SelectClipRgn to make the region into the clipping region for the specified device context. The following statements show how to create an L-shaped clipping region:

```
/* Create the vertical part */
Rgn1 = CreateRectRgn(10, 10, 50, 130);
/* Create the horizontal part */
Rgn2 = CreateRectRgn(50, 90, 90, 130);
/* Combine the regions */
CombineRgn(&Rgn3, Rgn1, Rgn2, RGN_OR);
/* Select the resulting region */
SelectClipRgn(hDC, Rgn3);
```

Using a clipping region ensures that all the drawing you do to the window will be inside the clipping region. You must also make sure that Windows does not draw outside the clipping region. Before repainting a window, Windows sends a WM_ERASEBKGND message to the program. If the result of this message is FALSE, Windows uses the brush in the window class information to draw the background. Windows does not know about your clipping region, so it fills in the whole window. To prevent this, you must handle the WM_ERASE-BKGND message by returning TRUE.

When the mouse is over a window, Windows sends messages to the program about mouse movements and button presses. If you change the shape of the window with a clipping region, you still get all of the messages for the entire rectangular window. Therefore, you should check to see if the mouse is inside the clipping region before handling any mouse messages. The Windows function PtInRgn returns TRUE if the point is in the region and FALSE if not.

The program in this solution creates an elliptical window. The window contains a single line of text that is enclosed in the clipping region. When the user presses the left mouse button the program exits. Figure 7-6 shows the program.

Figure 7-6
A Nonrectangular
Window

STEPS

1. Create a new project file called REGION.PRJ that includes the files REGION.CPP and STANDARD.DEF.

2. Create the source file REGION.CPP that includes this program:

```
#include <owl.h>

/* The main window */
class TMyWindow : public TWindow
{
    public:
        HRGN TheRegion;
        TMyWindow(PTWindowsObject Parent, LPSTR Title);
        virtual LPSTR GetClassName() {return "RegionClass";}
        virtual void GetWindowClass(WNDCLASS& AWndClass);
        virtual void SetupWindow();
        virtual void WMPaint(RTMessage) = [WM_FIRST+WM_PAINT];
        virtual void WMEraseBkgnd(RTMessage) = [WM_FIRST+WM_ERASEBKGND];
        virtual void WMLButtonDown(RTMessage) = [WM_FIRST+WM_LBUTTONDOWN];
};

TMyWindow::TMyWindow(PTWindowsObject Parent, LPSTR Title)
    : TWindow(Parent, Title)
{
    Attr.Style = WS_POPUP;
    Attr.X = 100;
    Attr.Y = 100;
    Attr.W = 200;
    Attr.H = 100;
}

void TMyWindow::GetWindowClass(WNDCLASS& AWndClass)
{
    TWindow::GetWindowClass(AWndClass);
    AWndClass.hIcon = NULL;
    AWndClass.hbrBackground = NULL;
}

/* Set up the main window */
void TMyWindow::SetupWindow()
{
    RECT Rect;

    TWindow::SetupWindow();
    GetClientRect(HWindow, &Rect);
    TheRegion = CreateEllipticRgnIndirect(&Rect);
}

/* Paint the window */
void TMyWindow::WMPaint(RTMessage)
{
    PAINTSTRUCT ps;
    HDC hDC;
    HBRUSH TheBrush;

    hDC = BeginPaint(HWindow, &ps);
    SelectClipRgn(hDC, TheRegion);
```

```
        TheBrush = CreateSolidBrush(0xFFFFFF);
        FillRgn(hDC, TheRegion, TheBrush);
        DeleteObject(TheBrush);
        TextOut(hDC, 10, 10
              , "This string will be stuffed inside the ellipse", 46);
        TheBrush = CreateSolidBrush(0xFF);
        FrameRgn(hDC, TheRegion, TheBrush, 3, 3);
        DeleteObject(TheBrush);
        EndPaint(HWindow, &ps);
}


/* Don't let Windows paint the background */
void TMyWindow::WMEraseBkgnd(RTMessage Msg)
{
        Msg.Result = (long) TRUE;
}


/* Close if clicked */
void TMyWindow::WMLButtonDown(RTMessage Msg)
{
        /* Make sure the click is in the region */
        if(PtInRegion(TheRegion, Msg.LP.Lo, Msg.LP.Hi))
            PostMessage(HWindow, WM_CLOSE, 0, 0L);
}


/* The application object class */
class TMyApp : public TApplication
{
        public:
            BOOL Running;
            TMyApp(LPSTR Name, HINSTANCE hInst, HINSTANCE hPrev
                  , LPSTR Cmnd, int Show)
                  : TApplication(Name, hInst, hPrev, Cmnd, Show) {};
            virtual void InitMainWindow();
};


/* Create the main window */
void TMyApp::InitMainWindow()
{
        MainWindow = new TMyWindow(NULL, "Regions");
}


int PASCAL WinMain(HINSTANCE hInst, HINSTANCE hPrev, LPSTR Cmnd, int Show)
{
        TMyApp App("", hInst, hPrev, Cmnd, Show);

        App.Run();
        return App.Status;
}
```

3. Use the *Run* command to compile and run the program

HOW IT WORKS

The constructor for the main window sets the window attribute to WS_POPUP. This tells Windows to create a window that does not have a border or title bar. This means that drawing the window is entirely up to the program. The constructor also sets the size of the window.

The SetupWindow member function creates the region. The function stores the handle to the region in the data member TheRegion so that other member functions can use it.

The WMPaint member function selects the region before drawing in the window. After drawing inside the ellipse, WMPaint draws a frame around the region. The frame must be the last step so that it covers anything drawn near the edge of the window.

The WMLButtonDown member function handles button presses from the user. Before doing anything, this function checks to see if the point is inside the clipping region. If so, it sends a WM_CLOSE message to end the program. Otherwise, it ignores the message.

COMMENT

You have to be careful when you put a nonrectangular window on top of another window. If the covered window does not change, everything will appear normal. But, if the covered window draws in its client area, it will not draw inside the rectangle of the window on top of it. In the case of the program in this solution, the corners of the bounding rectangle do not get updated.

The only way to completely prevent this problem is to control what is under the nonrectangular window. The only way to do that is to make the nonrectangular window a child window of a background window. Then, whenever you change the background window, you can hide the child window to make sure everything gets updated.

7.5 How Do I...
Use Complex Shapes as Windows?

Complexity: DIFFICULT

PROBLEM

Clipping regions are OK for regions that can be described as a collection of geometric shapes, but what do you do if the window shape is very complex? This solution shows how you can use bitmaps to create a window that can be any shape you can draw.

TECHNIQUE

You need to have two bitmaps of the image that you want to use as a window. The first is a mask that is white where the background should show through and black where the window is. If you combine this bitmap with the background using the SRCAND ROP, you get an image of the background with a hole in it where the window goes. The image bitmap should be white where the background should show through. When you combine the image with the previous bitmap using SRCPAINT, you get the background with the image in the hole created by the mask. Figure 7-7 illustrates the process.

This technique relies on the program being able to copy the current screen to a bitmap. One way to do this is to create a window that does not erase the background and that covers the area of the current screen you are interested in. Then you can get a device context for the window and BitBlt the window image to a bitmap.

The other way is to get a device context for the desktop window and copy the image directly. Before you can get a device context, you must have the window handle. The Windows function GetDesktopWindow returns the window handle of the desktop. You can pass this handle to GetDC to get the device context.

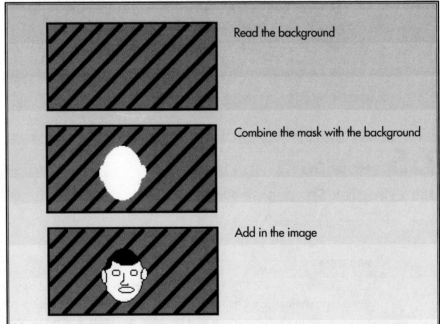

Figure 7-7
Making a
Bitmap
Window

The program in this solution creates a window with the bitmap from How-To 6.2. It moves this window across the top of the screen making holes in the background as required.

STEPS

1. Create a new project file called PLANE.PRJ that includes the files PLANE.CPP, PLANE.RES, and STANDARD.DEF.

2. Create the source file PLANE.CPP with this program:

```
#include <owl.h>

/* The main window */
class TMyWindow : public TWindow
{
    public:
    int XPos;
        HDC MemDC;
        HBITMAP TheBitmap;
        HDC BackDC;
        HBITMAP TheScreen;
        HDC MaskDC;
        HBITMAP TheMask;
        TMyWindow(PTWindowsObject Parent, LPSTR Title);
        ~TMyWindow();
        virtual void SetupWindow();
        virtual void WMTimer(RTMessage) = [WM_FIRST+WM_TIMER];
        virtual void WMPaint(RTMessage) = [WM_FIRST+WM_PAINT];
        virtual void WMEraseBkgnd(RTMessage) = [WM_FIRST+WM_ERASEBKGND];
};

/* Set the window style and position */
TMyWindow::TMyWindow(PTWindowsObject Parent, LPSTR Title)
    : TWindow(Parent, Title)
{
    Attr.Style = WS_POPUP;
    XPos = 640;              // The left edge of the image goes here
    Attr.X = 0;              // Make the window cover the top of the screen
    Attr.Y = 0;
    Attr.W = 640;
    Attr.H = 50;
}

/* Stop the timer and get rid of the bitmaps */
TMyWindow::~TMyWindow()
{
    KillTimer(HWindow, 1);
    DeleteDC(MemDC);
    DeleteObject(TheBitmap);
    DeleteDC(MaskDC);
    DeleteObject(TheMask);
    DeleteDC(BackDC);
    DeleteObject(TheScreen);
```

```
}

/* Set up the main window */
void TMyWindow::SetupWindow()
{
        HDC hDC;

        TWindow::SetupWindow();
        /* Create the airplane DC */
        hDC = GetDC(HWindow);
        MemDC = CreateCompatibleDC(hDC);
        TheBitmap = LoadBitmap(GetApplication()->hInstance, "Airplane");
        SelectObject(MemDC, TheBitmap);
        /* Create the mask DC */
        MaskDC = CreateCompatibleDC(hDC);
        TheMask = LoadBitmap(GetApplication()->hInstance, "TheMask");
        SelectObject(MaskDC, TheMask);
        ReleaseDC(HWindow, hDC);
        /* Create the DC to hold the screen information */
        hDC = GetDC(GetDesktopWindow());
        BackDC = CreateCompatibleDC(hDC);
        TheScreen = CreateCompatibleBitmap(hDC, 640, 50);
        SelectObject(BackDC, TheScreen);
        /* Save some of the main screen */
        BitBlt(BackDC, 0, 0, 640, 50, hDC, 0, 0, SRCCOPY);
        ReleaseDC(HWindow, hDC);
        SetTimer(HWindow, 1, 100, NULL);
}

/* Move the image */
void TMyWindow::WMTimer(RTMessage)
{
        XPos -= 5;
        InvalidateRect(HWindow, NULL, FALSE);
        if(XPos <= -130)
                PostMessage(HWindow, WM_CLOSE, 0, OL);
}

/* Make sure the window does not get erased */
void TMyWindow::WMEraseBkgnd(RTMessage Msg)
{
        Msg.Result = TRUE;
}

/* Handle the WM_PAINT message from Windows */
void TMyWindow::WMPaint(RTMessage)
{
        PAINTSTRUCT ps;
        HDC hDC;
        HDC TempDC;
        HBITMAP TempBitmap;

        /* Clear the ps structure */
        memset(&ps, 0x00, sizeof(PAINTSTRUCT));
        /* Get a device context handle */
```

```
        hDC = BeginPaint(HWindow, &ps);
        TempDC = CreateCompatibleDC(hDC);
        TempBitmap = CreateCompatibleBitmap(hDC, 130, 50);
        SelectObject(TempDC, TempBitmap);
        /* Put back the background */
        BitBlt(TempDC, 0, 0, 130, 50, BackDC, XPos, 0, SRCCOPY);
        /* Make a hole with the mask */
        BitBlt(TempDC, 0, 0, 130, 50, MaskDC, 0, 0, SRCAND);
        /* Put the airplane in the hole */
        BitBlt(TempDC, 0, 0, 130, 50, MemDC, 0, 0, SRCPAINT);
        /* Copy the bitmap to the screen */
        BitBlt(hDC, XPos, 0, 130, 50, TempDC, 0, 0, SRCCOPY);
        /* Free up the temp DC and bitmap */
        DeleteDC(TempDC);
        DeleteObject(TempBitmap);
        EndPaint(HWindow, &ps);
}


/* The application object class */
class TMyApp : public TApplication
{
    public:
        TMyApp(LPSTR Name, HINSTANCE hInst, HINSTANCE hPrev
            , LPSTR Cmnd, int Show)
            : TApplication(Name, hInst, hPrev, Cmnd, Show) {};
        virtual void InitMainWindow();
};

/* Create the main window */
void TMyApp::InitMainWindow()
{
    MainWindow = new TMyWindow(NULL, "The Plane");
}

int PASCAL WinMain(HINSTANCE hInst, HINSTANCE hPrev, LPSTR Cmnd, int Show)
{
    TMyApp App("", hInst, hPrev, Cmnd, Show);

    App.Run();
    return App.Status;
}
```

3. Create the resource file PLANE.RES with the bitmaps shown in Figure 7-8.

4. Use the *Run* command to compile and run the program.

HOW IT WORKS

Like the program in How-To 7.4, this program creates a WS_POPUP window so that Windows does not draw a border. The program also handles the WM_ERASEBKGND message to keep Windows from painting the window background.

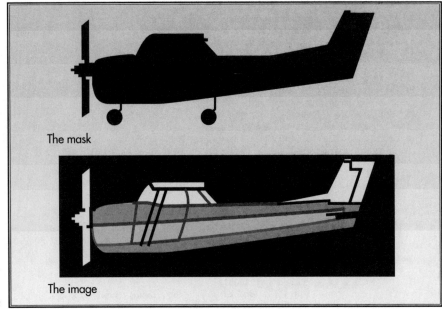

Figure 7-8
The Bitmap
For
PLANE.RES

The mask

The image

The SetupWindow member function creates the Device Contexts and bitmaps required for the program. The data members MemDC and TheBitmap are the Device Context and bitmap for the airplane image. MaskDC and TheMask hold the mask bitmap. The data members BackDC and TheScreen hold the background. The main window object destructor deletes these device contexts and bitmaps before the program exits.

SetupWindow also starts a timer that calls WMTimer every half second. This function changes the value of XPos to move the image to the left, and calls InvalidateRect to repaint the window in the new location. If XPos is less than -130, the image is off the left side of the screen and WMTimer stops the program.

The WMPaint member function paints the image on the screen. It creates its own memory Device Context and bitmap in which it creates the image. First, it copies the screen from BackDC. Next, it uses MaskDC to make a hole in the image. After that, WMPaint adds MemDC to the image. Finally, the function copies the complete image to the screen.

COMMENT

The program must read the screen before it puts the airplane bitmap on it. The reason for this is that once the image is drawn, there is no way to read the screen under the image. The drawback to reading the screen first is that if the screen changes while the image is moving across the screen, the changes do not get copied to the program's copy of the screen. Once the program exits, Windows updates the area under the program's window.

Storing Objects in Files 8

8

A common technique for saving data in a file using standard C is to put the data in a structure and write the structure to the file. To read the data, just read the data back into the same structure. The beauty of this technique is that once it is in memory, the data is available directly from the structure, you do not have to parse it any further.

Things get more complicated when there are pointers in the structure. In this case, you have to write special routines to read and write the data indicated by the pointers. Each structure needs its own set of routines to read and write the data. This is a perfect place to use the object-oriented encapsulation technique to bind the data to the routines that read and write the data.

8.1 Create a File Object

The Windows API includes functions for the usual file operations such as opening, reading, writing, and closing. The program in this solution assembles these functions into an object that you can use in your programs. By accessing files through an object, you can isolate your programs from the details of the file system. This gives several advantages (such as portability) to other operating systems, and the ability to tune the performance of the file routines without changing the program using the file object.

8.2 Save Different Objects in a File

The file object from the first solution in this chapter lets you use files to save and restore objects. If all of the objects that use the file object include read and write member functions, it is easy to save and restore many different types of objects to the same file. This solution shows how to make a file that includes different objects.

8.3 Read and Write Parts of the File

The format of the files created with the file object from the first solution includes a name tag for each object in the file. The reason for this is so that a program can search the file for the objects it needs. This solution shows how to give names to the objects in the file and read back selected objects.

8.1 How Do I...
Create a File Object?

Complexity: EASY

PROBLEM

If you write an MS-DOS program that uses the MS-DOS file functions, you must rewrite it every time you move the program to a new operating system. For example, to move the program to Windows, you should convert all of the calls to MS-DOS file functions to the corresponding Windows API functions.

This solution puts all of the operating system specific file functions into an object. Programs that use this object can be ported to other operating systems by simply changing the file object.

TECHNIQUE

Most programmers are familiar with handling files in programs. First you must open the file, then you read or write the data, and finally close the file. This solution puts all of these functions and more into an object called FileObject. The definition for this object is:

```
/* The file object definition */
class FileObject
{
     public:
             char FileName[260];                 // The name of the file
             BOOL Opened;                         // True when the file is open
             int FileHandle;                      // The MS-DOS file handle
             FileObject(LPSTR Name);              // Constructor
             ~FileObject();                       // Destructor
             void ChangeName(LPSTR Name);         // Select a new file
             void Save(LPSTR Name, int RecSize);  // Put a record header in the file
             int Load(LPSTR Name);                // Look for and read a record header
             int FindSection(LPSTR Name);         // Find a record header
             void Delete();                       // Delete the file
             BOOL Exists();                       // Returns true if the file exists
             void CopyFrom(LPSTR Dest, int Size); // Read data from the file
             void CopyTo(LPSTR Src, int Size);    // Write data to the file
             void OpenIt();                       // Open the file
             void CloseIt();                      // Close the file
};
```

The first thing a program that uses files needs to do is identify the file to use. The file object in this solution keeps the name of the file in the data member FileName. You can set the name in the constructor or change to another file by calling ChangeName. This statement identifies the file DATA.DAT as the file to use in the object MyFile:

```
FileObject MyFile("DATA.DAT");
```

You can read or write any kind of data to MS-DOS files in just about any format. FileObject files use the format shown in Figure 8.1. This format features records that include a record name, the size of the record, and the data for the record. The member function Save creates a record header in the file with the name and size given. For example, to create a record named "Betty" with a record size of 20, use this statement:

```
MyFile.Save("Betty", 20);
```

After calling Save, use the member function CopyTo to write data to the file. This function simply writes the data to the file following the record header.

The member function Load looks through the file for the specified record name in preperation for reading the record. After calling Load, your program can call CopyFrom to read the data.

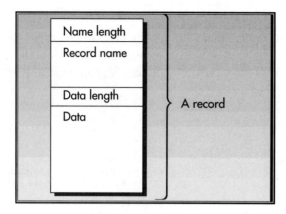

Figure 8-1
The File Format

Windows keeps portions of a file in memory while the file is open. This improves performance by reducing the number of disk reads and writes. The disadvantage is that if you do not close the file, portions of the file can get lost. To prevent data loss, you should call the CloseIt member function before exiting the program.

The program in this solution uses a FileObject object to save the size and position of the main window. If the file does not exist, the program creates a new window; otherwise, it uses the information from the file.

STEPS

1. Create a new project file called SAVEWIND.PRJ that includes the files SAVEWIND.CPP, SAVEWIND.RES, FILEOBJ.CPP, and STANDARD.DEF.

2. Create the source file SAVEWIND.CPP with this program:

```
/* Demonstrate the file object */
#include <io.h>
#include <owl.h>
#include "fileobj.h"

#define MID_SAVE        101

FileObject TheFile("window.sav");

/* Definition of the main window */
class TMyWindow : public TWindow
{
    public:
        TMyWindow(PTWindowsObject AParent, LPSTR ATitle);
        /* Handle messages from the menu */
        virtual void DoSave(RTMessage) = [CM_FIRST + MID_SAVE];
};

/* Initialize the menu */
```

```
TMyWindow::TMyWindow(PTWindowsObject AParent, LPSTR ATitle)
    : TWindow(AParent, ATitle)
{
    /* If file exists, load an object from it */
    if(TheFile.Exists())
    {
        TheFile.Load("Window");
        TheFile.CopyFrom((LPSTR) &Attr.X, sizeof(int));
        TheFile.CopyFrom((LPSTR) &Attr.Y, sizeof(int));
        TheFile.CopyFrom((LPSTR) &Attr.W, sizeof(int));
        TheFile.CopyFrom((LPSTR) &Attr.H, sizeof(int));
    }
    AssignMenu("FileMenu");
}

/* Save the window in a stream file */
void TMyWindow::DoSave(RTMessage)
{
    /* Get rid of the old file if it exists */
    TheFile.Delete();
    /* Save this object */
    TheFile.Save("Window", 8);
    TheFile.CopyTo((LPSTR) &Attr.X, sizeof(int));
    TheFile.CopyTo((LPSTR) &Attr.Y, sizeof(int));
    TheFile.CopyTo((LPSTR) &Attr.W, sizeof(int));
    TheFile.CopyTo((LPSTR) &Attr.H, sizeof(int));
}

/* Define the application object */
class TMyApp : public TApplication
{
    public:
        TMyApp(LPSTR ApName, HINSTANCE Inst, HINSTANCE PrevInst
            , LPSTR CmdLine, int CmdShow) : TApplication(ApName
            , Inst, PrevInst, CmdLine, CmdShow) {};
        virtual void InitMainWindow();
};

void TMyApp::InitMainWindow()
{
    MainWindow = new TMyWindow(NULL, "Persistant window");
}

int PASCAL WinMain(HINSTANCE Inst, HINSTANCE PrevInst, LPSTR CmdLine
    , int CmdShow)
{
    TMyApp TheApp("", Inst, PrevInst, CmdLine, CmdShow);

    TheApp.Run();
    return TheApp.Status;
}
```

   3. Create the source file FILEOBJ.CPP with this program:

```
/* File object routines */
#include <owl.h>
#include "fileobj.h"

/* Initialize a file object */
```

```
FileObject::FileObject(LPSTR Name)
{
     lstrcpy(FileName, Name);
     Opened = FALSE;
}

/* Get rid of the file object */
FileObject::~FileObject()
{
     CloseIt();
}

/* Save an object */
void FileObject::Save(LPSTR Name, int RecSize)
{
     int Size;

     /* Open the file if it is not already opened */
     OpenIt();
     /* Look for the section */
     if(FindSection(Name) != RecSize)
     {
          /* If section not found, go to the end of the file */
          _llseek(FileHandle, 0L, 2);
          /* Write the section name */
          Size = lstrlen(Name) + 1;
          _lwrite(FileHandle, &Size, sizeof(int));
          _lwrite(FileHandle, Name, Size);
          /* Write the size of the section */
          _lwrite(FileHandle, &RecSize, sizeof(int));
     }
}

/* Load an object */
int FileObject::Load(LPSTR Name)
{
     /* Open the file if it is not already opened */
     OpenIt();
     /* Look for the section */
     return FindSection(Name);
}

int FileObject::FindSection(LPSTR Name)
{
     int Size;
     char TmpStr[40];
   long Pos;

     /* Get the current position */
     Pos = _llseek(FileHandle, 0L, 1);
     /* While more data, keep looking */
     while(_lread(FileHandle, &Size, sizeof(int))==sizeof(int))
     {
          /* Get the section name */
          _lread(FileHandle, TmpStr, Size);
          Pos += (long) (sizeof(int) + Size);
          /* Get the size of the section */
          _lread(FileHandle, &Size, sizeof(int));
```

```
            /* See if this is the right section */
            if(!lstrcmp(TmpStr, Name))
                 return Size;
            /* Otherwise, skip this section */
            Pos += (long) (sizeof(int) + Size);
        _llseek(FileHandle, Pos, 0);
     }
     return 0;
}


/* Return true if the file exists */
BOOL FileObject::Exists()
{
     /* If the file is opened, it must exist */
     if(Opened)
          return TRUE;
     /* If it can be opened, it must exist */
     if((FileHandle = _lopen(FileName, OF_READWRITE|OF_SHARE_DENY_WRITE))!= -1)
     {
          _lclose(FileHandle);
          return TRUE;
     }
     return FALSE;
}


/* Open the file */
void FileObject::OpenIt()
{
     if(Opened)
     {
          /* Go to the begining of the file */
          _llseek(FileHandle, 0L, 0);
     }
     else
     {
          /* Open or create the file as required */
          if((FileHandle = _lopen(FileName
               , OF_READWRITE|OF_SHARE_DENY_WRITE)) == -1)
               FileHandle = _lcreat(FileName, 0);
          Opened = TRUE;
     }
}


/* Close the file */
void FileObject::CloseIt()
{
     /* If the file is opened, close it */
     if(Opened)
     {
          _lclose(FileHandle);
          Opened = FALSE;
     }
}


/* Write data to the file at the current location */
void FileObject::CopyTo(LPSTR Data, int Size)
{
     _lwrite(FileHandle, Data, Size);
```

══════311

```
}

/* Read data from the file */
void FileObject::CopyFrom(LPSTR Data, int Size)
{
     _lread(FileHandle, Data, Size);
}

/* Delete the file */
void FileObject::Delete()
{
     /* If the file is opened, close it */
     CloseIt();
     /* Delete the file */
     unlink(FileName);
}

/* Change the name of the file */
void FileObject::ChangeName(LPSTR Name)
{
     /* If there is already a file, close it */
     CloseIt();
     lstrcpy(FileName, Name);
}
```

4. Create the include file FILEOBJ.H with this definition:

```
/* The file object definition */
class FileObject
{
     public:
          char FileName[260];              // The name of the file
          BOOL Opened;                     // True when the file is open
          int FileHandle;                  // The MS-DOS file handle
          FileObject(LPSTR Name);          // Constructor
          ~FileObject();                   // Destructor
          void ChangeName(LPSTR Name);     // Select a new file
          void Save(LPSTR Name, int RecSize); // Put a record header in the file
          int Load(LPSTR Name);            // Look for and read a record header
          int FindSection(LPSTR Name);     // Find a record header
          void Delete();                   // Delete the file
          BOOL Exists();                   // Returns true if the file exists
          void CopyFrom(LPSTR Dest, int Size); // Read data from the file
          void CopyTo(LPSTR Src, int Size);    // Write data to the file
          void OpenIt();                   // Open the file
          void CloseIt();                  // Close the file
};
```

5. Create the resource file SAVEWIND.CPP with this menu:

```
FILEMENU MENU
BEGIN
     MENUITEM "&Save window", 101
END
```

6. Use the *Run* command to compile and run the program.

HOW IT WORKS

This program creates a file object named TheFile near the beginning of the program. The name of the file is window.sav. The constructor for the main window object uses the Exists member function to see if the file already exists. If the file exists, the constructor uses the Load and CopyFrom member functions to read the size and position information from the file. If the file does not exist, the program uses the default size and position for the main window.

You can use the standard controls to move and resize the window while the program is running. When you get a window you want to save, use the *Save window* menu command. This calls the DoSave member function which calls Save and CopyTo to save the window information in the file.

COMMENT

One of the first things that many programmers notice when they access files in a program that reading and writing small pieces of a file is very slow. This is because there is a certain amount of overhead for each call to the operating system. If you can read or write large blocks to the file at one time, you reduce the number of operating system calls and improve the performance of your program.

Gathering file reads and writes into large chunks can be difficult in a standard C program. The statements that read and write may be scattered all over the program. You need to come up with a way to associate buffer and pointer variables with each file. None of these problems apply to the file object. The functions you need to change are CopyTo and CopyFrom. Putting the buffer and pointer variables into the object automatically associates them with the correct file.

Object-oriented programming lets you make these changes to the object without having to make any changes to the main program. You need only update the definition of the object in the include file and in FILEOBJ.CPP. Then recompile and relink the main program.

8.2 How Do I...
Save Different Objects in a File?

Complexity: EASY

PROBLEM

You can use the object-oriented feature of polymorphism to make it easy to save different objects in a file using the FileObject class from the previous solution.

To do this, add member functions to the object that read and write the neccesary data for the object. A program can save an object that includes these member functions without knowing anything about the object.

TECHNIQUE

There are three member functions that you must add to an object to make it work with the FileObject class. The first member function is FileRead, which calls the CopyFrom member function in the FileObject object to get data from the file. The next function is FileWrite, which calls CopyTo to write data to the file. The last funciton is RecSize, which returns the number of bytes read or written by the first two functions.

The data that an object stores in the file is often the data that is created when the object is created. For example, an object representing an ellipse gets the co-ordinates of the bounding rectangle in the constructor. If the ellipse is saved in a file, you need a special constructor that calls the FileRead member function to get the coordinates.

The program in this example includes ellipse and rectangle objects that can be stored and retreived using a FileObject. There are menu commands to create new images such as in Figure 8.2, save the image in a file, and restore the images from a file.

STEPS

1. Create a new project file called OBJSAVER.PRJ that includes the files OBJSAVER.CPP, OBJSAVER.RES, FILEOBJ.CPP, and STANDARD.DEF.

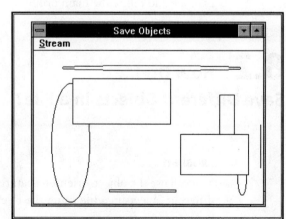

Figure 8-2

Elipse and Rectangle Objects

2. Create the source file OBJSAVER.CPP with this progam:

```
/* Show the file dialog object */
#include <owl.h>
#include <filedial.h>
#include <string.h>
#include <time.h>
#include <stdlib.h>
#include "fileobj.h"

#define IDM_NEW  101
#define IDM_OPEN 102
#define IDM_SAVE 103

FileObject TheFile("");

/* The objects to save on the stream */
class TEllipse
{
    public:
        RECT TheRect;
        TEllipse(RECT *ClientRect);
        TEllipse(FileObject *fo);
        virtual void Draw(HDC hDC);
        virtual void FileRead(FileObject *fo);
        virtual void FileWrite(FileObject *fo);
        virtual int RecSize() {return sizeof(RECT);};
};

/* Make a new ellipse */
TEllipse::TEllipse(RECT *ClientRect)
{
    /* Compute the upper left corner of the bounding rectangle */
    TheRect.left = random(ClientRect->right);
    TheRect.top = random(ClientRect->bottom);
    /* Compute the lower right corner of the bounding rectangle */
    TheRect.right = TheRect.left
        + random(ClientRect->right - TheRect.left);
    TheRect.bottom = TheRect.top
        + random(ClientRect->bottom - TheRect.top);
}

/* Create a new ellipse from file data */
TEllipse::TEllipse(FileObject *fo)
{
    FileRead(fo);
}

/* Draw the ellipses */
void TEllipse::Draw(HDC hDC)
{
    Ellipse(hDC, TheRect.left, TheRect.top
        , TheRect.right, TheRect.bottom);
}

void TEllipse::FileRead(FileObject *fo)
{
    fo->CopyFrom((LPSTR) &TheRect, sizeof(RECT));
}
```

```
void TEllipse::FileWrite(FileObject *fo)
{
      fo->CopyTo((LPSTR) &TheRect, sizeof(RECT));
}


class TRect
{
      public:
            RECT TheRect;
            TRect(RECT *ClientRect);
            TRect(FileObject *fo);
            virtual void Draw(HDC hDC);
            virtual void FileRead(FileObject *fo);
            virtual void FileWrite(FileObject *fo);
            virtual int RecSize() {return sizeof(RECT);};
};

/* Make a new Rectangle */
TRect::TRect(RECT *ClientRect)
{
      /* Compute the upper left corner of the bounding rectangle */
      TheRect.left = random(ClientRect->right);
      TheRect.top = random(ClientRect->bottom);
      /* Compute the lower right corner of the bounding rectangle */
      TheRect.right = TheRect.left
            + random(ClientRect->right - TheRect.left);
      TheRect.bottom = TheRect.top
            + random(ClientRect->bottom - TheRect.top);
}


/* Make a rectangle from file data */
TRect::TRect(FileObject *fo)
{
      FileRead(fo);
}


/* Draw the Rectangle */
void TRect::Draw(HDC hDC)
{
      Rectangle(hDC, TheRect.left, TheRect.top
            , TheRect.right, TheRect.bottom);
}


void TRect::FileRead(FileObject *fo)
{
      fo->CopyFrom((LPSTR) &TheRect, sizeof(RECT));
}


void TRect::FileWrite(FileObject *fo)
{
      fo->CopyTo((LPSTR) &TheRect, sizeof(RECT));
}


/* The main window object */
class TMyWindow : public TWindow
{
      public:
```

```
              char FileName[MAXPATH];
              long FileSize;
              TEllipse *TheEllipses[10];
              int EllipseCnt;
              TRect *TheRects[10];
              int RectCnt;

              TMyWindow(PTWindowsObject AParent, LPSTR ATitle);
              virtual void NewPict(RTMessage) = [CM_FIRST + IDM_NEW];
              virtual void OpenFile(RTMessage) = [CM_FIRST + IDM_OPEN];
              virtual void SaveFile(RTMessage) = [CM_FIRST + IDM_SAVE];
              virtual void WMPaint(RTMessage) = [WM_FIRST + WM_PAINT];
};

TMyWindow::TMyWindow(PTWindowsObject AParent, LPSTR ATitle)
        : TWindow(AParent, ATitle)
{
        randomize();
        EllipseCnt = 0;
        RectCnt = 0;
        lstrcpy(FileName, "pict.sav");
        AssignMenu("SaverMenu");
}

/* Create a new list of ellipses */
void TMyWindow::NewPict(RTMessage)
{
        RECT ClientRect;
        int i;

        /* Get rid of the old objects */
        for(i=0; i<EllipseCnt; ++i)
              delete TheEllipses[i];
        for(i=0; i<RectCnt; ++i)
              delete TheRects[i];
        /* Get the corners of the window */
        GetClientRect(HWindow, &ClientRect);
        EllipseCnt = random(10);
        for(i=0; i<EllipseCnt; ++i)
              TheEllipses[i] = new TEllipse(&ClientRect);
        RectCnt = random(10);
        for(i=0; i<RectCnt; ++i)
              TheRects[i] = new TRect(&ClientRect);
        InvalidateRect(HWindow, NULL, FALSE);
}

/* Select the file */
void TMyWindow::OpenFile(RTMessage)
{
        int i;

        lstrcpy(FileName, "*.sav");
        if(GetApplication()->ExecDialog(new TFileDialog(this
            , SD_FILEOPEN, FileName)) == IDOK)
        {
              /* Get rid of the old objects */
              for(i=0; i<EllipseCnt; ++i)
                    delete TheEllipses[i];
```

```
            for(i=0; i<RectCnt; ++i)
                delete TheRects[i];
            TheFile.ChangeName(FileName);
            TheFile.Load("Pict");
            TheFile.CopyFrom((LPSTR) &EllipseCnt, sizeof(int));
            for(i=0; i<EllipseCnt; ++i)
                TheEllipses[i] = new TEllipse(&TheFile);
            TheFile.CopyFrom((LPSTR) &RectCnt, sizeof(int));
            for(i=0; i<RectCnt; ++i)
                TheRects[i] = new TRect(&TheFile);
            InvalidateRect(HWindow, NULL, FALSE);
        }
}


/* Save the objects in a file */
void TMyWindow::SaveFile(RTMessage)
{
        int i;

        if(GetApplication()->ExecDialog(new TFileDialog(this
            , SD_FILESAVE, FileName)) == IDOK)
        {
            TheFile.ChangeName(FileName);
            TheFile.Save("Pict", sizeof(int) * 2
                + EllipseCnt * TheEllipses[0]->RecSize()
                + EllipseCnt * TheRects[0]->RecSize());
            TheFile.CopyTo((LPSTR) &EllipseCnt, sizeof(int));
            for(i=0; i<EllipseCnt; ++i)
                TheEllipses[i]->FileWrite(&TheFile);
            TheFile.CopyTo((LPSTR) &RectCnt, sizeof(int));
            for(i=0; i<RectCnt; ++i)
                TheRects[i]->FileWrite(&TheFile);
        }
}


/* Paint the ellipse object */
void TMyWindow::WMPaint(RTMessage)
{
        HBRUSH TheBrush;
        RECT ClientRect;
        int i;

        PAINTSTRUCT ps;
        HDC hDC;
        memset(&ps, 0x00, sizeof(PAINTSTRUCT));
        hDC = BeginPaint(HWindow, &ps);
        GetClientRect(HWindow, &ClientRect);
        TheBrush = CreateSolidBrush(0xFFFFFF);
        FillRect(hDC, &ClientRect, TheBrush);
        DeleteObject(TheBrush);
        for(i=0; i<EllipseCnt; ++i)
            TheEllipses[i]->Draw(hDC);
        for(i=0; i<RectCnt; ++i)
            TheRects[i]->Draw(hDC);
        EndPaint(HWindow, &ps);
}


class TMyApp : public TApplication
```

```
{
    public:
            TMyApp(LPSTR ApName, HINSTANCE Inst, HINSTANCE PrevInst
                , LPSTR CmdLine, int CmdShow) : TApplication(ApName
                , Inst, PrevInst, CmdLine, CmdShow) {};
            virtual void InitMainWindow();
};

void TMyApp::InitMainWindow()
{
    MainWindow = new TMyWindow(NULL, "Save Objects");
}

int PASCAL WinMain(HINSTANCE Inst, HINSTANCE PrevInst, LPSTR CmdLine
    , int CmdShow)
{

    TMyApp TheApp("", Inst, PrevInst, CmdLine, CmdShow);

    TheApp.Run();
    return TheApp.Status;
}
```

3. Copy FILEOBJ.CPP and FILEOBJ.H from How-To 8.1.

4. Use the procedure from How-To 3.2 to put the file save and open standard dialogs into the resource file OBJSAVER.RES. Then, add this menu resource:

```
SAVERMENU MENU
BEGIN
    POPUP "&Stream"
    BEGIN
        MENUITEM "&New", 101
        MENUITEM "&Load", 102
        MENUITEM "&Save", 103
    END

END
```

5. Use the *Run* command to compile and run the program.

HOW IT WORKS

The main window object includes two arrays of pointers. The first is a list of pointers to ellipse objects and the second is a list of pointers to rectangle objects. The member variables EllipseCnt and RectCnt tell how many objects are currently in each of the lists.

When the user selects the *New* menu command, the program creates a random number of ellipses and rectangles. Before it creates new objects, it uses the delete operator to get any existing objects out of memory. Then, the program calls the constructor for each of these objects to create random sized objects using the same techniques as in Chapter 6, "Graphics."

To save an image, the user selects the *Save* menu command. This command brings up the save file standard dialog to get a file name from the user. If the user exits the dialog box by pressing OK, the program puts the file name into the file object and writes information about the objects in the window to the file. The first step is to call the FileObject member function Save to create a record for the objects. The size includes two integers that give the number of ellipses and rectangles and the size of an ellipse object (given by the RecSize member function) times the number of ellipses and the size of a rectangle object times the number of rectangles. After creating the record, the program calls the FileWrite member function for each object in the window to write the data to the file.

The user can restore any saved image by selecting the *Load* command from the menu. The first thing this command does is to delete any existing objects. Then it brings up the Open file standard dialog to get a file name from the user. If the user selected OK, then the program copies the file name to the file object and calls the Load member function to get ready to read the file. The first read gives the number of ellipses in the file. The program creates the required ellipses by calling the ellipse object constructor. This constructor calls the FileRead member function to get the coordinates from the file. After all of the ellipses are read, the program does the same thing for the rectangles.

8.3 How Do I...
Read and Write Parts of the File?

Complexity: EASY

PROBLEM

In the previous solutions in this chapter, the programs read and wrote the complete file. This solution shows you how to use the names stored in the file to selectivly retrieve portions of the file. This lets you pick and choose the objects that should be in memory and those that can remain on the disk.

TECHNIQUE

The FileObject class presented in the first solution includes everything that you need to read and write portions of the file. Before writing a piece of the file, you should call the FileObject member function Save to put a marker in front of the data. Then when you read the file, use Load to find the marker in the file.

Each time you call Save, it looks for a record with the same name and size as the record you are about to save. This lets you overwrite existing records with new data. If there is not a suitable record in the file, FileObject puts the new record at the end of the file.

The Load member function searches from the begining to the end of the file looking for a record with the same name. The fact that the size of each record is included in the record header lets this function skip over records without having to know anything about the data in the record. When Load finds the right record, the file pointer is in the correct position to begin reading data.

The program in this solution lets you save different groups of ellipse objects to the file. Each time you save or restore a group, the program shows a dialog like the one in Figure 8.3 to get the name of the record.

STEPS

1. Create a new project file called PARTS.PRJ with the files PARTS.CPP, PARTS.RES, FILEOBJ.CPP, and STANDARD.DEF.

2. Create the source PARTS.CPP with this program:

```
/* Add an index to object files */
#include <owl.h>
#include <filedial.h>
#include <string.h>
#include <time.h>
#include <stdlib.h>
#include <edit.h>
#include "fileobj.h"

#define IDM_NEW   101
#define IDM_LOAD 102
#define IDM_SAVE 103

FileObject TheFile("COLLECT.SAV");

/* The objects to save on the stream */
class TEllipse
{
```

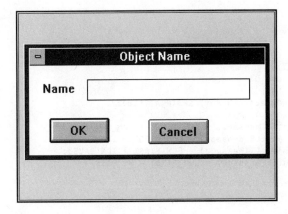

Figure 8-3
The Group
Name Dialog

```
      public:
            RECT TheRect;
            TEllipse(RECT *ClientRect);
            TEllipse(FileObject *fo);
            virtual void Draw(HDC hDC);
            virtual void FileRead(FileObject *fo);
            virtual void FileWrite(FileObject *fo);
};

/* Make a new ellipse */
TEllipse::TEllipse(RECT *ClientRect)
{
      /* Compute the upper left corner of the bounding rectangle */
      TheRect.left = random(ClientRect->right);
      TheRect.top = random(ClientRect->bottom);
      /* Compute the lower right corner of the bounding rectangle */
      TheRect.right = TheRect.left
            + random(ClientRect->right - TheRect.left);
      TheRect.bottom = TheRect.top
            + random(ClientRect->bottom - TheRect.top);
}

/* Make a new ellipse from data in the file */
TEllipse::TEllipse(FileObject *fo)
{
      FileRead(fo);
}

/* Draw the ellipses */
void TEllipse::Draw(HDC hDC)
{
      Ellipse(hDC, TheRect.left, TheRect.top, TheRect.right, TheRect.bottom);
}

void TEllipse::FileRead(FileObject *fo)
{
      fo->CopyFrom((LPSTR) &TheRect, sizeof(RECT));
}

void TEllipse::FileWrite(FileObject *fo)
{
      fo->CopyTo((LPSTR) &TheRect, sizeof(RECT));
}

class TMyWindow : public TWindow
{
      public:
            char ObjectName[40];
            TEllipse *TheEllipses[10];
            int EllipseCnt;
            TMyWindow(PTWindowsObject AParent, LPSTR ATitle);
            ~TMyWindow();
            virtual void NewPict(RTMessage) = [CM_FIRST + IDM_NEW];
            virtual void LoadObject(RTMessage) = [CM_FIRST + IDM_LOAD];
            virtual void SaveObject(RTMessage) = [CM_FIRST + IDM_SAVE];
            virtual void WMPaint(RTMessage) = [WM_FIRST + WM_PAINT];
};

/* The object name dialog */
class NameDlg : public TDialog
```

```
{
    public:
        NameDlg(PTWindowsObject AParent, LPSTR AResource);
};

/* Initialise the dialog controls and set up the transfer buffer */
NameDlg::NameDlg(PTWindowsObject AParent, LPSTR AResource)
    : TDialog(AParent, AResource)
{
    new TEdit(this, 101, 40);
    TransferBuffer = (void far *) &((TMyWindow *) Parent)->ObjectName;
}

TMyWindow::TMyWindow(PTWindowsObject AParent, LPSTR ATitle)
    : TWindow(AParent, ATitle)
{
    randomize();
    EllipseCnt = 0;
    lstrcpy(ObjectName, "First");
    AssignMenu("PartsMenu");
}

/* Be sure to close the file */
TMyWindow::~TMyWindow()
{
    TheFile.CloseIt();
}

/* Create a new list of ellipses */
void TMyWindow::NewPict(RTMessage)
{
    RECT ClientRect;
    int i;

    /* Get rid of the old objects */
    for(i=0; i<EllipseCnt; ++i)
        delete TheEllipses[i];
    /* Get the corners of the window */
    GetClientRect(HWindow, &ClientRect);
    EllipseCnt = random(10);
    for(i=0; i<EllipseCnt; ++i)
        TheEllipses[i] = new TEllipse(&ClientRect);
    InvalidateRect(HWindow, NULL, FALSE);
}

/* Select the Object */
void TMyWindow::LoadObject(RTMessage)
{
    int i;

    lstrcpy(ObjectName, "");
    if(GetApplication()->ExecDialog(
        new NameDlg((PTWindowsObject)this, "NameDialog")) == IDOK)
    {
        /* Get rid of the old objects */
        for(i=0; i<EllipseCnt; ++i)
            delete TheEllipses[i];
        if(TheFile.Load(ObjectName))
        {
            TheFile.CopyFrom((LPSTR) &EllipseCnt, sizeof(int));
```

```
                            for(i=0; i<EllipseCnt; ++i)
                                    TheEllipses[i] = new TEllipse(&TheFile);
                    }
                    else
                            EllipseCnt = 0;
                    InvalidateRect(HWindow, NULL, FALSE);
        }
}


/* Save the objects in a file */
void TMyWindow::SaveObject(RTMessage)
{
        int i;

        if(GetApplication()->ExecDialog
            (new NameDlg((PTWindowsObject)this, "NameDialog")) == IDOK)
        {
            TheFile.Save(ObjectName, sizeof(int)
                    + EllipseCnt * sizeof(RECT));
            TheFile.CopyTo((LPSTR) &EllipseCnt, sizeof(int));
            for(i=0; i<EllipseCnt; ++i)
                    TheEllipses[i]->FileWrite(&TheFile);
        }
}


/* Paint the ellipse object */
void TMyWindow::WMPaint(RTMessage)
{
        HBRUSH TheBrush;
        RECT ClientRect;
        int i;

        PAINTSTRUCT ps;
        HDC hDC;
        memset(&ps, 0x00, sizeof(PAINTSTRUCT));
        hDC = BeginPaint(HWindow, &ps);
        GetClientRect(HWindow, &ClientRect);
        TheBrush = CreateSolidBrush(0xFFFFFF);
        FillRect(hDC, &ClientRect, TheBrush);
        DeleteObject(TheBrush);
        for(i=0; i<EllipseCnt; ++i)
                TheEllipses[i]->Draw(hDC);
        EndPaint(HWindow, &ps);
}


class TMyApp : public TApplication
{
        public:
                TMyApp(LPSTR ApName, HINSTANCE Inst, HINSTANCE PrevInst
                    , LPSTR CmdLine, int CmdShow) : TApplication(ApName
                    , Inst, PrevInst, CmdLine, CmdShow) {};
                virtual void InitMainWindow();
};


void TMyApp::InitMainWindow()
{
        MainWindow = new TMyWindow(NULL, "File Parts");
}


int PASCAL WinMain(HINSTANCE Inst, HINSTANCE PrevInst, LPSTR CmdLine
```

```
     , int CmdShow)
{
     TMyApp TheApp("", Inst, PrevInst, CmdLine, CmdShow);

     TheApp.Run();
     return TheApp.Status;
}
```

3. Copy the files FILEOBJ.CPP and FILEOBJ.H from How To 8.1.

4. Create the resource file PARTS.RES with these resources:

```
PARTSMENU MENU
BEGIN
      POPUP "Index"
      BEGIN
            MENUITEM "&New", 101
            MENUITEM "&Load", 102
            MENUITEM "&Save", 103
      END

END

NAMEDIALOG DIALOG 18, 18, 138, 51
STYLE DS_MODALFRAME | WS_POPUP | WS_CAPTION | WS_SYSMENU
CAPTION "Object Name"
BEGIN
      CONTROL "Name", -1, "STATIC", SS_LEFT|WS_CHILD | WS_VISIBLE | WS_GROUP, 8, 9, 25, 8
      CONTROL "", 101, "EDIT", ES_LEFT|WS_CHILD|WS_VISIBLE|WS_BORDER|WS_TABSTOP, 34, 8, 95, 12
      CONTROL "OK", 1, "BUTTON", BS_DEFPUSHBUTTON |WS_CHILD|WS_VISIBLE|WS_TABSTOP, 12, 30, 35,14
      CONTROL "Cancel", 2, "BUTTON", BS_|WS_CHILD|WS_VISIBLE|WS_TABSTOP, 70, 31, 35, 14
END
```

5. Use the *Run* command to compile and run the program.

HOW IT WORKS

The difference between this program and the ones in the previous solutions is that this one includes a dialog object that gets the record name from the user. When the user selects the *Load* menu command, the program uses the dialog to get the name to pass to the Load member function. Then the program creates the objects with the constructor that reads the file. Saving works the same way, except the program calls the Save member function to position the record and FileWrite to save the data.

COMMENT

Searching through the entire file to find a record takes more and more time as the size of the file increases. One solution to this problem is to add an index of record names to the beginning of the file. This index can be used to locate the records instead of the searching method. Because the file routines are in an object, you can make this change without modifying the main program.

DDE
Connections 9

9

By exchanging data, you can add features from other applications to your own. For example, you can exchange data with a terminal emulation program to send and receive data with other computers. By using the terminal emulation program, you do not have to add a terminal emulation module to your program. The Dynamic Data Exchange (DDE) feature of Windows is a protocol that applications can use to exchange data.

Applications that use DDE set up *conversations* in which one application is the *server* and the other is the *client*. The server handles transactions from the client that establish conversations, exchange data, and execute commands. The client identifies the server and the data by name. If you know the names provided by any given server, you can make a DDE connection.

The data and names in DDE use shared memory segments and the Windows atom table. Before Windows version 3.1, DDE applications had to handle the shared memory and atom tables for each transaction. In addition, the application had to create special windows and handle extra messages. Windows 3.1 includes a simplified API for DDE that is fully compatible with older DDE programs. Windows 3.0 users can run programs that use the new API by adding the DDEML.DLL file from Windows 3.1.

This chapter shows how to use the Windows 3.1 API to develop programs that use DDE. This API is easier to use, and programs that use the API are more likely to be compatible with future revisions to DDE.

9.1 Create a DDE Server

The DDE server waits for transactions from clients and performs the requested service. Servers register a service name for the server and one or more topic names. Then, the server waits for connection transactions from clients. Once the client makes a connection, the server handles transactions to send and receive data and commands.

This solution shows how to create a server application that handles multiple topics. Each topic has three data items that the server can exchange with client applications.

9.2 Create a DDE Client

The DDE client program initiates transactions with the server. It requests a specific service and topic for a conversation. Then the client asks for data, and sends data and commands to the server. This solution shows how to make a client program that talks to the server in the first solution.

9.3 Get Updated Data from the Server

One problem with having the client request data from the server is that the client does not know when the server data changes. One solution is to request the data continuously, waiting for the data to change. The main drawback to this technique is that it uses up CPU time to keep polling.

This solution shows how to use the DDE *Advise* transaction to have the server inform the client when data changes. In this technique, the client has a callback function that Windows calls when the server sends an advise transaction.

9.4 Execute Commands on the Server

The DDE protocol includes a transaction for executing commands on the server. The commands can be part of a macro language used by the server or they can be used to execute menu commands. This solution shows how to implement the execute transaction.

9.1 How Do I...
Create a DDE Server?

Complexity: MODERATE

PROBLEM

Every DDE conversation has two sides, a server and a client. Although it is possible to make a program that is both a client and a server, the most common case is to make separate programs for each part. This solution shows how to make the server side of the conversation.

TECHNIQUE

The DDE server's job is to wait for a transaction from a client and act on that transaction. The server provides a callback function to handle DDE transactions. The program calls the Windows function DdeInitialize to tell Windows what function to use for callbacks. The prototype for the callback function is:

```
HDDEDATA CALLBACK DdeCallBack(UINT Type, UINT Format, HCONV TheConversation, HSZ Name1
, HSZ Name2, HDDEDATA DataHandle, DWORD Data1, DWORD Data2);
```

The name and data arguments to the callback function have different meanings depending on the type of transaction given in the Type argument. Table 9-1 lists the possible types and the meanings of the arguments for each type.

The Format argument gives the type of data for the transaction. The formats are the same as the ones used for the Clipboard. For this solution, the format is always CF_TEXT.

Once a conversation is established, it has a conversation handle that is passed in the argument TheConversation. DDE applications can have several conversations going on at once, so you must check the conversation handle to see for what conversation the transaction is intended.

The Windows function DdeInitialize tells Windows what function to use for DDE callbacks. The first argument to this function is a pointer to a double word that the function fills with an application instance identifier. You must keep this value (often called idInst) to pass to other DDE functions.

Each DDE server must have a name that clients can use to identify the server. Most servers use the program name as the server name. If you do not use the

Type	Arguments	Description
XTYP_ADVDATA	Name1=Topic	Data sent by the server to the
	Name2=Item	client.
	DataHandle=Advise data	
XTYP_ADVREQ	Name1=Topic	Sent to a server when server
	Name2=Item	calls DdePostAdvise.
	Data1=Transaction count	
XTYP_ADVSTART	Name1=Topic	Sent to server when client
	Name2=Item	wants to be advised.
XTYP_ADVSTOP	Name1=Topic	Sent to server when client does
	Name2=Item	not want to be advised anymore.
XTYP_CONNECT	Name1=Topic	Sent to server when a client
	Name2= Server name	wants a connection.
	Data1=Conversation context	
	Data2=Same instance flag	
XTYP_CONNECT	Name1=Topic	Sent to server when client
_CONFIRM	Name2=Item	confirms a conversation.
	Data2=Same instance flag	
XTYP_DISCONNECT	Data2=Same instance flag	Sent to server when the client
		disconnects.
XTYP_ERROR	Data1=Error value	Received on critical DDE error.
XTYP_EXECUTE	Name1=Topic	Sent to server for Execute
	DataHandle=Command	transaction.
XTYP_MONITOR	DataHandle=Event data	Sent to DDE debugging
	Data2=Event flag	programs.
XTYP_POKE	Name1=Topic	Sent to server with data to poke.
	Name2=Item	
	DataHandle=The data	
XTYP_REGISTER	Name1=Server name	Sent to all callbacks when a
	Name2=Server instance	server registers a name.
XTYP_REQUEST	Name1=Topic	Sent to server when the client
	Name2=Item	wants data.

(continued from page 332)

XTYP_UNREGISTER	Name1=Server name	Sent to all callbacks when a
	Name2=Server instance	server unregisters a name.
XTYP_WILDCONNECT	Name1=Topic	Sent to all servers when the
	Name2=Server name	client leaves out the server or
	Data1=Conversation context	topic name on a connection.
	Data2=Same instance flag	
XTYP_XACT_COMPLETE	Name1=Topic	Sent to client when a
	Name2=Item	transaction is complete.
	DataHandle=Transaction data	
	Data1=Transaction ID	
	Data2=Status flag	

Table 9-1 DDE Transaction Types

program name for the server, you need to include the server name in the documentation so that clients know what server to call.

Each server can have several topics. The topic name often refers to different files that the server can load. For example, a word processing DDE server can have topics for each document being edited. When the client makes a connection, it selects the topic along with the server to use.

In Windows, one application cannot access the data segment of another application. This means that you cannot pass the address of the service and topic names as you would with other Windows functions. DDE programs use *shared memory* and the *atom table* to pass data between applications. Shared memory is a memory block in the global heap that has the GMEM_DDESHARE flag set. Windows allows any application to use shared memory blocks. The atom table is a list of strings maintained by Windows. When an application adds a string to the atom table, Windows returns a unique handle for the string. Other applications can access the string by giving Windows the handle. The Windows function DdeCreateStringHandle adds a string to the atom table and returns a handle. This statement puts the string "My Name" into the atom table and puts the handle in the variable NameHandle:

```
NameHandle = DdeCreateStringHandle(idInst, "My Name", CP_WINANSI);
```

The last argument is a flag indicating the code page for the character set used. This is important for names in other languages that use extended ASCII characters. When you are done with the names, you must remove them from the atom table by calling DdeFreeStringHandle.

The server must register the service name and each topic name by calling the Windows function DdeNameService. The names must be converted to string handles with DdeCreateStringHandle before passing them to this function. The DdeNameService function can both register and unregister names depending on a flag passed to the function. When the names are registered, any client that attempts to connect to the registered names sends a XTYP_CONNECT transaction to the server's callback.

With DDE initialized and the names registered, there is nothing more for the server to do until a transaction comes in. Figure 9-1 illustrates the connection process. The first transaction that it can expect is an XTYP_CONNECT. The server needs to verify that the connection can be made and return TRUE if all is well. If the server returns TRUE, it will get an XTYP_CONNECT_CONFIRM transaction that gives the conversation handle for the connection. Your program should save the conversation handle to identify conversations in future transactions.

After a server is connected to a client, the server can expect several different transaction messages. This solution handles the XTYP_REQUEST, XTYP_POKE, XTYP_DISCONNECT, and XTYP_ERROR transactions. All servers should handle the XTYP_DISCONNECT (the client no longer wants a connection) and the XTYP_ERROR (there has been a critical error) transactions by releasing any resources used for the connection.

The XTYP_REQUEST transaction arrives when the client wants data from the server. The Name1 argument is the topic name and Name2 is the item name for the data to return. The item name identifies the specific data item to return. For example, if the server is a spreadsheet program, the item name is the cell to transfer. If the server can supply the requested data, it should use the DdeCreateDataHandle function to get a handle to put the data into a shared

Figure 9-1
Making a
DDE
Connection

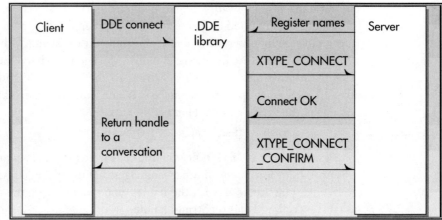

memory block and return the handle. This statement returns the data "Here is some data" to the client:

```
return DdeCreateDataHandle(idInst, "Here is some data", 18, 0, Name2, CF_TEXT, 0);
```

The numbers following the data string are the length of the data and the starting position in the data buffer. The last argument is a flag that sets the type of shared memory to use. Making this value 0 tells Windows to free the block after the data is transferred. The second to the last argument gives the format of the data. If you want to pass some other type of data, you need to use the correct format type here. For example, to pass a bitmap, you would use CF_BITMAP.

The XTYP_POKE transaction tells the server that the client wants to change a data item. In addition to the topic and item names, this transaction uses the DataHandle argument as the handle to the data to poke. If the data can be poked, the server should return TRUE. You must use the Windows function DdeGetData to convert the data handle back into the actual data. This statement gets the data received in a XTYP_POKE transaction:

```
DdeGetData(DataHandle, TmpStr, 80, 0);
```

The variable TmpStr is a buffer for the data. The next number is the length of the buffer and the last number is the offset for the data in the buffer.

The program in this solution is an MDI application in which each child window is a different DDE topic. The child windows have three lines of text that client programs can read through DDE. Figure 9-2 shows the program with several child windows.

STEPS

1. Create a new project called SERVER.PRJ that includes the files SERVER.CPP, SERVER.RES, and STANDARD.DEF.

2. Create the source file SERVER.CPP with this program:

```
/* SERVER.CPP A DDE Server */
#include <owl.h>
#include <mdi.h>
#include <edit.h>
#include <ddeml.h>

/* The application object for this program */
class TMyApp : public TApplication
{
    public:
        TMyApp(LPSTR AName, HANDLE Inst, HANDLE Prev
            , LPSTR lpCmdLine, int nCmdShow)
            : TApplication(AName, Inst, Prev, lpCmdLine, nCmdShow) {};
        virtual void InitMainWindow();
};
```

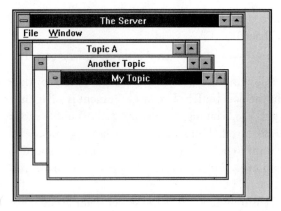

Figure 9-2
The Server
Program

```
/* The child window object */
class TMyMDIChild : public TWindow
{
     public:
             char TheData1[80];      // First data item for DDE
             char TheData2[80];      // Second data item for DDE
             char TheData3[80];      // Third data item for DDE
             HSZ  TopicHandle;       // Handle for the topic name string
             DWORD idInst;
             HCONV Conv;             // Handle for the DDE conversation
             TMyMDIChild(PTWindowsObject AParent, LPSTR WinName
                  , DWORD DDEInst);
             ~TMyMDIChild();
             virtual void SetData(LPSTR Data, int Which);
             virtual LPSTR GetData(int Which);
             virtual LPSTR GetClassName() {return "MyMDIChild";};
             virtual void GetWindowClass(WNDCLASS& AWndClass);
             virtual void WMPaint(RTMessage) = [WM_FIRST + WM_PAINT];
};

typedef TMyMDIChild _FAR *PChild;

/* Initialize a new topic window */
TMyMDIChild::TMyMDIChild(PTWindowsObject AParent, LPSTR WinName
     , DWORD DDEInst) : TWindow(AParent, WinName)
{
     Conv = NULL;
     idInst = DDEInst;
     TopicHandle = DdeCreateStringHandle(DDEInst, WinName, CP_WINANSI);
}

/* Clean up the topic */
TMyMDIChild::~TMyMDIChild()
{
     /* Disconnect if necessary */
     if(Conv)
           DdeDisconnect(Conv);
     DdeFreeStringHandle(idInst, TopicHandle);
}
```

```
/* Set one of the data items */
void TMyMDIChild::SetData(LPSTR Data, int Which)
{
     switch(Which)
     {
          case 1:
                  lstrcpy(TheData1, Data);
                  break;
          case 2:
                  lstrcpy(TheData2, Data);
                  break;
          case 3:
                  lstrcpy(TheData3, Data);
                  break;
     }
     /* Force a repaint */
     InvalidateRect(HWindow, NULL, FALSE);
}


/* Get the data from one of the data items */
LPSTR TMyMDIChild::GetData(int Which)
{
     switch(Which)
     {
          case 1:
                  return TheData1;
          case 2:
                  return TheData2;
          case 3:
                  return TheData3;
     }
     return NULL;
}


/* Set up the icon for the program */
void TMyMDIChild::GetWindowClass(WNDCLASS& AWndClass)
{
     TWindow::GetWindowClass(AWndClass);
     AWndClass.hIcon = LoadIcon(AWndClass.hInstance, "ChildPict");
}


/* Paint the data items in the middle of the child window */
void TMyMDIChild::WMPaint(RTMessage)
{
     PAINTSTRUCT ps;
     HDC hDC;
     RECT Rect;
     WORD Size;

     hDC = BeginPaint(HWindow, &ps);
     GetClientRect(HWindow, &Rect);
     /* Erase the window */
     FillRect(hDC, &Rect, GetStockObject(WHITE_BRUSH));
     /* Center the text */
     Size = GetTextExtent(hDC, TheData1, lstrlen(TheData1));
     TextOut(hDC, (Rect.right-LOWORD(Size))/2
             , (Rect.bottom-HIWORD(Size))/2 - HIWORD(Size)
```

```
                , TheData1, lstrlen(TheData1));
        Size = GetTextExtent(hDC, TheData2, lstrlen(TheData2));
        TextOut(hDC, (Rect.right-LOWORD(Size))/2
                , (Rect.bottom-HIWORD(Size))/2, TheData2, lstrlen(TheData2));
        Size = GetTextExtent(hDC, TheData3, lstrlen(TheData3));
        TextOut(hDC, (Rect.right-LOWORD(Size))/2
                , (Rect.bottom-HIWORD(Size))/2 + HIWORD(Size)
                , TheData3, lstrlen(TheData3));
        EndPaint(HWindow, &ps);
}


/* The frame window for the MDI application */
class TMyMDIFrame : public TMDIFrame
{
        public:
                /* Scratch variables for the dialogs */
                char NewTopic[80];      /* Topic name */
                char NewData1[80];      /* First data item */
                char NewData2[80];      /* Second data item */
                char NewData3[80];      /* Third data item */
                FARPROC CallBackInst;   /* Instance handle to the call back function */
                DWORD idInst;           /* The DDE instance handle */
                HSZ   ServiceName;      /* Handle to the name of this server */
                HSZ Items[3];           /* Handle for the item names */
                TMyMDIFrame(LPSTR ATitle);
                TMyMDIFrame();
                virtual LPSTR GetClassName() {return "MDIFrame";};
                virtual void GetWindowClass(WNDCLASS& AWndClass);
                virtual void SetupWindow();
                virtual PTWindowsObject CreateChild();
                static HDDEDATA FAR PASCAL _export CallBack(WORD, WORD, HCONV
                        , HSZ, HSZ, HDDEDATA, DWORD, DWORD );
};


TMyMDIFrame *FrameWindow;


/* Initialize variables */
TMyMDIFrame::TMyMDIFrame(LPSTR ATitle)
        : TMDIFrame(ATitle, "MDIMenu")
{
        ChildMenuPos = 1;
        NewTopic[0] = NewData1[0] = '\0';
        NewData2[0] = NewData3[0] = '\0';
        rameWindow = this;
}


/* Clean up the DDE stuff */
TMyMDIFrame::~TMyMDIFrame()
{
        DdeNameService(idInst, ServiceName, NULL, DNS_UNREGISTER);
        deFreeStringHandle(idInst, ServiceName);
        DdeFreeStringHandle(idInst, Items[0]);
        DdeFreeStringHandle(idInst, Items[1]);
        DdeFreeStringHandle(idInst, Items[2]);
        FreeProcInstance(CallBackInst);
}


/* Set up the program icon */
```

```
void TMyMDIFrame::GetWindowClass(WNDCLASS& AWndClass)
{
     TMDIFrame::GetWindowClass(AWndClass);
     AWndClass.hIcon = LoadIcon(AWndClass.hInstance, "DDEServer");
}


/* Initialize DDE service */
void TMyMDIFrame::SetupWindow()
{
     idInst = 0; // Initialize the instance number
     CallBackInst = MakeProcInstance((FARPROC) TMyMDIFrame::CallBack
          , GetApplication()->hInstance );
     * Set up DDE service */
     DdeInitialize(&idInst, (PFNCALLBACK) CallBackInst
          , APPCLASS_STANDARD, OL);
     ServiceName = DdeCreateStringHandle(idInst, "MyServer"
          , CP_WINANSI);
     Items[0] = DdeCreateStringHandle(idInst, "Item 1", CP_WINANSI);
     Items[1] = DdeCreateStringHandle(idInst, "Item 2", CP_WINANSI);
     Items[2] = DdeCreateStringHandle(idInst, "Item 3", CP_WINANSI);
     DdeNameService(idInst, ServiceName, NULL, DNS_REGISTER);
     TMDIFrame::SetupWindow();
}


/* Dialog for window name */
class TMyDlg : public TDialog
{
     public:
          TMyDlg(PTWindowsObject AParent, LPSTR AResource);
};


/* Initialize the dialog controls and set up the transfer buffer */
TMyDlg::TMyDlg(PTWindowsObject AParent, LPSTR AResource)
     : TDialog(AParent, AResource)
{
     new TEdit(this, 101, 80);
     new TEdit(this, 102, 80);
     new TEdit(this, 103, 80);
     new TEdit(this, 104, 80);
     TransferBuffer = (void far *) &((TMyMDIFrame *) Parent)->NewTopic;
}


/* Make a new topic window */
PTWindowsObject TMyMDIFrame::CreateChild()
{
     PTWindowsObject pw;

     if(GetApplication()->ExecDialog(
          new TMyDlg(this, "WindowName")) == IDOK)
     {
          pw = GetApplication()->MakeWindow(
               new TMyMDIChild(this, NewTopic, idInst));
          /* Copy the data to the new object */
          ((TMyMDIChild *) pw)->SetData(NewData1, 1);
          ((TMyMDIChild *) pw)->SetData(NewData2, 2);
          ((TMyMDIChild *) pw)->SetData(NewData3, 3);
          return pw;
     }
```

```
        return NULL;
}


/* Find the child for a topic */
BOOL
FirstTopic(Pvoid P, Pvoid D)
{
      return (DdeCmpStringHandles(((PChild) P)->TopicHandle
            , (HSZ) D) == 0);
}


/* Find the child for a conversation */
BOOL
FirstConv(Pvoid P, Pvoid D)
{
      return (((PChild) P)->Conv == (HCONV) D);
}



/* This is where all the DDE messages come in */
HDDEDATA FAR PASCAL TMyMDIFrame::CallBack(WORD Type, WORD
      , HCONV Conv, HSZ hsz1, HSZ hsz2, HDDEDATA hData, DWORD
      , DWORD)
{
      char TmpStr[80];
      int Item;
      PChild CurrentTopic;

      switch(Type)
      {
            /* The client is trying to make contact */
            case XTYP_CONNECT:
                if((CurrentTopic = (PChild)
                      (FrameWindow->FirstThat(FirstTopic, (Pvoid) hsz1)))
                      != NULL && CurrentTopic->Conv == 0)
                      return (HDDEDATA) TRUE;
                  return 0;
            /* Server library is confirming connection by giving the conversation handle */
            case XTYP_CONNECT_CONFIRM:
                if((CurrentTopic = (PChild)
                      (FrameWindow->FirstThat(FirstTopic, (Pvoid) hsz1)))
                      != NULL && CurrentTopic->Conv == 0)
                      CurrentTopic->Conv = Conv;
                break;
            /* The client wants to disconnect */
            case XTYP_DISCONNECT:
                if((CurrentTopic = (PChild)
                      (FrameWindow->FirstThat(FirstConv, (Pvoid) Conv))) != NULL)
                      CurrentTopic->Conv = 0;
                break;
            /* The client is sending data */
            case XTYP_POKE:
                CurrentTopic = (PChild)
                      (FrameWindow->FirstThat(FirstConv, (Pvoid) Conv));
                if(CurrentTopic)
                {
                      /* Look for the right item name */
                      for(Item=0; Item<3
```

```
                        && DdeCmpStringHandles(FrameWindow->Items[Item], hsz2)
                        ; ++Item);
                /* If all is well, put the data in the window */
                if(Item < 3)
                {
                        DdeGetData(hData, &TmpStr, 80, 0);
                        CurrentTopic->SetData(TmpStr, Item+1);
                        return (HDDEDATA)DDE_FACK;
                }
            }
            return DDE_FNOTPROCESSED;
        /* The client wants data */
        case XTYP_REQUEST:
            CurrentTopic = (PChild)
                    (FrameWindow->FirstThat(FirstConv, (Pvoid) Conv));
            if(CurrentTopic)
            {
                for(Item=0; Item<3
                        && DdeCmpStringHandles(FrameWindow->Items[Item], hsz2)
                        ; ++Item);
                /* Get the data to return */
                if(Item<3)
                {
                        return DdeCreateDataHandle(FrameWindow->idInst
                                , CurrentTopic->GetData(Item+1)
                                , lstrlen(CurrentTopic->GetData(Item+1))+1
                                , 0, hsz2, CF_TEXT, 0);
                }
            }
            return NULL;
        default :
            break;
    }
    return NULL;
}

/* Create the frame window */
void TMyApp::InitMainWindow()
{
  MainWindow = new TMyMDIFrame(Name);
}

/* Program entry point */
int PASCAL WinMain(HANDLE hInstance, HANDLE hPrevInstance, LPSTR lpCmdLine, int nCmdShow)
{
    TMyApp MyApp("The Server", hInstance
    , hPrevInstance, lpCmdLine, nCmdShow);

    MyApp.Run();
    return MyApp.Status;
}
```

   3. Create the resource file SERVER.RES with these resources:

```
MDIMENU MENU
BEGIN
    POPUP "&File"
    BEGIN
```

```
            MENUITEM "&New", 24339
            MENUITEM "&Exit", 24340
     END

     POPUP "&Window"
     BEGIN
            MENUITEM "&Cascade", 24337
            MENUITEM "&Tile", 24336
            MENUITEM "&Arrange icons", 24335
            MENUITEM "&Close all", 24338
     END

END

WINDOWNAME DIALOG 18, 18, 142, 99
STYLE DS_MODALFRAME | WS_POPUP | WS_CAPTION | WS_SYSMENU
CAPTION "New topic"
BEGIN
     CONTROL "Topic name", -1, "STATIC",SS_LEFT|WS_CHILD|WS_VISIBLE | WS_GROUP, 10, 12, 40, 8
     CONTROL "Item 1", -1, "STATIC",SS_LEFT | WS_CHILD | WS_VISIBLE | WS_GROUP, 10, 24, 25, 8
     CONTROL "Item 2", -1, "STATIC",SS_LEFT | WS_CHILD | WS_VISIBLE | WS_GROUP, 10, 36, 25, 8
     CONTROL "Item 3", -1, "STATIC",SS_LEFT | WS_CHILD | WS_VISIBLE | WS_GROUP, 10, 48, 25, 8
     CONTROL "", 101, "EDIT",ES_LEFT|WS_CHILD|WS_VISIBLE|WS_BORDER|WS_TABSTOP, 55, 10, 75, 12
     CONTROL "", 102, "EDIT", ES_LEFT|WS_CHILD|WS_VISIBLE|WS_BORDER|WS_TABSTOP, 55, 22, 75, 12
     CONTROL "", 103, "EDIT",ES_LEFT|WS_CHILD|WS_VISIBLE|WS_BORDER|WS_TABSTOP, 55, 34, 75, 12
     CONTROL "", 104, "EDIT",ES_LEFT|WS_CHILD|WS_VISIBLE|WS_BORDER|WS_TABSTOP, 55, 46, 75, 12
     CONTROL "OK", 1, "BUTTON", BS_DEFPUSHBUTTON|WS_CHILD|WS_VISIBLE|WS_TABSTOP, 15, 80, 40, 13
     CONTROL "Cancel", 2, "BUTTON",BS_PUSHBUTTON|WS_CHILD|WS_VISIBLE|WS_TABSTOP, 85, 81, 40, 13
END
```

Also add the icons DDEServer and ChildPict to the resource file. See Figure 9-3.

4. Use the *Make* command to compile the program. You must use a client program, such as the one in the next solution, to use this program.

HOW IT WORKS

The TMyMDIChild object class handles the child windows in this MDI application. The object includes three strings called TheData1, TheData2, and TheData3 to hold the data that this program can exchange with other programs through DDE. The topic name for the child window is the title of the window. The string handle for the window name goes in the data member TopicHandle.

The data members idInst and Conv identify the DDE conversation for the window. When the program creates a new child window, it copies the idInst to the child window so that the window can use functions from the Windows DDEML API. When a client program establishes a conversation with this program, the conversation handle goes into the member variable Conv.

The member functions SetData and GetData put data in and read data from the three data members. The program calls SetData when it creates the window

Program Icon

Child Icon

FIGURE 9-3
The DDEServer
Icons

or receives a poke transaction for the window. SetData copies the string to one of the data items based on the value of the argument Which.

The TMyMDIFrame object class handles the frame window for the MDI application. The first four data members in this object are strings to hold data from a dialog that gets information when the user creates a new child window.

The data member CallBackInst is the instance handle of the callback function. This variable is initialized in the SetupWindow member function.

The SetupWindow member function gets the program ready to receive DDE transactions from client programs. First, it tells Windows to use the callback function by calling DdeInitialize with the instance handle of the callback function. Next, the function creates the string handles for the server name and the item names. Finally, SetupWindow calls DdeNameService to register the name of the server. Note that the program passes NULL for the topic name. This tells Windows to pass on any connection request that mentions the server name.

When the user selects the *New* command, the program calls the CreateChild member function. The first step for this function is to run the WindowName dialog to get the name of the new topic and the initial values for the child window data items. When the user selects the OK button in the dialog, the transfer routines copy the data to the frame window object. Then, CreateChild creates a new child window and copies the data to it.

The CallBack member function receives all of the transactions from client programs. Because it is called from Windows, the implied argument this, which holds the address of the frame object, is not valid. That means that you cannot reference member functions and data without a pointer to the frame object. The constructor for the frame object copies a pointer to the object into a global variable called FrameWindow. The program must use this pointer to access the frame window object in the callback function.

The callback function handles several different transactions in the switch statement. When a client attempts to connect to this server, the server gets an XTYP_CONNECT transaction. The server looks through the child windows to find one that matches the topic requested. If it finds a matching topic, the program returns TRUE to establish the connection. If the client confirms the connection, Windows sends an XTYP_CONNECT_CONFIRM transaction to the server. The server looks for the window with the matching topic and copies the conversation handle to the child window. From now on, the server uses this handle to identify the conversation.

If the client is done with the connection, it sends an XTYP_DISCONNECT transaction. The server handles this by putting a 0 in the conversation handle to mark it as disconnected.

XTYP_POKE and XTYP_REQUEST handle data transfers to and from the server. The first step for both of these transactions is to find the right child window for the conversation. Next, the program identifies the data item by looking at the data item handle. Finally, the poke transaction gets data from the DDE transaction and puts it into the data item, and request transaction gets the data item and returns it to the client.

9.2 How Do I...
Create a DDE Client?

Complexity: MODERATE

PROBLEM

The server presented in the previous solution is not very useful by itself. Its true purpose is apparent only when it is combined with a client program that can access the data the server provides. This solution presents just such a client program.

TECHNIQUE

The first difference between a client and a server program is that a client program does not have to register any names. Because the client does not receive XTYP_CONNECT transactions, there is no need to register a name to which to connect. When you call DdeInitialize, you should specify the APPCMD_CLIENTONLY flag so that Windows does not allocate server resources for the program.

Another difference between client and server programs is in the callback function. The client program only needs to handle the XTYP_DISCONNECT and XTYP_ERROR transactions. There are other messages that a client might receive, but it is acceptable to ignore them.

The final difference is that the client program must initiate all DDE transactions. Instead of waiting for a connection, the client program must call the Windows function DdeConnect to link up with the server. To transfer data, the client must take action to get the data moved.

The program in this solution has several menu commands that perform the various DDE functions. Each menu selection brings up a dialog that gets information from the user to use in the transaction. Figure 9-4 shows the dialogs used in this program.

STEPS

1. Create a new project file called CLIENT.PRJ that includes the files CLIENT.CPP, CLIENT.RES, and STANDARD.DEF

2. Create the source file CLIENT.CPP with this program:

```
/* CLIENT.CPP A DDE Client */
#include <owl.h>
#include <edit.h>
#include <ddeml.h>

class TMyWindow : public TWindow
{
      public:
            char ServiceName[80];
            char TopicName[80];
            char ItemName[80];
            char Data[80];
            FARPROC CallBackInst;
            DWORD idInst;
            HCONV TheConv;
            HSZ   ServiceHandle;
            HSZ TopicHandle;
            TMyWindow(PTWindowsObject AParent, LPSTR ATitle);
            ~TMyWindow();
            virtual LPSTR GetClassName() {return "ClientWnd";};
            virtual void GetWindowClass(WNDCLASS& AWndClass);
            virtual void SetupWindow();
            static HDDEDATA FAR PASCAL _export CallBack(WORD, WORD, HCONV
                  , HSZ, HSZ, HDDEDATA, DWORD, DWORD );
            virtual void DoConnect(RTMessage) = [CM_FIRST+101];
            virtual void DoRequest(RTMessage) = [CM_FIRST+102];
            virtual void DoPoke(RTMessage) = [CM_FIRST+103];
};

TMyWindow *TheWindow;

/* Initialize variables */
TMyWindow::TMyWindow(PTWindowsObject AParent, LPSTR ATitle)
      : TWindow(AParent, ATitle)
{
      Attr.W = 150;
      Attr.H = 80;
      AssignMenu("ClientMenu");
      lstrcpy(ServiceName, "MyServer");
      lstrcpy(TopicName, "");
      lstrcpy(ItemName, "Item 1");
      lstrcpy(Data, "");
      ServiceHandle = NULL;
      TheWindow = this;
}
```

```
/* Clean up the DDE stuff */
TMyWindow::~TMyWindow()
{
     if(ServiceHandle)
     {
          /* Disconnect from the server */
          DdeDisconnect(TheConv);
          /* Free the string handles */
          DdeFreeStringHandle(idInst, ServiceHandle);
          DdeFreeStringHandle(idInst, TopicHandle);
     }
     FreeProcInstance(CallBackInst);
}


/* Set up the program icon */
void TMyWindow::GetWindowClass(WNDCLASS& AWndClass)
{
     TWindow::GetWindowClass(AWndClass);
     AWndClass.hIcon = LoadIcon(AWndClass.hInstance, "DDEClient");
}


/* Initialize DDE service */
void TMyWindow::SetupWindow()
{
     idInst = 0; // Initialize the instance number
     CallBackInst = MakeProcInstance((FARPROC) TMyWindow::CallBack
          , GetApplication()->hInstance );
     /* Set up DDE service */
     DdeInitialize(&idInst, (PFNCALLBACK) CallBackInst
          , APPCMD_CLIENTONLY, OL);
}


/* Dialog for server name */
class TConnectDlg : public TDialog
{
     public:
          TConnectDlg(PTWindowsObject AParent, LPSTR AResource);
};


/* Initialize the dialog controls and set up the transfer buffer */
TConnectDlg::TConnectDlg(PTWindowsObject AParent, LPSTR AResource)
     : TDialog(AParent, AResource)
{
     new TEdit(this, 101, 80);
     new TEdit(this, 102, 80);
     TransferBuffer = (void far *) &((TMyWindow *) Parent)->ServiceName;
}


/* Connect to a server */
void TMyWindow::DoConnect(RTMessage)
{
     if(ServiceHandle)
          MessageBox(HWindow, "Connection in progress", "DDE Client", MB_OK);
     else if(GetApplication()->ExecDialog(
          new TConnectDlg(this, "Connect")) == IDOK)
     {
          ServiceHandle = DdeCreateStringHandle(idInst
               , ServiceName, CP_WINANSI);
```

```
            TopicHandle = DdeCreateStringHandle(idInst
                , TopicName, CP_WINANSI);
            TheConv = DdeConnect(idInst, ServiceHandle
                    , TopicHandle, (PCONVCONTEXT) NULL);
            if(TheConv == NULL)
            {
                    DdeFreeStringHandle(idInst, ServiceHandle);
                    ServiceHandle = NULL;
                    DdeFreeStringHandle(idInst, TopicHandle);
                    MessageBox(HWindow, "No connection available"
                                , "DDE Client", MB_OK);
            }
        }
}


/* Dialog for requesting data */
class TRequestDlg : public TDialog
{
    public:
        TRequestDlg(PTWindowsObject AParent, LPSTR AResource);
};


/* Initialize the dialog controls and set up the transfer buffer */
TRequestDlg::TRequestDlg(PTWindowsObject AParent, LPSTR AResource)
    : TDialog(AParent, AResource)
{
    new TEdit(this, 101, 80);
    TransferBuffer = (void far *) &((TMyWindow *) Parent)->ItemName;
}


/* Request data from the server */
void TMyWindow::DoRequest(RTMessage)
{
    HSZ ItemHandle;
    HDDEDATA TheData;
    char TmpStr[80];

    if(ServiceHandle)
    {
        if(GetApplication()->ExecDialog(
            new TRequestDlg(this, "Request")) == IDOK)
        {
            ItemHandle = DdeCreateStringHandle(idInst, ItemName, CP_WINANSI);
            if((TheData = DdeClientTransaction(NULL, 0, TheConv
                , ItemHandle, CF_TEXT
                , XTYP_REQUEST, 5000, NULL)) != NULL)
            {
                DdeGetData(TheData, TmpStr, 80, OL);
                MessageBox(HWindow, TmpStr
                        , "DDE Client (XTYP_REQUEST)", MB_OK);
            }
            else
                MessageBox(HWindow, "No data", "DDE Client", MB_OK);
            DdeFreeStringHandle(idInst, ItemHandle);
        }
    }
    else
    MessageBox(HWindow, "No connection", "DDE Client", MB_OK);
}
```

```
/* Dialog for poking data */
class TPokeDlg : public TDialog
{
    public:
        TPokeDlg(PTWindowsObject AParent, LPSTR AResource);
};

/* Initialize the dialog controls and set up the transfer buffer */
TPokeDlg::TPokeDlg(PTWindowsObject AParent, LPSTR AResource)
    : TDialog(AParent, AResource)
{
    new TEdit(this, 101, 80);
    new TEdit(this, 102, 80);
    TransferBuffer = (void far *) &((TMyWindow *) Parent)->ItemName;
}


/* Poke data at the server */
void TMyWindow::DoPoke(RTMessage)
{
    HSZ ItemHandle;

    if(ServiceHandle)
    {
        if(GetApplication()->ExecDialog(
            new TPokeDlg(this, "Poke")) == IDOK)
        {
            ItemHandle = DdeCreateStringHandle(idInst, ItemName
                , CP_WINANSI);
            DdeClientTransaction(Data, lstrlen(Data)+1, TheConv
                , ItemHandle, CF_TEXT
                , XTYP_POKE, 5000, NULL);
            DdeFreeStringHandle(idInst, ItemHandle);
        }
    }
    else
        MessageBox(HWindow, "No Connection", "DDE Client", MB_OK);
}


/* This is where all the DDE messages come in */
HDDEDATA FAR PASCAL TMyWindow::CallBack(WORD Type, WORD
    , HCONV, HSZ, HSZ, HDDEDATA, DWORD, DWORD)
{
    char TmpStr[80];

    switch(Type)
    {
        case XTYP_DISCONNECT:
            MessageBox(TheWindow->HWindow, "Disconnected."
                , "DDE Client", MB_OK);
            TheWindow->TheConv = NULL;
            DdeFreeStringHandle(TheWindow->idInst, TheWindow->ServiceHandle);
            DdeFreeStringHandle(TheWindow->idInst, TheWindow->TopicHandle);
            TheWindow->ServiceHandle = NULL;
            break;
        case XTYP_ERROR:
            MessageBox(TheWindow->HWindow
```

```
                              , "DDE error", "DDE Client", MB_OK);
              break;
              default :
              break;
       }
       return NULL;
}

class TMyApp : public TApplication
{
       public:
              TMyApp(LPSTR AName, HINSTANCE Inst, HINSTANCE Prev
                  , LPSTR lpCmdLine, int nCmdShow)
                      : TApplication(AName, Inst, Prev, lpCmdLine, nCmdShow) {};
              virtual void InitMainWindow();
};

void TMyApp::InitMainWindow()
{
  MainWindow = new TMyWindow(NULL, Name);
}

int PASCAL WinMain(HINSTANCE hInstance, HINSTANCE hPrevInstance,
  LPSTR lpCmdLine, int nCmdShow)
{
       TMyApp MyApp("The Client", hInstance
       , hPrevInstance, lpCmdLine, nCmdShow);

       MyApp.Run();
       return MyApp.Status;
}
```

         3. Create the resource file CLIENT.RES with these resources:

```
CLIENTMENU MENU
BEGIN
       POPUP "&DDE"
       BEGIN
              MENUITEM "&Connect", 101
              MENUITEM "&Request", 102
              MENUITEM "&Poke", 103
              MENUITEM "&Exit", 24340
       END

END


CONNECT DIALOG 18, 18, 142, 69
STYLE DS_MODALFRAME | WS_POPUP | WS_CAPTION | WS_SYSMENU
CAPTION "Make connection"
BEGIN
       CONTROL "Server name", -1, "STATIC", SS_LEFT|WS_CHILD|WS_VISIBLE|WS_GROUP, 5, 12, 45, 8
       CONTROL "Topic name", -1, "STATIC", SS_LEFT|WS_CHILD|WS_VISIBLE | WS_GROUP, 5, 24,  45, 8
       CONTROL "", 101, "EDIT", ES_LEFT|WS_CHILD|WS_VISIBLE|WS_BORDER|WS_TABSTOP, 55, 10, 75, 12
       CONTROL "", 102, "EDIT", ES_LEFT | WS_CHILD | WS_VISIBLE | WS_BORDER | WS_TABSTOP
           , 55, 22, 75, 12
       CONTROL "OK", 1, "BUTTON", BS_DEFPUSHBUTTON | WS_CHILD | WS_VISIBLE | WS_TABSTOP
           , 15, 50, 40, 13
       CONTROL "Cancel", 2, "BUTTON", BS_PUSHBUTTON | WS_CHILD | WS_VISIBLE | WS_TABSTOP, 80, 50, 40,13
END
```

```
POKE DIALOG 18, 18, 142, 58
STYLE DS_MODALFRAME | WS_POPUP | WS_CAPTION | WS_SYSMENU
CAPTION "Poke Data"
BEGIN
    CONTROL "Item name", -1, "STATIC", SS_LEFT | WS_CHILD | WS_VISIBLE | WS_GROUP 5, 11, 45, 8
    CONTROL "Data", -1, "STATIC", SS_LEFT | WS_CHILD | WS_VISIBLE | WS_GROUP, 5, 23, 45, 8
    CONTROL "", 101, "EDIT", ES_LEFT|WS_CHILD|WS_VISIBLE | WS_BORDER | WS_GROUP | WS_TABSTOP, 55, 8, 75, 12
    CONTROL "", 102, "EDIT", ES_LEFT|WS_CHILD|WS_VISIBLE|WS_BORDER| WS_GROUP | WS_TABSTOP, 55, 20, 75, 12
    CONTROL "OK", 1, "BUTTON", BS_DEFPUSHBUTTON | WS_CHILD | WS_VISIBLE | WS_TABSTOP 15, 41, 40, 13
    CONTROL "Cancel", 2, "BUTTON", BS_PUSHBUTTON | WS_CHILD | WS_VISIBLE | WS_TABSTOP, 75, 41, 40, 13
END

REQUEST DIALOG 18, 18, 142, 48
STYLE DS_MODALFRAME | WS_POPUP | WS_CAPTION | WS_SYSMENU
CAPTION "Request data"
BEGIN
    CONTROL "Item name", -1, "STATIC", SS_LEFT | WS_CHILD | WS_VISIBLE | WS_GROUP, 5, 11, 45, 8
    CONTROL "", 101, "EDIT", ES_LEFT | WS_CHILD | WS_VISIBLE | WS_BORDER | WS_TABSTOP, 55, 9, 75, 12
    CONTROL "OK", 1, "BUTTON", BS_DEFPUSHBUTTON | WS_CHILD | WS_VISIBLE | WS_TABSTOP, 15, 30, 40, 13
    CONTROL "Cancel", 2, "BUTTON", BS_PUSHBUTTON | WS_CHILD | WS_VISIBLE | WS_TABSTOP, 75, 30, 40,13
END
```

Also include the icon DDEClient shown in Figure 9.5.

4. Use the *Run* command to compile and run the program. Also run the server program from the first solution in this chapter.

HOW IT WORKS

The object class TMyWindow handles the main window for the client program. The first four member variables get data from the dialog boxes. The idInst and TheConv members identify the DDE connection. ServiceHandle and TopicHandle are the handles for the server and topic names used to make the connection. If ServiceHandle is NULL, there is no active connection.

The constructor for TMyWindow puts default values into the member data items. It also initializes the ServiceHandle member to NULL. The destructor releases any resources being used and sends a disconnect transaction to the server if there is an active connection.

The SetupWindow member function initializes the DDE routines by calling DdeInitialize. There is no need to register names because this program does not do server operations.

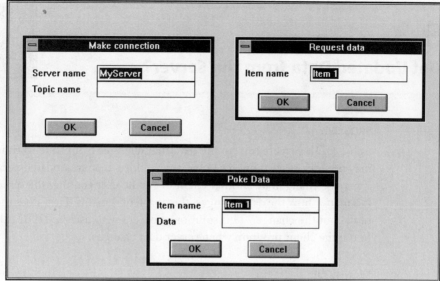

Figure 9-4
The Client
Program
Dialogs

When the user selects the *Connect* menu command, the program calls the DoConnect member function. First, the function checks the ServiceHandle member to see if there is already a connection in progress. If not, the program runs the Connect dialog to get the server and topic names from the user. DoConnect passes this information to the DdeConnect function to see if there are any servers that match. If a server responds, DoConnect stores the conversation handle in the member variable TheConv.

Once a conversation is running, the user can select the *Poke* or *Request* menu command. These commands call DoPoke and DoRequest, respectively. These functions check ServiceHandle to see if there is an active conversation, then bring up a dialog to get the topic and item names. In the case of DoPoke, the dialog also gets the data to poke. Finally, the function calls DDE functions to transfer the data.

Figure 9-5
The Icon
for the
DDEClient

COMMENT

This program is a very general implementation of a DDE client. It will work with just about any DDE server that uses text data items. If you use a program like Excel, that is a DDE server, you can try this program with it.

9.3 How Do I...
Get Updated Data from the Server?

Complexity: MODERATE

PROBLEM

Some DDE servers can supply data that changes from time to time. The data may be stock market quotes or weather reports that are updated periodically, or it may be changed by another client or by the user running the server program. No matter how the data changes, the problem remains: How does the client find out about the change? This solution shows how to use the DDE Advise feature to tell the client program when server data changes.

TECHNIQUE

As with any DDE transaction, setting up an advise loop starts with the client program. The client sends an XTYP_ADVSTART transaction to the server with the names of the topic and item to advise the client about. When the server sees this transaction, it sets a flag that tells it to call DdePostAdvise when the data changes.

When a server calls DdePostAdvise, Windows sends an XTYP_ADVREQ transaction to the server. This transaction is just like an XTYP_REQUEST transaction except that the client program did not make the request.

The server responds to the XTYP_ADVREQ by getting a data handle for the requested data and returning it to Windows. The DDE routines in Windows convert the returned value to an XTYP_ADVDATA transaction and send it to the client.

The client program handles the XTYP_ADVDATA transaction as if it were a server getting an XTYP_POKE message. It calls DdeGetData to get the data from the data handle and returns DDE_FACK to indicate that it got the data.

The two programs in this solution show how to add an advise loop to the programs from the first two solutions. The server includes a new dialog that lets you edit the data items. The client program has a new dialog that lets the user select which data items to be advised about. If the user selects one or more advise items and then edits the server data, the client displays the new data items in a message box.

STEPS

1. Create a new project file called ADVSVR.PRJ with the files ADVSVR.CPP, ADVSVR.RES, and STANDARD.DEF.

2. Create the source ADVSVR.CPP with this program:

```
/* ADVSVR.CPP A DDE Server */
#include <owl.h>
#include <mdi.h>
#include <edit.h>
#include <ddeml.h>

/* The application object */
class TMyApp : public TApplication
{
     public:
          TMyApp(LPSTR AName, HANDLE Inst, HANDLE Prev
               , LPSTR lpCmdLine, int nCmdShow)
               : TApplication(AName, Inst, Prev, lpCmdLine, nCmdShow) {};
          virtual void InitMainWindow();
};

/* Child window class */
class TMyMDIChild : public TWindow
{
     public:
          char TheData1[80];          // First data item
          char TheData2[80];          // Second data item
          char TheData3[80];          // Third data item
          BOOL Advise[3];             // Flag is true if server should advise
          HSZ  TopicHandle;           // Handle for topic name for this window
          DWORD idInst;
          HCONV Conv;
          TMyMDIChild(PTWindowsObject AParent, LPSTR WinName
               , DWORD DDEInst);
          ~TMyMDIChild();
          virtual void SetData(LPSTR Data, int Which);
          virtual LPSTR GetData(int Which);
          virtual LPSTR GetClassName() {return "MyMDIChild";};
          virtual void GetWindowClass(WNDCLASS& AWndClass);
          virtual void WMPaint(RTMessage) = [WM_FIRST + WM_PAINT];
          virtual void DoEdit(RTMessage) = [CM_FIRST + 101];
};

/* Frame window for the application */
class TMyMDIFrame : public TMDIFrame
{
     public:
          char NewTopic[80];          // Scratch data for dialog box
          char NewData1[80];
          char NewData2[80];
          char NewData3[80];
          FARPROC CallBackInst;       // Instance of the callback function
          DWORD idInst;
          HSZ  ServiceName;           // Handle to the name of the server
          HSZ Items[3];
          TMyMDIFrame(LPSTR ATitle);
          ~TMyMDIFrame();
          virtual LPSTR GetClassName() {return "MDIFrame";};
          virtual void GetWindowClass(WNDCLASS& AWndClass);
          virtual void SetupWindow();
          virtual PTWindowsObject CreateChild();
          static HDDEDATA FAR PASCAL _export CallBack(WORD, WORD, HCONV
               , HSZ, HSZ, HDDEDATA, DWORD, DWORD );
```

```
};

typedef TMyMDIChild _FAR *PChild;

/* Initialize a new topic window */
TMyMDIChild::TMyMDIChild(PTWindowsObject AParent, LPSTR WinName
    , DWORD DDEInst) : TWindow(AParent, WinName)
{
    /* Indicate that there is no conversation */
    Conv = NULL;
    idInst = DDEInst;
    /* No advise loops active yet */
    Advise[0] = Advise[1] = Advise[2] = FALSE;
    TopicHandle = DdeCreateStringHandle(DDEInst, WinName, CP_WINANSI);
}

/* Clean up the topic */
TMyMDIChild::~TMyMDIChild()
{
    /* Disconnect if necessary */
    if(Conv)
        DdeDisconnect(Conv);
    DdeFreeStringHandle(idInst, TopicHandle);
}

/* Copy data to one of the items */
void TMyMDIChild::SetData(LPSTR Data, int Which)
{
    switch(Which)
    {
        case 1:
            lstrcpy(TheData1, Data);
            break;
        case 2:
            lstrcpy(TheData2, Data);
            break;
        case 3:
            lstrcpy(TheData3, Data);
            break;
    }
    /* Force a repaint */
    InvalidateRect(HWindow, NULL, FALSE);
}

/* Get data from one of the items */
LPSTR TMyMDIChild::GetData(int Which)
{
    switch(Which)
    {
        case 1:
            return TheData1;
        case 2:
            return TheData2;
        case 3:
            return TheData3;
    }
    return NULL;
}
```

```
/* Set up the icon for the child windows */
void TMyMDIChild::GetWindowClass(WNDCLASS& AWndClass)
{
    TWindow::GetWindowClass(AWndClass);
    AWndClass.hIcon = LoadIcon(AWndClass.hInstance, "ChildPict");
}

/* Center the three data items in the child window */
void TMyMDIChild::WMPaint(RTMessage)
{
    PAINTSTRUCT ps;
    HDC hDC;
    RECT Rect;
    DWORD Size;

    hDC = BeginPaint(HWindow, &ps);
    GetClientRect(HWindow, &Rect);
    /* Erase the window */
    FillRect(hDC, &Rect, GetStockObject(WHITE_BRUSH));
    /* Center the text */
    Size = GetTextExtent(hDC, TheData1, lstrlen(TheData1));
    TextOut(hDC, (Rect.right-LOWORD(Size))/2
         , (Rect.bottom-HIWORD(Size))/2 - HIWORD(Size)
         , TheData1, lstrlen(TheData1));
    Size = GetTextExtent(hDC, TheData2, lstrlen(TheData2));
    TextOut(hDC, (Rect.right-LOWORD(Size))/2
         , (Rect.bottom-HIWORD(Size))/2, TheData2, lstrlen(TheData2));
    Size = GetTextExtent(hDC, TheData3, lstrlen(TheData3));
    TextOut(hDC, (Rect.right-LOWORD(Size))/2
         , (Rect.bottom-HIWORD(Size))/2 + HIWORD(Size)
         , TheData3, lstrlen(TheData3));
    EndPaint(HWindow, &ps);
}

/* Dialog To edit data */
class TEditDlg : public TDialog
{
    public:
        TEditDlg(PTWindowsObject AParent, LPSTR AResource);
};

/* Initialize the dialog controls and setup the transfer buffer */
TEditDlg::TEditDlg(PTWindowsObject AParent, LPSTR AResource)
    : TDialog(AParent, AResource)
{
    new TEdit(this, 101, 80);
    new TEdit(this, 102, 80);
    new TEdit(this, 103, 80);
    TransferBuffer = (void far *) &((TMyMDIChild *) Parent)->TheData1;
}

/* Handle the edit menu item */
void TMyMDIChild::DoEdit(RTMessage)
{
    int i;

    if(GetApplication()->ExecDialog(
```

```
              new TEditDlg(this, "EditData")) == IDOK)
    {
          for(i=0; i<3; ++i)
                if(Advise[i])
                {
                      DdePostAdvise(idInst, TopicHandle
                            , ((TMyMDIFrame *) Parent)->Items[i]);
                }
          InvalidateRect(HWindow, NULL, FALSE);
    }
}


TMyMDIFrame *FrameWindow;    // Pointer to the frame window

/* Initialize variables */
TMyMDIFrame::TMyMDIFrame(LPSTR ATitle)
    : TMDIFrame(ATitle, "MDIMenu")
{
    ChildMenuPos = 1;
    NewTopic[0] = NewData1[0] = '\0';
    NewData2[0] = NewData3[0] = '\0';
    FrameWindow = this;
}


/* Clean up the DDE stuff */
TMyMDIFrame::~TMyMDIFrame()
{
    DdeNameService(idInst, ServiceName, NULL, DNS_UNREGISTER);
    DdeFreeStringHandle(idInst, ServiceName);
    DdeFreeStringHandle(idInst, Items[0]);
    DdeFreeStringHandle(idInst, Items[1]);
    DdeFreeStringHandle(idInst, Items[2]);
    FreeProcInstance(CallBackInst);
}


/* Set up the program icon */
void TMyMDIFrame::GetWindowClass(WNDCLASS& AWndClass)
{
    TMDIFrame::GetWindowClass(AWndClass);
    AWndClass.hIcon = LoadIcon(AWndClass.hInstance, "DDEServer");
}


/* Initialize DDE service */
void TMyMDIFrame::SetupWindow()
{
    idInst = 0; // Initialize the instance number
    CallBackInst = MakeProcInstance((FARPROC) TMyMDIFrame::CallBack
          , GetApplication()->hInstance );
    /* Set up DDE service */
    DdeInitialize(&idInst, (PFNCALLBACK) CallBackInst
          , APPCLASS_STANDARD, 0L);
    ServiceName = DdeCreateStringHandle(idInst, "MyServer"
          , CP_WINANSI);
    Items[0] = DdeCreateStringHandle(idInst, "Item 1", CP_WINANSI);
    Items[1] = DdeCreateStringHandle(idInst, "Item 2", CP_WINANSI);
    Items[2] = DdeCreateStringHandle(idInst, "Item 3", CP_WINANSI);
    DdeNameService(idInst, ServiceName, NULL, DNS_REGISTER);
    TMDIFrame::SetupWindow();
}
```

```
/* Dialog for window name */
class TMyDlg : public TDialog
{
     public:
          TMyDlg(PTWindowsObject AParent, LPSTR AResource);
};

/* Initialize the dialog controls and set up the transfer buffer */
TMyDlg::TMyDlg(PTWindowsObject AParent, LPSTR AResource)
     : TDialog(AParent, AResource)
{
     new TEdit(this, 101, 80);
     new TEdit(this, 102, 80);
     new TEdit(this, 103, 80);
     new TEdit(this, 104, 80);
     TransferBuffer = (void far *) &((TMyMDIFrame *) Parent)->NewTopic;
}

/* Make a new topic window */
PTWindowsObject TMyMDIFrame::CreateChild()
{
     PTWindowsObject pw;

     if(GetApplication()->ExecDialog(
          new TMyDlg(this, "WindowName")) == IDOK)
     {
          pw = GetApplication()->MakeWindow(
               new TMyMDIChild(this, NewTopic, idInst));
          /* Copy the data to the new object */
          ((TMyMDIChild *) pw)->SetData(NewData1, 1);
          ((TMyMDIChild *) pw)->SetData(NewData2, 2);
          ((TMyMDIChild *) pw)->SetData(NewData3, 3);
          return pw;
     }
     return NULL;
}

/* Find the child for a topic */
BOOL
FirstTopic(Pvoid P, Pvoid D)
{
     return (DdeCmpStringHandles(((PChild) P)->TopicHandle
          , (HSZ) D) == 0);
}

/* Find the child for a conversation */
BOOL
FirstConv(Pvoid P, Pvoid D)
{
     return (((PChild) P)->Conv == (HCONV) D);
}


/* This is where all the DDE messages come in */
HDDEDATA FAR PASCAL TMyMDIFrame::CallBack(WORD Type, WORD
     , HCONV Conv, HSZ hsz1, HSZ hsz2, HDDEDATA hData, DWORD
     , DWORD)
{
```

```
char TmpStr[80];
int Item;
PChild CurrentTopic;

switch(Type)
{
    /* The client is trying to make contact */
    case XTYP_CONNECT:
        if((CurrentTopic = (PChild)
            (FrameWindow->FirstThat(FirstTopic, (Pvoid) hsz1)))
            != NULL && CurrentTopic->Conv == 0)
            return (HDDEDATA) TRUE;
        return 0;
    /* The server library is confirming the connection */
    case XTYP_CONNECT_CONFIRM:
        if((CurrentTopic = (PChild)
            (FrameWindow->FirstThat(FirstTopic, (Pvoid) hsz1)))
            != NULL && CurrentTopic->Conv == 0)
            CurrentTopic->Conv = Conv;
        break;
    /* The client wants to disconnect */
    case XTYP_DISCONNECT:
        if((CurrentTopic = (PChild)
            (FrameWindow->FirstThat(FirstConv, (Pvoid) Conv))) != NULL)
            CurrentTopic->Conv = 0;
        break;
    /* The client is sending data */
    case XTYP_POKE:
        CurrentTopic = (PChild)
            (FrameWindow->FirstThat(FirstConv, (Pvoid) Conv));
        if(CurrentTopic)
        {
            /* Look for the right item name */
            for(Item=0; Item<3
                && DdeCmpStringHandles(FrameWindow->Items[Item], hsz2)
                ; ++Item);
            /* If all is well, put the data in the window */
            if(Item < 3)
            {
                DdeGetData(hData, &TmpStr, 80, 0);
                CurrentTopic->SetData(TmpStr, Item+1);
                return (HDDEDATA)DDE_FACK;
            }
        }
        return DDE_FNOTPROCESSED;
    case XTYP_ADVREQ:         // Send changed data to the client
    case XTYP_REQUEST:        // Return requested data to the client
        CurrentTopic = (PChild)
            (FrameWindow->FirstThat(FirstConv, (Pvoid) Conv));
        if(CurrentTopic)
        {
            for(Item=0; Item<3
                && DdeCmpStringHandles(FrameWindow->Items[Item], hsz2)
                ; ++Item);
            /* Get the data to return */
            if(Item<3)
            {
                return DdeCreateDataHandle(FrameWindow->idInst
```

```
                        , CurrentTopic->GetData(Item+1)
                        , lstrlen(CurrentTopic->GetData(Item+1))+1
                        , 0, hsz2, CF_TEXT, 0);
                    }
                }
                return NULL;
        case XTYP_ADVSTART:         // Set up an advise loop
                CurrentTopic = (PChild)
                    (FrameWindow->FirstThat(FirstTopic, (Pvoid) hsz1));
                if(CurrentTopic)
                {
                    for(Item=0; Item<3
                        && DdeCmpStringHandles(FrameWindow->Items[Item]
                            , hsz2)
                        ; ++Item);
                    if(Item<3)
                    {
                        CurrentTopic->Advise[Item] = TRUE;
                        return TRUE;
                    }
                }
                return NULL;
        default :
                break;
    }
    return NULL;
}


/* Initialize the main window */
void TMyApp::InitMainWindow()
{
    MainWindow = new TMyMDIFrame(Name);
}


/* Program entry point */
int PASCAL WinMain(HANDLE hInstance, HANDLE hPrevInstance,
  LPSTR lpCmdLine, int nCmdShow)
{
    TMyApp MyApp("The Server", hInstance
    , hPrevInstance, lpCmdLine, nCmdShow);

    MyApp.Run();
    return MyApp.Status;
}
```

3. Copy the resource file SERVER.RES from How To 9.1 to the file ADVSVR.RES. Then change the menu resource to:

```
MDIMENU MENU
BEGIN
    POPUP "&File"
    BEGIN
        MENUITEM "&New", 24339
        MENUITEM "Edit &data", 101
        MENUITEM "&Exit", 24340
    END

    POPUP "&Window"
```

```
        BEGIN
            MENUITEM "&Cascade", 24337
            MENUITEM "&Tile", 24336
            MENUITEM "&Arrange icons", 24335
            MENUITEM "&Close all", 24338
        END

END
```

and add this dialog resource:

```
EDITDATA DIALOG 18, 18, 142, 70
STYLE DS_MODALFRAME | WS_POPUP | WS_CAPTION | WS_SYSMENU
CAPTION "Edit data"
BEGIN
        CONTROL "Item 1", -1, "STATIC", SS_LEFT | WS_CHILD | WS_VISIBLE | WS_GROUP, 10, 8, 25, 8
        CONTROL "Item 2", -1, "STATIC", SS_LEFT | WS_CHILD | WS_VISIBLE|WS_GROUP, 10, 22, 25, 8
        CONTROL "Item 3", -1, "STATIC", SS_LEFT | WS_CHILD |WS_VISIBLE | WS_GROUP, 10, 35, 25, 8
        CONTROL "", 101, "EDIT", ES_LEFT|WS_CHILD|WS_VISIBLE|WS_BORDER|WS_TABSTOP, 55, 7, 75, 12
        CONTROL "", 102, "EDIT", ES_LEFT|WS_CHILD|WS_VISIBLE|WS_BORDER|WS_TABSTOP, 55, 19, 75, 12
        CONTROL "", 103, "EDIT", ES_LEFT|WS_CHILD|WS_VISIBLE|WS_BORDER|WS_TABSTOP, 55, 31, 75, 12
        CONTROL "OK", 1, "BUTTON", BS_DEFPUSHBUTTON|WS_CHILD|WS_VISIBLE|WS_TABSTOP, 15, 53, 40, 13
        CONTROL "Cancel", 2, "BUTTON", BS_PUSHBUTTON|WS_CHILD|WS_VISIBLE|WS_TASTOP, 85, 52, 40,13
END
```

4. Use the *Make* command to compile the program.

5. Create a new project file called ADVCLI.PRJ with the files ADVCLI.CPP, ADVCLI.RES, and STANDARD.DEF.

6. Create the source ADVCLI.CPP with this program:

```
/* ADVCLI.CPP A DDE Client */
#include <owl.h>
#include <checkbox.h>
#include <edit.h>
#include <ddeml.h>

/* The application window */
class TMyWindow : public TWindow
{
    public:
            char ServiceName[80];          // Data for the dialog boxes
            char TopicName[80];
            char ItemName[80];
            char Data[80];
                WORD Advise[3];
            FARPROC CallBackInst;          // Instance of the call back function
            DWORD idInst;
                HCONV TheConv;
            HSZ   ServiceHandle;
            HSZ TopicHandle;
            TMyWindow(PTWindowsObject AParent, LPSTR ATitle);
                ~TMyWindow();
            virtual LPSTR GetClassName() {return "ClientWnd";};
            virtual void GetWindowClass(WNDCLASS& AWndClass);
            virtual void SetupWindow();
            static HDDEDATA FAR PASCAL _export CallBack(WORD, WORD, HCONV
                , HSZ, HSZ, HDDEDATA, DWORD, DWORD );
```

```
            virtual void DoConnect(RTMessage) = [CM_FIRST+101];
            virtual void DoRequest(RTMessage) = [CM_FIRST+102];
            virtual void DoPoke(RTMessage) = [CM_FIRST+103];
            virtual void DoAdvise(RTMessage) = [CM_FIRST+104];
};

TMyWindow *TheWindow;        // Pointer to the window for the callback function

/* Initialize variables */
TMyWindow::TMyWindow(PTWindowsObject AParent, LPSTR ATitle)
     : TWindow(AParent, ATitle)
{
     int i;

     /* Make a small window */
     Attr.W = 150;
     Attr.H = 80;
     /* Put in the menu */
     AssignMenu("ClientMenu");
     /* Initialize the dialog data */
     lstrcpy(ServiceName, "MyServer");
     lstrcpy(TopicName, "");
     lstrcpy(ItemName, "Item 1");
     lstrcpy(Data, "");
     ServiceHandle = NULL;
     TheWindow = this;
     for(i=0; i<3; ++i)
          Advise[i] = 0;
}

/* Clean up the DDE stuff */
TMyWindow::~TMyWindow()
{
     if(ServiceHandle)
     {
          /* Disconnect from the server */
          DdeDisconnect(TheConv);
          /* Free the string handles */
          DdeFreeStringHandle(idInst, ServiceHandle);
          DdeFreeStringHandle(idInst, TopicHandle);
     }
     FreeProcInstance(CallBackInst);
}

/* Set up the program icon */
void TMyWindow::GetWindowClass(WNDCLASS& AWndClass)
{
     TWindow::GetWindowClass(AWndClass);
     AWndClass.hIcon = LoadIcon(AWndClass.hInstance, "DDEClient");
}

/* Initialize DDE service */
void TMyWindow::SetupWindow()
{
     idInst = 0; // Initialize the instance number
     CallBackInst = MakeProcInstance((FARPROC) TMyWindow::CallBack
          , GetApplication()->hInstance );
     /* Set up DDE service */
     DdeInitialize(&idInst, (PFNCALLBACK) CallBackInst
```

```
                     , APPCMD_CLIENTONLY, OL);
}


/* Dialog for server name */
class TConnectDlg : public TDialog
{
    public:
            TConnectDlg(PTWindowsObject AParent, LPSTR AResource);
};


/* Initialize the dialog controls and set up the transfer buffer */
TConnectDlg::TConnectDlg(PTWindowsObject AParent, LPSTR AResource)
    : TDialog(AParent, AResource)
{
    new TEdit(this, 101, 80);
    new TEdit(this, 102, 80);
    TransferBuffer = (void far *) &((TMyWindow *) Parent)->ServiceName;
}


/* Connect to a server */
void TMyWindow::DoConnect(RTMessage)
{
    if(ServiceHandle)
        MessageBox(HWindow, "Connection in progress", "DDE Client", MB_OK);
    else if(GetApplication()->ExecDialog(
        new TConnectDlg(this, "Connect")) == IDOK)
    {
        /* Set up the selected names */
        ServiceHandle = DdeCreateStringHandle(idInst, ServiceName, CP_WINANSI);
        TopicHandle = DdeCreateStringHandle(idInst, TopicName, CP_WINANSI);
        /* Attempt a connection */
        TheConv = DdeConnect(idInst, ServiceHandle, TopicHandle, (PCONVCONTEXT) NULL);
        /* Make sure the connection was successful */
        if(TheConv == NULL)
        {
            DdeFreeStringHandle(idInst, ServiceHandle);
            ServiceHandle = NULL;
            DdeFreeStringHandle(idInst, TopicHandle);
            MessageBox(HWindow, "No connection available"
                        , "DDE Client", MB_OK);
        }
    }
}


/* Dialog for requesting data */
class TRequestDlg : public TDialog
{
    public:
            TRequestDlg(PTWindowsObject AParent, LPSTR AResource);
};


/* Initialize the dialog controls and set up the transfer buffer */
TRequestDlg::TRequestDlg(PTWindowsObject AParent, LPSTR AResource)
    : TDialog(AParent, AResource)
{
    new TEdit(this, 101, 80);
    TransferBuffer = (void far *) &((TMyWindow *) Parent)->ItemName;
}
```

```
/* Request data from the server */
void TMyWindow::DoRequest(RTMessage)
{
      HSZ ItemHandle;
      HDDEDATA TheData;
      char TmpStr[80];

      if(ServiceHandle)
      {
            if(GetApplication()->ExecDialog(
                  new TRequestDlg(this, "Request")) == IDOK)
            {
                  ItemHandle = DdeCreateStringHandle(idInst, ItemName, CP_WINANSI);
                  if((TheData = DdeClientTransaction(NULL, 0, TheConv, ItemHandle, CF_TEXT
                        , XTYP_REQUEST, 5000, NULL)) != NULL)
                  {
                        DdeGetData(TheData, TmpStr, 80, 0L);
                        MessageBox(HWindow, TmpStr
                              , "DDE Client (XTYP_REQUEST)", MB_OK);
                  }
                  else
                        MessageBox(HWindow, "No data", "DDE Client", MB_OK);
                  DdeFreeStringHandle(idInst, ItemHandle);
            }
      }
      else
      MessageBox(HWindow, "No connection", "DDE Client", MB_OK);
}

/* Dialog for poking data */
class TPokeDlg : public TDialog
{
      public:
            TPokeDlg(PTWindowsObject AParent, LPSTR AResource);
};

/* Initialize the dialog controls and set up the transfer buffer */
TPokeDlg::TPokeDlg(PTWindowsObject AParent, LPSTR AResource)
      : TDialog(AParent, AResource)
{
      new TEdit(this, 101, 80);
      new TEdit(this, 102, 80);
      TransferBuffer = (void far *) &((TMyWindow *) Parent)->ItemName;
}

/* Poke data at the server */
void TMyWindow::DoPoke(RTMessage)
{
      HSZ ItemHandle;

      if(ServiceHandle)
      {
            if(GetApplication()->ExecDialog(
                  new TPokeDlg(this, "Poke")) == IDOK)
            {
                  ItemHandle = DdeCreateStringHandle(idInst, ItemName
                        , CP_WINANSI);
                  DdeClientTransaction(Data, lstrlen(Data)+1, TheConv
                        , ItemHandle, CF_TEXT
```

```
                            , XTYP_POKE, 5000, NULL);
                    DdeFreeStringHandle(idInst, ItemHandle);
            }
      }
      else
            MessageBox(HWindow, "No Connection", "DDE Client", MB_OK);
}

/* Dialog for starting and stopping advise loops */
class TAdvDlg : public TDialog
{
      public:
            TAdvDlg(PTWindowsObject AParent, LPSTR AResource);
};

/* Initialize the dialog controls and set up the transfer buffer */
TAdvDlg::TAdvDlg(PTWindowsObject AParent, LPSTR AResource)
      : TDialog(AParent, AResource)
{
      PTGroupBox TheGroup;
      int i;

      TheGroup = new TGroupBox(this, 101);
      for(i=0; i<3; i++)
            new TCheckBox(this, 102+i, TheGroup);
      TransferBuffer = (void far *) &((TMyWindow *)
            Parent)->Advise;
}

/* Tell the server what items to advise on */
void TMyWindow::DoAdvise(RTMessage)
{
      HSZ ItemHandle;
      WORD OldAdvise[3];
      int i;
      char TmpStr[10];

      if(ServiceHandle)
      {
            /* Copy the current advise flags to see if they change */
            for(i=0; i<3; ++i)
                  OldAdvise[i] = Advise[i];
            if(GetApplication()->ExecDialog(
                  new TAdvDlg(this, "Advise")) == IDOK)
            {
                  lstrcpy(TmpStr, "Item 0");
                  /* Look at each advise flag */
                  for(i=0; i<3; ++i)
                  {
                        ++(TmpStr[5]);
                        /* If advise loop turned on */
                        if(Advise[i] && !OldAdvise[i])
                        {
                              ItemHandle = DdeCreateStringHandle(idInst
                                    , TmpStr, CP_WINANSI);
                              DdeClientTransaction(NULL
                                    , 0, TheConv
                                    , ItemHandle, CF_TEXT
                                    , XTYP_ADVSTART, 5000, NULL);
```

```
                                     DdeFreeStringHandle(idInst, ItemHandle);
                        }
                        /* If advise loop turned off */
                        else if(!Advise[i] && OldAdvise[i])
                        {
                                ItemHandle = DdeCreateStringHandle(idInst
                                        , TmpStr, CP_WINANSI);
                                DdeClientTransaction(NULL
                                        , 0, TheConv
                                        , ItemHandle, CF_TEXT
                                        , XTYP_ADVSTOP, 5000, NULL);
                                DdeFreeStringHandle(idInst, ItemHandle);
                        }
                }
            }
        }
    }
    else
        MessageBox(HWindow, "No Connection", "DDE Client", MB_OK);
}


/* This is where all the DDE messages come in */
HDDEDATA FAR PASCAL TMyWindow::CallBack(WORD Type, WORD
        , HCONV, HSZ, HSZ, HDDEDATA TheData, DWORD
        , DWORD)
{
    char TmpStr[80];

    switch(Type)
    {
        /* Data from the advise loop */
        case XTYP_ADVDATA:
                DdeGetData(TheData, TmpStr, 80, 0);
                MessageBox(TheWindow->HWindow, TmpStr, "Advised data", MB_OK);
                return (HDDEDATA) DDE_FACK;
        case XTYP_DISCONNECT:
                MessageBox(TheWindow->HWindow, "Disconnected.", "DDE Client", MB_OK);
                TheWindow->TheConv = NULL;
                DdeFreeStringHandle(TheWindow->idInst, TheWindow->ServiceHandle);
                DdeFreeStringHandle(TheWindow->idInst, TheWindow->TopicHandle);
                TheWindow->ServiceHandle = NULL;
                break;
        case XTYP_ERROR:
                MessageBox(TheWindow->HWindow, "DDE error", "DDE Client", MB_OK);
                break;
        default :
                break;
    }
    return NULL;
}


class TMyApp : public TApplication
{
    public:
        TMyApp(LPSTR AName, HINSTANCE Inst, HINSTANCE Prev
                , LPSTR lpCmdLine, int nCmdShow)
                : TApplication(AName, Inst, Prev, lpCmdLine, nCmdShow) {};
        virtual void InitMainWindow();
};
```

```
void TMyApp::InitMainWindow()
{
    MainWindow = new TMyWindow(NULL, Name);
}


int PASCAL WinMain(HINSTANCE hInstance, HINSTANCE hPrevInstance,
  LPSTR lpCmdLine, int nCmdShow)
{
    TMyApp MyApp("The Client", hInstance
           , hPrevInstance, lpCmdLine, nCmdShow);

    MyApp.Run();
    return MyApp.Status;
}
```

7. Copy the resource file CLIENT.RES from How-To 9.2 to the file ADVCLI.RES. Then change the menu resource to:

```
CLIENTMENU MENU
BEGIN
      POPUP "&DDE"
      BEGIN
            MENUITEM "&Connect", 101
            MENUITEM "&Request", 102
            MENUITEM "&Poke", 103
            MENUITEM "&Advise", 104
            MENUITEM "&Exit", 24340
      END

END
```

and add this dialog resource:

```
ADVISE DIALOG 18, 18, 97, 92
STYLE DS_MODALFRAME | WS_POPUP | WS_CAPTION | WS_SYSMENU
CAPTION "Advise"
BEGIN
      CONTROL "Items", 101, "BUTTON", BS_GROUPBOX | WS_CHILD | WS_VISIBLE, 13, 10, 70, 51
      CONTROL "Item 1",102, "BUTTON", BS_AUTOCHECKBOX|WS_CHILD|WS_VISIBLE|WS_GROUP, 19, 22, 45, 12
      CONTROL "Item 2", 103, "BUTTON", BS_AUTOCHECKBOX | WS_CHILD | WS_VISIBLE, 19, 34, 35,12
      CONTROL "Item 3", 104, "BUTTON", BS_AUTOCHECKBOX | WS_CHILD | WS_VISIBLE, 19, 46, 35, 12
      CONTROL "Ok", 1, "BUTTON", BS_DEFPUSHBUTTON | WS_CHILD | WS_VISIBLE, 8, 73, 35, 13
      CONTROL "Cancel", 2, "BUTTON", BS_PUSHBUTTON | WS_CHILD | WS_VISIBLE, 55, 73, 35, 13
END
```

8. Use the *Run* command to compile and run the program. Also run the ADVSVR.EXE program.

HOW IT WORKS

The server program is similar to SERVER.CPP from How-To 9.1. The first difference is that the child window object now has a data member called Advise. This data member is an array of flags that indicate which data items need to be passed to the client when they change. The child window object also includes a new member function, DoEdit, to handle the edit dialog.

The constructor for the child window initializes the Advise flags to FALSE. The callback function changes the settings of the Advise flags when it receives an XTYP_ADVSTART or XTYP_ADVSTOP transaction from the client. When the user selects the *Edit* menu command, the program calls DoEdit to bring up the edit dialog. For each item with a true Advise flag, DoEdit calls DdePostAdvise to set up for sending the data.

Calling DdePostAdvise causes Windows to send an XTYP_ADVREQ transaction to the callback function. The server uses the same routine as for XTYP_REQUEST transactions to send the data to the client program.

The ADVCLI.CPP program also includes Advise flags to indicate which items have advise loops. In this program, the user sets the Advise flags with the advise dialog in the member function DoAdvise. When the user changes the state of an Advise flag, the client program sends an XTYP_ADVSTART or XTYP_ADVSTOP transaction to the server to start or stop an advise loop.

The callback function in the client program handles XTYP_ADVDATA transactions from the server. First, the program gets the data from the data handle with DdeGetData. Then, it displays the data in a message box. The last step is to return DDE_FACK to Windows indicating that the transfer is complete.

9.4 How Do I...
Execute Commands on the Server?

Complexity: MODERATE

PROBLEM

Applications can do more than just transfer data with DDE. For example, a DDE client can send commands to the server to open a file or change fonts or any other command the server provides. The XTYP_EXECUTE transaction type lets a client program send commands to the server program. The server is responsible for parsing the commands from the client, so the possible commands depend on what the server allows. This solution shows how to send commands from the client to the server.

TECHNIQUE

The XTYP_EXECUTE transaction is easy to implement. At the client end, you send a string with the commands to the DdeClientTransaction function. The server gets the command in its callback loop. The server uses DdeGetData to get the command, then it parses and executes the command.

The program in this solution is based on the programs from How-To 9.1 and 9.2. The new server program handles the XTYP_EXECUTE transaction by displaying the command in a message box. The new client program has a dialog box that lets the user enter the command to execute.

STEPS

1. Create a new project file called EXECSVR.PRJ with the files EXECSVR.CPP, EXECSVR.RES, and STANDARD.DEF.

2. Create the source file EXECSVR.CPP with this program:

```
/* EXECSVR.CPP A DDE Server */
#include <owl.h>
#include <mdi.h>
#include <edit.h>
#include <ddeml.h>

class TMyApp : public TApplication
{
    public:
        TMyApp(LPSTR AName, HANDLE Inst, HANDLE Prev
                , LPSTR lpCmdLine, int nCmdShow)
                : TApplication(AName, Inst, Prev, lpCmdLine, nCmdShow) {};
        virtual void InitMainWindow();
};

class TMyMDIChild : public TWindow
{
    public:
        char TheData1[80];
        char TheData2[80];
        char TheData3[80];
        HSZ  TopicHandle;
        DWORD idInst;
        HCONV Conv;
        TMyMDIChild(PTWindowsObject AParent, LPSTR WinName
                , DWORD DDEInst);
        ~TMyMDIChild();
        virtual void SetData(LPSTR Data, int Which);
        virtual LPSTR GetData(int Which);
        virtual LPSTR GetClassName() {return "MyMDIChild";};
        virtual void GetWindowClass(WNDCLASS& AWndClass);
        virtual void WMPaint(RTMessage) = [WM_FIRST + WM_PAINT];
};

typedef TMyMDIChild _FAR *PChild;

/* Initialize a new topic window */
TMyMDIChild::TMyMDIChild(PTWindowsObject AParent, LPSTR WinName
    , DWORD DDEInst) : TWindow(AParent, WinName)
{
    Conv = NULL;
    idInst = DDEInst;
    TopicHandle = DdeCreateStringHandle(DDEInst, WinName, CP_WINANSI);
}
```

```
/* Clean up the topic */
TMyMDIChild::~TMyMDIChild()
{
      /* Disconnect if necessary */
      if(Conv)
            DdeDisconnect(Conv);
      DdeFreeStringHandle(idInst, TopicHandle);
}


void TMyMDIChild::SetData(LPSTR Data, int Which)
{
      switch(Which)
      {
            case 1:
                  lstrcpy(TheData1, Data);
                  break;
            case 2:
                  lstrcpy(TheData2, Data);
                  break;
            case 3:
                  lstrcpy(TheData3, Data);
                  break;
      }
    /* Force a repaint */
    InvalidateRect(HWindow, NULL, FALSE);
}

LPSTR TMyMDIChild::GetData(int Which)
{
      switch(Which)
      {
            case 1:
                  return TheData1;
            case 2:
                  return TheData2;
            case 3:
                  return TheData3;
      }
      return NULL;
}

void TMyMDIChild::GetWindowClass(WNDCLASS& AWndClass)
{
      TWindow::GetWindowClass(AWndClass);
      AWndClass.hIcon = LoadIcon(AWndClass.hInstance, "ChildPict");
}

void TMyMDIChild::WMPaint(RTMessage)
{
      PAINTSTRUCT ps;
      HDC hDC;
      RECT Rect;
      DWORD Size;

      hDC = BeginPaint(HWindow, &ps);
      GetClientRect(HWindow, &Rect);
      /* Erase the window */
      FillRect(hDC, &Rect, GetStockObject(WHITE_BRUSH));
      /* Center the text */
      Size = GetTextExtent(hDC, TheData1, lstrlen(TheData1));
```

```
        TextOut(hDC, (Rect.right-LOWORD(Size))/2
                , (Rect.bottom-HIWORD(Size))/2 - HIWORD(Size)
                , TheData1, lstrlen(TheData1));
        Size = GetTextExtent(hDC, TheData2, lstrlen(TheData2));
        TextOut(hDC, (Rect.right-LOWORD(Size))/2
                , (Rect.bottom-HIWORD(Size))/2, TheData2, lstrlen(TheData2));
        Size = GetTextExtent(hDC, TheData3, lstrlen(TheData3));
        TextOut(hDC, (Rect.right-LOWORD(Size))/2
                , (Rect.bottom-HIWORD(Size))/2 + HIWORD(Size)
                , TheData3, lstrlen(TheData3));
        EndPaint(HWindow, &ps);
}


class TMyMDIFrame : public TMDIFrame
{
        public:
                char NewTopic[80];
                char NewData1[80];
                char NewData2[80];
                char NewData3[80];
                FARPROC CallBackInst;
                DWORD idInst;
                HSZ   ServiceName;
                HSZ Items[3];
                TMyMDIFrame(LPSTR ATitle);
                ~TMyMDIFrame();
                virtual LPSTR GetClassName() {return "MDIFrame";};
                virtual void GetWindowClass(WNDCLASS& AWndClass);
                virtual void SetupWindow();
                virtual PTWindowsObject CreateChild();
                static HDDEDATA FAR PASCAL _export CallBack(WORD, WORD, HCONV
                        , HSZ, HSZ, HDDEDATA, DWORD, DWORD );
};


TMyMDIFrame *FrameWindow;

/* Initialize variables */
TMyMDIFrame::TMyMDIFrame(LPSTR ATitle)
        : TMDIFrame(ATitle, "MDIMenu")
{
        ChildMenuPos = 1;
        NewTopic[0] = NewData1[0] = '\0';
        NewData2[0] = NewData3[0] = '\0';
        FrameWindow = this;
}


/* Clean up the DDE stuff */
TMyMDIFrame::~TMyMDIFrame()
{
        DdeNameService(idInst, ServiceName, NULL, DNS_UNREGISTER);
        DdeFreeStringHandle(idInst, ServiceName);
        DdeFreeStringHandle(idInst, Items[0]);
        DdeFreeStringHandle(idInst, Items[1]);
        DdeFreeStringHandle(idInst, Items[2]);
        FreeProcInstance(CallBackInst);
}


/* Set up the program icon */
void TMyMDIFrame::GetWindowClass(WNDCLASS& AWndClass)
{
```

```
        TMDIFrame::GetWindowClass(AWndClass);
        AWndClass.hIcon = LoadIcon(AWndClass.hInstance, "DDEServer");
}


/* Initialize DDE service */
void TMyMDIFrame::SetupWindow()
{
        idInst = 0; // Initialize the instance number
        CallBackInst = MakeProcInstance((FARPROC) TMyMDIFrame::CallBack
                , GetApplication()->hInstance );
        /* Set up DDE service */
        DdeInitialize(&idInst, (PFNCALLBACK) CallBackInst
                , APPCLASS_STANDARD, OL);
        ServiceName = DdeCreateStringHandle(idInst, "MyServer"
                , CP_WINANSI);
        Items[0] = DdeCreateStringHandle(idInst, "Item 1", CP_WINANSI);
        Items[1] = DdeCreateStringHandle(idInst, "Item 2", CP_WINANSI);
        Items[2] = DdeCreateStringHandle(idInst, "Item 3", CP_WINANSI);
        DdeNameService(idInst, ServiceName, NULL, DNS_REGISTER);
        TMDIFrame::SetupWindow();
}


/* Dialog for window name */
class TMyDlg : public TDialog
{
        public:
                TMyDlg(PTWindowsObject AParent, LPSTR AResource);
};


/* Initialize the dialog controls and set up the transfer buffer */
TMyDlg::TMyDlg(PTWindowsObject AParent, LPSTR AResource)
        : TDialog(AParent, AResource)
{
        new TEdit(this, 101, 80);
        new TEdit(this, 102, 80);
        new TEdit(this, 103, 80);
        new TEdit(this, 104, 80);
        TransferBuffer = (void far *) &((TMyMDIFrame *) Parent)->NewTopic;
}


/* Make a new topic window */
PTWindowsObject TMyMDIFrame::CreateChild()
{
        PTWindowsObject pw;

        if(GetApplication()->ExecDialog(
                new TMyDlg(this, "WindowName")) == IDOK)
        {
                pw = GetApplication()->MakeWindow(
                        new TMyMDIChild(this, NewTopic, idInst));
                /* Copy the data to the new object */
                ((TMyMDIChild *) pw)->SetData(NewData1, 1);
                ((TMyMDIChild *) pw)->SetData(NewData2, 2);
                ((TMyMDIChild *) pw)->SetData(NewData3, 3);
                return pw;
        }
        return NULL;
}


/* Find the child for a topic */
```

```
BOOL
FirstTopic(Pvoid P, Pvoid D)
{
      return (DdeCmpStringHandles(((PChild) P)->TopicHandle
            , (HSZ) D) == 0);
}


/* Find the child for a conversation */
BOOL
FirstConv(Pvoid P, Pvoid D)
{
      return (((PChild) P)->Conv == (HCONV) D);
}



/* This is where all the DDE messages come in */
HDDEDATA FAR PASCAL TMyMDIFrame::CallBack(WORD Type, WORD
      , HCONV Conv, HSZ hsz1, HSZ hsz2, HDDEDATA hData, DWORD
      , DWORD)
{
      char TmpStr[80];
      int Item;
      PChild CurrentTopic;

   switch(Type)
      {
            /* The client is trying to make contact */
            case XTYP_CONNECT:
                  if((CurrentTopic = (PChild)
                        (FrameWindow->FirstThat(FirstTopic, (Pvoid) hsz1)))
                        != NULL && CurrentTopic->Conv == 0)
                        return (HDDEDATA) TRUE;
                  return 0;
            case XTYP_CONNECT_CONFIRM:
                  if((CurrentTopic = (PChild)
                        (FrameWindow->FirstThat(FirstTopic, (Pvoid) hsz1)))
                        != NULL && CurrentTopic->Conv == 0)
                        CurrentTopic->Conv = Conv;
                  break;
            case XTYP_DISCONNECT:
                  if((CurrentTopic = (PChild)
                        (FrameWindow->FirstThat(FirstConv, (Pvoid) Conv))) != NULL)
                        CurrentTopic->Conv = 0;
                  break;
            case XTYP_POKE:
                  CurrentTopic = (PChild)
                        (FrameWindow->FirstThat(FirstConv, (Pvoid) Conv));
                  if(CurrentTopic)
                  {
                        /* Look for the right item name */
                        for(Item=0; Item<3
                              && DdeCmpStringHandles(FrameWindow->Items[Item], hsz2)
                              ; ++Item);
                        /* If all is well, put the data in the window */
                        if(Item < 3)
                        {
                              DdeGetData(hData, &TmpStr, 80, 0);
                              CurrentTopic->SetData(TmpStr, Item+1);
```

```
                        return (HDDEDATA)DDE_FACK;
                    }
                }
                return DDE_FNOTPROCESSED;
          case XTYP_EXECUTE:
                DdeGetData(hData, TmpStr, 80, 0);
                MessageBox(FrameWindow->HWindow, TmpStr, "DDE Execute", MB_OK);
          return (HDDEDATA) DDE_FACK;
          case XTYP_REQUEST:
                CurrentTopic = (PChild)
                      (FrameWindow->FirstThat(FirstConv, (Pvoid) Conv));
                if(CurrentTopic)
                {
                    for(Item=0; Item<3
                          && DdeCmpStringHandles(FrameWindow->Items[Item], hsz2)
                          ; ++Item);
                    /* Get the data to return */
                    if(Item<3)
                    {
                          return DdeCreateDataHandle(FrameWindow->idInst
                                , CurrentTopic->GetData(Item+1)
                                , lstrlen(CurrentTopic->GetData(Item+1))+1
                                , 0, hsz2, CF_TEXT, 0);
                    }
                }
                return NULL;
          default :
                break;
    }
    return NULL;
}


void TMyApp::InitMainWindow()
{
    MainWindow = new TMyMDIFrame(Name);
}


int PASCAL WinMain(HANDLE hInstance, HANDLE hPrevInstance,
  LPSTR lpCmdLine, int nCmdShow)
{
    TMyApp MyApp("The Server", hInstance
    , hPrevInstance, lpCmdLine, nCmdShow);

    MyApp.Run();
    return MyApp.Status;
}
```

3. Copy the resource file SERVER.RES to EXECSVR.RES.

4. Use the *Make* command to compile the program.

5. Create a new project file called EXECCLI.PRJ with the files EXECCLI.CPP, EXECCLI.RES, and STANDARD.DEF.

6. Create the source file EXECCLI.CPP with this program:

```
/* EXECCLI.CPP A DDE Client */
#include <owl.h>
#include <edit.h>
```

```
#include <ddeml.h>

class TMyWindow : public TWindow
{
     public:
             char ServiceName[80];
             char TopicName[80];
             char ItemName[80];
             char Data[80];
             FARPROC CallBackInst;
             DWORD idInst;
             HCONV TheConv;
             HSZ   ServiceHandle;
             HSZ TopicHandle;
             TMyWindow(PTWindowsObject AParent, LPSTR ATitle);
             ~TMyWindow();
             virtual LPSTR GetClassName() {return "ClientWnd";};
             virtual void GetWindowClass(WNDCLASS& AWndClass);
             virtual void SetupWindow();
             static HDDEDATA FAR PASCAL _export CallBack(WORD, WORD, HCONV
                  , HSZ, HSZ, HDDEDATA, DWORD, DWORD );
             virtual void DoConnect(RTMessage) = [CM_FIRST+101];
             virtual void DoRequest(RTMessage) = [CM_FIRST+102];
             virtual void DoPoke(RTMessage) = [CM_FIRST+103];
             virtual void DoExec(RTMessage) = [CM_FIRST+104];
};

TMyWindow *TheWindow;

/* Initialize variables */
TMyWindow::TMyWindow(PTWindowsObject AParent, LPSTR ATitle)
     : TWindow(AParent, ATitle)
{
     Attr.W = 150;
     Attr.H = 80;
     AssignMenu("ClientMenu");
     lstrcpy(ServiceName, "MyServer");
     lstrcpy(TopicName, "");
     lstrcpy(ItemName, "Item 1");
     lstrcpy(Data, "");
     ServiceHandle = NULL;
     TheWindow = this;
}

/* Clean up the DDE stuff */
TMyWindow::~TMyWindow()
{
     if(ServiceHandle)
     {
          /* Disconnect from the server */
          DdeDisconnect(TheConv);
          /* Free the string handles */
          DdeFreeStringHandle(idInst, ServiceHandle);
          DdeFreeStringHandle(idInst, TopicHandle);
     }
     FreeProcInstance(CallBackInst);
}
```

```
/* Set up the program icon */
void TMyWindow::GetWindowClass(WNDCLASS& AWndClass)
{
     TWindow::GetWindowClass(AWndClass);
     AWndClass.hIcon = LoadIcon(AWndClass.hInstance, "DDEClient");
}

/* Initialize DDE service */
void TMyWindow::SetupWindow()
{
     idInst = 0; // Initialize the instance number
     CallBackInst = MakeProcInstance((FARPROC) TMyWindow::CallBack
          , GetApplication()->hInstance );
     /* Set up DDE service */
     DdeInitialize(&idInst, (PFNCALLBACK) CallBackInst
          , APPCMD_CLIENTONLY, OL);
}

/* Dialog for server name */
class TConnectDlg : public TDialog
{
     public:
          TConnectDlg(PTWindowsObject AParent, LPSTR AResource);
};

/* Initialize the dialog controls and set up the transfer buffer */
TConnectDlg::TConnectDlg(PTWindowsObject AParent, LPSTR AResource)
     : TDialog(AParent, AResource)
{
     new TEdit(this, 101, 80);
     new TEdit(this, 102, 80);
     TransferBuffer = (void far *) &((TMyWindow *) Parent)->ServiceName;
}

/* Connect to a server */
void TMyWindow::DoConnect(RTMessage)
{
     if(ServiceHandle)
          MessageBox(HWindow, "Connection in progress", "DDE Client", MB_OK);
     else if(GetApplication()->ExecDialog(
          new TConnectDlg(this, "Connect")) == IDOK)
     {
          ServiceHandle = DdeCreateStringHandle(idInst
               , ServiceName, CP_WINANSI);
          TopicHandle = DdeCreateStringHandle(idInst
          , TopicName, CP_WINANSI);
          TheConv = DdeConnect(idInst, ServiceHandle
               , TopicHandle, (PCONVCONTEXT) NULL);
          if(TheConv == NULL)
          {
               DdeFreeStringHandle(idInst, ServiceHandle);
               ServiceHandle = NULL;
               DdeFreeStringHandle(idInst, TopicHandle);
               MessageBox(HWindow, "No connection available"
                         , "DDE Client", MB_OK);
          }
     }
}
```

```
/* Dialog for requesting data */
class TRequestDlg : public TDialog
{
    public:
            TRequestDlg(PTWindowsObject AParent, LPSTR AResource);
};

/* Initialize the dialog controls and set up the transfer buffer */
TRequestDlg::TRequestDlg(PTWindowsObject AParent, LPSTR AResource)
    : TDialog(AParent, AResource)
{
    new TEdit(this, 101, 80);
    TransferBuffer = (void far *) &((TMyWindow *) Parent)->ItemName;
}


/* Request data from the server */
void TMyWindow::DoRequest(RTMessage)
{
    HSZ ItemHandle;
    HDDEDATA TheData;
    char TmpStr[80];

    if(ServiceHandle)
    {
        if(GetApplication()->ExecDialog(
            new TRequestDlg(this, "Request")) == IDOK)
        {
            ItemHandle = DdeCreateStringHandle(idInst, ItemName, CP_WINANSI);
            if((TheData = DdeClientTransaction(NULL, 0, TheConv
                , ItemHandle, CF_TEXT
                , XTYP_REQUEST, 5000, NULL)) != NULL)
            {
                DdeGetData(TheData, TmpStr, 80, 0L);
                MessageBox(HWindow, TmpStr
                    , "DDE Client (XTYP_REQUEST)", MB_OK);
            }
            else
                MessageBox(HWindow, "No data", "DDE Client", MB_OK);
            DdeFreeStringHandle(idInst, ItemHandle);
        }
    }
    else
    MessageBox(HWindow, "No connection", "DDE Client", MB_OK);
}


/* Dialog for poking data */
class TPokeDlg : public TDialog
{
    public:
            TPokeDlg(PTWindowsObject AParent, LPSTR AResource);
};

/* Initialize the dialog controls and set up the transfer buffer */
TPokeDlg::TPokeDlg(PTWindowsObject AParent, LPSTR AResource)
    : TDialog(AParent, AResource)
{
    new TEdit(this, 101, 80);
```

```
        new TEdit(this, 102, 80);
        TransferBuffer = (void far *) &((TMyWindow *) Parent)->ItemName;
}


/* Poke data at the server */
void TMyWindow::DoPoke(RTMessage)
{
        HSZ ItemHandle;

        if(ServiceHandle)
        {
                if(GetApplication()->ExecDialog(
                        new TPokeDlg(this, "Poke")) == IDOK)
                {
                        ItemHandle = DdeCreateStringHandle(idInst, ItemName
                                , CP_WINANSI);
                        DdeClientTransaction(Data, lstrlen(Data)+1, TheConv
                                , ItemHandle, CF_TEXT
                                , XTYP_POKE, 5000, NULL);
                        DdeFreeStringHandle(idInst, ItemHandle);
                }
        }
        else
                MessageBox(HWindow, "No Connection", "DDE Client", MB_OK);
}


/* Dialog for executing a command */
class TExecDlg : public TDialog
{
        public:
                TExecDlg(PTWindowsObject AParent, LPSTR AResource);
};

/* Initialize the dialog controls and set up the transfer buffer */
TExecDlg::TExecDlg(PTWindowsObject AParent, LPSTR AResource)
        : TDialog(AParent, AResource)
{
        new TEdit(this, 101, 80);
        TransferBuffer = (void far *) &((TMyWindow *) Parent)->Data;
}


/* Send a command to the server */
void TMyWindow::DoExec(RTMessage)
{
        if(ServiceHandle)
        {
                if(GetApplication()->ExecDialog(
                        new TExecDlg(this, "Execute")) == IDOK)
                {
                        DdeClientTransaction(Data, lstrlen(Data)+1, TheConv
                                , NULL, CF_TEXT, XTYP_EXECUTE, 5000, NULL);
                }
        }
        else
                MessageBox(HWindow, "No Connection", "DDE Client", MB_OK);
}

/* This is where all the DDE messages come in */
```

```
HDDEDATA FAR PASCAL TMyWindow::CallBack(WORD Type, WORD
    , HCONV, HSZ, HSZ, HDDEDATA, DWORD
    , DWORD)
{
    char TmpStr[80];

    switch(Type)
    {
        case XTYP_DISCONNECT:
            MessageBox(TheWindow->HWindow, "Disconnected."
                , "DDE Client", MB_OK);
            TheWindow->TheConv = NULL;
            DdeFreeStringHandle(TheWindow->idInst, TheWindow->ServiceHandle);
            DdeFreeStringHandle(TheWindow->idInst, TheWindow->TopicHandle);
            TheWindow->ServiceHandle = NULL;
            break;
        case XTYP_ERROR:
            MessageBox(TheWindow->HWindow
                , "DDE error", "DDE Client", MB_OK);
            break;
        default :
            break;
    }
    return NULL;
}


class TMyApp : public TApplication
{
    public:
        TMyApp(LPSTR AName, HINSTANCE Inst, HINSTANCE Prev
            , LPSTR lpCmdLine, int nCmdShow)
            : TApplication(AName, Inst, Prev, lpCmdLine, nCmdShow) {};
        virtual void InitMainWindow();
};

void TMyApp::InitMainWindow()
{
    MainWindow = new TMyWindow(NULL, Name);
}

int PASCAL WinMain(HINSTANCE hInstance, HINSTANCE hPrevInstance,
    LPSTR lpCmdLine, int nCmdShow)
{
    TMyApp MyApp("The Client", hInstance
        , hPrevInstance, lpCmdLine, nCmdShow);

    MyApp.Run();
    return MyApp.Status;
}
```

7. Copy the resource file CLIENT.RES to EXECCLI.RES and change the menu resource to:

```
CLIENTMENU MENU
BEGIN
    POPUP "&DDE"
```

```
        BEGIN
                MENUITEM "&Connect", 101
                MENUITEM "&Request", 102
                MENUITEM "&Poke", 103
                MENUITEM "E&xecute", 104
                MENUITEM "&Exit", 24340
        END

END
```

and add this dialog resource:

```
EXECUTE DIALOG 18, 18, 142, 46
STYLE DS_MODALFRAME | WS_POPUP | WS_CAPTION | WS_SYSMENU
CAPTION "Execute"
BEGIN
        CONTROL "Command", -1, "STATIC", SS_LEFT | WS_CHILD |WS_VISIBLE | WS_GROUP, 5, 12, 45, 8
        CONTROL "", 101, "EDIT", ES_LEFT|WS_CHILD|WS_VISIBLE|WS_BORDER|WS_TABSTOP, 55,10,75,12
        CONTROL "OK", 1, "BUTTON", BS_DEFPUSHBUTTON|WS_CHILD|WS_VISIBLE|WS_TABSTOP, 15, 30, 40, 13
        CONTROL "Cancel", 2, "BUTTON", BS_PUSHBUTTON|WS_CHILD|WS_VISIBLE|WS_TABSTOP, 80, 30, 40, 13
END
```

8. Use the *Run* command to compile and run the program. Also run the EXECSVR.EXE program.

HOW IT WORKS

The difference between these programs and the ones in How-To 9.1 and 9.2 is that the client program includes the DoExec member function and the server handles the XTYP_EXECUTE transaction. The DoExec member function uses the TExecDlg object to get the command string from the user. Then, it passes the command to the server with the Windows function DdeClientTransaction. The server gets the XTYP_EXECUTE transaction in the callback function. The server uses the Windows function DdeGetData to get the command from the data handle. Then it calls MessageBox to display the command on the screen.

COMMENT

The transaction between the server and client programs in this solution is not very exciting. You can see more of the power of the execute transaction by using the client program to access other DDE programs. For example, enter the server name PROGMAN and the topic name PROGMAN. Then use the execute command to execute the statement, [CreateGroup(New Group)]. This command tells program manager to create a new group named, "New Group." Check the Windows help text for more information about commands that you can send to Program Manager.

Object Linking
and Embedding 10

10

Windows version 3.1 includes two new ways for programs to communicate with each other. The first is called drag-and-drop. The user can select files in the file manager and drag them to a drag-and-drop program that is running on the Windows desktop. When the user drops the files on the program, Windows sends messages to the program, giving it the file names.

The other communication method is called Object Linking and Embedding (OLE). A client program can use OLE to exchange data with a server program. The difference between OLE and DDE (see Chapter 9, "DDE Connections") is that an OLE client can call functions in the server to handle the data. This means that the client does not have to know the format of the data, because it can let the server do things such as editing or drawing the object.

An OLE server encapsulates data and functions into objects that client programs can use. There are two types of objects in OLE programs, *embedded* and *linked*. With embedded objects, the server sends the data for the object to the client and the client embeds the data in its own documents. With linked objects, the server only sends the name of the object to the client. The client uses the name when referring to the object.

OLE clients should use embedded objects when the document needs its own copy of the data. Use linked objects if you want the data to be updated automatically when the server changes the object. For example, you can use OLE to write a report that includes some figures from a spreadsheet. If you want the report to always include the data from the day you wrote the report, use an embedded object. On the other hand, if you want the report to always show the most current data, you can use a linked object.

Older Windows programs shared data via DDE and the Clipboard. These mechanisms are relatively easy to implement and use, but they suffer from a major drawback. The programs at both ends of the connection must understand the format of the data. This is fine if you write both the client and server, but it limits the usefulness of your programs with other applications. OLE reduces this problem by letting the client ask the server to do many of the common actions on the data, such as displaying the data on the screen or printer. This means that many more programs can work with an OLE server than with the Clipboard or a DDE program.

10.1 Get Drag-and-Drop Files

This solution shows how you can make your program accept file names that the user dropped on it. You can use this feature to make file viewers, backup utilities, editors, and many other programs that use files. Your programs get all the power of the file manager for locating files without you having to add very much extra code.

10.2 Create an OLE Client

This solution shows how to create a program that can access OLE servers, such as the Windows Paint program. A nice feature for programs, such as word processors and databases, is to allow the user to add drawings to the text or data record. By using OLE, these programs can use the Paint program for editing these drawings.

10.3 Create an OLE Server

The other half of an OLE connection is the server. This solution shows how to make a simple OLE server. Just about any program that collects or edits data can be turned into an OLE server. When you make a program into an OLE server, it becomes a tool that can be used by other programs. For example, a text editor that you convert to an OLE server can be used by OLE clients for any text editing chores the client may have. Another example is a program that gets data from an on-line database. By making the program an OLE server, you can set up spreadsheets and report generators that are updated automatically when the program gets new data.

10.1 How Do I...
Get Drag-and-Drop Files?

Complexity: EASY

PROBLEM

The file dialog in many programs is not the easiest way to find a file buried in some subdirectory whose name you cannot remember. The Windows file manager is a much better tool for hunting down that file. The problem is that once you find the file, you have to write down the path for the file, go back to your application, and then enter the path in the file dialog. Drag-and-drop simplifies the process by letting you click on selected files and drag them to the application, then drop the files into the application. This solution is a program that accepts dropped files and copies them to a disk.

TECHNIQUE

Before your program gets any drag-and-drop messages, you must register the window by calling DragAcceptFiles. When the user drags files over a registered window, the mouse cursor changes indicating that the files can be dropped. If the user releases the mouse button while the mouse cursor is over the window, Windows sends a WM_DROPFILES message to the window.

The word parameter in the WM_DROPFILES message is a handle to a shared memory area that contains the names of the files just dropped. The format of the memory in this area is not documented, but Windows provides the DragQueryFile routine to get file names. You pass the handle to the memory, the index of the file name, a buffer for the file name, and the size of the buffer. The return value is the number of bytes in the file name, or the number of files if the index is 0xFFFF.

You can find out the location of the mouse cursor when the user dropped the files by calling DragQueryPoint. You can do different things to the files depending on the place where the user dropped the file. This code fragment shows how to get the mouse position:

```
if(DragQuereyPoint(DropHandle, &APoint))
      wsprintf(TmpStr, "Files dropped at: %d, %d", APoint.x, APoint.y);
```

The argument &APoint is the address of a POINT type structure. The mouse position is in Window coordinates. DragQueryPoint returns TRUE if the point is in the client area of the window. In this example, the program puts the position into TmpStr if the point is in the client area.

After processing a WM_DROPFILES message, a program should call the Windows function DragFinish to free the shared memory block.

The program in this solution copies files to drive A.

STEPS

1. Create a new project called DROPPER.PRJ that includes the files DROPPER.CPP, DROPPER.RES, and STANDARD.DEF.

2. Create the source file DROPPER.CPP with this program:

```
/* DROPPER.CPP receive drag and drop items */
#include <owl.h>
#include <shellapi.h>

/* The main window object */
class TMyWindow : public TWindow
{
      public:
            TMyWindow(PTWindowsObject, LPSTR);
            virtual LPSTR GetClassName() {return "FlopDrop";};
            virtual void GetWindowClass(WNDCLASS &);
            virtual void SetupWindow();
            virtual void ShutDownWindow();
            virtual void Paint(HDC, PAINTSTRUCT &);
            virtual void WMDropFiles(RTMessage) = [WM_FIRST + WM_DROPFILES];
            virtual void WMLButtonDown(RTMessage) = [WM_FIRST + WM_LBUTTONDOWN];
};

/* Initialize variables */
TMyWindow::TMyWindow(PTWindowsObject AParent, LPSTR ATitle)
      : TWindow(AParent, ATitle)
{
      Attr.Style = WS_POPUP;
      Attr.W = 64;
      Attr.H = 64;
}

/* Set up the program icon */
void TMyWindow::GetWindowClass(WNDCLASS& AWndClass)
{
      TWindow::GetWindowClass(AWndClass);
      AWndClass.hIcon = LoadIcon(AWndClass.hInstance, "DropIcon");
}
```

```
/* Start accepting files */
void TMyWindow::SetupWindow()
{
    TWindow::SetupWindow();
    DragAcceptFiles(HWindow, TRUE);
}

/* Stop accepting files */
void TMyWindow::ShutDownWindow()
{
    DragAcceptFiles(HWindow, FALSE);
    TWindow::ShutDownWindow();
}

/* Show the bitmap in the main window */
void TMyWindow::Paint(HDC hDC, PAINTSTRUCT&)
{
    HDC MemDC;
    HBITMAP TheBitmap, OldBmp;

    /* Load the bitmap */
    TheBitmap = LoadBitmap(GetApplication()->hInstance, "DropPict");
    /* Draw the bitmap */
    MemDC = CreateCompatibleDC(hDC);
    OldBmp = (HBITMAP) SelectObject(MemDC, TheBitmap);
    BitBlt(hDC, 0, 0, 64, 64, MemDC, 0, 0, SRCCOPY);
    DeleteObject(SelectObject(MemDC, OldBmp));
    DeleteDC(MemDC);
}

/* Handle file drop message */
void TMyWindow::WMDropFiles(RTMessage Msg)
{
    HDROP TheDrop;
    int FileCnt;
    char Buffer[512];
    int i, j;
    HFILE Src, Dest;
    int Size;

    /* Get the handle to the dropped data */
    TheDrop = (HDROP) Msg.WParam;
    /* Find out how many files there are */
    FileCnt = DragQueryFile(TheDrop, 0xFFFF, NULL, 0);
    /* Get each file */
    for(i=0; i<FileCnt; ++i)
    {
        /* Get the file name */
        DragQueryFile(TheDrop, i, Buffer, 512);
        /* Confirm the copy with the user */
        if(MessageBox(HWindow, Buffer, "Copy file", MB_OKCANCEL)==IDOK)
        {
            /* Open the file */
            Src = _lopen(Buffer, READ);
            Buffer[0] = 'A';
            /* Search for last '\' */
            for(j=lstrlen(Buffer)-1; j>3 && Buffer[j] != '\\'; --j);
```

```
                    /* Squeeze out the path */
                    if(j>3)
                            lstrcpy(&Buffer[3], &Buffer[j+1]);
                    /* Open a file on the floppy */
                    if((Dest = _lcreat(Buffer, 0)) == HFILE_ERROR)
                    {
                            MessageBox(HWindow, Buffer, "Cannot create", MB_OK);
                            _lclose(Src);
                    }
                    else
                    {
                            do {
                                    Size = _lread(Src, Buffer, 512);
                                    _lwrite(Dest, Buffer, 512);
                            } while(Size == 512);
                            _lclose(Src);
                            _lclose(Dest);
                    }
            }
    }
    DragFinish(TheDrop);
}


/* Quit when the user presses the button */
void TMyWindow::WMLButtonDown(RTMessage)
{
    PostMessage(HWindow, WM_CLOSE, 0, 0L);
}


class TMyApp : public TApplication
{
    public:
            TMyApp(LPSTR AName, HINSTANCE Inst, HINSTANCE Prev
                    , LPSTR lpCmdLine, int nCmdShow)
                    : TApplication(AName, Inst, Prev, lpCmdLine, nCmdShow) {};
            virtual void InitMainWindow();
};

void TMyApp::InitMainWindow()
{
    MainWindow = new TMyWindow(NULL, "Dropper");
}


int PASCAL WinMain(HINSTANCE hInstance, HINSTANCE hPrevInstance,
  LPSTR lpCmdLine, int nCmdShow)
{
    TMyApp MyApp("", hInstance, hPrevInstance, lpCmdLine, nCmdShow);

    MyApp.Run();
    return MyApp.Status;
}
```

3. Create the resource file DROPPER.RES with the bitmap and icon in Figure 10-1.

4. Use the *Run* command to compile and run the program.

HOW IT WORKS

The SetupWindow member function for the main window in this program calls the DragAcceptFiles routine to register the window. You cannot call this function from the constructor because it needs the window handle, which is not available in the constructor.

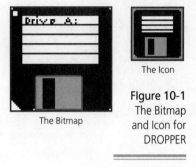

The Icon

Figure 10-1
The Bitmap
and Icon for
DROPPER

The Bitmap

The program uses the message response member function WMDropFiles to handle the WM_DROP-FILES message. First, the routine copies the word parameter to the variable TheDrop. Then, the routine calls DragQueryFiles with an index of 0xFFFF to get the number of files dropped. Next, the routine calls DragQueryFiles for each file to get the name of the file. This file name is a complete path, so it can be opened no matter what the current directory is. The routine makes the destination file name by removing all of the path from after the drive name to the last backslash. Then it changes the drive name to 'A.' When the files are open, the routine copies the file by reading from the source file and writing to the destination file. When the file is copied, the routine closes the files and calls DragFinish.

10.2 How Do I...
Create an OLE Client?

Complexity: MODERATE

PROBLEM

An OLE client application can use servers to make itself more useful. For example, a database that can include OLE objects in a record can store text, formulas, graphics, or anything else that your servers handle. This solution shows how to make an OLE client that uses the Windows Paint program as a server to edit graphics.

TECHNIQUE

An OLE client program calls the OLE client library to maintain objects associated with a server. The first thing the client does is to register a document with

FUNCTION	OLE TYPE	DATA SOURCE
OleClone	Same as source	Another object.
OleCopyFromLink	Embedded	A linked object.
OleCreate	Embedded	The server.
OleCreateFromClip	Embedded	The Clipboard.
OleCreateFromFile	Embedded	A file.
OleCreateFromTemplate	Embedded	Another object (new object has no data).
OleCreateInvisible	Embedded	The server (the server is not shown to the user).
OleCreateLinkFromClip	Linked	The Clipboard.
OleCreateLinkFromFile	Linked	A file.

Table 10-1 Functions for Creating OLE Objects

the client library using the Windows function OleRegisterClientDoc. This function assigns a document handle for the document that you can use with other OLE functions that use documents. Any OLE objects used by the client must be associated with a previously registered document.

There are several ways for a client program to create an OLE object. The method to use depends on the source of the data and whether the object is a linked or embedded object. Table 10-1 lists the functions that create objects.

To create a new object, the client program must tell the client library the client document that uses the object, the address of an OLECLIENT structure for the object, the address of the pointer to the object data, the name of the object, and the name of the server for the object.

The document for the object is the one registered at the beginning of the program. The OLECLIENT structure holds the address of the callback function that the server uses to inform the client of changes to the object. The client library fills in the pointer to the object data so that you can pass this information to other OLE functions. The object name must be unique in the document. The name of the server comes from the Windows registration database.

The Windows registration database keeps track of the OLE servers available and the types of files they use. OLE clients can look up the available servers by checking the registration database. Windows version 3.1 includes a program called REGEDIT.EXE that lets you see and edit the registrations. Figure 10-2 shows the registration information for the Windows Paint program.

Programs can access the registration database through the Windows 3.1 API. An OLE client program can use the RegOpenKey and RegEnumKey routines to get a list of the available servers. This routine shows how:

```
HKEY TheRoot;
char TmpStr[80];
DWORD i
long cb;

/* Open the root level key */
if(RegOpenKey(HKEY_CLASSES_ROOT, NULL, &TheRoot) == ERROR_SUCCESS)
{
      /* Look up each root level key */
      for(i=0; RegEditEnumKey(TheRoot, i, TmpStr, sizeof(TmpStr)) == ERROR_SUCCES; ++i)
      {
            /* Skip extension associations */
            if(TmpStr[0] != '.')
                  /* Put the server name in a list box */
                  SendDlgItemMessage(hDlg, IDC_SERVERS, LB_ADDSTRING, 0
                        , (LONG)(LPSTR) TmpStr);
      }
}
```

Once you know the server, you can call a function, such as OleCreate, to create an embedded object from the server. Your program passes all of the required information to OleCreate, which sends the data to the OLE client library, which passes the data to the OLE server library which passes the data to the server. After the server creates the object, possibly letting the user edit the object, the server returns the object data to the client program. During this lengthy process, the client program may not alter the document or use the object data in any other OLE calls. The client may not simply wait for the process to complete because Windows expects the client to handle messages. To handle this situation, you have to supply a routine that checks for a completed OLE function

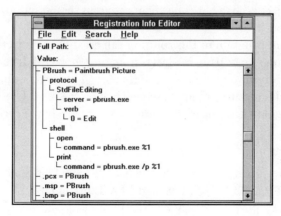

Figure 10-2
The Windows
REGEDIT.EXE
Program

and processes messages. The FinishOLECmnd routine in the sample program is an example of such a function.

The other way to create an object shown in the program in this solution is to use the Clipboard. In this case, the object already exists and includes information about the server. Therefore, the client program does not have to look up the server in the registration database. The client passes information about the call-back function, the client document, the name of the object, and the address of a pointer to the object data to the Windows function OleCreateFromClip. You must call FinishOLECmnd to wait for the creation to complete.

Each server has a list of verbs that you, the client, can use to operate on the object. For example, the first verb may edit the data and another may play the object. To access these verbs, use the Windows function OleActivate. You pass this function the address of the object data, the verb number, and information about where to display the object. The CMActivate member function in the sample program shows how to use CMActivate.

One of the more common things to do with an object is to draw it on the screen or printer. The Windows function OleDraw sends commands to the server to draw the object in a specified device context, such as the client window or on the printer. You must pass a pointer to the object to draw, a handle to the device context, and a bounding rectangle that tells the server where to draw the object. The sample program uses OleDraw to handle the WM_PAINT message from Windows. In this case, the program fills the client window with the object.

One piece of information that a client program sends to the server when it creates an object is the address of a callback function. The server uses this func-tion to inform the client program when it does something with an object. For ex-ample, when the server saves the object, it calls the callback function to tell the client that the object is changed. The client program should redraw the object using the new data.

The OLE client program in this solution can create new objects using the Windows Paint program or paste in objects from the Clipboard. It keeps track of the last object displayed so that it can undo changes. The current object fills the client window and is updated when the server changes the data. There are menu commands for creating new objects or using the server to edit the current object.

STEPS

1. Create a new project called OCLIENT.PRJ that includes the files OCLIENT.CPP, OCLIENT.RES, and STANDARD.DEF.

2. Create the source file OCLIENT.CPP with this program:

```
/* OLECLI.CPP AN OLE Client */
#include <owl.h>
#include <ole.h>

#define CM_PBRUSH      101
#define CM_UNDO        102
#define CM_CUT         103
#define CM_COPY        104
#define CM_PASTE       105
#define CM_CLEAR       106
#define CM_ACTIVATE    107

HINSTANCE TheInst;
typedef int FAR PASCAL (*TCallBack)(LPOLECLIENT, OLE_NOTIFICATION, LPOLEOBJECT);

void FinishOLECmnd(OLESTATUS Ret, LPOLEOBJECT Object, int Location);
void Check(OLESTATUS Ret, int Location);


_CLASSDEF(TMyClient)

/* The main window */
class TMyWindow : public TWindow
{
     public:
           OLESTATUS Ret;              // Status of the last OLE function
           LHCLIENTDOC ClientDoc;      // Handle to the client document
           char DocName[260];          // Name of the document
           char ObjectName[260];       // Name of the object
           char UndoObjectName[260];   // Name of the object to undo
           PTMyClient TheClient;       // OLEClient structure
           BOOL ObjectLoaded;          // True if an object is loaded
           BOOL UndoObjectLoaded;      // True if there is an undo object
           LPOLEOBJECT Object;         // Pointer to the object
           LPOLEOBJECT UndoObject;     // Pointer to the undo object
           int NextObjectNumber;
           TMyWindow(PTWindowsObject, LPSTR);
           virtual LPSTR GetClassName() {return "OLEClient";};
           virtual void GetWindowClass(WNDCLASS &);
           virtual void SetupWindow();
           virtual void ShutDownWindow();
           virtual void Paint(HDC, PAINTSTRUCT &);
           void CloseCurrentOle();
           void BackupObject();
           virtual void WMInitMenu(RTMessage) = [WM_FIRST+WM_INITMENU];
           virtual void CMPBrush(RTMessage) = [CM_FIRST + CM_PBRUSH];
           virtual void CMUndo(RTMessage) = [CM_FIRST + CM_UNDO];
           virtual void CMCut(RTMessage) = [CM_FIRST + CM_CUT];
           virtual void CMCopy(RTMessage) = [CM_FIRST + CM_COPY];
           virtual void CMPaste(RTMessage) = [CM_FIRST + CM_PASTE];
           virtual void CMClear(RTMessage) = [CM_FIRST + CM_CLEAR];
           virtual void CMActivate(RTMessage) = [CM_FIRST + CM_ACTIVATE];
           LPSTR GetNextObjectName();
           int CallBack(LPOLECLIENT, OLE_NOTIFICATION, LPOLEOBJECT);
};

/* Data structure for callbacks */
struct TMyClient : OLECLIENT
```

```
{
     TMyWindow *TheWindow;          // Pointer to the main window
     TMyClient(TMyWindow *, HINSTANCE HInst = 0);
     LPOLECLIENTVTBL ClientVtbl;
};

/* Initialize variables */
TMyWindow::TMyWindow(PTWindowsObject AParent, LPSTR ATitle)
     : TWindow(AParent, ATitle)
{
     Ret = OLE_OK;
     ClientDoc = 0;
     ObjectLoaded = FALSE;
     UndoObjectLoaded = FALSE;
     TheClient = NULL;
     Object = NULL;
     UndoObject = NULL;
     lstrcpy(DocName, "noname.ole");
     UndoObjectName[0] = '\0';
     ObjectName[0] = '\0';
     AssignMenu("OLEMenu");
     NextObjectNumber = 0;
}

/* Set up the program icon */
void TMyWindow::GetWindowClass(WNDCLASS& AWndClass)
{
     TWindow::GetWindowClass(AWndClass);
     AWndClass.hIcon = LoadIcon(AWndClass.hInstance, "OleClient");
}

/* Initialize OLE service */
void TMyWindow::SetupWindow()
{
     TWindow::SetupWindow();
     Ret = OleRegisterClientDoc(GetApplication()->Name, DocName, 0, &ClientDoc);
     Check(Ret, 105);
     TheClient = new TMyClient(this);
}

/* Clean up OLE objects */
void TMyWindow::ShutDownWindow()
{
     CloseCurrentOle();
     if(TheClient)
          delete TheClient;
     TWindow::ShutDownWindow();
}

/* Draw the picture */
void TMyWindow::Paint(HDC hDC, PAINTSTRUCT&)
{
     LPOLEOBJECT DrawObject = NULL;
     RECT Rect;

     if(ObjectLoaded)
          DrawObject = Object;
```

```
        else if(UndoObject)
            DrawObject = UndoObject;
        if(DrawObject)
        {
            GetClientRect(HWindow, &Rect);
            Ret = OleDraw(DrawObject, hDC, &Rect, NULL, 0);
            FinishOLECmnd(Ret, DrawObject, 104);
        }
}

/* Get rid of the object */
void TMyWindow::CloseCurrentOle()
{
    if(Object)
    {
        Ret = OleDelete(Object);
        FinishOLECmnd(Ret, Object, 106);
    }
    if(UndoObject)
    {
        Ret = OleDelete(UndoObject);
        FinishOLECmnd(Ret, Object, 107);
    }
    Object = UndoObject = NULL;
    ObjectLoaded = UndoObjectLoaded = FALSE;
    InvalidateRect(HWindow, NULL, TRUE);
}

/* Make a backup copy of an object */
void TMyWindow::BackupObject()
{
    if(Object)
    {
        Ret = OleClone(Object, (LPOLECLIENT) TheClient, ClientDoc
            , GetApplication()->Name, &UndoObject);
        FinishOLECmnd(Ret, Object, 100);
        lstrcpy(UndoObjectName, ObjectName);
        lstrcpy(ObjectName, GetNextObjectName());
        UndoObjectLoaded = ObjectLoaded;
    }
}

/* Adjust the menu for current status */
void TMyWindow::WMInitMenu(RTMessage Msg)
{
    HMENU TheMenu;
    WORD EnableUndo;

    TheMenu = (HMENU) Msg.WParam;
    if((Object != UndoObject) && (UndoObject != NULL))
        EnableUndo = MF_ENABLED;
    else
        EnableUndo = MF_GRAYED;
    EnableMenuItem(TheMenu, CM_UNDO, EnableUndo);
    EnableMenuItem(TheMenu, CM_COPY, (ObjectLoaded?MF_ENABLED:MF_GRAYED));
    EnableMenuItem(TheMenu, CM_CUT, (ObjectLoaded?MF_ENABLED:MF_GRAYED));
    Ret = OleQueryCreateFromClip("StdFileEditing", olerender_draw, 0);
```

```
        EnableMenuItem(TheMenu, CM_PASTE, ((Ret==OLE_OK)?MF_ENABLED:MF_GRAYED));
        EnableMenuItem(TheMenu, CM_CLEAR, (ObjectLoaded?MF_ENABLED:MF_GRAYED));
        EnableMenuItem(TheMenu, CM_ACTIVATE, (ObjectLoaded?MF_ENABLED:MF_GRAYED));
        DrawMenuBar(HWindow);
}


/* Create a new object using the Paint program */
void TMyWindow::CMPBrush(RTMessage)
{
        BackupObject();
        ObjectLoaded = FALSE;
        lstrcpy(ObjectName, GetNextObjectName());
        /* Create an OLE object for painting */
        Ret = OleCreate("StdFileEditing", (LPOLECLIENT) TheClient
                , "PBRUSH", ClientDoc, GetApplication()->Name, &Object
                , olerender_draw, 0);
        FinishOLECmnd(Ret, Object, 101);
        /* Send the object name to the server */
        Ret = OleSetHostNames(Object, GetApplication()->Name, ObjectName);
        FinishOLECmnd(Ret, Object, 102);
}


/* Undo the last edit by replacing the object with the old object */
void TMyWindow::CMUndo(RTMessage)
{
        LPOLEOBJECT Swap;
        BOOL FSwap;

        if(UndoObject && UndoObject != Object)
        {
                Swap = Object;
                Object = UndoObject;
                UndoObject = Swap;
                FSwap = ObjectLoaded;
                ObjectLoaded = UndoObjectLoaded;
                UndoObjectLoaded = FSwap;
                InvalidateRect(HWindow, NULL, TRUE);
        }
}


/* Put the object in the clipboard, then delete it */
void TMyWindow::CMCut(RTMessage Msg)
{
        CMCopy(Msg);
        CloseCurrentOle();
}


/* Copy the object to the clipboard */
void TMyWindow::CMCopy(RTMessage)
{
        if(OpenClipboard(HWindow) && EmptyClipboard())
        {
                Ret = OleCopyToClipboard(Object);
                Check(Ret, 103);
                CloseClipboard();
        }
}
```

```
/* Handle the paste command from the menu */
void TMyWindow::CMPaste(RTMessage)
{
    if(OpenClipboard(HWindow))
    {
        BackupObject();
        lstrcpy(ObjectName, GetNextObjectName());
        Ret = OleCreateFromClip("StdFileEditing"
            , (LPOLECLIENT) TheClient, ClientDoc, ObjectName
            , &Object, olerender_draw, 0);
        Check(Ret, 108);
        ObjectLoaded = TRUE;
        CloseClipboard();
        InvalidateRect(HWindow, NULL, TRUE);
    }
}


/* Handle the clear command from the menu */
void TMyWindow::CMClear(RTMessage)
{
    CloseCurrentOle();
}


/* Handle the edit command from the menu */
void TMyWindow::CMActivate( RTMessage )
{
    RECT Rect;

    BackupObject();
    GetClientRect(HWindow, &Rect);
    Ret = OleActivate(Object , OLEVERB_PRIMARY, TRUE
        , TRUE , HWindow , &Rect);
    FinishOLECmnd(Ret, Object, 109);
    InvalidateRect(HWindow, NULL, TRUE);
}


/* Create a unique object name */
LPSTR TMyWindow::GetNextObjectName()
{
    static char Buffer[260];

    wsprintf(Buffer, "Object #%03d", NextObjectNumber++);
    return Buffer;
}


/* This is where the window gets OLE Messages */
int TMyWindow::CallBack(LPOLECLIENT, OLE_NOTIFICATION OleNotify
    , LPOLEOBJECT)
{
    switch(OleNotify)
    {
        case OLE_CHANGED:
        case OLE_SAVED:
            ObjectLoaded = TRUE;
            InvalidateRect(HWindow, NULL, TRUE);
            break;
    }
    return TRUE;
```

```
}

/* Get information from the server */
int FAR PASCAL _export TheCallBack(LPOLECLIENT Client
    , OLE_NOTIFICATION Notify, LPOLEOBJECT Object)
{
    return ((TMyClient *)Client)->TheWindow->CallBack(Client
        , Notify, Object);
}

/* Create a new Vtbl */
TMyClient::TMyClient(TMyWindow *Owner, HINSTANCE HInst)
{
    TheWindow = Owner;
    if(!ClientVtbl)
    {
        ClientVtbl = new OLECLIENTVTBL;
        if(HInst==0)
            ClientVtbl->CallBack = TheCallBack;
        else
            ClientVtbl->CallBack = (TCallBack) MakeProcInstance(
                (FARPROC)TheCallBack, HInst);
    }
    lpvtbl = ClientVtbl;
}


class TMyApp : public TApplication
{
    public:
        OLECLIPFORMAT LinkForm;
        OLECLIPFORMAT NativeForm;
        OLECLIPFORMAT OwnerForm;
        TMyApp(LPSTR AName, HINSTANCE Inst, HINSTANCE Prev
            , LPSTR lpCmdLine, int nCmdShow)
            : TApplication(AName, Inst, Prev, lpCmdLine, nCmdShow) {};
        virtual void InitMainWindow();
        virtual void InitInstance();
};

/* Get Windows messages while waiting for an OLE operation to finish */
void FinishOLECmnd(OLESTATUS Ret, LPOLEOBJECT Object, int Location)
{
    MSG msg;

    if(Ret == OLE_WAIT_FOR_RELEASE)
    {
        while((Ret=OleQueryReleaseStatus(Object)) == OLE_BUSY)
            if(GetMessage(&msg, NULL, NULL, NULL))
            {
                TranslateMessage(&msg);
                DispatchMessage(&msg);
            }
        if(Ret == OLE_OK)
            return;
    }
    Check(Ret, Location);
}

/* If there is an error, display the message */
void Check(OLESTATUS Ret, int Location)
```

```
{
    char TmpStr[80];
    char ErrStr[80];

    if(Ret != OLE_OK)
    {
        LoadString(TheInst, (UINT) Ret, ErrStr, 80);
        wsprintf(TmpStr, "Error: %s at: %d", ErrStr, Location);
        MessageBox(GetFocus(), TmpStr, "OLE Client", MB_OK);
    }
}


void TMyApp::InitMainWindow()
{
    MainWindow = new TMyWindow(NULL, "OLE Client Program");
}


void TMyApp::InitInstance()
{
    TApplication::InitInstance();
    LinkForm = RegisterClipboardFormat("ObjectLink");
    NativeForm = RegisterClipboardFormat("Native");
    OwnerForm = RegisterClipboardFormat("OwnerLink");
}


int PASCAL WinMain(HINSTANCE hInstance, HINSTANCE hPrevInstance
    , LPSTR lpCmdLine, int nCmdShow)
{
    TMyApp MyApp("OleClient", hInstance
        , hPrevInstance, lpCmdLine, nCmdShow);

    TheInst = hInstance;
    MyApp.Run();
    return MyApp.Status;
}
```

3. Create the resource file OCLIENT.RES with these resources:

```
OLEMENU MENU
BEGIN
    POPUP "&OLE"
    BEGIN
        MENUITEM "Create &PBRUSH", 101
        MENUITEM "&Edit object", 107
        MENUITEM "&Undo", 102
        MENUITEM "&Cut", 103
        MENUITEM "C&opy", 104
        MENUITEM "Pa&ste", 105
        MENUITEM "C&lear", 106
    END
END


STRINGTABLE LOADONCALL MOVEABLE DISCARDABLE
BEGIN
    2, "OLE Busy"
    3, "OLE Attempt to use real mode"
    4, "OLE Low memory"
    5, "OLE Stream error"
    6, "OLE Non static object expected"
```

```
     7, "OLE Critical data missing"
     8, "OLE Drawing error"
     9, "OLE Invalid metafile"
    10, "OLE User aborted"
    11, "OLE Clipboard failure"
    12, "OLE Unavailable format"
    13, "OLE Invalid object"
    14, "OLE Invalid link/render option"
    15, "OLE Invalid protocol"
    16, "OLE Invalid pointer"
    17, "OLE Objects not equal"
    18, "OLE Invalid handle"
    19, "OLE General Error"
    20, "OLE Invalid class"
    21, "OLE Invalid command syntax"
    22, "OLE Unsupported data format"
    23, "OLE Invalid colors"
    24, "OLE Not a linked object"
    25, "OLE Client document contains objects"
    26, "OLE Bad buffer size"
    27, "OLE Invalid drive letter"
    28, "OLE Network error"
    29, "OLE Invalid name"
    30, "OLE Server could not load template"
    31, "OLE Server could not load document"
    32, "OLE Server could not create instance"
    33, "OLE Server document not opened"
    34, "OLE Object not opened"
    35, "OLE Could not launch server"
    36, "OLE No server connection"
    37, "OLE Termination error"
    38, "OLE Execute error"
    39, "OLE Show error"
    40, "OLE Error in verb"
    41, "OLE Missing item"
    42, "OLE Unknown item format"
    43, "OLE Server does not support renaming"
    44, "OLE Unable to poke data to the server"
    45, "OLE Server could not render native data"
    46, "OLE Server could not render presentation data"
    47, "OLE Server blocked"
    48, "OLE Unregistered server"
    49, "OLE Document already registered"
    50, "OLE Invalid task"
    51, "OLE Object is out of date"
    52, "OLE Cannot update client"
    53, "OLE Update error"
    54, "OLE Unrecognized format"
    55, "OLE Cannot load object from another OS"
END
```

4. Use the *Run* command to compile and run the program.

HOW IT WORKS

When Windows starts this program, ObjectWindows calls the member function InitInstance, which registers the Clipboard formats used by OLE programs.

Then, the program creates the main window, which includes information for contacting an OLE server. The program uses OleRegisterClientDoc in the SetupWindow member function to set up the client document. The function puts the handle to the document in the member variable ClientDoc.

The next thing SetupWindow does is create a TMyClient structure. This structure is an extension of the OLECLIENT structure that OLE client programs use to keep track of an object. If the client program allowed more than one OLE object, it would allocate a structure for each object. The data required by OLE in this structure is a pointer to an OLECLIENTVTBL structure that contains the address of the client's callback routine. The extra data used in this program gives the address of the main window object, and the address of a special callback for the TMyClient object.

When Windows calls the client's callback function, it provides the OLE-CLIENT structure for the object that changed. Because this program added the address of the main window object, the program can call a routine in the main window object. This procedure means that the implied argument this is valid in the main window callback function (unlike in the callback for DDE functions).

Once the client document is registered and the OLECLIENT structure is ready, the program can begin using OLE objects. If the user selects the create menu function, the program calls the member function CMPBrush, which calls OLECreate to create a new embedded object. Another way to create an object is to use a server to put an object in the Clipboard and select the *Paste* command. In this case, the program calls OLECreateFromClip to create the object.

The *Paste* menu command is available only when there is an object in the Clipboard. The member function WMInitMenu determines which menu items are enabled. The client program uses the Windows function OleQueryCreateFromClip to see if the Clipboard contains an object.

There are two sets of variables that handle objects in this program. The handle for the main object is called Object, and the second object is called UndoObject. Whene the program changes Object, it copies information about the object to UndoObject. The *Undo* menu command, which calls the CMUndo member function, swaps the UndoObject and the main object.

Some OLE functions return immediately, but continue processing. The program calls FinishOLECmnd after calling one of these functions to process messages until the processing is done. Other functions do not return until they are done. In this case, the program called Check to see if the function generated any errors. If there is an error, Check uses the error code as a key to the string table in the resource file to get a string to display.

10.3 How Do I...
Create an OLE Sever?

PROBLEM

If you have a program that handles data, you may be able to increase its usefulness by making it an OLE server. For example, if you have a program that plays waveform files, you can make it an OLE server and add sound capability to any program that can be an OLE client. This solution shows you how to create a simple OLE server that edits triangles.

TECHNIQUE

OLE servers use a three layer hierarchy to describe an object. At the top is the server level. This level includes functions and data that affect the server itself. The next level is the document level which handles all of the objects on which the server is working. The lowest level is the object level which handles the objects sent to clients. At each level there is a structure used by the OLE server to tell the OLE server library about the functions the server provides.

The first thing that a server does is allocate the OLE structures and put the addresses of the callback functions into these structures. Note that if you do not use the smart callbacks option you must use the Window MakeProcInstance function to get the address to store in the structures.

Once the structures are ready, you can call OleRegisterServer to register the server. This function checks to see whether the server is in the registration database. You should make the entries in the registration database shown in Figure 10-3.

There are several command line options that Windows uses when it starts a server. If the server will be creating an embedded object, the command line includes the option /Embedding. If there is a document name for the object, it appears on the command line also. The server program must look for these options to determine with what type of object it will work. For example, if /Embedding is in the command line, the server should hide its main window. If there is a document name, the server should call OleRegisterServerDoc to register the document.

After getting the server set up, the rest of the interaction is the result of the server library calling callback functions. Table 10-2 lists the callback functions used.

The program in this solution is a simple OLE server that lets the user edit triangles, and paste them to the Clipboard to be included in other programs.

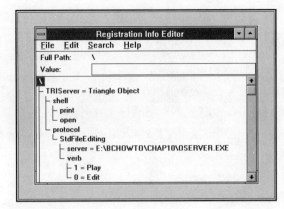

Figure 10-3
The Registration
Database Entry for
This Server

STEPS

1. Create a project file called OSERVER.PRJ that includes the files OSERVER.CPP, OSERVER.RES, and STANDARD.DEF.

2. Create the source file OSERVER.CPP with this program:

```
/* OSERVER.CPP An OLE Server */
#include <owl.h>
#define SERVERONLY
#include <ole.h>
#include <shellapi.h>
#include <string.h>

typedef struct {
     int Version;
     struct {
          int x;
          int y;
     } Corners[3];
} TRIANGLE;

/* Object structure functions */
LPVOID FAR PASCAL _export QueryProtocol(LPOLEOBJECT, LPSTR);
OLESTATUS FAR PASCAL _export Release(LPOLEOBJECT);
OLESTATUS FAR PASCAL _export Show(LPOLEOBJECT, BOOL);
OLESTATUS FAR PASCAL _export DoVerb(LPOLEOBJECT, UINT, BOOL, BOOL);
OLESTATUS FAR PASCAL _export GetData(LPOLEOBJECT, WORD, LPHANDLE);
OLESTATUS FAR PASCAL _export SetData(LPOLEOBJECT, OLECLIPFORMAT, HANDLE);
OLESTATUS FAR PASCAL _export SetTargetDevice(LPOLEOBJECT, HANDLE);
OLESTATUS FAR PASCAL _export SetBounds(LPOLEOBJECT, LPRECT);
OLECLIPFORMAT FAR PASCAL _export EnumFormats(LPOLEOBJECT, OLECLIPFORMAT);
OLESTATUS FAR PASCAL _export SetColorScheme(LPOLEOBJECT, LPLOGPALETTE);

/* Document structure functions */
OLESTATUS FAR PASCAL _export Save(LPOLESERVERDOC);
OLESTATUS FAR PASCAL _export Close(LPOLESERVERDOC);
OLESTATUS FAR PASCAL _export SetHostNames(LPOLESERVERDOC, LPSTR, LPSTR);
OLESTATUS FAR PASCAL _export SetDocDimensions(LPOLESERVERDOC, LPRECT);
OLESTATUS FAR PASCAL _export GetObject(LPOLESERVERDOC, LPSTR, LPOLEOBJECT FAR *, LPOLECLIENT);
OLESTATUS FAR PASCAL _export Release(LPOLESERVERDOC);
OLESTATUS FAR PASCAL _export SetColorScheme(LPOLESERVERDOC, LPLOGPALETTE);
```

OLESERVER	FUNCTIONS
Function Name	Description
Open	Open a file and edit it.
Create	Make a new object and edit it.
CreateFromTemplate	Make a new object based on data from a file.
Edit	Create a new object for editing. The data comes from SetData.
Exit	Close the server.
Release	Close the document.
Execute	Execute a DDE command.

OLESERVERDOC	FUNCTIONS
Function Name	Description
Save	Save the document.
Close	Close the document.
SetHostNames	Set the name for the client and the document.
SetDocDimensions	Set the location in the device context for the object.
GetObject	Create a new object.
Release	Close the document.
SetColorScheme	Set a new color palette.
Execute	Execute a DDE command.

OLEOBJECT	FUNCTIONS
Function Name	Description
QueryProtocol	Return the protocols handled by this server.
Release	Close the object.
Show	Show the server window.
DoVerb	Execute one of the verbs for this object.
GetData	Return the data for an object in the requested format.
SetData	Put data into the object.
SetTargetDevice	Indicate the device for the data.
EnumFormats	List the formats provided by the server.
SetColorScheme	Set a new color palette.

Table 10-2 The Server Callback Functions

```
OLESTATUS FAR PASCAL _export Execute(LPOLESERVERDOC, HANDLE);

/* Server structure functions */
OLESTATUS FAR PASCAL _export Open(LPOLESERVER, LHSERVERDOC, LPSTR, LPOLESERVERDOC FAR *);
OLESTATUS FAR PASCAL _export Create(LPOLESERVER,LHSERVERDOC,LPSTR,LPSTR,LPOLESERVERDOC FAR *);
OLESTATUS FAR PASCAL _export CreateFromTemplate(LPOLESERVER,LHSERVERDOC
      ,LPSTR,LPSTR,LPSTR, LPOLESERVERDOC FAR *);
OLESTATUS FAR PASCAL _export Edit(LPOLESERVER,LHSERVERDOC,LPSTR,LPSTR, LPOLESERVERDOC FAR *);
OLESTATUS FAR PASCAL _export Exit(LPOLESERVER);
OLESTATUS FAR PASCAL _export Release(LPOLESERVER);
OLESTATUS FAR PASCAL _export Execute(LPOLESERVER, HANDLE);

OLESERVERVTBL TheServerVTBL = {
     Open,
     Create,
     CreateFromTemplate,
     Edit,
     Exit,
     Release,
     Execute
};
OLESERVER TheServer = {&TheServerVTBL};
OLESERVERDOCVTBL TheDocumentVTBL = {
     Save,
     Close,
     SetHostNames,
     SetDocDimensions,
     GetObject,
     Release,
     SetColorScheme,
     Execute
};
OLESERVERDOC TheDocument;
OLEOBJECTVTBL TheObjectVTBL = {
     QueryProtocol,
     Release,
     Show,
     DoVerb,
     GetData,
     SetData,
     SetTargetDevice,
     SetBounds,
     EnumFormats,
     SetColorScheme
};
OLEOBJECT TheObject = {&TheObjectVTBL};

class TMyWindow : public TWindow
{
     public:
          TRIANGLE TheTriangle;
          int CurCorner;
          char FileName[260];
          char DocName[260];
          BOOL Embedded;
          LHSERVER ServerHandle;
          LHSERVERDOC DocumentHandle;
          RECT DataRect;
          TMyWindow(LPSTR ATitle);
          virtual LPSTR GetClassName() {return "OLEServer";};
```

```
                virtual void GetWindowClass(WNDCLASS& AWndClass);
                virtual void Paint(HDC, PAINTSTRUCT&);
                virtual void DrawObject(HDC);
                virtual void WMLButtonDown(RTMessage);
                /* Menu operations */
                virtual void DoCopy(RTMessage) = [CM_FIRST + 101];
};

/* Pointer to the window that the callbacks can use */
TMyWindow *TheWindow;

/* The application object */
class TMyApp : public TApplication
{
    public:
            OLECLIPFORMAT Native, OwnerLink, ObjectLink;
            TMyApp(LPSTR AName, HANDLE Inst, HANDLE Prev
                , LPSTR lpCmdLine, int nCmdShow)
                : TApplication(AName, Inst, Prev, lpCmdLine, nCmdShow) {};
            virtual void InitInstance();
            void Wait(BOOL &WaitFlag);
            void Error(int ErrorCode);
};

/* Initialize variables */
TMyWindow::TMyWindow(LPSTR ATitle)
    : TWindow(NULL, ATitle)
{
    TheWindow = this;
    AssignMenu("ServerMenu");
    CurCorner = 0;
    Embedded = FALSE;
    FileName[0] = '\0';
    lstrcpy(DocName, "TriDoc");
}

/* Set up the program icon */
void TMyWindow::GetWindowClass(WNDCLASS& AWndClass)
{
    TWindow::GetWindowClass(AWndClass);
    AWndClass.hIcon = LoadIcon(AWndClass.hInstance, "OLEServer");
}

/* Paint the triangle */
void TMyWindow::Paint(HDC hDC, PAINTSTRUCT&)
{
    int i;

    GetClientRect(HWindow, &DataRect);
    DrawObject(hDC);
}

/* Draw the object in DataRect */
void TMyWindow::DrawObject(HDC hDC)
{
    int i;

    FillRect(hDC, &DataRect, GetStockObject(WHITE_BRUSH));
    MoveTo(hDC, TheTriangle.Corners[2].x, TheTriangle.Corners[2].y);
    for(i=0; i<3; i++)
```

```
        LineTo(hDC, TheTriangle.Corners[i].x, TheTriangle.Corners[i].y);
}

/* Key a mouse button press */
void TMyWindow::WMLButtonDown(RTMessage Msg)
{
        TheTriangle.Corners[CurCorner].x = Msg.LP.Lo;
        TheTriangle.Corners[CurCorner].y = Msg.LP.Hi;
        CurCorner = (CurCorner + 1)%3;
        InvalidateRect(HWindow, NULL, FALSE);
}

/* Copy the triangle to the clipboard */
void TMyWindow::DoCopy(RTMessage)
{
        HANDLE Handle;
        TRIANGLE *Tri;
        LPSTR p;

        if(OpenClipboard(HWindow))
        {
                EmptyClipboard();
                Handle = GlobalAlloc(GMEM_DDESHARE, sizeof(TRIANGLE));
                Tri = (TRIANGLE *) GlobalLock(Handle);
                *Tri = TheTriangle;
                GlobalUnlock(Handle);
                SetClipboardData(((TMyApp *)GetApplication())->Native, Handle);
                Handle = GlobalAlloc(GMEM_DDESHARE, 15 + lstrlen(DocName));
                p = (LPSTR) GlobalLock(Handle);
                lstrcpy(p, "TRIServer");
                p += 10;
                lstrcpy(p, DocName);
                p + lstrlen(DocName) + 1;
                *p++ = '1';
                *p++ = '\0';
                *p = '\0';
                GlobalUnlock(Handle);
                SetClipboardData(((TMyApp *)GetApplication())->OwnerLink, Handle);
                SetClipboardData(((TMyApp *)GetApplication())->ObjectLink, Handle);
                CloseClipboard();
        }
}

/* The client wants to save the document */
OLESTATUS FAR PASCAL _export Save(LPOLESERVERDOC)
{
        return OLE_OK;
}

/* Close the current document */
OLESTATUS FAR PASCAL _export Close(LPOLESERVERDOC)
{
        OleRevokeServerDoc(TheWindow->DocumentHandle);
        return OLE_OK;
}

/* The client sent the name */
OLESTATUS FAR PASCAL _export SetHostNames(LPOLESERVERDOC, LPSTR Client
        , LPSTR Doc)
{
```

```
        char TmpStr[100];

        lstrcpy(TheWindow->DocName, Doc);
        wsprintf(TmpStr, "Triangle server - %s in %s", Doc, Client);
        TheWindow->SetCaption(TmpStr);
        return OLE_OK;
}

/* The client sent the location and size of the object */
OLESTATUS FAR PASCAL _export SetDocDimensions(LPOLESERVERDOC, LPRECT Rect)
{
        TheWindow->DataRect = *Rect;
        return OLE_OK;
}

/* Create an Object */
OLESTATUS FAR PASCAL _export GetObject(LPOLESERVERDOC, LPSTR, LPOLEOBJECT FAR *, LPOLECLIENT)
{

        return OLE_OK;
}

/* The client is done with the object */
OLESTATUS FAR PASCAL _export Release(LPOLESERVERDOC)
{
        return OLE_OK;
}

/* Set a color scheme */
OLESTATUS FAR PASCAL _export SetColorScheme(LPOLESERVERDOC, LPLOGPALETTE)
{
        return OLE_OK;
}

/* Handle DDE execute commands */
OLESTATUS FAR PASCAL _export Execute(LPOLESERVERDOC, HANDLE)
{
        return OLE_OK;
}

/* Inform the server library that this program handles the
StdFileEditing protocol */
LPVOID FAR PASCAL _export QueryProtocol(LPOLEOBJECT, LPSTR Prot)
{
        return lstrcmp(Prot, "StdFileEditing")?NULL:(LPVOID)&TheObject;
}

/* The client no longer needs the object */
OLESTATUS FAR PASCAL _export Release(LPOLEOBJECT)
{
        return OLE_OK;
}

/* Show the object */
OLESTATUS FAR PASCAL _export Show(LPOLEOBJECT, BOOL Focus)
{
        TheWindow->Show(SW_SHOWNORMAL);
        if(Focus)
                SetFocus(TheWindow->HWindow);
```

```
            return OLE_OK;
}


/* Do a verb */
OLESTATUS FAR PASCAL _export DoVerb(LPOLEOBJECT, UINT TheVerb
     , BOOL ShowIt, BOOL Focus)
{
     switch(TheVerb)
     {
          case 0:
                return ShowIt?Show(&TheObject, Focus):OLE_OK;
          case 1:
                return OLE_OK;
          default:
          return OLE_ERROR_DOVERB;
     }
}


/* Return data to the client */
OLESTATUS FAR PASCAL _export GetData(LPOLEOBJECT, WORD Format
     , LPHANDLE DataHandle)
{
     TRIANGLE *Tri;

     if(Format == ((TMyApp *)(TheWindow->GetApplication()))->Native)
     {
          *DataHandle = GlobalAlloc(GMEM_DDESHARE, sizeof(TRIANGLE));
          Tri = (TRIANGLE *) GlobalLock(*DataHandle);
          *Tri = TheWindow->TheTriangle;
          GlobalUnlock(*DataHandle);
          return OLE_OK;
     }
     return OLE_ERROR_FORMAT;
}


/* Set the data for the object */
OLESTATUS FAR PASCAL _export SetData(LPOLEOBJECT, OLECLIPFORMAT
     , HANDLE DataHandle)
{
     TRIANGLE *Tri;

     Tri = (TRIANGLE *) GlobalLock(DataHandle);
     TheWindow->TheTriangle = *Tri;
     GlobalUnlock(DataHandle);
     return OLE_OK;
}


/* Get the target device */
OLESTATUS FAR PASCAL _export SetTargetDevice(LPOLEOBJECT, HANDLE)
{
     return OLE_OK;
}


OLESTATUS FAR PASCAL _export SetBounds(LPOLEOBJECT, LPRECT)
{
     return OLE_ERROR_GENERIC;
}


/* Return the formats handled by this server */
```

```
OLECLIPFORMAT FAR PASCAL _export EnumFormats(LPOLEOBJECT
     , OLECLIPFORMAT LastFormat)
{
     if(LastFormat == 0)
          return ((TMyApp *) (TheWindow->GetApplication()))->Native;
     if(LastFormat == ((TMyApp *) (TheWindow->GetApplication()))->Native)
          return ((TMyApp *) (TheWindow->GetApplication()))->OwnerLink;
     if(LastFormat == ((TMyApp *) (TheWindow->GetApplication()))->OwnerLink)
          return ((TMyApp *) (TheWindow->GetApplication()))->ObjectLink;
     return NULL;
}

/* The client is setting the palette to use with the object */
OLESTATUS FAR PASCAL _export SetColorScheme(LPOLEOBJECT, LPLOGPALETTE)
{
     return OLE_OK;
}

/* Open an existing file */
OLESTATUS FAR PASCAL _export Open(LPOLESERVER, LHSERVERDOC, LPSTR, LPOLESERVERDOC FAR *)
{
     return OLE_OK;
}

/* Create a new object */
OLESTATUS FAR PASCAL _export Create(LPOLESERVER, LHSERVERDOC, LPSTR,LPSTR, LPOLESERVERDOC FAR *)
{
     int i;

     for(i=0; i<3; ++i)
          TheWindow->TheTriangle.Corners[i].x
               = TheWindow->TheTriangle.Corners[i].y = 0;
     OleRegisterServerDoc(TheWindow->ServerHandle, TheWindow->DocName
          , &TheDocument, &TheWindow->DocumentHandle);
     return OLE_OK;
}

/* Create a new object based on another object */
OLESTATUS FAR PASCAL _export CreateFromTemplate (LPOLESERVER, LHSERVERDOC, LPSTR, LPSTR, LPSTR,
LPOLESERVERDOC FAR *)
{
     int i;

     for(i=0; i<3; ++i)
          TheWindow->TheTriangle.Corners[i].x
               = TheWindow->TheTriangle.Corners[i].y = 0;
     OleRegisterServerDoc(TheWindow->ServerHandle, TheWindow->DocName
     , &TheDocument, &TheWindow->DocumentHandle);
     return OLE_OK;
}

/* Edit an object */
OLESTATUS FAR PASCAL _export Edit(LPOLESERVER,LHSERVERDOC,LPSTR, LPSTR, LPOLESERVERDOC FAR *)
{
     int i;

     for(i=0; i<3; ++i)
```

```
                TheWindow->TheTriangle.Corners[i].x
                    = TheWindow->TheTriangle.Corners[i].y = 0;
        TheWindow->Show(SW_HIDE);
        return OLE_OK;
}


/* Close down the server */
OLESTATUS FAR PASCAL _export Exit(LPOLESERVER)
{
        TheWindow->Show(SW_HIDE);
        OleRevokeServer(TheWindow->ServerHandle);
        PostMessage(TheWindow->HWindow, WM_QUIT, 0, 0);
        return OLE_OK;
}


/* Release the server */
OLESTATUS FAR PASCAL _export Release(LPOLESERVER)
{
        PostMessage(TheWindow->HWindow, WM_QUIT, 0, 0);
        return OLE_OK;
}


/* Handle DDE Execute commands */
OLESTATUS FAR PASCAL _export Execute(LPOLESERVER, HANDLE)
{
        return OLE_OK;
}


/* Initialize the server and the main window */
void
TMyApp::InitInstance()
{
        LPSTR p;

        MainWindow = new TMyWindow("OLE Server");
        MainWindow = MakeWindow(MainWindow);
        /* Register the clipboard formats */
        Native = RegisterClipboardFormat("Triangle");
        OwnerLink = RegisterClipboardFormat("OwnerLink");
        ObjectLink = RegisterClipboardFormat("ObjectLink");
        /* Get the command line arguments */
        p = lpCmdLine;
        ((TMyWindow *) MainWindow)->Embedded = FALSE;
        while(*p && *p != ' ')          // Skip white space
                ++p;
        if(*p && (*p != '-' || *p != '/'))      // Check for option
        {
                ++p;
                if(_fstrncmp(p, "Embedding", 9) == 0)
                {
                        ((TMyWindow *) MainWindow)->Embedded = TRUE;
                        p += 9;
                        nCmdShow = SW_HIDE;     // Hide window
                }
        }
        while(*p && *p != ' ')          // Skip white space
                ++p;
```

```
    if(*p)       // Check for the file name
          lstrcpy(((TMyWindow *) MainWindow)->FileName, p);
    if(OleRegisterServer("TriServer", &TheServer
          , &((TMyWindow *)MainWindow)->ServerHandle, hInstance
          , OLE_SERVER_MULTI) == OLE_ERROR_CLASS)
          MessageBox(NULL, "Server not registered", "TriServer", MB_OK);
    /* Show the main window if not embedded */
    if(MainWindow)
          MainWindow->Show(nCmdShow);
    else
          Status = EM_INVALIDMAINWINDOW;
}


/* Wait for OLE operations to complete */
void
TMyApp::Wait(BOOL &WaitFlag)
{
    MSG   Msg;
    BOOL  OLEMessages = FALSE;

    while(!WaitFlag)
    {
          /* Do OLE Messages */
          OleUnblockServer(((TMyWindow *)MainWindow)->ServerHandle
                , &OLEMessages);
          if(!OLEMessages)
          {
                /* Do Windows messages */
                if(GetMessage(&Msg, NULL, NULL, NULL))
                {
                      TranslateMessage(&Msg);
                      DispatchMessage(&Msg);
                }
          }
    }
}


/* Handle errors from the OLE Library */
void
TMyApp::Error(int ErrorCode)
{
    char TmpStr[80];

    if(ErrorCode == 100)
          lstrcpy(TmpStr, "Cannot register clipboard formats");
    else if(ErrorCode == 101)
          lstrcpy(TmpStr, "Cannot create VTBL thunks");
    else
    {
          TApplication::Error(ErrorCode);
          return;
    }
    MessageBox(0, TmpStr, "Triangle Server", MB_OK | MB_ICONSTOP);
    PostAppMessage(GetCurrentTask(), WM_QUIT, 0, 0);
}
```

```
int PASCAL WinMain(HANDLE hInstance, HANDLE hPrevInstance
     , LPSTR lpCmdLine, int nCmdShow)
{
     TMyApp MyApp("OLE Server", hInstance
          , hPrevInstance, lpCmdLine, nCmdShow);

     MyApp.Run();
     return MyApp.Status;
}
```

3. Create the resource file OSERVER.RES with this menu resource and the icon from Figure 10.4.

```
SERVERMENU MENU
BEGIN
     POPUP "&File"
     BEGIN
          MENUITEM "&Exit", 24340
     END
     POPUP "&Edit"
     BEGIN
          MENUITEM "&Copy", 101
     END
END
```

Figure 10-4
The Server
Program Icon

4. Use the *Run* command to compile and run the program.

HOW IT WORKS

The triangle editor part of this program is a standard ObjectWindows program that handles the WMLButtonDown message by moving one of the corners of a triangle to the mouse position. The triangle corners are in the TRIANGLE structure called TheTriangle. There is also a member function to copy the triangle data and server information to the Clipboard. When a client program sees this information in the Clipboard, it can create a new object from the data and use this server to edit the object.

This program is a server because of the OLE structures of callback functions defined at the beginning of the program and the addition of code to the TMyApp object that registers the program as a server.

The program uses the InitInstance member function to register Clipboard formats, register the server, and check the command line to see whether or not the object is embedded. Once this happens, the server library calls the callback routines to make things happen.

All of the callback functions are defined, although many of them do nothing but return a successful result. Functions that interact with the triangle data use the global variable TheWindow to get at the window object.

Index

& (in menu definition), 52

A

accelerator keys, providing for, 52
accelerator table, 10
AddFontResource(), 252
AddString(), 105
ADVSVR.PRJ, 352-367
aliasing, 199-200
Alt-key detection, 177
AnimatePalette(), 259
  example of use, 262
anonymous unions, 34
AnsiToOem(), 94
Arc(), 232
  example of use, 234
ASOUND.WAV, 201
AssignMenu(), 122
  example of use, 125
atom table, 333
Attr structure, 35, 42
ATTRMNU.PRJ, 150-153

B

backgrounds
  enabling, 40, 42
  opaque vs. transparent, 222, 231
banding (in printing), 207
BeginPaint(), 31
  example of use, 29, 84
BitBlt(), 239-240
  example of use, 241
BITMAP.PRJ, 240-243
bitmaps
  creating, 239
  as menu items, 157-161
  and non-rectangular windows, 295-301

bitmaps *(cont.)*
  drawing, 239-240
  removing from memory, 161
  storing in memory, 239-243
  storing in resource file, 239
.BMP file extension, 18
BN_CLICKED, 114
BN_DOUBLECLICKED, 114
Borland C++
  compatibility note, *vii*
  editor, 17
  modifying AUTOEXEC.BAT file for, 5
  modifying CONFIG.SYS file for, 5
  options needed for ObjectWindows, 5-6
  programming tools, basics of using, 16-20
  setting up for ObjectWindows, 4-6
  speedbar buttons, 14
brushes
  basics, 40, 42
  bitmapped, 222
  default attributes, 220
  styles, 222
Build all command, 17
BUTTON.PRJ, 115-118
buttons, 114-118
Buttons structure, 115, 118
BWCC.DLL, 271-272

C

callback functions
  DDE prototype, 331
  DDE server, 343
  OLE server (table), 404
Cancel button handling, 15
CanClose(), 10, 81
CapsLock state detection, 177
CF_FIRST, 15

Books have a substantial influence on the destruction of the forests of the Earth. For example, it takes 17 trees to produce one ton of paper. A first printing of 30,000 copies of a typical 480 page book consumes 108,000 pounds of paper which will require 918 trees!

Waite Group Press™ is against the clear-cutting of forests and supports reforestation of the Pacific Northwest of the United States and Canada, where most of this paper comes from. As a publisher with several hundred thousand books sold each year, we feel an obligation to give back to the planet. We will therefore support and contribute a percentage of our proceeds to organizations which seek to preserve the forests of planet Earth.

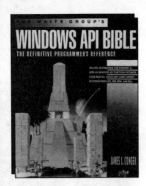

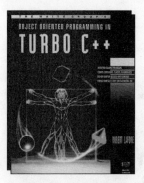

BREAK into Windows Programming

Subscribe to **Windows Tech Journal**,
the new magazine of tools and techniques for
Windows programmers.

(see other side for more information)

Plan for a programming breakthrough.

To get your free issue and start your no-risk subscription, simply fill out this form and
send it to **Windows Tech Journal**, PO Box 70087, Eugene OR 97401-0143 or
you can FAX it to 503-746-0071.
You'll get a full year—12 issues in all—of Windows tools and techniques for only **$29.95**.
If you're not completely satisfied write "no thanks" on the subscription bill.
The free issue is yours to keep and you owe nothing.

NAME _____

COMPANY _____

ADDRESS _____

CITY _____ STATE _____ ZIP _____

PHONE _____

For fastest service call **800-234-0386** or FAX this card to **503-746-0071**.

NOTES

NOTES

NOTES

NOTES

Companion Disk Order Form

Filling out this order form may change your life, help you impress your friends, and perhaps even influence people. The companion disk for *ObjectWindows How-To* is organized by chapter and includes all the program listings contained in this book, all pre-tested and debugged. The companion disk ensures that you spend more time programming and less time debugging.

To order by phone call 800-368-9369 or Fax 415-924-2576

or send to Waite Group Press, 200 Tamal Plaza, Corte Madera, CA 94925

Name

Company

Address
Street Address Only, No P.O. Box

City   State   ZIP   —

Daytime Phone

Quantity and Type

Name	Item #	Disk Size	Quantity	Price	
ObjectWindows How-To	CD016	3.5"	☐	x $15.00	
companion disk	CD516	5.25"	☐	x $15.00	

Sales Tax—California addresses add 7.25% sales tax.

Shipping—Price includes First Class shipping within the Continental U.S. Add $10 Canada, or $15 Foreign for shipping and handling. Allow 3 to 4 weeks. Prices subject to change. Purchase orders subject to credit approval, and verbal purchase orders will not be accepted.

Sales Tax

Shipping

Total Due

Method of Payment

Checks or money orders, payable to The Waite Group. To pay by credit card, complete the following:

☐ Visa   ☐ MasterCard   Card Number

Cardholder's Name _____   Exp. Date

Cardholder's Signature _____

Phone Number _____

SATISFACTION REPORT CARD

Please fill out this card if you wish to know of future updates to *ObjectWindows How-To*, or to receive our catalog.

WAITE GROUP PRESS™

Company Name: _____

Division/Department: _____ Mail Stop: _____

Last Name: _____ First Name: _____ Middle Initial: _____

Street Address: _____

City: _____ State: _____ Zip: _____

Daytime telephone: (___) _____

Date product was acquired: Month _____ Day _____ Year _____ Your Occupation: _____

Overall, how would you rate *ObjectWindows How-To*?

☐ Excellent ☐ Very Good ☐ Good
☐ Fair ☐ Below Average ☐ Poor

What did you like MOST about this book? _____
_____
_____

What did you like LEAST about this book? _____
_____
_____

How did you use this book (problem-solver, tutorial, reference…)?
_____

What programming tools do you use to write Windows applications?
☐ Borland/Turbo C++ ☐ MS-C++ ☐ Windows Software Dev. Kit
☐ MS-QuickC ☐ Other _____

What is your level of computer expertise?
☐ New ☐ Dabbler ☐ Hacker
☐ Power User ☐ Programmer ☐ Experienced Professional

What computer languages are you familiar with? _____
_____

Please describe your computer hardware:
Computer _____ Hard disk _____
5.25" disk drives _____ 3.5" disk drives _____
Video card _____ Monitor _____
Printer _____ Peripherals _____
Sound Board _____ CD ROM _____

Where did you buy this book?
☐ Bookstore (name): _____
☐ Discount store (name): _____
☐ Computer store (name): _____
☐ Catalog (name): _____
☐ Direct from WGP ☐ Other _____

What price did you pay for this book? _____

What influenced your purchase of this book?
☐ Recommendation ☐ Advertisement
☐ Magazine review ☐ Store display
☐ Mailing ☐ Book's format
☐ Reputation of Waite Group Press ☐ Other _____

How many computer books do you buy each year? _____

How many other Waite Group books do you own? _____

What is your favorite Waite Group book? _____
_____

Is there any program or subject you would like to see Waite Group Press cover in a similar approach? _____
_____

Additional comments? _____
_____
_____
_____

☐ **Check here for a free Waite Group catalog**

ObjectWindows How-To

BUSINESS REPLY MAIL
FIRST CLASS MAIL   PERMIT NO. 9   CORTE MADERA, CA

POSTAGE WILL BE PAID BY ADDRESSEE

Waite Group Press, Inc.
Attention: *Object Windows How-To*
200 Tamal Plaza
Corte Madera, CA 94925

FOLD HERE